The Proms

The Proms

❧ A NEW HISTORY ❧

Edited by
JENNY DOCTOR
and
DAVID WRIGHT

Consultant Editor
NICHOLAS KENYON

with 155 illustrations, 42 in colour
compiled by Elisabeth Agate

Thames & Hudson

To the memory of Cyril Ehrlich (1925–2004)

Frontispiece *BBC Prom at the Royal Albert Hall, 19 July 2006*

First published in the United Kingdom in 2007
by Thames & Hudson Ltd, 181A High Holborn,
London WC1V 7QX

www.thamesandhudson.com

British Library Cataloguing-in-Publication Data
A catalogue record for this book is available from the British Library

ISBN-13:   978-0-500-51352-1
ISBN-10:   0-500-51352-X

Printed and bound in Singapore by C S Graphics Pte Ltd

Contents

Preface

THE STORY OF THE PROMS: WHAT COULD BE MORE STRAIGHTFORWARD? An oft-told narrative, reaching back over a century, with a dazzling array of orchestras, conductors and soloists: the greatest musicians in the world performing for audiences of thousands in the Queen's Hall or the Royal Albert Hall, and to millions more around the world through radio, television and now the internet. It is a story of ever-increasing success, from the adventurous beginnings in the 1895 season to the sophistication of the present-day Proms with its big-screen relays and international stars. It is a heart-warming story that involves the education of the British public, an ever-growing enthusiasm for great music, a struggle against financial odds, and since 1927 the continuing involvement of the BBC, guiding and nurturing public taste.

Yet the story of the Promenade Concerts is far from being that simple. The Proms presents very different faces at different times, and it is not easy to judge whether the continuities of the story are greater than the discontinuities. The Edwardian seasons were completely different from the Proms of the 1950s; and the BBC Proms of the twenty-first century are a world apart from the series that the BBC took on in 1927. The Proms has often been presented, in historical accounts and in the publicity for each season, as a carefully preserved entity handed down across the generations. But it is actually quite a challenge to reconcile the very different identities and characters of the Proms across more than a century with the conventional representation of the season as a seamless continuum.

These questions about the nature and identity of the Proms lie at the heart of this book, which grew out of a series of papers given at the 'Music in Britain' seminar held at the Institute of Historical Research in London. It reflects a growing interest in public concert-giving as a subject for serious musical study – an interest that has taken too long to establish itself in a discipline that has traditionally been concerned with works and composers rather than the performance and concert context. One result is that there are now many different constructions of the Proms story; the question is whether they all feed into a larger, overarching identity. The most direct way to discuss the Proms is to set down the record of who played, what they played, and when they played it. From that we would gain some statistical sense of artists and repertory. But what that type of narrative does not give us is the sense of *why* it was that these things happened. So whereas most Proms histories have set out by stressing the idea that the Proms is about continuity, this book emphasizes various points of discontinuity – those moments of disruption when participants had to make significant decisions about the future of the series, and when the outcome hung in the balance. There were plenty of moments in the early years when the Proms might have folded, like many ventures of a similar kind. Equally, what might have happened if the modern phenomenon of broadcasting had not provided the Proms with subsidy, an outstanding orchestra and a vastly increased audience base through the 1930s and 40s? What would have been the series' fate if Malcolm Sargent had not cut such an imposing figure on television, giving a glamorous image to the unadventurous Proms of the 1950s? Or if William Glock had not appeared in 1960 to turn around the Proms' fortunes again, to create a newly modernized and exciting festival that achieved international distinction? If these things had not happened, would the Proms have fizzled out, relegated as a grand idea that had had its day? Without Glock's intervention, would the static repertory and disappointing performance standards have continued to hold the attention of audiences who were becoming used to cheaper, more convenient substitutes through the technologies of recording and broadcasting? Equally, would the Proms seem as welcoming and accessible to the wider range of audiences that they reach today had not the BBC taken full advantage of technological innovation to develop digital TV broadcasts, big-screen Proms in the Park and internet access alongside the regular nightly broadcasts of the concerts on Radio 3?

Those who go to the Proms, or listen to or watch its broadcasts, represent multifarious audiences, with a diversity of musical enthusiasms and preferences. To different listeners, decade by decade, the Proms has meant something quite individual; after all, even in the communal experience of an intense performance at the Queen's Hall or the Royal Albert Hall, everyone hears it differently. This is ever more so in an age when what was traditionally identified as the 'classical music audience' has become subsumed within far more volatile and flexible (but arguably larger) groups of audiences for diverse musics. For many the world over, the Proms has come to mean the television experience of the Last Night; for others it is the opportunity to hear fresh and familiar music in new conjunctions, with the Last Night merely a curious, or perhaps embarrassing, aberration. For many in the live audience, experience of the Proms centres around the unique nature of the Prommers, a committed and at times eccentric community ever-present in the arena and gallery of the Royal Albert Hall; for others internationally, the Proms is more simply about the excitement of live performance communicated through the convenience of broadcasting for home enjoyment.

Given that it was clearly necessary to situate the Proms against these cultural and musical backgrounds rather than simply to describe the contents of the concerts, and given how recently developed are some of these areas of research, it became difficult to imagine a single author undertaking a substantial contextual history. There are already a number of informative single-authored texts relating to the Proms, which offer much detailed description and discussion about events and performances that took place. Given this wealth of

The Proms audience conducted by Sir Malcolm Sargent at the Last Night of the Proms, 20 September 1952.

published information, we took a different approach, inviting a group of distinguished scholars – each experienced in exploring British musical and cultural life in a way particularly suited to their subject – to write accounts of the Proms as they saw it from different perspectives. Moreover, since the Proms has been documented for decades in pictures as well as music and print, we decided to take advantage of this rich visual legacy and interleave our discussions with images – which act as visual entertainment, of course, but are also fascinating as cultural indicators.

A great pleasure of producing this book has been the strong collaboration between the contributors. From initial discussions we developed a series of themes, starting with the concerts themselves, always a wonderfully vivid barometer of their times; the economics of the season, exploring how the commercial realities of presenting concerts have affected the Proms at various stages; the pressures of the box office, and how they have been managed alongside the commitment to adventurous repertory; and the institutional pressures, which since 1927 have centred around the BBC – creating a symbiotic relationship between two cultural survivors. Through a series of chapters taking different points of view and assuming different approaches, the contributors have examined the questions of why and how the Proms as a series of concerts celebrating the old and the new in music – as an institution, as a brand, and as a vibrant, relevant part of British culture – has managed to survive, against the odds.

As we mark the eightieth anniversary of the alliance between the BBC and the Proms – the stimulus for creating the book at this time – we very much hope that the intersection of ideas within it may provide readers with new ways of thinking about the series. Our ambition has been not to produce a definitive history, but rather to offer possible explanations and raise questions that will open the fascinating cultural context of the Proms to further investigation. We hope the book may help to stimulate new ideas about the writing of performance history, about concerts and the contexts of performance: the Proms in all its range, diversity and longevity has been ideal as a proving ground for this kind of study.

Our book, then, marks a stage in the history of the Proms. From its metropolitan beginnings in the 1890s, it now achieves a global impact in the twenty-first century. Always a fertile meeting ground for musicians and music-lovers, for established composers and new musical creators, for those gathering to hear performers in concert halls or joined through broadcast experiences around the world – given their international following today, may the Proms continue to inspire long into the future.

Jenny Doctor, Nicholas Kenyon and David Wright
October 2006

The Proms:
An Industrious Revolution

PAUL KILDEA

Of course I do not go in for being musical ... I only care for music – a very different thing. But still I will say this for myself – I do know when I like a thing and when I don't. Some people are the same about pictures. They can go into a picture gallery ... and say straight off what they feel, all round the wall. I never could do that. But music is so different to pictures, to my mind. When it comes to music I am as safe as houses, and I assure you, Tibby, I am by no means pleased by everything. There was a thing – something about a faun in French – which Helen went into ecstasies over, but I thought it most tinkling and superficial, and said so, and I held to my opinion too.

MRS MUNT IN *HOWARDS END*, E. M. FORSTER[1]

WHEN E. M. FORSTER'S NOVEL *HOWARDS END* WAS PUBLISHED IN 1910, THE Queen's Hall Promenade Concerts were a mere fifteen years old. The series was born of the entrepreneur Robert Newman's desire to 'run nightly concerts and train the public by easy stages ... Popular at first, gradually raising the standard until I have *created* a public for classical and modern music.'[2] Forster's novel, on the other hand – particularly in the above scene, which follows on from a concert of Mendelssohn, Beethoven, Brahms and Elgar in the Queen's Hall in London – was born of the desire to satirize grand popularizing gestures such as Newman's and those to whom he was appealing. In *Howards End* Forster carefully sketches the gradual erosion yet ultimate survival of class distinction in England at the turn of the last century. He draws together aristocratic Victorian capitalists, enlightened bourgeoisie and the working class, and through them disturbs the smooth surface of English social propriety. More specifically, their worlds collide at the altar of high culture. Aristocrats view high culture as the vehicle of patronage (whatever scant interest they may show in it), the knowledgeable bourgeoisie see it as their love, the workers their aspiration. In a story more of sadness than liberation, Forster makes it explicit that this high culture is often a prize rather than a genuine passion, political not artistic in its function.

The sting in this tale sits a little uncomfortably with the older Forster, the one who wrote and spoke for the mass-audience BBC and whose books sold in quantities to a large, literate public. But in this first decade of the twentieth century, following a century of population explosion and industrialization,

Forster aligned himself with the emerging intellectual consensus that identified mass culture as the greatest possible threat to civilization. 'Everywhere the mediocre are combining in order to make themselves master', wrote Friedrich Nietzsche in the 1880s.[3] Forster's distaste for the growth, debasement, needs and innovations of the middle classes was similarly pronounced at an early age. He was twenty-nine when in his 1908 diary he wrote: 'Science, instead of freeing man … is enslaving him to machines … God what a prospect! The little houses that I am used to will be swept away, the fields will stink of petrol, and the air ships will shatter the stars.'[4] This was the price of advancement. The trophies of industrialization would destroy the soul of the individual and then of civilization itself; no aspect of traditional European high culture would be left untouched.

Promenade concert conducted by Sir Henry Wood, Queen's Hall, 1922.

Intellectuals in this same era wrote of 'crowds' destroying public places – the places, in John Carey's words, 'created by civilization for the best people'.[5] Far more loaded words than 'crowd' were added to their armoury: rabble,

mob, caste, mass, sheep and herd were just some of them. There were of course genuine responses to the rise of the masses in England and their desire to populate the places created for the best people. Think for a moment of the theatres that appeared in such numbers throughout the nineteenth century, their erection testimony to some form of cultural ideal, their easy destruction usually the result of nothing more than a carelessly flung match. The inclusion in these theatres of cheap seats was recognition of these new and emerging audiences, of those without season subscriptions, of those who would never inherit a box above the stalls. Yet even in a century of such swift demographic changes, these same new theatres were careful to retain the demarcation between stalls and balconies that had characterized such buildings for two hundred years. Design obeyed conventional desire, and the separation of the different parts of the hall, reinforced through careful pricing, on the whole prevented the various layers of society from interacting. No matter that the model no longer suited the era; the hierarchies of politics and class were played out even in the leisure of the elite. Thus even one of the most noble of arts, architecture, continued to reinforce social discrimination (*such* a twentieth-century word). Although exposure to the culture of the elite was permitted, full participation clearly was not.

Following the opening of the Queen's Hall in 1893 Newman identified the opportunity for a new social experiment amid London's culturally barren summers. The experiment was borrowed and adapted from partially success-ful ventures in London in the previous half century: the stalls, traditionally the domain of the moneyed if not necessarily the cultured, would be given over to those without conspicuous wealth or family. Moreover, such access to the heart of the hall was granted in exchange for a 'popularly priced' ticket. In the same year as the Hall's inauguration, George Bernard Shaw had described the effect of this social revolution in promenade concerts held at Covent Garden. 'The shilling public can watch performance much more closely, since it can get right up to the platform instead of having to observe the pianist's fingers or "that marvellous fiddle bow" from afar across a vast space of half-guinea and five-shilling stalls.'[6] It was not simply proximity that excited this 'shilling public'. They were physically taking over their betters' territory. Moreover, they were doing it in a way again borrowed from populist experi-ments in nineteenth-century concert seasons. Seats were removed and audiences promenaded around the stalls against a backdrop of orchestral music. ('The general freedom of circulation round the orchestra and from the gallery to the floor practically gives the shilling the run of the house', said Shaw with approval.) And with this one act the accepted formality and regi-mentation of presenting serious music was turned on its head.

Given the magnificent new concert hall, the precedents for such popular promenade concerts and the acceptance that London concert life was not all it could be, perhaps an enterprising individual other than Newman would soon enough have identified an opportunity and acted accordingly. Yet Newman got there first. He would hardly have cared that initially his series was as much a social ritual as an artistic experience, if not more. Time would change this, he was confident. Meanwhile, he had seen commercial opportunity where Forster and his fellow intellectuals saw only sprawling masses and encroachment on 'their' culture. And not even Newman's genuine love of music, his real sense of evangelism regarding this culture that belonged most rightly to the 'best people', would have earned him plaudits from Forster and his peers. Make no mistake: what Newman undertook was not simply a battle for the hearts and minds of the newly educated, but an attempt to lay siege to the culture itself.

Any history of the concerts originated in 1895 by Newman and his intrepid conductor Henry Wood is no mere promenade in the park. The story of the Proms constitutes a narrative of enormous complexity.[7] It is a detective story as much as it is a volume of social anthropology. It is a study of class and nationalism as much as it is an examination of the commodification of culture. It is at times a history of music piracy, of unions and unification, of tyranny and technology. In the hundred years since Forster's novel appeared, what he delineated and mocked has come of age: a culture once owned and tended to by the cultivated elite is now considered, rightly, the spoils of democracy. How this position was arrived at forms the backbone of this book – not merely because it deals with the only concert-giving institution in London whose lineage stretches back unbroken to the 1890s,[8] but because the Proms is historically the most subversive undertaking in British art music.

Yet what was once a Trojan horse wheeled into the very centre of British musical life – with not one but two targets: the elite whose culture was to be appropriated and the masses whose taste was to be shaped – is today a popular festival. This too forms the substance of this book. How did such a radical venture become a mainstream event? What remains today of Newman's pioneering determination to change popular taste rather than bow down before it? Is it possible that success leaves the Proms hostage to its own position of commercial and cultural eminence within the art-music world?

It does not need stating that the story of the Proms is peculiarly English. Music in nineteenth-century England formed a sorry contrast to the highly developed and professional industries on the Continent. It was amateur and often shoddy; at its best, it was derivative of other cultures and countries. Thus Newman's aspirations would have been irrelevant to the people of Vienna, the subjects of the German Empire or, later, the citizens of the Weimar Republic. The last thing Newman wanted was the emperor's new clothes, a make-believe culture; instead he was after the great German symphonies, the tangible artistic spoils of his empire. Yet without the notions of amateurism that threaded their way through English music in the nineteenth century, without the opportunity that came from the industry's relatively unformed condition, it is unlikely that Newman would have been best placed to spark his cultural revolution. Well-established hierarchies and constrictions of taste, such as those in place in Austria and Germany, would not have allowed him much elbow room. The comedy of Wood's enlistment to Newman's cause is a case in point:

'I have decided to run those Promenade concerts I told you about last year.
I want you to be the conductor of a permanent Queen's Hall Orchestra. …'
'But you have never seen me conduct.'
'Oh, yes I have! … I mean to run you and *make* you. The public will support
us. The time is ripe for an English conductor … and now … can you put up a
little capital – say two or three thousand pounds?'
'I'm afraid not. I haven't such a sum to risk, and I don't know anyone who has.'
'Never mind! I'll see what can be done, *for I mean to run those concerts!*'[9]

Although more Evelyn Waugh than Bernard Shaw and no doubt embellished through decades of retelling, it nevertheless captures the muddled, very English, derring-do aspirations of the new venture.

However English is the broad picture, the Proms is also very much a child of a great city, one with a specific artistic profile and social infrastructure. Of course, in the century since *Howards End* appeared, the impact of the Proms has moved beyond this one capital city, altering the make-up of national culture and international festivals along the way through a combination of ambition, technology, reputation and hubris. The origins of these national changes, however, are in a series of concerts devised for a single city. In thinking of London's history in the past century it is impossible to look at Forster's characters and their interaction without wry amusement quickly giving way to recognition. Class is fundamental to English society. More particularly, the conflict between the hierarchies of class is felt never more strongly than in the rough and tumble of urban life. It is a trope in our art, our politics and our hopes.

This chapter's epigraph is intended as a thumb-sketch of bourgeoisie aspirations in the first decade of the twentieth century, part comedy and part anthropology. Although Mrs Munt's 'I may not know much about art' outlook is recognized today as a cliché of cultural philistinism *par excellence*, its currency in this context was by no means wide when Forster was writing.[10] How it became so is an important part of Proms history. This book is at heart more than a chronicle of personalities and repertories. It is an exploration of how the ownership of musical high culture in England shifted inexorably; when and why it altered under the influences of rapid social and industrial change; and how we arrived at a radically new demography of those who own our musical life.

* * * *

The intellectual consensus to which Forster subscribed, however much in its infancy, needs to be understood if the audacity of Newman's undertaking is to be given its full due. Characters such as Leonard Bast in *Howards End*, whose attempt to ingratiate himself into the culture of his superiors ends in ignominy and death, were commonplace in late nineteenth-century literature. Many intellectuals did not even bother presenting their arguments at one remove through fictional characters. Ezra Pound, that big intellectual bully boy, summarized the arguments of cultural ownership when in 1914 he said, 'The artist has no longer any belief or suspicion that the mass, the half-educated simpering general … can in any way share his delights.'[11] Author George Gissing went further still, not confining his contempt to the masses alone, but extending it to those who attempted to enlighten them. In his novel *Our Friend the Charlatan*, he mocks a worthy character, May Tomalin, for planning a series of high-brow concerts for the poor. 'It isn't our object to *amuse* people', Tomalin declares. 'We want to train their intelligence. … We have to show them how bad and poor their taste is, that they may strive to develop a higher and nobler [taste].'[12] Gissing had no argument with nobility being the core of high art; few intellectuals did. But he certainly believed in what today we would perhaps term cultural apartheid. In this environment, Newman emerges as a cross between Gissing's May Tomalin and P. T. Barnum, the brilliant American purveyor of high and low art and anything in between.

Nevertheless, something was happening to popular taste. First of all, it was recognized; then it was given a platform. Perhaps more accurately, it was its commercial potential that was recognized. Carey thinks that this was attributable to the fault of the new popular newspapers that sprang up in the last decades of the nineteenth century;[13] given the intellectual ire they attracted, he is surely right. Intellectuals slapped them down with ever-increasing derision, hating both their poor quality and what they represented. Criticized for what they were *not*, the new newspapers were nonetheless a cultural barometer, an indication of taste and leisure, of sophistication and pleasure. They were a product of either commercial cynicism or genius in a climate of greater literacy. Their success was measured not by the conventional critical and intellectual apparatus but by sales figures alone. The *Daily Mail* was only one product of this *fin-de-siècle* frenzy, appearing in the year following Newman's first Queen's Hall season; yet within the space of a few years it had become market leader. Newspaper and concert series may have both drunk from the same trough, but how different were their aspirations. 'A newspaper is to be made to pay', said Lord Northcliffe, the publisher of the *Mail*. 'Let it deal with what interests the mass of people.'[14] Naturally, Newman wanted Northcliffe's subscribers, but was determined not simply to give them what they wanted ('popular at first, gradually raising the standard'). Rather, both he and Wood were intent on giving the public something slightly more than it thought it wanted.

If this all sounds familiar, in all its convoluted nobility, that is because it is. John Reith articulated Newman's argument with more eloquence and power in the 1920s with reference to the new BBC – 'to inform, educate, and entertain' – thus providing an intellectual framework the impact of which remains with us today. There is a point of further significance for cultures other than the newspaper industry. The concept of the greatest power being derived from the largest circulation translated effortlessly to the British *and* American film industries in the 1930s and beyond with telling consequence. Popular culture was quickly equated with visible numbers, and numbers on a scale far exceeding anything that had come before. Notions of excellence and artistic objectivity that had governed the presentation and economy of elite culture before the twentieth century were now challenged by this popular new commercial model. The walls of Troy were not yet crumbling, and would not for some years, but the city was clearly under siege. The notion of an absolutist culture, of a canon of literature and great art that had prevailed for a century, was no longer impenetrable. The relativist culture we recognize in music today, in which high art is so often judged on the economic and aesthetic criteria of popular culture, is a partial and unforeseen legacy of these turn-of-the-century shifts. Wood and Newman may have introduced their new audiences to great canonic works, but they were also carefully attuned to what audiences did and did not like at the fringes of the canon, and reacted accordingly.

There have been since Newman's time (Chapter 2) many and various attempts either to reinforce or chip away at his original aspiration for the Queen's Hall Promenade Concerts. Following Newman's death in 1926, Wood took over the sole artistic responsibility for the series. Neither this nor the BBC's assumption of responsibility for the Proms in the following year affected the core structure or aspirations of the concerts (Chapter 3). The steady-as-she-goes seasons following Wood's death in 1944, amid major BBC structural changes – some good, notably the enlistment of more than one orchestra to the Proms' cause – and Sir Malcolm Sargent's tiresome vanity and workaday musicianship, perhaps diluted Newman's founding principles (Chapter 4). William Glock's era of 1960–73, and that of his successor, Robert Ponsonby, whose final official season was 1985, clearly reinforced the Proms' remit (Chapter 5). The era of John Drummond (1986–95) was one of cultural absolutism, while that of Nicholas Kenyon (1996 onwards) has relied more on a two-way dialogue between the Proms and its audiences than Glock aspired to (Chapter 7). Yet Drummond's moderated autocracy and Kenyon's continual innovations have resonances with components of the Proms' early years.

For whatever truth there is in such broad-brush critiques, it is wrong to analyse one period with the criteria of another. Nothing was standing still, least of all cultural reference points: wars, technological advancements, politics, transport, education and patriotism all influenced contemporary notions of high art and popular culture to a greater extent. Such social progress of course influenced the operations and rationale of the Proms. The cult of the movie star, fostered by Hollywood's studio system from the late 1920s onwards, found its contemporary reflection in the postwar celebration of the international virtuoso. Long-playing records made these virtuoso artists collectable commodities, while commercial aviation ensured their portability – their occasional earthly appearance vital for the verification and survival of their cult, something perhaps cribbed from any number of established religions. Radio broadcasts were critical in creating the notion of the Proms as a festival for the masses – an important departure from the principle behind Bayreuth, Salzburg and, later, Aldeburgh, each of which celebrated a modified exclusivity as an artistic and commercial necessity.

New public transport networks brought audiences in to the Queen's Hall, and then to the Royal Albert Hall, from all over London and beyond – the middle classes from their houses in the suburbs or the Home Counties, the aspiring classes from closer to the capital's centre. Wars affected the structural viability of orchestras and their choice of repertory and artists, as patriotism battled with and triumphed over the canon of great Austro-Germanic works in different British music organizations, the Proms a notable exception. The growth of socialism and a decline in religious belief helped to ensure that the English vogue for oratorios did not extend much beyond Elgar. The triumph of capitalism reinforced the ascendancy of the market place; in matters cultural this empowered consumers and brought them ever closer to producers.

In the different orchestras, standards rose and fell – the former through the conductor Henry Wood's tenacity, the latter as young men enlisted or were conscripted. The women who took their places, particularly in 1939, found social emancipation through opportunities hitherto never afforded them. And where there was once cultural drought, soon enough there was flood: competition, opportunism, wealth and entrepreneurship found their combined expression in the formation of new orchestras that lured away players in great numbers from the Proms' resident band. The first of these was the London Symphony Orchestra, which was founded as early as 1904. Wood survived this challenge, but it was only in 1930, with the formation of the BBC Symphony Orchestra and its establishment as the Proms' in-house orchestra, that the series attained greater security. Yet the inaugural concert of the London Philharmonic Orchestra at the Queen's Hall in 1932 represented new competition. Of far more consequence was the 1945 formation of the Philharmonia by part tartar, part genius Walter Legge. This new venture, and the postwar restructuring of other ensembles damaged by the 1939–45 conflict, had a catastrophic impact on the BBC Symphony Orchestra's make-up. And so it continued. In such changing social and cultural circumstances, one distinct era in Proms history cannot be judged so easily against another.

These changes are only the most visible manifestations of the very public intersection of high culture, social history and economics. Underlining such massive shifts for all of the last century was a less visible force. As Chapter 3 makes clear, any history of the Proms is also a history of modernism in Britain, so neatly are the chronologies of both interconnected. The direct impact of modernism is harder to trace than that of the microphone or the aeroplane, although it is possible to put forward here a few dates and a few milestones that will be explored in the course of the book. When Newman inaugurated the Proms in 1895, Richard Strauss was still ten years off completing *Salome*, his great expressionist outpouring, which today remains a modernist touchstone.[15] Even sympathetic critics at its Dresden première considered the opera a new departure in art, an embracement of the decadent and depraved. In 1895 Strauss's *Also sprach Zarathustra* was still a year away – it too a sensational, modernist work in its time. In other words, Newman's 'manifesto' was conceived at the peak of high romanticism and with knowledge of a public taste

London Underground
poster, 'At the Proms',
by Tony Sarg, 1913
(quoting from The
Merchant of Venice,
Act V, Scene 1),

for popular light music, little more. Although clearly a visionary and educated at the Royal Academy of Music, Newman could not have been prepared for how quickly Strauss and his younger colleagues, notably Schoenberg, would shift the musical ground from underneath him.

The signs of change were already present in this decade, if scarcely visible. By 1895 Strauss had composed his tone poems *Macbeth*, *Don Juan*, *Tod und Verklärung* and *Till Eulenspiegel*. These pieces, Strauss's 'music of the future', represented a loosening of his ties with the totems of high romanticism and a huge step towards his expressionist works of the early twentieth century. With *Also sprach Zarathustra* (1896), originally subtitled 'Symphonic optimism in *fin-de-siècle* form, Dedicated to the 20th Century', Strauss's modernist credentials were established beyond question. Nietzsche's poet *Zarathustra* has been pressed into all sorts of unsavoury apprenticeships since his first complete appearance in the early 1890s, notably by the failed painter and dictator Hitler, who found much to his liking in *Zarathustra*'s references to a super race. Strauss used the work for less sinister purpose, and what his *Zarathustra* thus spake is a sort of Enlightenment–humanist vision, an implicit rejection of religion and an elevation of humankind to its highest station. With this work Strauss had his Martin Luther moment: he had nailed his reform theses to the church door in conscious provocation of the parishioners who passed through it, and now stood back to watch their response.

Strauss's *Zarathustra* and other tone poems are illustrative of the fine line trod by Wood in his choice of modern music. Whereas Strauss's earlier tone poems were advocated by Wood from the beginning of the Proms onwards, *Zarathustra* had to wait until 1922 for its Proms première – and was not repeated in the concerts until 1960. Wood was nervous of letting this wolf inside the chicken pen; he was adventurous, catholic in taste, yet not consciously provocative. As a result of his programming choices, in these early Proms a handful of composers such as Strauss flew in under the radar and were subsequently embraced by populist audiences. Wood's advocacy helped prepare and educate audiences, certainly. And it cannot be said that the flight was always smooth. Schoenberg's *Five Orchestral Pieces* was hissed by Promenaders at its 1912 première – although this response, at least in part a consequence of Wood contending with the orchestra's hostility, seems almost sycophantic in comparison to the reception afforded the première of Stravinsky's *The Rite of Spring* in Paris the following year. Moreover, in these early years Wood was careful to select new works outside the more brutal, primitivist experiments in contemporary music or from the more radical tinkerings with tonality. Notwithstanding these provisos, there was still an unexpected rapport between the new audiences and new music. Strauss became a firm favourite of Proms' audiences, and the repeat performance of Schoenberg's *Five Orchestral Pieces* a year and a half after its première, this time under the composer's direction, was an event of significance in the London concert calendar. Even the British première of Debussy's *Prélude à l'après-midi d'un faune* in the 1904 Proms season, to which Forster's Mrs Munt refers with neither appreciation

(Unfit for treasons, stratagems & spoils)

T THE PROMS.

BY THE

UNDERGROUND

HUMOURS OF LONDON Nº 9.

ELECTRIC RAILWAY HOUSE, BROADWAY, WESTMINSTER.   JOHNSON, RIDDLE & CO. LTD. LONDON, S.E.   4.5/8/ —1350-8-13

ROYAL ALBERT HALL
15 JULY – 10 SEPTEMBER

Chief Executive: Patrick Deuchar

HUNDREDTH

ADAPTED FROM DESIGN BY LEE-ELLIOTT. PHOTOGRAPH BY BARON

"PROMS"

SEASON

nor understanding, was in reality more of a success with the Promenaders, many of whom wrote directly to Wood requesting its immediate return.[16] Thus the work entered the Proms' repertory.

In their campaign to broaden audience tastes, Wood and Newman were not beyond firing pre-emptive shots across the bow. The 1913 printed programme contained the following: 'Fortunately the Promenade audience has now been educated to such sound and liberal tastes that it is possible to organise programmes of a very high order and to include a good many novelties, provided the experimental note is not over-emphasised.'[17] With its mixture of flattery and genuine respect, it is possible to recognize in this one sentence the covenant already in place between Wood, Newman and their audiences, one that was to endure in different forms and with different balances for generations. Moreover, its existence suggests that Newman was able to adapt quickly and convincingly to the changing musical aesthetics often enthusiastically peddled by Wood. In any given year in these first decades there was a good number of 'novelties', none of which was markedly lighter in substance than those presented at the same time by the Royal Philharmonic Society, whose brow was set somewhat higher. Individual programmes in this era came to look as though they had not been put together by Wood's cat, as early ones did. And if performance standards were not always remarkable – an outcome of Wood's musical limitations and the difficult circumstances in which each arduous season was rehearsed and performed – there was no shortage of ideas, commitment and innovation.

Of course, as modernism shed its old skins, the substance of this covenant between consumer and supplier changed. Each chapter in this book demarcates different stages in its development, from the relationship's origins (Chapter 2) to the postmodern version we have today (Chapter 7). And at each stage in its history this changing pact between the Proms and its audiences has had the strongest possible cultural ramifications. For example, the conservative programming in the 1950s, in the context of the avant-garde experimentation of Darmstadt and other Continental centres, laid the ground for Glock's revolution. Glock identified and responded to new audiences who would replace those whom he knew would not survive the more extreme consequence of his cultural *coup d'état* (Chapter 5). And with them a new pact was formed.

And after Glock? Well, every action has its equal and opposite reaction, which arguably explains Britain's art-music climate today, in which the power of the consumer has never been stronger. 'I may not know much about art, but …' Perhaps this was also the fault of Benjamin Britten who, at the height of his self-doubt in the 1960s, argued that something in our culture had destroyed the 'holy triangle of composer, performer and listener'.[18] Composers were no longer writing for audiences, that much he was certain. But listeners too had to take their responsibilities seriously, never more so than in the age of radio and recordings. 'Music demands more from a listener than simply the possession of a tape-machine or a transistor radio. It demands some preparation, some effort, a journey to a special place, saving up for a ticket, some homework on the programme perhaps, some clarification of the ears and sharpening of the instincts.'[19] Britten would no doubt be glad of certain progress made since then on this front – although I suspect he would have been as perplexed as I was when, during my tenure as artistic director of London's Wigmore Hall, I was forcibly told by a regular audience member that the hall was a shop, that I was the shopkeeper whose single role was to stock it with the produce for which there was evident demand, and where of course the customer was always right.

* * * *

The differences between *fin-de-siècle* Britain and its counterpart in the new millennium are greater than the similarities. Britain is today a country scarred by its imperial triumphs and traumatized by its failures. It therefore comes as no surprise that Britain's relationship with its culture has changed considerably, especially so in the field of serious music. Surely it is self-evident that when faced with complex new scores the customer cannot be expected to be right? Taking this argument one step further, as is done in Chapter 7, if audiences are now equal partners in the process of canon building, what are the implications not only for new repertory, but also for great works previously and unjustly ignored by programmers or misunderstood by audiences? What would an audience of Mrs Munts leave us with today? Certainly not Debussy's *Prélude à l'après-midi d'un faune*, let alone the essays in more aggressive modernism that have featured at the Proms since 1895.

In many instances and institutions, democracy has replaced nineteenth-century cultural hierarchies with the more immediate values and mechanisms of the commercial market. The social role of artists has changed markedly in consequence. Of the early twentieth century in Britain the historian D. L. LeMahieu wrote: 'Artists despised a public they refused to court and asserted their superiority over a human aggregate understandably indifferent to their leadership.'[20] There are other decades to which these words would easily fit – the surly distance between artist and audience outlined by LeMahieu was similarly attacked by Britten in his 1964 lecture.[21] But such sentiments could not be applied to music in Britain today. Mass audiences now have the power to consecrate works – think of Górecki's Third Symphony or Taverner's *The Protecting Veil* – where formerly they were simply guests at the table, supping on whatever they were served. They also consecrate artists: think of that handful of young pianists now with huge careers and recording contracts, who would never have survived the critical apparatus and the accepted hierarchies of taste in the period before the recording industry's domination and the large-scale commercialization of art music. It is true that as long ago as 1850 Barnum generated a mass American audience for the Swedish soprano Jenny Lind, but she could really sing.

Whether or not the current situation is desirable is a question quite distinct from how we got here. A striking aspect of the Proms' history is its element of ebb and flow. There has not been a sole trajectory, notwithstanding whatever

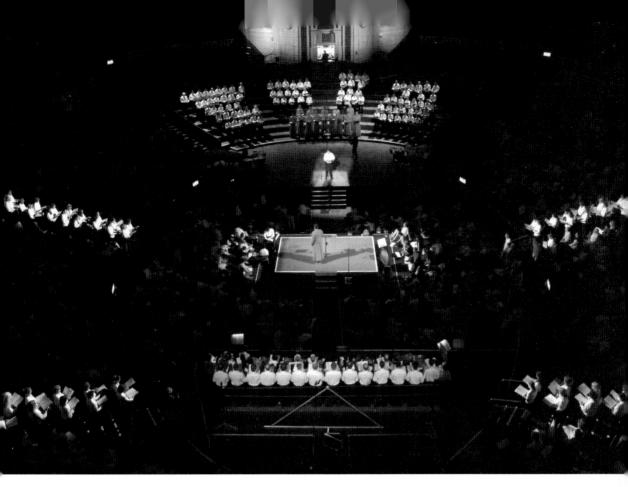

A unique arena: John Tavener, The Veil of the Temple, *world première of the concert version, Royal Albert Hall, 1 August 2004.*

similarities in repertory and programme-building there have been in different eras. Instead, the philosophy, taste and knowledge of each director have reacted with the cultural expectations of each period, low and high, to unique effect. These defined eras either melded into each other or formed markedly distinct cultural juxtapositions. The BBC's first year, in 1927, was only marginally different from 1926. Glock initiated root-and-branch reform in 1960, which was continued by his successor, Robert Ponsonby, and then taken in a new, more international direction by his successor, John Drummond. In the BBC era, different directors have been attracted to different elements of John Reith's mantra, 'to inform, to educate, to entertain'. It has been these shifts in directorial outlook, be they autocratic or democratic in personality, and the consequent chemical reaction within British culture, that has taken the Promenade concerts to where they are now.

There are numerous aspects of serious music in Britain in the twenty-first century, indeed of the industry that provides our culture with its infrastructure, that derive from Proms practices. For as the Proms cemented its role at the centre of British musical life, so too did it come to exert its own powers of consecration. However, what we take for granted today in the wider presentation and consumption of art music in this country often grew from clumsy experimentation or good fortune as much as from the founders' firm

pedagogic principles. From its beginning, when the recording industry was in its infancy, the Proms had set out to present 'standard repertory' to audiences that may never have heard it performed by a full symphony orchestra. The notion of 'standard repertory' was then in flux, but its consolidation in the early twentieth century is part of the Proms' history. The Beethoven symphonies formed the backbone of most years' programmes. Brahms, too, appeared frequently; his symphonies were carefully rotated, sometimes across different years but more often after 1926 as a complete cycle. Although this may give the appearance of checklist programming, something more complex was actually at work in these early years. Wood identified a fundamental need to acquaint audiences with the framework of Western orchestral music if they were ever to understand and appreciate the more challenging aspects of his programming. Yet the presentation of a full cycle of Sibelius' seven symphonies in 1945, the first season following Wood's death, and that of Vaughan Williams' five symphonies in the following year was something quite distinct from Wood's commitment to what would soon be recognized as core nineteenth-century repertory. With two *contemporary* cycles, the Proms took a bold step towards the 'completionism' that we recognize today as fundamental to orchestral programming in Britain and abroad: the performance of whole cycles of almost *anything* by almost *anyone* – not as an offshoot of a defined educational philosophy, but as monument-building. If an individual work is flawed, such flaws are disguised when the piece is made a building block of something far greater. This was a completely different way of approaching and *hearing* modern music, in which the cumulative effect somehow transformed the impact of each individual work. And although this venture by the Proms into complete cycles of contemporary works was not a success in the mid-1940s, by the end of the century such enterprises would be commonplace in British concert halls.

Wood's complete or near-complete cycles of the great nineteenth-century symphonies – the model for the Vaughan Williams and Sibelius programmes – had further far-reaching consequences. Different audiences were attracted by different composers which led to the introduction of composer nights and season tickets. This allowed popular engagement with the 'great composers', those whose works were the foundations of the evolving canon. More vitally, the scale of the Proms' operations allowed the broad essays into eighteenth- and nineteenth-century orchestral repertory that were simply impossible for other concert organizations. The sheer repetition of works from year to year was fundamental to the creation of a core repertory in the early twentieth century; as the century progressed, so too did this repertory expand. Mountains were to be climbed, the Proms suggested, some higher or more treacherous than others. Scale is the important factor here – in the emerging performance traditions of individual works, certainly, but also in the formation of the canon, which itself came to resemble a constellation, with new stars being discovered yearly.

In this cause the Proms and their directors were aided by the new long-playing record, it too a product of the *zeitgeist* and war-driven technology. Following its introduction in America in 1948 and its quick adoption in Britain, the increased capacity of the LP allowed the playing of large-scale works to be less disruptive to the listener, notably the symphonies that had hitherto suffered in recordings through countless snips and turns. And as conductors and soloists set about recording great works for the first or near-first time, audiences started collecting albums with a zeal bordering on mania. As LP prices dropped, new audiences were actively targeted by both record companies and gramophone manufacturers. Needless to say, such marketing was aimed at audiences similar to those who attended the Royal Albert Hall or listened to its broadcasts each season in great numbers. Here was the true commercialization of elite culture, an opportunity for audiences to 'own' its jewels and to develop a relationship with them independently from the programming philosophies and timetables of broadcasters and concert organizers alike. One spin-off was a general raising of expectations and standards. Glock in particular, whose reign commenced soon after the inception of stereo recording, was sensitive to the challenges and opportunities presented by the gramophone record.

"This is a 33⅓ r.p.m. microgroove high-fidelity antistatic L.P. of some Mozart or something."

Cartoon by Quentin Blake, from Punch *(22 August 1956).*

There are downsides to completionism. It emphasizes repertory over the interpreter, a trend noticed by the businessman Klaus Heymann, who in 1986 responded by forming the record label Naxos – his own Newmanesque marriage of culture and commercial opportunity. Heymann's company in the new millennium is far more sophisticated in its market identification and its recording philosophy than it was at the time of its formation: music is not *quite* the commodity it appeared to be early on, a product to be shifted in bulk regardless of quality or interpreter; but Naxos is still a repertory-driven company. And the Proms, although signing up enthusiastically to completionist programming, has never explored the flip side of this particular coin, the disregard for the role of the interpreter.

On the one hand it has not subscribed to simple checklists of repertory without reference to a full concert experience (Britten's triangle once more). And on the other, the commercially bred and shamelessly titled 'celebrity concert' – in truth not the highest point of Western cultural evolution, but which nonetheless plagues British concert halls and radio stations alike – is not an aspect of Proms thinking. It has steered a middle course, programming great artists and events with high box-office appeal but avoiding the circus tricks associated with 'crossover artists' and other offshoots of the commercialization of art music.

There was arguably more behind this explosion of interest in the unknown than the invention of the LP and its altogether smarter younger sister, the stereo recording. And here, too, the Proms was intricately involved. If the sad and lonely war memorials erected throughout Britain after the First World War were intended as a silent reproach to the inhumanity of total war, memorial culture post-1945 took a different form. It was more optimistic, for one thing. And it revelled in the large scale – a return to nineteenth-century memorial culture, which equated heroism with size. Britain would rebuild its bombed capital city, and if the scale of its aspirations often outdid that of the new buildings themselves, this was only an unfortunate offshoot of a decimated economy. In this environment, in which the country's leaders had been determined to beat its enemy not just on the front line but on the cultural home front as well, physical evidence of the triumph of democracy over totalitarianism was needed in postwar Britain as surely as it had been over the skies of Dresden and Berlin or on the North Sea.

The postwar formation of the Arts Council, the BBC's Third Programme, a permanent opera company at Covent Garden and the Aldeburgh and Edinburgh festivals, as well as the construction of the Royal Festival Hall, are only the most obvious steps towards postwar cultural aspiration. Indeed, this marriage of culture and industry – exemplified in the 1951 Festival of Britain – was altogether a new feature of the arts in Britain. The Royal Albert Hall, originally used by the Proms temporarily to plug the gap left by the destruction of the Queen's Hall in 1941, was soon emblematic of both the scale and the democracy of Britain's cultural aspirations. After the intimacy of the Queen's Hall, music that would fill the Royal Albert Hall would be seen as a badge of triumph, a monument to British resilience – and would soon satisfy the BBC as well, with its far greater potential income from ticket sales. The change was not immediate, but the combination of these various factors after the war ignited in those who ran the Proms a desire to formulate a grand culture of their own, all the while essentially colonizing those of other countries, Germany included. Britain would be gracious in victory.

Enough has been written about the Last Night of the Proms in later chapters for it to delay us only slightly here. At its worst, it is a signal that Forster's concerns for 'his' culture were justified. At its best, it is a reminder that all artistic endeavours evolve continuously, never more so than those with entrenched traditions. On the Last Night of the Proms in 2005, conductor Paul Daniel scored points off the Australians in the audience by referring to the Ashes series that would end three days later in victory for the English

Last Night of the Proms, 14 September 1991, conducted by Andrew Davis, with Dame Gwyneth Jones.

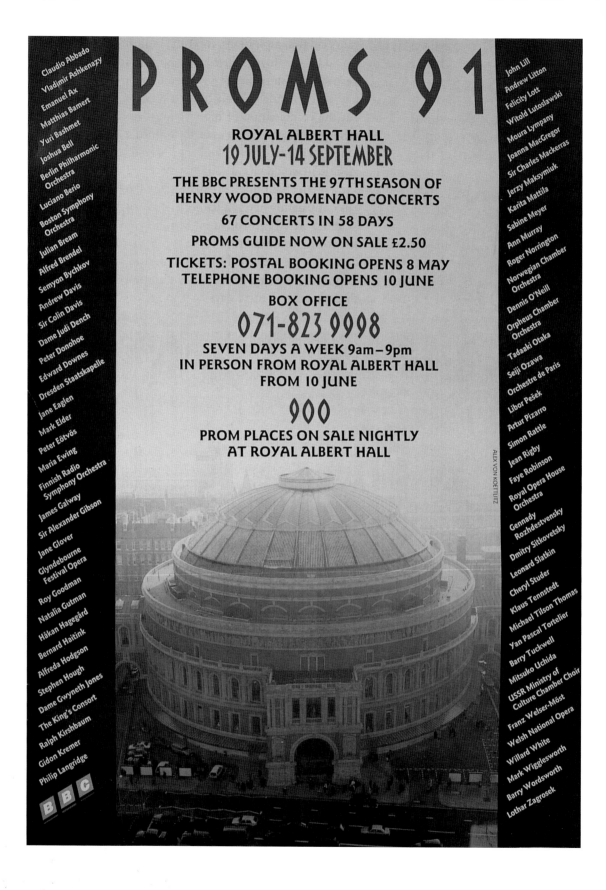

PROMS 91

ROYAL ALBERT HALL
19 JULY–14 SEPTEMBER

THE BBC PRESENTS THE 97TH SEASON OF
HENRY WOOD PROMENADE CONCERTS

67 CONCERTS IN 58 DAYS

PROMS GUIDE NOW ON SALE £2.50

TICKETS: POSTAL BOOKING OPENS 8 MAY
TELEPHONE BOOKING OPENS 10 JUNE

BOX OFFICE
071-823 9998
SEVEN DAYS A WEEK 9am–9pm
IN PERSON FROM ROYAL ALBERT HALL
FROM 10 JUNE

900
PROM PLACES ON SALE NIGHTLY
AT ROYAL ALBERT HALL

ALEX VON KOETLITZ

Claudio Abbado
Vladimir Ashkenazy
Emanuel Ax
Matthias Bamert
Yuri Bashmet
Joshua Bell
Berlin Philharmonic Orchestra
Luciano Berio
Boston Symphony Orchestra
Julian Bream
Alfred Brendel
Semyon Bychkov
Andrew Davis
Sir Colin Davis
Dame Judi Dench
Peter Donohoe
Edward Downes
Dresden Staatskapelle
Jane Eaglen
Mark Elder
Peter Eötvös
Maria Ewing
Finnish Radio Symphony Orchestra
James Galway
Sir Alexander Gibson
Jane Glover
Glyndebourne Festival Opera
Roy Goodman
Natalia Gutman
Håkan Hagegård
Bernard Haitink
Alfreda Hodgson
Stephen Hough
Dame Gwyneth Jones
The King's Consort
Ralph Kirshbaum
Gidon Kremer
Philip Langridge

John Lill
Andrew Litton
Felicity Lott
Witold Lutoslawski
Moura Lympany
Joanna MacGregor
Sir Charles Mackerras
Jerzy Maksymiuk
Karita Mattila
Sabine Meyer
Ann Murray
Roger Norrington
Norwegian Chamber Orchestra
Dennis O'Neill
Orpheus Chamber Orchestra
Tadaaki Otaka
Seiji Ozawa
Orchestre de Paris
Libor Pesek
Artur Pizarro
Simon Rattle
Jean Rigby
Faye Robinson
Royal Opera House Orchestra
Gennady Rozhdestvensky
Dmitry Sitkovetsky
Leonard Slatkin
Cheryl Studer
Klaus Tennstedt
Michael Tilson Thomas
Yan Pascal Tortelier
Barry Tuckwell
Mitsuko Uchida
USSR Ministry of Culture Chamber Choir
Franz Welser-Möst
Welsh National Opera
Willard White
Mark Wigglesworth
Barry Wordsworth
Lothar Zagrosek

BBC

cricket team. The Australians took this with evident good grace. Yet what was more unexpected was that any Australians were there *at all*, displaying their flag inside the Victorian auditorium alongside those of so many other countries. Perhaps they were a natural offshoot of the more diverse view of contemporary Britain held by Nicholas Kenyon, whose Last Night celebrations have harnessed new technologies to highlight each of the four nations of the United Kingdom in place of the more broad-brushed Britishness of yore. In any case, the Ashes series was not the most important battle in which Britain was then involved. In that week of further escalations in the violence perpetrated by and against British soldiers in Iraq, it seemed incongruous that Australians or anyone else would wish to celebrate Britain's great imperial foundations, in which much of the tea party of the Last Night has its origins.

But the representation of so many other countries on this peculiarly British night is at the least indicative of changing Proms traditions. Each of the artistic directors since Sargent's show-pony era of Last Nights has found himself wrestling with his conscience and his audience on this very matter. Glock tried to alter the content by introducing commissioned works and dropping some favourites, but was forced to retreat; for Ponsonby and Drummond it was a battle too hard, until Drummond programmed Birtwistle's *Panic* on his last Last Night in 1995. Change, therefore, has been slow and subtle – helped in the Kenyon years by the innovation and application of technology and by Britain's evolving sense of politics and history. Not everyone applauds these alterations to time-honoured rituals. The official Proms website today crackles with correspondence from disappointed Prommers, many looking back to happier times ('But, can we PLEASE have Rule Britannia! reinstated in full, with a soloist in the famous Union Jack dress? And, if we must have Danny Boy and the like, please DO NOT put them in the middle of Fantasia On British Sea Songs').

Perhaps those on both sides of the debate protest too much. Adherence to this ragbag of invented traditions and gestures, the origins of which are scarcely known by those who enact them, is little different from adherence to the rituals that define Britain's official church and government, even if its social consequence is less. It is hardly worlds away from the entrenched and idiosyncratic traditions associated with Vienna's New Year's Concerts. Moreover, even today audiences of 'serious' art music ritualize concerts and recitals, never more so than in Britain. Those who sneer at Last Nighters or the supposed populist philosophy of the Proms are more often than not the same people who enter other concert auditoriums pre-programmed, determined that only they and those blessed with the same special knowledge will be witnesses to An Important Event. This is cultural one-upmanship at its worst, its admixture of blind ritual and religiosity arguably more damaging than anything thrown up by the Last Night of the Proms. The response of these audiences is preordained, regardless of the quality of the actual performance. And nothing or no one will convince them that this time the emperor really was naked.

In this, the Proms has been true to its democratic aim. As this book relates, it has done far more than that. In his somewhat worthy autobiography, Henry Wood wrote of the reaction of orchestral players to him as a young conductor: 'And look how he works us! Why in the old days, the conductor would say: "Fifth Symphony, Beethoven, gentlemen! We don't need to rehearse *that*! We all *know* it!" "Aye, and how we all yelled *No*!"'[22] Wood insisted that they *did* need to rehearse Beethoven, and much else besides; his skills as a planner and rehearsal conductor thus initiated a new era of orchestral playing and standards. This is his legacy today. He has bequeathed us a somewhat backward-looking culture in which the best possible performances of largely canonic repertory are given by distinguished interpreters. Considering aspects of the British music scene in the late nineteenth century, this legacy alone marks Wood out as a true radical. His own aspirations, however, were greater than this. Through his genuine commitment to 'novelties' he created a template for a century of programme-building that in today's climate of caution and conformity looks ever more innovative. He and Newman caught the spirit of their time and, like Richard Strauss, another revolutionary with blood on his hands, together forged their own symphonic optimism in *fin-de-siècle* form.

Sir Henry Wood (centre) with John Gough (right, BBC Pacific Programmes Organiser) and Hubert Clifford (left, BBC Empire Music Director) in the ruins of the bombed Queen's Hall, May 1941.

Building an Orchestra, Creating an Audience

ROBERT NEWMAN AND THE QUEEN'S HALL
PROMENADE CONCERTS, 1895–1926

LEANNE LANGLEY

1895 WAS A GOOD YEAR FOR EXPERIMENTS. In Bologna, Guglielmo Marconi successfully carried out the first wireless telegraph transmission, assuring the birth of radio. In London, Robert Newman launched a series of summer orchestral concerts at the newly opened Queen's Hall, shaping the phenomenon we know as the Proms. Neither of these innovators started from scratch or worked in a vacuum. Both drew on earlier efforts and sought continual practical improvements. Passionate about the potential in their achievements, both also acted as entrepreneurs to develop and promote their ideas. They had to: Italian and British governments gave little support to scientific or cultural endeavour in the late nineteenth century. The comparison goes further. Marconi spent much of his childhood in Bedfordshire and later established the Marconi Wireless Telegraph Company in London. He won a Nobel prize for physics and died in 1937 with an international reputation. Newman, who studied singing in Italy and stockjobbing in London, emerged as one of the most astute music administrators in Europe. He died in 1926, respected as chief founder and manager of the Queen's Hall Orchestra, the Promenade Concerts, Sunday Orchestral Concerts and Saturday Symphony Concerts, though eclipsed in celebrity by Sir Henry Wood.

*Henry J. Wood
in 1902, aged 33,
cultivating an image
as a serious artist,
tinged with humour.*

Wood was in fact Newman's most famous creation and the public face of the Proms.

Despite the parallels, there is no suggestion that Marconi and Newman ever met, no evidence that in 1895 they were even aware of each other. Science and technology had impacted on music and public entertainment for centuries – through instrument-making and music printing, for example – and the two spheres were soon to collide through advances in sound recording and radio in the early twentieth century. But when Newman designed his promenade experiment as a way of getting people into that vast and empty hall in Upper Regent Street, he was of course not remotely concerned about the concerts' longer-term future through some nebulous, nationwide musical service 'over the airwaves', with its new mode of individual listening and mass public address. Not yet. By the same logic, the growing musical, educational and social importance of the Queen's Hall Promenade Concerts between 1895 and 1926 had nothing whatever to do with what would become the British Broadcasting Corporation. Indeed, the reverse is closer to reality: any early prestige enjoyed by the infant broadcasting industry in the late 1920s came at least partly through its close association with the much-loved, nationally celebrated promenade concerts started by Newman at Queen's Hall.

It was the *survival* of the series into the crucial summer of 1927, without Newman but still conducted by Wood, his closest colleague from the original experiment, that linked the Proms to radio and the BBC – successfully as it happened, and so emotively that a later generation might almost believe that the concerts had barely existed before then. 'Takeover', 'rescue', even 'salvation' were not too strong to apply, given the series' precarious financial position, widely known at the time, and the devastating impact of Newman's unexpected death in late 1926. That Wood himself thought of the change not in terms of rescue but of the Corporation's 'entrance' with the Proms is a telling distinction.[1] From his point of view, the concerts were an established fixture in the national diary; the BBC, an unknown quantity, was simply their fifth sponsor since 1895. The political and musical ramifications of these differing angles on the Newman–Wood years will be apparent below and in later chapters. What is incontestable is that new life ensued after 1927, for the concerts and for broadcasting. Robert Newman surely imagined as much, since there is every reason to believe that well before his death he not only

*Opposite Robert
Newman, c. 1910,
founder of the Proms
and for thirty-one
years manager of
the Queen's Hall
Orchestra.*

understood the benefits of transferring the Proms to a national broadcasting body, but himself took some of the first steps to explore such a possibility, securing his life's achievement and Wood's career.[2] In that sense, his 1895 experiment did cross with Marconi's, consciously. The Queen's Hall Promenade Concerts founded by Newman underpinned the cultural policy of the new BBC and helped make broadcasting acceptable to a wide public. In turn, the concerts' transition from private to corporate management, from on-site event to public broadcast, appeared part of a seamless continuity belying the personal anxieties on all sides.

Survival is hardly remarkable in Britain, however, or a sign of robust health or importance: it is far too common. Indeed, the Queen's Hall Proms had had their difficulties twice before the 1920s but pulled through, so that the notion of endurance was a golden thread in their historiography well ahead of the BBC rescue.[3] Onward from 1927, it was only a short step to the celebration of Wood's long conducting career – half a century by 1938 – and then of fifty years of the Queen's Hall Promenades themselves (and Wood's seventy-fifth birthday) in 1944. Between those two dates Hitler destroyed the hall but not the concerts, which again survived by reappearing at an older temple to British technology and culture, the Royal Albert Hall. A growing lore on the Proms phenomenon, increasingly conflated with Wood himself (he died in August 1944), now began to find imagined continuities in the past, as each celebratory book or pamphlet sought to fill in the 'historical background' by referring to Victorian and even Georgian traditions of promenading at a range of informal London concerts, outdoors and in. Colourful illustrations of Vauxhall Gardens and of the Paris-inspired entertainments of Jullien and Rivière; descriptions of popular waltzes, quadrilles and cornet solos; bemused or embarrassed references to the free flow of drink, the cheap tickets and the occasional symphony movements thrown in for education's sake – all these elements and more found their way into that great British success story that culminated in the 'Henry Wood Promenade Concerts' and the elevation of Wood to cultural icon. The narrative is familiar and rarely questions the momentum that seems to connect Vauxhall with the Albert Hall, Jullien with Wood, the whole Proms tradition with British pride and a good night out. Even late twentieth-century writers, aware of Wood's shortcomings or interested in more recent music, have hardly disputed – or sought to explain – the Queen's Hall part of the narrative: Newman is little more than a stalwart functionary, the hall a tragic loss, and the 10th of August 1895, the first First Night, a kind of misty 'national moment'.

One underlying problem here is not just the point of view and tone in the received literature but a reluctance by modern historians to take the Proms seriously, to place them critically against a wider sweep of contemporary culture within Britain. Yet looking at urban and social identity together with national concert life more broadly may well present things in a different light. Above all, what the Queen's Hall Promenade Concerts actually achieved before 1915, levering the musical culture of Victorian Britain into modernity and classical music itself into a place of wide public recognition on a par with literature, theatre and art, may emerge with new clarity. For without doubt the Proms was a key driver in the national shift from choral, mostly sacred repertory to secular orchestral music, from individual music-making and mixed-bag taste to corporate listening and coherent programming, indeed in the very definition of 'high' and 'popular'. Moreover, exploring what Robert Newman was really trying to do, and what he accomplished against the odds, shows that the Queen's Hall Promenades excelled because they were a major *dis*continuity with tradition, a subversion of prevailing concert patterns that within ten years had totally changed the public perception of orchestral music in Britain. Establishing the orchestral medium as attractive to thousands of new listeners not only brought serious concerts and box-office takings into something like equilibrium in London (for a while), but also helped make orchestral music the new professional norm, viable and stimulating for indigenous composers, career conductors, and a pool of players second to none in the world. It was never straightforward, of course. Educating taste often came at the expense of polished performances. Managing and maintaining a house orchestra brought its own crises. A catastrophic world war nearly destroyed everything.

How all this relates to 1895, and how Robert Newman's experiment developed over its first twenty-five years, is largely a forgotten story. To recover it we should start with the hall itself, a building that readily explains why Newman was interested in the promenade idea.

Queen's Hall, Langham Place

Queen's Hall was conceived as an 'events space' for both serious and popular music at a time of unprecedented growth in the entertainment industry, the mid-1880s. Theatres and music halls had been springing up all over London, often with related drinking and dining facilities. Department stores, skating rinks and professional sporting venues were similarly on the rise, meeting and stimulating the demand for leisure activity on more than one social level. Partly the result of urbanization and a deflationary trend creating greater prosperity for the working and middle classes from the 1870s,[4] this invigorated business environment gained further from new transport links – Londoners were steadily populating the suburbs in the late nineteenth century – and a generous supply of music providers, too. Here London was uniquely well served, with its international repute as a music capital (some would say 'the' music capital of Europe, open to all comers), two major conservatories (the Royal College of Music had opened in 1883, joining the Royal Academy of Music of 1823), other music schools, a wealth of private instructors, and increasing numbers of skilled performers. Concert hall provision had always been haphazard, though, more so than in regional cities with firm cultural ambitions such as Birmingham, Manchester, Glasgow and Leeds. By the late 1880s, the common remark that London had no centrally located venue 'sufficiently large and convenient to meet the extended and ever growing musical

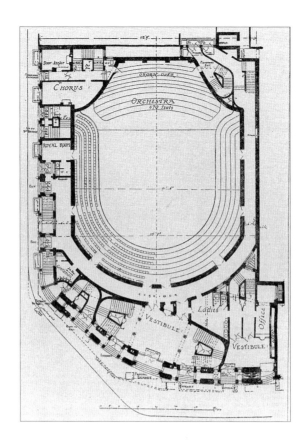

Plan, at street level, of the proposed new concert hall in Langham Place, from The Builder (14 February 1891).

Opposite Queen's Hall interior, 1894, ornately decorated (above), and exterior, c. 1905, with box office on the far right (below).

requirements of the present day' was hard to deny.[5] St James's Hall, located between Regent's Street and Piccadilly and built in the late 1850s by the music publishers Chappell, came closest; but after thirty years it was too small for large forces, uncomfortable for audiences and notoriously unsafe, cited more than once by the Metropolitan Board of Works (from 1889 the London County Council) for breach of fire regulations.

Enter a private consortium with expertise in banking, property development, architecture, theatre management and music: at its head was the financier Francis Ravenscroft, founder of the Birkbeck Bank (and a benefactor of what would become Birkbeck College).[6] Despite severe hurdles over a six-year period, including the withdrawal of most of his advisers, Ravenscroft built the hall many had dreamt of, on a prime corner site at the top of Regent Street, just south of All Souls' Church and opposite the Langham Hotel. It was an ornate, imposing structure seating almost 3,000. On its opening in November 1893, the hall was acclaimed as much for its modern amenities as for its exuberant style and acoustic success.[7] The total effect can only be imagined now: a huge, resonant space with a wide but shallow stepped platform at the east end (away from Regent Street); two balconies and curved open corridors around three sides; a sunken arena at basement level, with individual removable seats; broad stone staircases with seventeen exits onto three streets (for state-of-the-art safety); a premier location near Underground and bus routes, fashionable shops, department stores and restaurants; a long, curved

open frontage for carriages, with parking available; a special press room for reporters and music critics; airy refreshment spaces, bars and comfortable toilet areas for everyone; a full kitchen in the basement and a small chamber hall (seating 500), with adjoining conservatory, in the roof; and last but not least, a box office selling tickets to any show in town. One might well conclude that 'customers', not merely music-lovers, were expected at this place, and that the very experience of going into it was part of the attraction.

The trouble was that getting people in the door in their hundreds and thousands depended more on the product inside than on any novelty of building design, yet Ravenscroft had absolutely no grip on what he was selling. A luxurious space to be let out for wedding breakfasts, City dinners, children's parties and musical entertainment, yes, but by whom, how and when? Queen's Hall lacked a clear identity in 1893; even its name had been changed hastily from the originally projected 'Victoria Concert Hall' to avoid confusion with that better-known Victoria Music Hall across the river (the Old Vic), suggesting that its character and direction were uncertain at the outset.[8] Without a lessee just a few weeks before the opening, Ravenscroft was desperate to hire someone, anyone, to run the hall. He turned for advice to Frederic Cowen, the only musician on his original board, who in turn recommended a former athlete, stockjobber and baritone just then trying his hand at musical agency work, Robert Newman.[9] It was a lucky chance, no more, but was soon to prove one of the most effective appointments in the history of British music.

A JOY OF THE DOG-DAYS: THE PROMENADE CONCERTS
WHICH BENEFIT THE SANDWICH-MAN AS WELL AS THE MUSIC-LOVER

Sandwich men outside Door 13 of Queen's Hall in Riding House Street, evoking the energy and immediacy of Newman's publicity effort in the early 1900s.

From day one, Newman knew he had a problem, or rather several – attracting promoters, attracting the public, and building a sustainable programme of his own events. He seems at first to have taken the job for a year, on salary plus a percentage of receipts.[10] Then, from late 1894, he became Ravenscroft's full tenant – lessee of the building and manager, at his own risk, of the whole operation. Experimentation and an open mind were always in Newman's own interest as he felt his way forward. This attitude, with an apparently genuine concern to serve the customer – to find out what audiences wanted and let them have it gradually, building trust between provider and consumer – helps explain his success at creating the hall's liberal ethos (precisely what his critics, usually old partisans of St James's Hall, disliked: 'pandering to the box office'). Indeed, Newman's every step seemed to alternate experiment, adjustment, experiment, adjustment, with no preconceived class agenda, political ideology, genre preference, music publisher or piano-maker calling the shots. This in itself – a kind of free trade in concerts – was almost revolutionary in London and stemmed directly from the size of Queen's Hall and the need to make it pay its own way. For, despite appearances of democracy and public responsiveness, there was little altruism here: Newman was a commercial animal, shrewdly promoting events and managing people like shares on the market. His nine-year winning streak, to 1902, suggests he knew exactly what he was doing.

Continuities

With the manager's late start and artists' reluctance to hire an untried venue, bookings were slow to arrive in the 1893–4 season. Within six months of opening, however, four key events had helped tap potential audiences and set a seal of approval on the new hall: a spectacularly successful 'Cav and Pag' (unstaged) on a Saturday afternoon in January; three invited appearances of the Bach Choir (rent-free, in return for advice on acoustics during construction); the permanent transfer of the august Philharmonic Society concerts from St James's Hall (their first, in February 1894, included the eagerly awaited English première of Tchaikovsky's Sixth Symphony); and a short Wagner series in April (conducted by Felix Mottl ahead of Hans Richter's annual visit to London). Newman was stealing a march on his competitors. Drawing good press notices and catering for several advanced tastes, he was also learning to work with, and sometimes against, London seasonal expectations. The hall would face a virtual blank in August and September, for example, unless he could concoct something in-house: as everyone knew, London subscription concerts and big-name artist appearances were futile once the social elite had left town.

It was at this juncture, as early as February or March 1894, that Newman began to think seriously about promenade concerts, the one model that would certainly work in low season with its lesser-known (cheaper) performers, relaxed atmosphere and open social access. The hall's floor space and visual appeal, including its beautiful ceiling, might be ideal for promenades. More important, proms could be used to lure hundreds of punters who might otherwise never hear of Queen's Hall or set foot inside it – resident Londoners seeking light evening entertainment, foreign and provincial visitors on excursion, any music-lovers not belonging to the taste groups Newman was already courting. The key requisites would be personnel and capital. Luckily, Fred Cowen was at hand. An experienced conductor with knowledge of good players, he had worked well with Newman on precisely this sort of series the previous summer at Covent Garden (in effect securing the manager his Queen's Hall post). It seemed an obvious partnership to repeat. Yet neither of them had the cash to risk.[11] Newman then approached a young accompanist and vocal coach just back from a celebrity tour, Henry J. Wood, about his views and possible involvement in the scheme. Although interested and receptive to Newman's ideas, Wood was similarly unable to contribute.[12] There were no proms in 1894.

By February 1895 the manager had made up his mind to go ahead. As the story goes, Newman called on Wood, announced his intentions, asked for financial input from his chosen director designate and, when disappointed, replied, 'Never mind! I'll see what can be done, *for I mean to run those concerts!*'[13] That same day it was not Newman but Wood whose excitement at a vocal lesson uncovered a willing sponsor – Dr George Cathcart, a Harley Street throat specialist. Not only impressed with Wood's teaching and communication skills, Cathcart had a radical agenda of his own: he wanted any such public concerts in the new venue to be given at 'French pitch' – slightly lower than what was then customary in England and healthier for singers' voices – and for Wood to be engaged as sole conductor, giving him a fair chance in all repertory including Wagner.[14] Both conditions proved their worth, and Cathcart received full credit for his role in starting the Queen's Hall Promenades.[15] Before the deal was finally struck, however, and the summer dates booked, Newman arranged a trial concert on Saturday night, 23 March 1895. The first-ever Queen's Hall 'Grand Promenade Concert' – conducted by Henry J. Wood, with unnamed orchestra, four vocal soloists, three instrumental soloists, an organist and the Band of the Coldstream Guards (directed by C. Thomas) – this event reflected longstanding promenade practice.[16] To Newman, it was the new location and conductor who were on test, not the concert model.

The nature and pedigree of that model, and the influence it would have exerted in 1895, are worth exploring. Some of Newman's first orchestral players, for example, had performed at the Covent Garden proms for twenty years or more, including W. H. Eayres, Frye Parker, Charles Ould, W. H. Hann, J. Anderson and, famously, Howard Reynolds the cornet player.[17] And there were other continuities besides, as shown by the aspects of the promenade tradition listed below, all of which were well established before 1895. Each point is traceable in surviving programmes, press reports or personal memoirs from at least the 1870s – some as far back as the 1840s, 50s and 60s – at various London theatres including the Lyceum, Her Majesty's and Covent Garden.[18]

Parallels with the first Queen's Hall series, as well as with later Proms traditions, are striking.

- ⚘ A promenade concert was a long evening's entertainment, from 8 to 11 or 11.30 pm, often held nightly (except Sunday) for several weeks in late summer or autumn, in a physical space that encouraged listeners to walk around during the performance; moving in and out of the music's range – leaving, then returning at will – was entirely acceptable for standing concert-goers.

- ⚘ A large orchestra prominently displayed, sometimes supplemented by a military or wind band, was the main attraction; seeing the sound source and appreciating its fullness were part of the visceral excitement.

- ⚘ Cornet solos, which had their roots in Philippe Musard's Paris concerts of the 1830s, offered displays to catch the ear, just as instrumental solos in operatic medleys, begun in the 1840s, offered audiences the chance to 'spot' favourite players and recognize distinct timbres.

- ⚘ Elaborate floral decorations, greenery, palms or even décor painted with scenic views (e.g. 'a Persian Palace', or 'Switzerland') might be added as visual attractions, whether to mimic the outdoors or create an illusion of coolness and an informal mood.

- ⚘ An emphasis on refreshments, especially liquid, often came from the concert promoter's main business: for many years in the 1860s and 70s, the promenade sponsor at Covent Garden was Gatti's Grand Café in the Strand, which regularly made more profit on drink than on ticket sales, as in the music hall industry; food and drink, placed on long tables behind the orchestra, were accessible during the performance.

- ⚘ A promenade's first part contained its most serious musical elements, while the second had a more popular, miscellany feel – often dance music or vocal numbers; the evening progressed so that a range of expectations could be fulfilled.

- ⚘ For educational purposes, classical works were introduced into frankly popular programmes gradually – e.g. single symphony movements, then the whole; they seem to have been valued as part of the rich mix, not feared or avoided.

- ⚘ Themed nights were common and often fell into regular patterns – 'Classical Night' on Wednesdays and 'Popular Night' on Saturdays both had long histories before 1895 – although there were also many one-offs, such as Mozart Night, Scotch Ballad Night, Rossini Night, Gounod Night, Military Night; the theme applied to the first half of the concert only.

- ⚘ Special commissions or other new works might be introduced each season and played or sung as appropriate, even by the audience, on succeeding nights (with publication and supplier information advertised in the programme). Political topicality was sometimes a spur to new British work; foreign novelties were warmly welcomed (e.g. Siegfried's Funeral March from *Götterdämmerung*, with its new tubas, in the mid-1870s).

❧ For decades before 1895, a shilling was the standard entry price each night and allowed the visitor to promenade or take an unreserved seat. Season tickets at a guinea were also available, taking the price of a single evening's entertainment down to a few pence; the notion of transferability, encouraging season-ticket holders to pass around their tickets, seems to have been introduced in the late 1880s by way of a small book of detachable tickets.

❧ Audience behaviour warnings to train casual listeners were printed in the nightly programme or displayed on signs, largely to discourage encores and to ensure the running order kept to time; smoking was usually permitted, as in a music hall, though sometimes in restricted areas.

❧ Published criticism of promenade concerts came from above and below, in the form of elite condescension about how vulgar it all was (e.g. from the *Musical Times*, academics and organists), or working-class disdain about how heavy orchestral music seemed compared with a few good tunes (*The Era* and other music hall sources).

The obvious conclusion to draw from this list, apart from the clear links with showbusiness, is that in the promenade model Newman found a familiar package that would attract the widest possible audience, diverse in age, level of musical sophistication and social class. Whether he also felt deeply motivated to teach the masses to 'love great music' (as Wood later claimed) is another question altogether – slightly suspect and probably irrelevant, certainly in the 1890s.[19] Newman's first aim was to promote the hall and make the finances work. Since the fulcrum of his plan, and its greatest expense, would be the hiring of a full orchestra six nights a week, the manager soon turned to logistics and business strategy.

A New Function for Promenades

One problem for students of the early Queen's Hall Proms has always been a lack of original documentation. Although such material surely existed in the manager's office at Langham Place, there is now no archive of letters, contracts or business ledgers giving detailed insight into Proms planning, public attendance or finance. Nor is there a known cache of personal papers for Newman or any of his successor proprietors for the period 1902–26 (see Table 1 below, p. 65).[20] To get an idea of how things developed, one has to piece together odd scraps of information from the letters of Wood, his associates and other musicians, from memoirs, newspapers and journals and, of course, from published programmes. Along with sources relating to the building of Queen's Hall, including public records, and other concerts at the same venue and beyond, these make a jigsaw of evidence from which reasonable inferences can be drawn. Consulting wider culture is essential because all along Newman was running a multi-use building, not just a concert hall; he was an artist's agent, not just a series promoter; and the promenade concerts were only one strand of his growing, year-round business. His great genius lay in linking all the strands effectively, characteristically turning problems into opportunities and, as lessee, thinking laterally about how to unite the entire Queen's Hall enterprise.

Once committed to the promenade project under Cathcart's conditions, Newman had one over-arching goal – to build a first-rate house orchestra out of a scratch orchestra, which is what Wood took on when he agreed to the arrangement. The young director had to train his chosen players in a huge body of music, not just old favourites, on minimal amounts of time and money. This in itself sharpened his 'scientific' rehearsal techniques – the careful checking and marking of every part beforehand, exactly timed slots for each piece and each soloist, a precise tuning check before rehearsal began ('the ritual of the fork'), and so on.[21] Newman had reckoned, rightly, that the job could be done *well enough* if the same players, all of them good readers, played together every night for eight or ten weeks in the season; extensive rehearsal would be unnecessary because the performances would contribute to the rehearsal process. Indeed, for each week of concerts – six performances – there were only three morning rehearsals; for these nine sessions, the players received 45 shillings (5 shillings a session).[22] Continuity of membership over the season was vital. So was repeating much of the same music and using piano or organ rather than orchestra to accompany many of the vocal solos. Omitting the usual military contingent with its own director made a further saving and met Cathcart's stipulation about conductorship, while hiring an orchestra slightly smaller than usual, perhaps 75 or 80 players rather than the 100+ at Covent Garden, most certainly cut costs. *Voilà* – cheap labour.

The real stumbling block had been Cathcart's insistence on French pitch. In principle, the doctor was right. English pitch had crept up over the nineteenth century to about a semitone higher than anywhere else in Europe, and there was no agreed standard even within Britain; variation in the tuning of instruments, including pianos, and the strain placed on singers were perceived as real problems.[23] But Newman resisted. Not only did he actually prefer the old system; he also knew the proposed change would mean big expenditure on new wind instruments from the Continent (where *diapason normal* was standard) and on repitching the Queen's Hall organ to match. In the end Cathcart paid for the wind instruments, which the players later happily repurchased, but Newman had to shell out for the organ. No wonder he exploited the situation, turning his investment into headlines and promoting Queen's Hall as leading national change. In August 1895 he announced that the promenade orchestra and all other groups performing at the hall, including the Philharmonic Society and the Bach Choir, would thenceforth adopt French pitch (equivalent to $a' = 439$ at 68°F) – which they did. The move aroused public curiosity (whatever did 'French' pitch sound like?).

Henry J. Wood conducting, cartoon by Spy, published in Vanity Fair (1907).

Equally important, it opened Queen's Hall to future collaboration with entire foreign orchestras, not just visiting conductors. At Newman's invitation, the Lamoureux and Colonne bands from Paris were first on the platform, winning accolades in 1896–7, Lamoureux's orchestra even playing *with* the Queen's Hall Orchestra during Newman's first London Musical Festival in May 1899. Linking one strand of his business to another, the manager had solved a problem while raising excitement and musical expectations at the same time.

But what about the likely long-term response from an uncertain, indeterminate promenade audience? Even on tight margins, how could anyone hope to make a profit from so elaborate and expensive a scheme as running – sustaining – a large orchestra? One answer is this: in gaining a foothold on the London calendar and marshalling his own forces, Newman was building a brand. He had begun with a 'Queen's Hall Choir' in 1894, but its concerts lacked public support and the group transmuted into a Queen's Hall Choral Society for occasional large-scale performances.[24] It was the more modern and exciting notion of a permanent orchestra based at a purpose-built hall – unimaginable in London, truly radical and fraught with risk – that presented the greatest potential for developing new audiences at just this moment. Since the 1880s there had been growing enthusiasm for week-night subscription orchestral concerts at St James's Hall conducted by the formidable Hans Richter, among others, and, from even earlier, Saturday afternoon concerts at the Crystal Palace in suburban Sydenham conducted by August Manns.[25] Public and critical reception, not least by George Bernard Shaw, was good enough to justify continued support of these often revelatory orchestral series. Yet timing, ticket price, programme or location had in effect divided the existing audience for such concerts into separate loyalty groups: Rosa Newmarch, who knew the territory, observed that few of the habitués of one London orchestral series ever met those of another, and hardly ever at the same concerts.[26] It was one of Robert Newman's signal insights that from the beginning he targeted not the conglomerate audience of established orchestral concerts, but a far larger, metropolitan audience living mostly in the new suburbs – generally of modest means and few preconceived expectations, but with genuine intellectual and social aspirations. Late summer was perfect for his purpose, because at promenades almost anything was allowed, including an unknown English conductor. If success followed and the hall became known, the manager could gradually spin out separate instrumental or orchestral series for specialist tastes ('new products' under the same brand name), using the same core players in new combinations – as indeed he did. The fiduciary value of Queen's Hall, its name alone a guarantee of excellence, would thus become firmly established in logical stages. Henry Wood was to spearhead the plan, starting with the Promenades, and his role would develop in tandem with that of the other hired musicians.

The broad diversity of the Promenade audience was in fact one of its most conspicuous traits from the outset – real connoisseurs and total novices,

'A Début at the Promenades', drawing by C. H. Taffs, from The Graphic *(24 October 1908), in which a crowded audience, mixed in age, sex and social class, joins the conductor in applauding a new singer.*

practising musicians and ordinary event-seekers, the well behaved, the inattentive, students, the elderly, office workers and bus drivers, soldiers ('khaki'), single women and couples, bankers, solicitors, clerks and clerics, civil servants, the man on the street escaping the rain. And the wide mix did not disappear as the programmes gradually became more serious.[27] This breadth was unlike the audience for any other series we know about, high or low. It owed as much to Newman's assiduous cultivation of casualness as to the sprawling multifariousness of London and its lack of a 'town hall' mentality. The manager wanted people to attend for their own enjoyment and stimulation, not to be seen or because it was the thing to do; he also wanted them to come back time after time, bringing friends and passing the pleasure along – hence his continued use of transferable season tickets, which in turn helped promote the concerts' value as educative. By 1908, the Queen's Hall Promenade Concerts had not only helped establish an unequivocal top brand for the building, they had also achieved for London what local choral societies and orchestras had already done in regional music centres, which is to say they gave the city a unique cultural institution, using locally based players, that fostered the general and continuous love of music in its own residents.[28] In an inversion of the usual assumptions about musical leadership emanating from London, the Proms at last put the capital – as an English city of ordinary music-loving people, not an international honeypot attracting foreign musical stars – on the national cultural map. It had been a long time coming.[29]

Working Dynamics, Practicalities

Creating a brand – using promenade concerts to train players and listeners, any of whom might go on to other activities at the same hall – was clearly the tie-in that made Newman's package excel where previous proms had just repeated themselves. But how did the process work in practice, and what role did Wood actually fulfil? Team sport and music hall suggest some possible analogies, as does the notion of the Proms as a laboratory or workshop, trying out, then channelling, new artists and new music. Each concert, and each season, constituted a set of relationships being played out in the hall, subtly shifting and changing in the search for better musical experiences (whatever that might mean at different times). Every night was part of the ongoing experiment.

Teamwork

Newman was boss and Wood's professional manager. As far as we know, they planned programmes together, Wood submitting his musical ideas to Newman for presentational refinement.[30] Teamwork infused the whole system, along with careful handling of individual strengths, a quick and flexible response to market signals, and an utterly professional attitude to corporate strategy, including the deployment of artists. In the early years, soloists of repute, singers and instrumentalists alike, were often hired for several dates in one season, not just a single appearance. Functioning a bit like a company, they were placed as needed, sometimes up to ten times in the season. Notable individual examples include the pianist Frederick Dawson (who appeared six times in 1895), the cellist W. H. Squire (eight times in 1899), the pianist Adela Verne (five times in 1900), the violinist Leonora von Stosch and the young pianist Wilhelm Backhaus (nine and ten times, respectively, in 1901), and a remarkable 13-year-old piano prodigy known simply as Solomon (ten times in 1915), each promoted on a roster which they shared with many others in the given season. Such a team approach not only lent efficiency to Newman and Wood – booking one artist for several appearances almost certainly kept the unit cost down besides easing repertory selection and rehearsal – it fostered audience rapport too. Listeners looked for the familiar face, voice or style of each performer and learned to appreciate them through visual repetition, but also to trust them when the music changed. With listener experience came discrimination, as a number of anonymous jottings in extant programmes can show. Some particularly frank remarks from 1919 include these: 'Great disappointment for lovely song. I do not like her at all. Her voice was drowned. Bad enunciation' (on Liszt's 'The Loreley', sung by Miss Hilda Blake), or: 'I love this opera. She has quite the best voice I've heard this season ... quite a delight' (on Miss Phyllis Smith, singing Puccini's 'Vissi d'arte'), or even: 'This I love & Wood does well, but not as well as L. R.' (on Bantock's *Pierrot of the Minute*, favouring Landon Ronald's interpretation).[31] With consumers like this one, clearly a comparison-shopper, who needed professional critics?

The tight-knit team idea of the mid- and late-1890s gradually loosened as more and more young artists presented themselves for audition – for it soon became desirable, career-wise, to make one's début at the Proms. Wood listened to streams of aspirants, from 1896 giving several weeks of his time each year to nothing else, talent-scouting for Newman.[32] Hundreds of musicians received engagements. In the 1907 season alone, no fewer than 105 soloists were featured across the ten weeks – chiefly new sopranos and pianists, but also orchestral principals. Again, the orchestra was presented as a team made of distinct individuals; learning to spot them was an audio-visual exercise focusing new listeners' attention. Those who knew the sound of each instrument and who was playing from within the larger body could keep up and stay in the game. It was for just such an exercise, or spectator sport, that the 'operatic fantasia' slot opening nearly every concert's second half was retained as late as 1904, the same tradition prompting Wood's song medleys, not least the *Fantasia on British Sea Songs*, from 1905.[33] For the *Sea Songs'* première – the centenary of the battle of Trafalgar on 21 October 1905 – the successive solo instruments with the players' names were printed in the programme so that everyone could follow along; and even for ordinary fantasia slots the players and their instruments were usually named in sectional order. This was no concession to cheap taste (as Wood later claimed about the cornet solos), but a way in for learners, a deliberate training device not unlike Benjamin Britten's *Young Person's Guide to the Orchestra* half a century later. The effect must have been liberating, subverting the star-driven ethos of other orchestral concerts whereby fantastic celebrities with unique mental mastery of 'great music' were expected to be silently appreciated (and paid) for all their virtuosity, implying

1. GRAND FANTASIA - "Faust" - - - *Gounod*
Solos by Messrs. ARTHUR W. PAYNE (Violin), H. LYELL-TAYLER (Violin), A. E. FERIR (Viola), JACQUES RENARD ('Cello), J. HAYDN WAUD (Contra Bass), A. FRANSELLA (Flute), J. WILCOCKE (Piccolo), J. L. FONTEYNE (Oboe), M. GOMEZ (Clarinet), E. F. JAMES (Bassoon), A. BORSDORF (Horn), T. COLTON (Trombone), WALTER REYNOLDS (Euphonium), C. HENDERSON (Tympani), Miss MIRIAM TIMOTHY (Harp), and ARTHUR SMITH (Cornet).

The opera "Faust" (based on the first part only of Goethe's great dramatic poem) is not only the greatest work of its composer, but is also one of the finest and most universally appreciated operas written during the nineteenth century. It was produced in 1859 at the Théâtre Lyrique, Paris, and was played for the first time in England at Her Majesty's Theatre, Haymarket, in June, 1863. Among the first pieces from the opera 'to catch the public ear was the "Soldiers' Chorus." So popular indeed was this piece during the "Sixties" that it became almost a public nuisance—little else was to be heard. The "Faust" legend (one of the most permanently pregnant of modern humanity's myths) had often been utilized for musical purposes before Gounod took it in hand, and has since been treated by Boito, whose "Mefistofele" (produced in 1868) is an attempt to deal with Goethe's poem in a more philosophical spirit than that shown by his predecessors.

Programme detail from the opening of Part II for 11 September 1901, listing soloists' names and instruments for the 'Grand Fantasia' on Gounod's Faust.

a huge gap between them and the listeners. At the Queen's Hall Promenades, audiences were encouraged to identify with professional musicians as real people. Whether seen and heard enjoying their work, or having difficulty with a memory slip, staying together, even audibly reacting to each other, each musician was a partner in the performance, reaching out to each listener.[34] On every side a human bond was created, so that positive reassurance was easy and natural between platform and promenade. By all accounts, players enjoyed that rapport as much as listeners did.

One of Wood's roles was to hold everything together on the night. With his impeccable timing, white carnation, stage presence and easy versatility, he was little short of a real music hall chairman, noted for his sensitive accompanying on the piano, the organ or with full orchestra. But he was by no means the only colourful figure on the rostrum, nor indeed the concerts' only conductor. Composers, especially if close at hand, were often invited to conduct their own works: Elgar conducted his new *Coronation Ode* in late October 1902 (incorporating 'Land of Hope and Glory', its first Proms performance); Ethyl Smyth directed her overture to *The Wreckers* in August 1913; Percy Pitt and Frederic Cowen appeared within two nights of each other in September 1914. At times a principal violinist took over the baton, whether in Wood's absence owing to illness or an outside engagement – as in 1902, when Arthur Payne often conducted (Payne was orchestral leader, late 1895–1903) – or by way of the management's effort to distance Wood from the more popular end of the repertory – as in 1903 and 1904, when Henry Lyell-Tayler often conducted a concert's second half (Lyell-Tayler was principal second violin, 1901–4). Occasionally other arrangements had to be made. For part of the 1908 season when Wood and the Queen's Hall Orchestra (QHO) were at the Sheffield Festival, Newman and his managerial colleagues hired the entire New Symphony Orchestra, conducted by no less a figure than Edouard Colonne. In 1911 and 1912, Sir George Henschel directed a few Proms while Wood was in Norwich or Birmingham. That Henry Wood's presence was ultimately crucial, however, is clear: his 1902 absence, from mid-October to early November, affected Promenade takings, partly precipitating a direct challenge to the wider menace of the London deputy system. For generations, the custom had been to accept players' students and nominated colleagues as deputies at rehearsals (and even performances) while the players themselves took more lucrative engagements elsewhere. In late spring 1904 Newman and Wood finally forbade this practice in the QHO.[35] Continuity of personnel turned out to be as important as the frequency of concerts, since it enabled performance levels to rise.

The orchestra
From its modest size of around 80 players in 1895, the orchestra had grown to 90 for the 1896 season, and 103 a year later. The age profile came down as Wood replaced old-timers with new blood, boosting both his authority and (more gradually) the playing standard; still only twenty-eight years old in

The Queen's Hall Orchestra with Henry J. Wood, c. 1903–4, photographed during their main season (note the chairs in arena), with female harpists prominent at front right.

1897, he had to be tough over the attendance and punctuality of men many years his senior, a firmness Newman staunchly supported.[36] Orchestral auditions included sight-reading from several types of music – *Parsifal* or *Ride of the Valkyries*, for instance; a scherzando movement with rapid time changes; and definitely something in manuscript. In 1951 Eugene Goossens, who played first violin for Wood in 1912–16, left a vivid record of his own audition, remembering 'the perspiration pouring down and my knees shaking, … feeling like a victim stretched on the rack'. He flunked the manuscript piece but passed the audition, recalling Wood's final words to him: 'Go and tell Mr. Newman you're engaged. First violin. Very good indeed. But watch those MS. sheets. Dear, dear, dear: we constantly play new works. All from MS. parts. Practise reading manuscript all the time. Dear me, watch those MSS!'[37] Besides confirming the need for excellent music-reading skills, this vignette hints at the pivotal role played by new material in the Proms before 1915, a practical aspect of the early concerts not widely appreciated later. That is, with very good players, 'new works' – either truly new or just newly arranged (a Leo sinfonia, say, or a Bach suite) – were not only positively helpful in attracting curious popular listeners and press reporters: as manuscripts, they were cheaper to perform than standard classical or romantic repertory because they involved no payments to publishers.[38] Moreover, a continuous stream of new works, whatever the style, gave Wood the upper hand in training his players – instilling discipline, broadening experience and asserting a general's command over potentially restive troops (no trite image in the twilight of empire or indeed, in London's freelance orchestral environment when labour was starting to organize itself). The Queen's Hall Orchestra, built by Newman and

Wood, was the first-ever permanent orchestra to be established in central London, but its survival relied on a fusion of strong management, business innovation and member loyalty. The balance, which was never easy, disintegrated in 1904. Under the enlightened sponsorship and vision of Edgar Speyer, it was re-established with an emphasis on innovation in the years before the Great War, the heyday of the QHO in both repertory and performing standard.

Wood was proud of his players, worked them hard, and always maintained that the orchestra's international mix was a strength, yielding performances that were 'brilliant and temperamental', showing '*nuance* and fire' – by which he meant colourful, interesting and dangerous rather than careful, consistent and inspired.[39] Reports of rough ensemble at the Proms, not uncommon, were usually attributed to short rehearsal time, Wood himself admitting that the standard was likely to be better at his Saturday Symphony concerts.[40] But a loose ensemble sound – much looser than would be acceptable in the 1930s and 40s, let alone in the age of the compact disc – was also typical of even the finest players in this period; ramshackle performances, or 'just getting through', could for some listeners still produce evenings of characterful music-making.[41] The positive trade-off, for Promenade audiences and players alike, was breadth of exposure and thorough grounding in practically the entire orchestral repertory, including, according to Goossens, the 'meatier things in the contemporary symphonic repertory'.[42] Eric Coates, principal viola in the QHO between 1912 and 1919, recalled that Wood was at the peak of his energy in this period and 'spared no effort to keep the standard of the performances at its very highest'.[43] Goossens thought no conductor of the day combined better musicianship with a finer stick technique. He went further:

> Even though I played under other men with greater "box office" names than H. J. W. (Nikisch, Mengelberg, Steinberg, Safonoff), I never encountered a sincerer artist or a more resourceful, experienced, and versatile conductor than the beloved head of the Queen's Hall Orchestra. The debt owed him by the last two generations of English composers alone is a fantastic one, and that of the British public to him is quite incalculable.[44]

Among Wood's other players in various Promenade seasons up to 1920 were dozens of well-known musicians, indigenous and Continental. The following selective list is small but representative: Henri Verbruggen (principal first violin, 1904–7),[45] Arthur Catterall (principal first violin, 1909–14), W. H. Reed (violin), Frederick Stock (violin), Dora Garland (first violin), Basil Cameron (violin), Charles Woodhouse (violin, then principal first from 1920), Hugo Hundt (principal second violin), Lionel Tertis (principal viola), Siegfried Wertheim (principal viola), Philip Sainton (principal viola), W. H. Squire (principal cello), Jacques Renard (principal cello), C. Warwick Evans (principal cello), John Barbirolli (cello), J. H. Waud (principal double-bass), Adolf Lotter (principal double-bass), Albert Fransella (principal flute), Desiré Lalande (principal oboe), Henri du Busscher (principal oboe), Leon Goossens (principal oboe), Manuel Gomez (principal clarinet), Haydn Draper (principal clarinet), E. F. and W. G. James (bassoons), Adolph Borsdorf (principal horn), Alfred and Aubrey Brain (horns), Oskar Borsdorf (horn), Walter Morrow (trumpet and cornet), John Solomon (principal trumpet), Arthur Falkner (trombone), T. H. Gutteridge (trombone), Walter Reynolds (tuba and euphonium), Miriam Timothy (harp) and Alfred Kastner (harp).

The genial and accomplished Percy Pitt, a close friend of Wood's, worked as Proms accompanist from 1896 to 1905, besides serving as occasional composer, arranger, note-writer and adviser, a model of in-house efficiency. He shared the accompanist's role with Frederick B. Kiddle, a skilled organist, in 1904 and 1905, after which Kiddle took over. Since up to a quarter of the pieces on any Proms programme in the early years might be accompanied by piano or organ alone (especially in the lighter second halves), this job was an important one. Pitt further achieved minor celebrity as celesta player in Tchaikovky's *Nutcracker* suite, first performed in England at one of Newman's Saturday-series Promenades on 17 October 1896 and often thereafter; during his later work at Covent Garden and for the BBC Pitt retained influential contact with Wood.

As for the orchestra's female contingent, Wood was pleased to be the first conductor in London to admit women to his rank and file. He hired six women for the string department in 1913 – Dora Garland, Jessie Grimson, E. M. Dudding, and Jean Stewart, violins; S. Maturin and Rebecca Clarke, violas – and started them with the Saturday Symphony series in October that year. Because Newman considered the Promenade season too strenuous for them, however (even Goossens admitted the work was 'back-breaking'),[46] they did not play in the Proms orchestra until 1916, when a total of twelve women helped filled the desks left vacant by some twenty-seven QHO players on active service. In 1917 Garland won accolades as a soloist at the Proms, and a year later took Arthur Beckwith's place as leader for a period ('one of the signs of the times', according to a music journal).[47] Her achievement was a considerable advance over reports of Miriam Timothy's appeal twenty years earlier. Shrewdly, Newman had noticed that the carpet on the promenade floor near the platform on Miss Timothy's side of the orchestra – harpists sat at the very front of the stage – required more repairs than that in any other part of the hall. More candidly, Wood observed 'she was a beautiful girl … able to express her sense of artistry in her dress'. The two observations added up, Wood

Henry J. Wood and Percy Pitt, c. 1894–6, close in age, outlook and musical sympathies.

thought: 'Miriam undoubtedly was an attraction to the male Promenaders.'[48] So much for the lure of great music.

Creating demand

Advertising, programme notes and applause – aspects of regular communication between concert-givers and audiences – make a fascinating study in themselves, showing the immediacy and tightness of the Proms operation but also management's astuteness in creating and responding to demand. In the earliest years, programmes were sketched out in late spring and advertised only a week at a time in the newspapers and on the back of each nightly programme; changes to advertised programmes were not uncommon and rarely remarked. Public announcements were used instead for big promotional effect. 'Increased Orchestra, Increased Floral Decorations, The Most Refined Musical Entertainment, at One Shilling, in the Coolest Hall in London', trumpeted the *Daily Telegraph* on 21 August 1895: it had been Cathcart's bright idea to put a fountain in the centre of the arena, with blocks of ice in it. Two weeks later a confident-sounding echo, 'In Consequence of the Brilliant Success' (3 September), alluded to possible extension of the 1895 season to 'the first week in October or longer'. Though appearing to put the length of the run in the public's hands, this tack in fact signalled desperation. The series was facing certain financial loss, the only question being how big or small it might turn out to be.[49] But who would have known that from the advertising?

Once the concerts had become more firmly established, a form of advance prospectus was instituted. The earliest appears to be a folded leaflet of 1902 simply listing the orchestral works to be performed for the first time in London and the artists engaged for that season.[50] Daily advertising of each programme meanwhile continued in the papers. By 1907 at least (possibly as early as 1903), the nightly programmes were more or less fixed and printed in a full prospectus available to the public in June; evidence from 1913 shows that at that time 40,000 such prospectuses were circulated to interested parties, including regular subscribers who would be 'naturally annoyed' if alterations were made.[51] Annoyed! Annoyance was an excellent sign, even better than frayed carpet. Indeed the Proms' transformation from music hall to symphony concert is nowhere more evident than in this simple shift towards accountability and a known audience. A product of quality was now wanted by large numbers willing to pay, so the pressure to deliver – or explain – had clearly grown. On several occasions, an announced new work was cancelled because the orchestral parts had not arrived *that morning*, astonishingly close by modern standards but normal practice in the Proms rehearsal schedule; management duly inserted an apologies slip explaining any substitution in the evening's programme.[52]

With the onset of world war just before the start of the twentieth season, Wood's ability to deliver exact programmes, many featuring new European music and artists, became seriously handicapped. Keen to maintain contact with its public, QHO Ltd reminded patrons to check the newspapers every

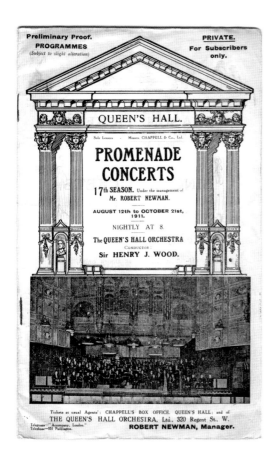

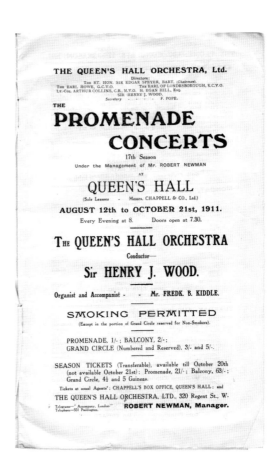

day. In 1914 the full programme for each evening appeared daily in seven papers – *The Times, Daily Telegraph, Standard, Morning Post, Daily Chronicle, Daily Express* and *Daily Graphic* – while the week's prospectus, in digest, was printed once in each of six papers – Saturday in the *Daily Telegraph*, Monday in *The Times*, Tuesday in the *Standard*, Wednesday in the *Morning Post*, Thursday in the *Daily Express* and Friday in the *Daily Chronicle*. A similar but less lavish pattern was adopted in 1915 and 1916, after which concert-goers were urged merely to acquire the prospectus at the hall's central ticket office. In the nature of ephemeral advertising, very few prospectuses survive from before the 1920s, a record that bears no relation to the series' high public profile at this time.

Proms programme notes over the first twenty-five years are a different matter – regular as clockwork, essentially educative and all along deliberately aimed at popular listeners whatever the musical content on a given night. If less important now for their analytic substance than for what they reveal about logistics, the notes nevertheless contain some of E. F. Jacques's and Rosa Newmarch's most widely read material and give an insight into how the series developed its following. At London concerts from well before the 1890s, 'analytic programmes' had been solid mementos of transient musical experience – objects to scribble on, take away and read again, share round, even collect and bind up for later study.[53] But the notes in Queen's Hall Promenade programmes were necessarily extremely brief, the paper as thin as newsprint. Just as preparation time was limited for the orchestra, so explanatory space for concert-goers was restricted. In the four-page broadsheet (price twopence), only the upper two-thirds of the two inner pages could contain programme information, which would often include up to eighteen or twenty items in early years. The rest of the space carried advertising matter – largely for beer, water and spirits before 1903, pianos, music schools and sheet music after – with the back page almost wholly devoted to Queen's Hall events, including future Proms.

Descriptions of the pieces to be heard, then, far from supplying aural roadmaps or thoughtful essays in the manner of George Grove's celebrated notes, aimed to give basic information on composers and works – or for vocal numbers, the words only – in a reader-friendly style. Occasionally the descriptions were glossed with hints about how to behave at the concerts. In 1908, for example, whenever Wood presented a Haydn symphony, many of which were new to the Proms at this date, the notes warned that it would be played without break. Wood's intention was to suppress any automatic applause for individual movements and encourage longer-range listening for the drama and shape of symphonic form. Haydn was, after all, 'father of the symphony', and a symphony was different from a concerto (in which intermediate applause for a soloist was still appropriate).[54] In addition, inside the top of the printed programme ran two standard headers. On the left, a notice indicated where non-smokers could sit in the hall – smoking (implicitly by men) was permitted in most areas, the assumption being that a majority of listeners in a relaxed atmosphere would either do so themselves or not object to others smoking; in the right-hand header, Newman gave a strong hint against the persistent demand for encores, which sometimes made the concerts run beyond their advertised finishing time of 11 o'clock.[55] Applause, it seems, arose so readily from some parts of the audience, as at ballad concerts, that clapping and shouts of ' 'Core!' often meant very little, besides causing monotony for other parts of the same audience.[56] Attempts to regulate it were required; training the new listenership followed on from training the orchestra. It was

Notice about the new hall's amenities, from the inaugural Promenade programme, 10 August 1895 (the 'Supper' service was soon discontinued).

UNDERGROUND

THE WAY FOR ALL

ELECTRIC RAILWAY HOUSE, BROADWAY, WESTMINSTER.

JOHNSON, RIDDLE & C? L? LONDON S.E.

Please keep this carefully for me

QUEEN'S
Sole Lessees

HALL, W.
Messrs. CHAPPELL & CO., Ltd.

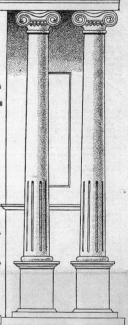

THE QUEEN'S HALL ORCHESTRA, Ltd.

Edgar Speyer, Esq., *Chairman.*

Directors —
The Earl Howe, G.C.V.O.
Lt.-Col. Arthur Collins, C.B.
H. Egan Hill, Esq.
Henry J. Wood, Esq.

Secretary - F. Pope.

PROMENADE CONCERTS

AUGUST 6th to OCTOBER 21st, 1904.

Every Evening at 8. Doors open at 7.30.

FRIDAY, OCTOBER 7th, 1904, at 8 p.m.

Miss BETTY BOOKER.

Mr. W. A. PETERKIN.

Solo Pianoforte - Mrs. NORMAN O'NEILL.

QUEEN'S HALL ORCHESTRA

Principal Violin - Mr. H. VERBRUGGHEN.
Organist & Accompanist - Mr. FREDERICK B. KIDDLE.

Conductor - Mr. HENRY J. WOOD.

Promenade, 1/-; Balcony, 2/-; Grand Circle (numbered & reserved), 3/- & 5/-
Season Tickets (Transferable), available till October 21st.—Promenade, 21/-;
Balcony, 42/-; Grand Circle, 3 & 5 Guineas.

SMOKING PERMITTED (except in the portion of Grand Circle reserved for non-smokers)

The QUEEN'S HALL ORCHESTRA, Ltd., 320 Regent St., W.
ROBERT NEWMAN, Manager.

PRICE TWOPENCE.

Front page of the
programme for
7 October 1904,
showing a trend
towards music-related
advertising as well as
this particular owner's
view of the document.

almost as if, for Newman and Wood, priming the manner of audience response was the first step in a larger strategy, suggesting more subtle repertory- or programme-shaping to come.

In approach and use of language, the notes naturally varied with each writer, from Edgar F. Jacques (1895–1901) and the partnerships of Jacques and Percy Pitt (1902–3), and Pitt and Alfred Kalisch (1904–7), to Rosa Newmarch (1908–18; with Eric Blom, 1919–26).[57] At one point Newman hired Pitt surreptitiously to help Jacques, who, often too lightweight, began to fall behind in his supply of new notes around 1900. Old material could be recycled as often as the repeated works they described, since Baines & Scarsbrook, the printers, kept a running collection with any paragraph ready at a moment's notice. But Wood's stream of novelties increased the flow and the deadline pressure significantly. Real trouble occurred when, more than once, there was only a single manuscript copy of a new work to be studied quickly by both conductor and note-writer.[58] Pitt soon replaced Jacques, but had to be helped himself when he started working at Covent Garden in 1903; his assistant Alfred Kalisch, an opera translator and critic with a legal background, proved efficient but wordy. With tone veering towards the tedious in 1905–6, and musical examples proliferating, management decided to make a change; getting the programme notes right was fundamental to audience-building. The directors approached Newmarch, a well-known and sensitive musical writer close to Wood. She would surely understand how to draw in the reader with intelligent persuasion rather than dry description. Wood's confidential letter to her of 5 June 1907 explains:

My dear Rosa,
In a long conversation I had with Sir Edgar Speyer and Mr. Newman on Saturday afternoon, we decided that we must make a change in the writers of the analytical programmes at Queens Hall, as the stuff they have been writing for the last season or two is really of no use to us, as it is purely technical, and the musical examples have become so numerous that we lose pounds upon these programmes.

What we require is simple, short notices, without musical examples, giving the mood and dramatic purport of the piece, and not mentioning first and second subjects, modulations and episodes, as the public have no time in the concert-room to read such things; and although Jacques' programmes were not ideal, the public liked them very much better because they were more chatty. For the Wagner items I should like to see short extracts from his own literary works, and for the Overture to 'Tannhauser', the Prelude to 'Lohengrin' and those sort of pieces, his own analyses. …

Everything is ready and printed, so that you have got a clear two months before you, and could write these analytical notes wherever you were staying, as we make no changes once the concerts start; and if you could do the first three or four weeks programmes, so long as you kept a fortnight or three weeks in advance of the 'Proms' there would be no necessity for you to do the whole ten weeks straight off the reel. …

You clearly understand that we want … short notes of 10 or 12 lines for the ordinary overture and symphonic poem, but for the symphonies you are free to write as much as you like … something in the style that Tchaikovsky wrote for his 4th symphony: there is an admirable analytical programme, yet it never mentions the key, etc., but only tells the dramatic story.

As Sir Edgar Speyer and Mr. Newman said there was nobody who could do the work so well as you, if you could only spare the time.[59]

In the event Rosa could not take the job until the following year, but her sense of the brief and its underlying purpose was clear, her output effective. Rather than 'write down' to the uninitiated, she took her training role seriously. Robert Newman soon asked her to help with other forms of Queen's Hall publicity.

Responding to demand

Rosa Newmarch,
c. 1936, Wood's
champion and
colleague, eloquent
advocate of Russian
and Czech music, and
energetic writer of
Proms programme
notes, 1908–18.

Newman's injunction against indiscriminate encores did not mean that he was averse to all shows of enthusiasm. On the contrary, no one was more eager to extend a success, repeat a new work or reuse a compelling artist than he was, alike for efficiency, expansion of the repertory and customer trust. Responding to demand was the correlative of creating it. Examples are plentiful, including the second performance, unscheduled but given within eight days of the first, of Tchaikovsky's intermezzo 'The Battle of Poltava' (from *Mazeppa*), in August 1904; a repeat ('By request') of Stanford's *Five Songs of the Sea*, two days after the cycle and its singer, Robert Burnett, had been 'greatly applauded', in September 1905; a repeat of Arensky's Variations for Strings on a Theme of Tchaikovsky, in October 1906 – which had made such 'a hit' on its first outing that it brought many written requests for further hearings; and Sibelius's *Finlandia* ('What a furore *that* created! It was a revelation to London'), first given at the Proms on 13 October 1906 and immediately scheduled for the last night thirteen days later.[60] Such 'redemanded' works, so called in seasonal summaries, registered quite differently from planned subsequent performances (such as the three of Strauss's *Symphonia Domestica* at the 1905 Proms), as well as from any popular favourites merely encored.

Strong feeling on the night was not totally disregarded, however. Wood's most memorable on-the-spot repeat was undoubtedly the double encore for Elgar's *Pomp and Circumstance* March No. 1, given at the Proms on 22 October 1901 only four days after the work's première in Liverpool. A. J. Jaeger, Elgar's ally at Novello, and Wood both recalled its remarkable reception in Queen's Hall – the conductor vividly:

The people simply rose and yelled. I had to play it again – with the same result; in fact, they refused to let me go on with the programme. After considerable delay, while the audience roared its applause, I went off and fetched Harry Dearth who was to sing *Hiawatha's Vision* (Coleridge-Taylor); but they would not listen. Merely to restore order, I played the march a third time. And that, I may say, was the one and only time in the history of the Promenade concerts that an orchestral item was accorded a double encore.[61]

The implication is that vocal items were more likely to receive such encores (exactly the problem Wood and his colleagues were trying to address). That on this occasion the audience positively ignored a vocal work in favour of a new orchestral one must have hit home – though within a year the very vocality of that orchestral item would alter its use forever. As 'Land of Hope and Glory', the texted finale of Elgar's *Coronation Ode*, the piece got a warm response again at the larger work's first London performance, the Queen's Hall Sunday Afternoon concert of 26 October 1902. Elgar conducted. Although not a Prom, this concert overlapped with the closing days of the 1902 Promenade season and served a similar, if slightly more 'polite', audience. W. H. Reed, reporting from his seat in the first violins, described what happened:

> At the close the enthusiasm was such that Elgar was brought five times to the platform; then a voice from the gallery was heard: 'Let's have the last part again.' Quiet was only restored when Robert Newman … came forward to express the composer's gratitude for the splendid reception of his work, and to beg the audience to allow the programme to proceed, at the same time stating that on [a] following Sunday afternoon, the 9th, which happened to be the king's birthday, the *Ode* would again be performed under the composer's direction.[62]

No encore for the great tune this time, but a dramatic intervention by the manager instead. His counter-offer to the eager crowd – vintage Newman, this – was nothing less than a triple promise of a full repeat performance, the composer's reappearance, and a celebration of the king's birthday in one afternoon. The *Ode* was indeed given on that successive Sunday (9 November 1902, the day after the Last Night of the Proms), and yet again two weeks later at a prestigious Queen's Hall Saturday Symphony concert (22 November), Elgar conducting both. What Newman did not say to his Sunday patrons was that the complete *Ode*, under the composer, was also to be given at an intervening Promenade concert on a Friday night (31 October, a Beethoven night including the Ninth Symphony) – in fact the *Ode*'s first performance in London 'in its original form with military band'.[63] Using the full panoply of Queen's Hall series available, the manager thus packaged things individually, taking care to protect an attractive new work's 'drawing-power' at the top end of the market by maintaining clear distinctions below.

It was this integration of the hall's activity, extending the value of rehearsal investment and dovetailing one series with another, that ultimately allowed the Proms to become much more than a summer entertainment. Already by 1900 it was a workshop or feeder series for the entire Queen's Hall system – the point of entry for nearly all new works and artists, which were then channelled according to potential, to be dropped, reused at the Proms or shifted up and

'The Promenade
Concerts – a Popular
night at Queen's Hall':
drawing by Thomas
Downey, c. 1898, of
both animated
informality and
serious listening under
the grand circle.

further rehearsed. Who decided? Largely Wood and what these days would be
called his focus group, the Promenade audience (another reason for teaching
them how to listen). The conductor's role as barometer in this process was
central, for he alone was intermediary between orchestra and audience, aware
of what he could push players to achieve and listeners to appreciate. Just as
'effectiveness' was a key criterion in his performing decisions,[64] so the hierarchy of Queen's Hall series offered a coherent pathway for new repertory. In
1945 Adrian Boult recalled how it worked:

> The plan with novelties was usually this. Anything that looked like being worth
> while was put down for a Prom. If that went well it found its way to a Sunday
> concert the following autumn. But if the work seemed exceptionally important
> it would go straight into a Symphony Concert, and the Composer might be asked
> to conduct.[65]

To cite only a few illustrations: from the 1906 Prom season *Finlandia* skated
straight to the succeeding Saturday Symphony concerts, while from 1907
Elgar's new *Pomp and Circumstance* March No. 4 went to the Sunday after-
noon series; from 1911, Ravel's *Pavane pour une infante défunte* graced both the
Sunday and Saturday series, as Johan Svendsen's *Zorahayda* and Enescu's
Romanian Rhapsody No. 1 enriched the Symphony concerts; from the 1912
Proms Ravel's *Ma mère l'oye* suite and Sinigaglia's *Piemonte* suite went immediately to the Symphony series, whereas Arnold Schoenberg's *Five Orchestral
Pieces*, after its much-remarked première under Wood at the Prom of 3 September 1912 (with unusual but clear audience hissing), was deemed important
enough for further rehearsal: it made a notable success in the following year's

Symphony concerts, conducted by the composer.[66] The key point is that the whole system worked by encouraging innovation, gradually, from the bottom up: neither elite subscribers nor a populist box office were allowed to control repertory choice and direction.

Well before the 1910s, while still under his own entrepreneurial steam, Newman had tried additional ways of extending the Proms' good effects – first, to keep Promenaders in the habit of going to Queen's Hall once a week by mounting Saturday night Proms through the winter and spring of 1896–7; and second, more cost efficient, to plug the gap at the end of the year with a winter holiday version of every-night Proms, from 26 December 1901 to 1 February 1902. Though good experiments, neither idea worked well enough to justify continuation.[67] In any case, in early 1902 Newman's widening ambitions exceeded his mastery of the risks; he became so over-extended beyond Queen's Hall, from the Albert Hall and Crystal Palace to the Comedy Theatre in Panton Street, that he totally ran out of steam. He was bankrupt by May, and the Proms' future passed into other hands.

Challenge and Change

Edgar Speyer's entry on the scene in spring 1902 was quiet but momentous. He had just married the American violinist Leonora von Stosch, a Proms artist on Newman's books. Hearing of the manager's difficulty and himself having ample funds, musical sense and a wish to please his bride, he stepped forward.

'Insatiate: Sir Edgar Speyer meditating … a yet wider control of our traction', drawing by Max Beerbohm, an affectionate lampoon of the small man who was making big changes across London.

It was a sea change for Newman and Wood. Not only Speyer's money, but his advice and artistic vision prevented the whole enterprise from collapsing in a narrower direction – funded potentially by a British music publisher or composing interest, according to Wood.[68] Speyer moreover encouraged Newman and Wood to raise their game, underwriting the promenade concerts to the tune of some £2,000 a year, and the Sunday and Saturday series besides.[69] This upward shift through private subsidy helps explain a number of related achievements at Queen's Hall in the period 1902–14, including the deputy-system challenge of 1904 – which triggered the start-up of the rival London Symphony Orchestra – and an eager pursuit of internationally recognized composers including Elgar, Debussy and Strauss. Orchestral concert activity in fact shot up everywhere in this period: by 1908 London alone had five symphony orchestras.

Yet no strategy of the company Speyer initiated, Queen's Hall Orchestra Ltd, was more important than its marriage of innovation with education in Proms programming, as the Haydn and Schoenberg examples above both show. The chairman's day job in the City offered a parallel if much larger challenge. His investment bank Speyer Brothers, with associates in the USA and shareholders in Britain, New York, Boston, Amsterdam, Frankfurt and Paris, was financing the electrification of the Metropolitan District Railway as well as building three new tube lines and working hard to attract millions of passengers onto the modernized system.[70] The soft-spoken Sir Edgar (active Liberal, baronet from 1906, privy councillor from 1909) increased take-up and negotiated pitfalls in both industries, London concerts and urban transport, until mid-1915, when national zealots hounded him out of the country for his German business connections.[71] Neither George V nor Herbert Asquith could dissuade him from leaving, although kind words from Shaw and, later, Elgar may have given some comfort.[72] He settled in New York, taking his wife and three daughters with him. Leonora worked out her anger through writing, winning the Pulitzer Prize for Poetry in 1927 with, aptly enough, *Fiddler's Farewell*.

The Queen's Hall Orchestra and the Proms meanwhile fell into their own pit of economic and artistic difficulties, from which they would not emerge for more than a decade. Speyer's patronage had been the life-blood of Queen's Hall music for thirteen years. With his loss and the intensification of wartime conditions, Wood began to overtake Newman in psychological leadership of the Promenades. But from 1915 both men were in any case subject to the limited goals of the businessman who had held the hall's lease since late 1902, William Boosey of Chappell & Co., and who now, in a default position, agreed to guarantee the concerts largely for patriotic reasons.[73] Although Boosey renamed the band 'The New Queen's Hall Orchestra' and in his own way kept the Proms afloat despite obvious losses, stimulating orchestral culture was a low priority with him, even at odds with the thrust of his piano and sheet-music business. Letting the hall, perhaps selling it outright, remained closer to his idea of a profitable endgame.[74] The resulting dilution of character in the Proms, understandable during tough times, was however little affected by the cessation of war: the sense of drift continued, and led nowhere. As losses mounted, so did personal and professional tensions: galloping postwar inflation and, not least, the perceived threat to musicians' employment presented by broadcasting in the early 1920s were both deeply felt. By 1918, repetitiveness in Proms programming alongside the apparent neglect of British composers, that old lament in national music, had joined a litany of complaints about what was wrong with the concerts.[75]

For his part, Newman did not give up. 'White and old' with a paralysed eye, and personally affected by the loss of a son in the war (whom he saw die), he nevertheless continued to pursue alliances that might restore momentum. Getting Ferruccio Busoni to play Chappell pianos at Queen's Hall in 1919 was one such strategy.[76] Appealing to Edward Speyer – older cousin of Sir Edgar and distinctly more conservative as a musical patron – was another, in 1924. Wood approached him. This Speyer's firm classical tastes, his advice *against* new music, and probably his money too (or the hope of it) lay behind at least part of the 1924 season.[77] Between 1919 and 1924 it seems likely that once, maybe twice, Boosey threatened to pull the plug on failing Queen's Hall promotions. Various rescue plans, public and private, were set in motion to inhibit the proprietor from dropping the Proms and Wood with them, or to generate alternative support in case he did. Wood's election as an RCM Fellow in February 1924, boosting his stature with the music establishment; press leaks about the Proms' precariousness, inviting speculation over the possibility of civic subsidy since the concerts conceivably constituted a public service in London; above all, an arranged royal visit in October 1924 during the last week of the Proms' thirtieth season, conferring the highest possible seal of national approval on the concerts (not the first time a king and queen had appeared in person to dispel doubt over a Newman series)[78] – all these actions could be read as deliberate manoeuvres against impending destruction. They worked, for a while.

But it was already clear to Robert Newman that such stop-gaps could not continue, that Boosey was a serious obstacle and the way forward might lie in some kind of mutually productive arrangement with the British Broadcasting Company.[79] His old employee Percy Pitt was an insider there: from May 1924 he was Director of Music, responsible for the content of all broadcast concerts and the obvious route by which to gain a foothold on Wood's behalf. If Pitt were to approach Wood for any public concerts the new company might be contemplating, the door would at least be opened to collaboration, crucially from the BBC side. For the predicament Newman and Wood both faced was two-pronged. Boosey, a connoisseur of light music and the ballad, not only had no real interest in running serious orchestral concerts and was tired of wasting money on them ('profit' had been a moot point since before 1902, whatever the growing perception of the Proms' success). He also resolutely refused the use of Queen's Hall and his own Chappell artists to any concert-givers, including broadcasters, whom he deemed unfair competitors by virtue of their non-commercial finance and exemption from entertainment tax. Yet it was precisely the hall, with its central location, prestige connections and crystalline acoustic, that the BBC most wanted – not Wood, and certainly not an existing series widely known to be loss-making.[80] Newman surely perceived this dilemma and would have seen that the hall (the 'brand'), its reputation high among all levels of the concert-going public, was his best bargaining tool. Discreet and well regarded by everyone, he would need only to encourage the relevant parties, including Wood and Boosey, to think in their long-term self-interest, over several months perhaps, in order to reach consensus. What he could not have known is that it would take his own death nearly three years later to focus minds and effect the transfer he envisaged.

In fact the existing paper trail, such as it is, points exactly to this kind of gradual process, by turns cautious, hopeful, reactionary, confused – certainly time-consuming by Newman's standards; modern bureaucracy had arrived. Pitt and John Reith, keen to break Boosey's embargo, first approached Wood about his availability and attitude to broadcasting generally, over lunch in early July 1924; Newman, still Boosey's employee, then arranged a secret meeting with Reith alone to convey his own openness, in October; by May 1925 Boosey had evidently been talked round to allowing broadcasting from the hall subject to a negotiated fee, a pleasant surprise to Reith.[81] No clear action was forthcoming, and after the 1925 season Boosey issued a strong hint about converting Queen's Hall into a picture house.[82] Bluff or not, this thunderbolt brought Wood and Reith into serious discussion for the first time, in mid-February 1926. Though deliberations were cordial, the proposal was unconnected with the Proms and in any case Reith delayed his offer (a three-year conducting contract for twenty concerts a year), causing Wood, his pride hurt, to make other commitments: he was in demand in the USA and the English regions, after all. The old team of Boosey, Newman and Wood then carried on for a further Prom season (shortened by a week), probably looking elsewhere for collaborators. It was only when Newman became ill, in August 1926, and died on 4 November that the tone and dynamic of crisis genuinely changed. Newman's death was a numbing shock to everyone connected with Queen's Hall, exposing more palpably than ever before the stabilizing yet progressive role he had played in London music for more than thirty years.[83] The loss stoked public sympathy for Wood and open conjecture about the concerts. Robert Newman *was* the Proms. In early March 1927 Boosey issued an unambiguous statement that Chappell's would no longer run the Queen's Hall Promenades or symphony concerts.

Wood later claimed it was Percy Pitt who convinced him to keep going with the Proms. Pitt indeed kept Wood's name warm inside the BBC when others there doubted his usefulness or saw the risk of running even a single Promenade season as prohibitive and unjustifiable.[84] Among the conductor's other supporters were Walford Davies and especially Filson Young, who wrote clearly of the advantage an association with Wood would confer: 'I cannot think of any appointment that would so add to the prestige and standing of the B.B.C. with the musical public.'[85] Reith's attitude was more complex. He saw difficulties with the vast public sentiment attaching to Wood and his Queen's Hall concerts, yet also potential honour in some form of corporation rescue; the kudos or advertising value alone of such a 'big public gesture' (Reith's words, 10 March 1927) might be well worth the price. And so it was. 'Saving the Promenades', devised from early in the BBC's serious negotiations as both puff of its beneficence and signal of its own importance and musical ambitions, floated into public consciousness – and broadcasting history – and stayed there.[86] Meanwhile the elaborate dance between Boosey and the BBC about Queen's Hall, and between the Corporation and Wood about his expected 'comprehensive' role with them, whirled on until June. The initial agreement was for one season only, a short one, but at last a working solution was reached, inaugurating the epoch-making 'fourth phase' of the Queen's Hall Promenade Concerts.[87] It was the first one without the founder in place. And though wonderful music would now reach potentially millions of new listeners, considerable doubt remained: no one had any idea how radio might affect the attendance and vitality of all concerts. Wood just kept going, and welcomed the BBC on board.

Repertory Patterns

To summarize the choice of music presented between 1895 and 1919 is a tall order, given the swings in seasonal length (six to eleven weeks), changes in concert function and finance, shifts in national temper, and the sheer number of pieces performed over this quarter-century. There are some 1,435 programmes in total, or roughly 57 concerts a season. In each season, Wood estimated he gave something like 500 works, so that building up his own library with literally thousands of individual parts was essential for managing the day-to-day running of the concerts.[88] A catalogue of that library in any year might be one way to take in the Proms repertory at a given moment, just as

TABLE 1 Proms ownership and management, 1895–1926

DATE	QH LESSEE	QH MANAGER	CHIEF PROMS PROMOTER	ORCHESTRA MANAGER
1895	R. Newman	R. Newman	G. Cathcart	R. Newman
1896–1902	R. Newman	R. Newman	R. Newman	R. Newman
1902–1914	Chappell & Co.	R. Newman (to 1904), then C. Streatfeild, then R. Humphreys	Edgar Speyer, for QHO Ltd	R. Newman
1915–1926	Chappell & Co.*	R. Humphreys (to 1928)	Chappell & Co., with New QHO	R. Newman, with W. W. Thompson (from 1916)

* in 1920 Chappell's acquired the main lease from the Crown, previously having sublet from the Ravenscroft family

successive lists of novelties give a feel for the concerts' adventurousness. Yet however one approaches the challenge, simple descriptors seem inadequate; the very idea of a 'Proms repertory' resists definition, for even favourite pieces came and went, along with novelties and fillers, 'canonic' works and dross. Instead, some basic principles of programming and the patterns that emerged under each management offer the clearest view of how Proms taste developed. Table I summarizes the management periods before 1927.

At all periods, Newman's overriding principle was to make each programme so attractive that no one would want to miss a single concert. With the available time to fill, roughly sixteen hours a week, this required some ingenuity in the 1890s. The breadth of the promenade tradition, indeed of mixed-bag Victorian programmes generally, offered a good start: popular and classical, vocal and instrumental, solo and concerted pieces, integral works and 'selections' could be juxtaposed as normal companions. But Newman also needed structuring devices to divide the time meaningfully, to set up and reward a sense of expectation in variegated audiences and inject drive into each week. Careful repetition of favourite pieces and frequent introduction of new ones became his corollary principles which, when added to the shaping provided by solo artists and nightly themes, gave him the flexibility to try out a huge range of material. He and Wood were quick to learn.

Wagner orchestral 'chunks', assimilable, impressive and familiar to many from Richter's concerts, were a goldmine. They immediately drew some parts of the audience well enough to sustain a regular Wagner night on their own (usually Mondays), while lighter French, Italian and German overtures, waltzes and marches appealed to other listeners, operatic pot-pourris and English songs to still others – none of these tastes being mutually exclusive; most second halves remained miscellanies. Even the 'Classical Night' idea (at first Wednesdays, later Fridays), which embraced serious favourites like Schubert's 'Unfinished' Symphony or Mendelssohn's 'Italian' in complete versions, was never allowed to become a ghetto, hiving off Mozart, Schubert, Beethoven or Mendelssohn, or indeed the symphony or concerto, from other kinds of music. Any of those composers in turn, especially Beethoven (and others alone or in combination, including Sullivan, Tchaikovsky, Gounod, Schumann, Brahms and Liszt), might be allocated his own night; Beethoven as a Friday-night draw worked well from 1896 but still was not fixed. Similarly, 'Popular Night' (traditionally Saturdays but potentially Tuesdays or Thursdays as well), though a receptacle for anything already well liked, could also become a sly testing ground for the new – say, works by Lalo, Pitt or 'Gluck–Mottl', as occurred in 1900. Newman's categories were suggestive, not rigid; the whole idea was to encourage a sense of adventure and discovery.

By the same token, the manager learned the hard way that promoting British composers overtly or collectively, as he did in 1898 and 1901, was doomed as a regular theme; listeners at this date simply stayed away, prejudiced against solid blocks of the home article. Wood found it much better to sandwich a new English or Scottish piece between familiar standards, integrating the best of new British works into the mainstream gradually.[89] And indigenous composers did have a chance: over the first seven seasons, the conductor gave some fifty-seven British pieces a first hearing, an average of about one a week.[90] If their total impact was modest, one reason may be that the most attractive of several new waves in the 1890s, from Russia, had exotic appeal. Not only Tchaikovsky but Rimsky-Korsakov, Glazunov, Arensky, Cui and Musorgsky struck a personal chord with Wood (partly under Newmarch's cosmopolitan influence, from 1897) and he took up their cause with verve, adding Balakirev, Borodin and Rachmaninov in short order. By 1914, Tchaikovsky would even approach Beethoven in total number of Proms performances – an extraordinary rise – although neither of them came anywhere near Wagner, whose real and fashionable hold on London orchestral audiences continued through the Great War and beyond (despite an ill-judged attempt by William Boosey, in August 1914, to boycott German music).[91]

With the ownership change of 1902, a number of subtle but clear innovations suggest Speyer's sharper approach. The first known prospectus, that of 1902, may have been his idea, to reassure Promenaders, focus planning and set a higher presentational standard that would attract higher-paying subscribers. Former crowd-pulling gimmicks such as the instrumental solo spots and interval cinematographs ('animated photographs', shown upstairs in the Small Hall since 1896) began to be dropped. And the programmes themselves showed fresh ambition. In 1902 all the Tchaikovsky symphonies (not just the favourite Fourth, Fifth and Sixth) were given in order, roughly one a week; Brahms's First Symphony received its Proms première; Beethoven's Ninth – in by now the third year for a complete Beethoven cycle – was for once given with its choral finale;[92] and a complete Haydn symphony (No. 92, 'Oxford')

Advertisement for the Polytechnic Animated Photographs, upstairs in the Small Hall, during the interval on 11 September 1901 – another sensory experience (6d. extra) to increase movement within the building.

INTERVAL OF TWENTY MINUTES

DURING WHICH

THE POLYTECHNIC ANIMATED PHOTOGRAPHS will be shown in the SMALL HALL. Admission Sixpence. This evening's series will include the following subjects, reproduced with all the actual movements of real life:—

1.—HENLEY REGATTA, 1901.—The film starts by showing the banks of the river at Henley, closely packed by thousands of spectators, awaiting the finish of the race between the American crew from Philadelphia and the Leander Rowing Club. As the camera slowly rotates the river is shown packed with craft of every size and description, all huddled together behind the booms, whilst along the course, stretching between those two long rows of boats, the rival eights can be seen racing towards the winning-post. Leander having won the race, both eights can be seen resting on their oars, apparently having rowed themselves out to the very last ounce. The concluding portion of the film shows the course covered with boats, all dodging each other in a sort of mazy dance, a pleasing feature being the wonderful costumes of the ladies and the great variety of sunshades displayed.

2.—THE SANTOS - DUMONT STEERABLE BALLOON. (*a*) Emerging from the shed. (*b*) In mid-air.

3.—THE GREAT PARIS - BERLIN MOTOR - CAR RACE.—Showing the Passports on the Belgian Frontier.

4.—TORPEDO-BOAT DESTROYERS PASSING THROUGH THE MANCHESTER SHIP CANAL.

5.—RAILWAY PANORAMA from BEAULIEU to MONACO.

6.—PANORAMA OF THE GRAND CANAL, VENICE, FROM THE PESARO TO THE GHETTO DISTRICT.—The film starts by showing many hundreds of structures; the Palace of Pesaro, one of the finest buildings along the Canal; the magnificent Palaces, Vendramin Calergi, where Richard Wagner, the great composer, died in 1883; Ca' D'Oro of the 14th century, a palace of grand structure; the Church of San Simone Piccolo, dating from the 10th century, built in imitation of the Pantheon; &c. At this point a splendid view was obtained of an intersecting canal, with its many bridges, running through Ghetto district.

7.—FEEDING THE PIGEONS, ST. MARK'S PLACE, VENICE.

8.—PLAITING THE MAYPOLE. (BARN DANCE.)—The girls attired in white are seen weaving the ribbons suspending from the pole into a plait, and forms one of the prettiest pictures that one could ever wish to see.

9.—SEA CAVE.

---

was programmed for the first time. Such a conscious symphonic accent might be seen as educational, ideological or both; it was not done in isolation and never with a heavy hand. In a parallel move, the number of individual items on a typical programme was progressively pruned – from something like eighteen or twenty in the 1890s to more like ten or twelve in the early 1900s – while operatic fantasias were targeted for gradual removal. From 1905 these were replaced by incidental music or tone poems that still offered virtuoso display but were more substantial and modern in feel, such as Strauss's *Till Eulenspiegel*. Unusual in being both cutting-edge and popular – *Till* appeared on a Saturday programme as early as September 1903 and was given on three successive nights in October 1904 – this piece symbolized the new spirit of the Speyer era as well as genuine interest in Strauss's work, from *Don Juan*, *Don Quixote* and *Tod und Verklärung* to *Heldenleben*, several songs, the early Horn Concerto, the Waltz from *Rosenkavalier* and more. Wood's first Strauss première had been in 1895, but the rate at which the composer's other works were introduced and repeated from 1903 onwards is particularly striking. If Speyer's personal affinity explains part of that attention, including expenditure on extra rehearsal, it must also be said that the music's wit and technique, orchestral resource and sheer beauty were now appreciated by some of the most advanced listeners in Europe, at the Proms.

The concerts began to acquire their international reputation at precisely this period; they were virtually symphony concerts from 1905, broad based and modern at the same time.[93] Educational efforts were paying off too, and audiences, often full houses,[94] were receptive to almost anything. Wood's story about how quickly the Promenaders took to Debussy's *Prélude à l'après-midi d'un faune* is a little misleading, however. He introduced it in 1904 – 'I shall never forget the riveted attention of the Promenade … the beauty … the atmosphere … created the deepest impression. In fact I received more letters asking for a repetition than I had ever received before on the production of a novelty' – but it was not until 1908, after subsequent performances in 1906 and 1907, that the work became a firm favourite, opening the way for other Debussy pieces.[95] Advocacy and repetition were essential for players and listeners alike. All the more staggering, then, is the amount and quality of other new European music introduced in the Speyer period – by Mahler, Reger, Schoenberg, Franck, Fauré, Bruneau, D'Indy, Ravel, Sibelius, Busoni, Sinigaglia, Enescu, Glière, Scriabin, Delius, Stravinsky, Dohnányi and Bartók, for example – as well as American music. Much of it lasted. And while the international list grew, there was no loss of pace in the British one. Out of some 220 new British works given in the first twenty-five years of the Proms, more than a hundred belong to the Speyer era, including music by Bantock, Bax, York Bowen, Bridge, Coleridge-Taylor, Walford Davies, Elgar, Balfour Gardiner, German, Harty, Holbrooke, Stanford, Quilter, Cyril Scott and Vaughan Williams, the real push in this direction beginning in 1903. At the same time, Wood was exploring to a lesser degree baroque and classical repertory (often promoted as new and interesting, never 'canonic'), a strand that would grow in importance in the war years, while old and new popular favourites, symphonic, vocal or theatrical, supported the steady middle ground of Proms taste. Beethoven symphony cycles continued more or less regularly (the piano concertos were also given in order in 1907), often with extra performances of the Fifth Symphony. That work, however, to some listeners the quintessential Proms piece at this time,[96] only barely topped Tchaikovsky's Sixth in number of performances to 1914, while Grieg's *Peer Gynt* suite beat both of them put together. Plurality as a keynote did not mean weakness. The musical range, artistic quality and performing standard were all exceptional in Speyer's period – 'a time of wonderful expansion and unostentatious educational value,' according to Rosa Newmarch, 'a period of modernism and … productive idealism'.[97] Such a level would not be reached again until after 1927.

To cast light on some of these patterns, Table 2 shows the cumulative representation of thirty-two selected composers from 1895 to the end of Speyer's regime, measured in total number of individual performances. Comparisons are intriguing. The figures derive from analysis of the full set of programmes owned by the BBC. A performance is not necessarily of an entire work; the total number of all Proms performances for this period is 16,127.

The repertory story between 1915 and 1919 is rather different but not without interest; the war and its immediate aftermath – a time when everyone struggled just to carry on – brought retrenchment and then stasis. From 1915 season tickets were discontinued and programmes became shorter, novelties fewer, but the artists remained of high calibre. Comparative newcomers such as Solomon, Benno Moiseiwitsch and Albert Sammons joined favourites including Fanny Davies, Irene Scharrer, Myra Hess, Gervase Elwes and Robert Radford. Determination to keep the concerts going prompted experiments with format and timing, from matinées in October 1915 (which failed) and earlier evening start times in 1916 to shortened intervals and much lighter, brief second halves containing only an overture, two or three English songs and a march. The prevalence of Chappell ballads was understandably a strong

TABLE 2 Total number of performances of 32 selected composers, 1895–1914

Wagner	2383	A. Thomas	229	R. Strauss	139
Beethoven	681	Brahms	220	Schumann	119
Tchaikovsky	611	Berlioz	209	Sibelius	79
Sullivan	508	Elgar	208	Stanford	63
Gounod	487	Verdi	199	Haydn	44
Mozart	390	Bizet	188	Debussy	39
Mendelssohn	315	Rossini	187	Bantock	38
Liszt	295	Grieg	180	Rimsky-Korsakov	33
Saint-Saëns	269	Dvořák	162	Purcell	30
Schubert	248	Bach	157	Musorgsky	25
Weber	236	E. German	139		

feature as Boosey sought to recoup part of his investment through sheet-music sales, pushing the popular songs of Montague Phillips, Haydn Wood, Guy d'Hardelot, Teresa del Riego and others (he insisted on the use of Chappell pianos, too). It was genuinely felt that 'something had to be conceded to the psychological condition of audiences largely made up of soldiers on leave and civilians rather weary of air raids',[98] and in fact a couple of serious shrapnel incidents occurred during the 1917 season. Yet the incongruities must have told. By stressing ballad culture so much, Boosey, who would have seen little value in educating popular taste for higher things anyway, effectively split the keen orchestral audience built up before the war. It was a backwards move.

Although Wood had purposefully arranged the national anthems of Allied countries to begin successive concerts in 1915, this routine became tired and was shelved the following year. Meanwhile, in the absence of brand new German and Austro-Hungarian music – and the proscription of any such established works that would have produced fees for 'enemy' publishers (e.g. by Mahler or Strauss, much of Bartók, and the symphonies of Sibelius) – the conductor sought alternative sources through British, American, French, Belgian, Spanish, Russian, Finnish, Swiss, Italian and Australian networks. These produced some attractive novelties by composers relatively new to the Proms, such as Charles Martin Loeffler, Joseph Jongen, Granados and Butterworth (both of whom had died in 1916), Prokofiev, Vladimir Rebikov, J. A. Carpenter, G. F. Malipiero, Howard Carr, C.-M. Widor and Dorothy Howell, as well as revivals or new works by more familiar composers, particularly British, including Bax, Bridge, Coates, Delius, Elgar, Balfour Gardiner, Mackenzie, Ronald and Quilter. Also relatively familiar were pieces by Grainger, MacDowell, Scriabin, Lyadov, Albéniz, Franck and Lalo.[99] But despite bright spots and occasional good houses, there was a decided sameness, even sentimentality, about the repetition of so many very old stand-bys in programmes that for all the world looked like shorter versions of evenings from the 1890s. As the Promenades' edge ebbed away, ticket prices went up – three times, in 1916, 1918 and 1919, when basic entry to the promenade reached two shillings.

Signs of a possible turn came with Wood's search for older material he could rescore for large orchestra. His interest in J. S. Bach above all – some of the Brandenburgs had been heard at the Proms since 1905, other concertos and instrumental works earlier – resulted in versions of a 'Concerto for 2 violins in C Minor', Wood's own 'Suite no. 6', and a Violin Concerto in G minor (after BWV 1056) presented 'for the first time in England', all of which helped sow the seeds of a Bach cult at the Proms. Quite against the first opinions of people like Newmarch and Newman, who thought promoting Bach was a retrograde step (they associated his music with pedantic Victorian organ recitals and oratorio culture, even with bitter medicine taken to make one better), this composer turned out to be what many listeners wanted after the devastation of war, and after Tchaikovsky and Strauss had lost their flash.[100] Not for the first time, Wood detected an opening, a voice and a spirit for new times that could perhaps move his players and audiences forward.

Situating the pre-1927 Proms in their own world without reference to what came later is impossible; we know too well what happened. But approaching the story forwards from the context of a nineteenth-century concert experiment, rather than backwards from a broadcasting success, at least puts things in logical order. Events unfold, enabling the recovery of fresh information and a better understanding of a lost time and place: in seeing how the Queen's Hall Promenades worked, we begin to see why they mattered. Without doubt they offered a more novel, viscerally exciting experience than any of the home-grown traditions that fed them – music hall, ballad concerts, parlour culture, wind bands, seaside music, the English organ tradition, even oratorio. All those practices, those sounds, were old stuff in the 1890s, as were occasional 'high-class' orchestral concerts for select auditors, whereas musically adventurous full-orchestral concerts with an emphasis on entertainment were absolutely unparalleled. And they were not only new but peculiar: the sheer volume and colour of sound would have been breathtaking to many, the enjoyment a pleasant surprise.

That the concerts quickly attracted a wide and enthusiastic audience is often put down to cheap entry. At little over fourpence a concert, spreading a one-guinea season ticket across sixty nights, the price was indeed cheap, dirt cheap (newspapers cost a penny in 1895, cigarettes sixpence a pack). But can price alone explain what is more remarkable – that so many of those listeners returned night after night, week after week, year after year, as if in some ritual observance? Rosa Newmarch found a better explanation in the release of emotions after 'a generation nurtured upon an occasional oratorio and Sunday evening organ recitals was permitted to intoxicate itself upon Tchaikovsky, Grieg, and Schubert'. Calling the early Queen's Hall years 'the "ice-melting" period' in British musical life, she concluded:

> Hitherto British youth – especially masculine youth – had been shy of showing any feeling for music. Now they 'gave themselves away' unreservedly. ... The early Promenade Concerts taught a far greater number of people to feel music than to appreciate it intellectually. ... Without these thrills there might have been no living growth of taste and enthusiasm. ... That the 'Proms' may fairly claim to be the one institution in our musical life absolutely free from pedantry, preciousness and all forms of affectation, is probably due to this opening of the sluice-gates at the beginning. The first period of the concerts was, above all, educative of the emotions.[101]

Young people were perhaps Newman's chief target all along, or at least came to symbolize that deep-rooted, thrilling discovery of music so many listeners associated with their first experience of Queen's Hall. Evocative memoirs paint the scene from several angles. Eugene Goossens was 'seated behind a potted palm among the first violins', watching 'that sea of upturned eager faces avidly drinking in everything we had to offer – through a thick haze of tobacco smoke'.[102] Victor Gollancz always stood 'in almost exactly the same spot … about a couple of yards from the bank of flowers that hemmed off the orchestra, and a little to the left'. Thinking it impossible to miss a night, he realized 'with a sense of continual expectation, that day after day throughout the lifetime ahead of me there would be a whole new world to grow familiar with'.[103] Thomas Burke remembered the floor not as a place where 'you could do any promenading' but where there was 'a jam, mainly of young men and women, most of the young men wearing straw hats'.[104] C. E. M. Joad described an occasional seat in the balcony as 'one of the hardest and most uncomfortable seats in London', but wrote of his gratitude for the 'new possibilities of aesthetic experience', his 'awakened consciousness' and especially 'the cunning with which [Wood] contrived year after year to insinuate comparatively unknown pieces … among the musical "chestnuts"; pieces which we should never have gone to hear of our own volition'.[105] Joad also wrote vividly, as Gollancz did, of the hall's social significance, its familiarity, convivial atmosphere and even its smell, of his sense of homecoming every year and Wood's 'large friendliness'– all despite 'the heat, the stuffiness, the upright posture, the concentration [and] the emotional stresses induced by the music'.[106]

Professional journalists were not passive. Some praised the Promenades' educational efficacy while others, more cynical, admired the breadth of programming and etiquette that allowed them to come in and go out at will, avoiding music they didn't like. But ultimately it was common listeners, not critics, whose judgments really counted, however divergent and headlong they might be – a scenario brilliantly summoned up in A. H. Sidgwick's story of 1914, *The Promenade Ticket: A Lay Record of Concert-Going.*[107] A group of seven young people, including two females and more than one level of musical sophistication, share a transferable season ticket one summer; between them they produce a diary of reactions to the sixty concerts – all imagined but drawing recognizably on the music and conventions of around 1904–11. As a lampoon of class, taste, gender and social relations, the story amuses; as a celebration of musical enjoyment it excels, which may explain why the book was reprinted five times to 1945. On collective Promenade taste and its value, the main character asserts:

> [This audience] loves the Brandenburg concertos, and the Mozart symphonies, and heaps of Handel, and all the symphonies, concertos, and overtures of Beethoven, and lots of Schubert, and some Schumann, and all the Wagner it can hear, and a good deal of Liszt, and two concertos and three symphonies of Tschaikowsky, and plenty more. The musical experience of this audience, taken as a whole, is fairly comprehensive. The Promenades alone go on every night for ten weeks, and many of us hold season tickets. If you continue year after year aggregating this very sound and catholic mass of musical experience, after a time some of it is bound to stick – to take form within you and grow into concrete musical sensibility. Multiply yourself by 1500 or so, and you get a body of taste and critical capacity not to be sneezed at. The Promenades are really forming an educated musical democracy, and its judgments are becoming important factors in contemporary music.[108]

AUGUST 1906. A STRAW HAT SEASON.

THOS. DOWNEY. del.

Cartoon by Thomas Downey, from the Illustrated Sporting and Dramatic News *(15 September 1906), showing the Promenade floor as a jam, the bulk of keen listeners young men, and Henry Wood their congenial guide.*

Robert Newman and Henry Wood would have agreed with him. Audience-building through continual revision and updating, without neglecting the musical groundwork new listeners needed, was the key. As Newman juggled three different but interlocking concert series, Wood managed as many repertory strands, both men keeping several products and tastes in play so that cross-influence on all concert-goers was not only possible but likely. Meanwhile, the genuine surge of interest in orchestral music both fed and reflected social aspirations in this period. The concerts' cultural work was thus doubly important, introducing beauty to people who may never have glimpsed it before, as well as fostering a larger musical transformation across Great Britain. Ultimately the Queen's Hall Promenades, more than any other single force between 1870 and 1920, established orchestral music as a norm, not a freak or a rarity, in the lives of thousands of ordinary Britons. For that alone Robert Newman deserves his own place in history, next to Wood, and our engagement with the full measure of their achievement.

A New Dimension

THE BBC TAKES ON THE PROMS, 1920–44

JENNY DOCTOR

> A myth is a story – a certain kind of story – about gods and goddesses, [about] questing heroes … about the origins of creation and natural phenomena, about deep time past … Frequently the stories puzzle at the meaning and purpose of it all, and they show quite extraordinary inventiveness in their responses. … Their immortal adventures provide explanatory stories for the origins of things and their interconnections.[1]

BY THE LATE 1920S, THE STORY OF THE QUEEN'S HALL PROMENADE CONCERTS had already been told many times. Each summer, as part of the rhythm of this annual event within the London seasonal calendar, the full story of the Proms was told and retold – in newspaper articles introducing that season's concerts, in the *Radio Times*, *BBC Handbooks*, and as introductory articles in the concert programmes. The myth of the Proms thus evolved, as layer upon layer of print encoded the sequence of events and confirmed not only 'the way it was', but reinforced the Proms as a unique, national icon, anchored in a continuous past, characterized by what had become cherished traditions and evincing an inevitability for the present and future.

Four highly significant events transformed the Proms in the years between 1920 and 1944. First, financial doldrums plagued all concert-giving in the years immediately following the First World War, threatening the Proms' survival once again. Second, from these threats sprang the 'phoenix' of broadcasting in 1927, which added an entirely new dimension to the Promenade Concerts. Significantly, the series conformed to what had become by then the tried and true Proms 'formula', yet broadcasting extended the audience base and introduced an entirely different context of performance, delivery and reception. Moreover, the BBC Symphony Orchestra, formed in 1930, provided a remarkable instrument with which to achieve performance excellence. Third, the Second World War forced the traditional configuration of the Proms as concert series to change, especially following the loss of the Queen's Hall in 1941, which led the Proms to its new home in the Royal Albert Hall. Finally, the most essential transformation came with Sir Henry Wood's death in 1944. When the full tale is told, the second quarter-century of the Promenade Concerts is once again about the series' survival, but now as an intersection of iconic institutions – Wood, the Queen's Hall, the Proms itself and the new player, the BBC.

'Broadcasting as the
Artist Sees it, VI:
"We are now going
over to the Savoy … "',
drawing by Alfred
Thompson from Radio
Times (12 August
1927). The Savoy
dance band was heard
by listeners each
evening as a segue
from the Prom
broadcast from the
Queen's Hall.

Interwar Modernization

The period from the early 1920s to near the end of the Second World War covers twenty-five years that for Western society encompassed a breathtaking kaleidoscope of technological, cultural, social and ethical change. It was a time in which ever-evolving notions of modernism challenged the tenets of tradition as never before – while at the same time courting and utilizing those same traditions as a means of cultivating a sense of continuity.

Modernism serves as a key to understanding the Proms during the second half of Henry Wood's time as conductor, as it did for the first half. Not only is it an international art term, encompassing the many avant-garde styles and movements that proliferated during the first half of the twentieth century; it may also be used in a broader, cultural context, to describe a world of industrial development and mechanization, and an increasingly urbanized and secularized society. 'Modern living … was now about distance, speed, consumption, communication and mechanisation.'[2]

As turn-of-the-century British society was transformed by the expansion of consumer culture, with its increased leisure opportunities and by the notion of a 'mass market', the founding of the Queen's Hall Promenade Concerts represented an innovative, new approach to concert-giving, a successful symbol of modernity. A quarter-century later, in the years of reconstruction following the First World War, how did the Proms measure up to the new conceptions of modernity that in effect redefined British culture yet again?

In the history of the twentieth century, the Great War marked a watershed, after which the social and economic structures of Europe and the Western world were irreversibly altered. The developments and horrific realities of modern warfare from 1914 to 1918 transformed human existence in fundamental, soul-wrenching ways. Yet in the years following the war, as surviving cultural remnants came to terms with what had happened and searched for ways forward, there were technological developments that crossed over from being strategic wartime applications into peacetime inventions and conventions, significantly altering, stabilizing and modernizing life.

In particular this period was marked by the development and increasing popularity of sound technologies. Gramophone recordings had begun to influence the music market even before the war; and, after 1926, sound quality improved greatly as mechanical means of recording were replaced by an all-electric system.[3] Competition intensified and prices dropped, as recordings became mass-produced commodities aimed at mass markets, contributing vigorously to the final breakdown of nineteenth-century piano culture. 'The once despised toy was taking over the market for home music. … By 1928, shares in gramophone companies were "the liveliest of stock exchange propositions".'[4] In the interwar years, the relationship between music and consumerism shifted course, the market turning decisively away from live performance as a primary means of access. As prices dropped, sound technologies cut through invisible class barriers as through material domestic walls, permeating and becoming an inherent part of the daily routine of consumers of all classes and tastes.

Cinema, too, was a technological competitor that flourished as a result of increased leisure time and expendable income. During the First World War and the decade after, the 'silent' cinema provided audiences with an important means of experiencing popular music, the main features borrowing from 'more than a hundred compositions'.[5] Moreover, the many cinemas provided much employment – by 1929, up to four-fifths of the country's musicians worked in cinemas.[6] But with the proliferation of sound films in the 1930s, the scene changed once more. For many performing musicians, the 'talkies' were economically disastrous, 'speedily [throwing] very nearly all these people out of employment'.[7] The sound cinema grew in influence, remaining a prime competitor to concert-going throughout the interwar period. In fact, the competing mesh of leisure options seemed relatively limitless, including 'cocktail parties, Monopoly, bridge, whist, motor-car excursions, jigsaw puzzles, tennis and (especially in the 1920s) seances'.[8]

Alongside the gramophone and the cinema, the radio represented the third development in sound technology that profoundly transformed patterns of domestic life. In 1922 the British Broadcasting Company was established as a monopoly organization, developing the educational capabilities of broadcasting and the commercial radio market while keeping control of transmissions within the UK bandwidth.[9] Rapidly increasing sales of radio equipment and of the required licences for using it – issued by the BBC for 10 shillings a year –

NOW WHO SAYS THAT WE'RE NOT A MUSICAL NATION?

Cartoon by Fougasse, from Punch *(5 November 1928).*

led to soaring audience figures. In time, radio listening became an essential daily activity: around 20 per cent of British households were hooked by the time the Company became a Corporation at the end of 1926, increasing to 50 per cent by 1933 and rising to 71 per cent by the end of 1938.[10]

It took some time to win over suspicious music-lovers, critics and professional musicians, who objected to radio and the BBC on aesthetic grounds. Sound quality was much inferior to that of live music, particularly before adequate electric microphones and valve receivers significantly improved matters from around 1925.[11] But distaste may also be blamed on broadcasting's democratic nature: transmissions cut across class divisions in an entirely indiscriminate way, and a high proportion of the daily output was considered too 'low-brow' to be of interest.

If the objective, mass appeal of department stores helped define modernity in 1900 – bringing 'traditional luxuries and concepts of leisure to a new public'[12] – then radio may provide a parallel metaphor for the 1920s and 30s. The variety of features, educational talks, information, drama, literature and, most significantly, musics broadcast each day were calculated both to educate and to appeal to the 'Ordinary Listener',[13] the modern concept of mass 'catering' and cultural education leaping beyond all boundaries, right into each listener's home.

Modern musical entertainments were no longer necessarily social events involving travel, time and special knowledge or expertise. In fact, the nearly constant availability and choice of music, independent of live presentation, is a vital characteristic of 1920s modernity. In the interwar years, the power balance in the music entertainment industry shifted further away from a supplier-led market towards one in which consumer flexibility, choice and home access had caught the popular imagination.

The Orchestral Concert Industry

Developments in the concert industry, as in all spheres, shadowed the larger picture of social and economic recovery, and these contexts provide an important background to the Promenade Concerts themselves. At the end of the war, European economies were highly unstable, leading to 'unrelieved gloom'[14] in 1920 and 1921, and to widespread unemployment. But trends began to turn, and in 1924 the economic position greatly improved. This rapid recovery was credited in part to government initiatives, but was due even more 'to new inventions of various kinds – notably the internal combustion engine, wireless telegraphy and telephony, electrical development, more intense specialisation and division of labour and mass electrical production'.[15] One gets a sense of the vast scale of popularity for these symbols of modernity, radio (as 'wireless telephony') among them: the inventions stimulated such a mass purchase of commodities that they helped to counteract the effects of enormous wartime debts.

Postwar economic conditions had specific ramifications for London music-making. In general, London 'concerts raged day after day, at 3, 5, and 8 o'clock', and the concert halls 'were devoted to an endless stream of recitals' and orchestral concerts.[16] But the economics of such abundance was stark: 'it is a sheer impossibility that such numbers … could under any circumstances pay, as there is not the public to support them'.[17] For urban orchestras performing art music, financial realities were especially grim, since they did not benefit from the 'golden age' of opportunities enjoyed by cinema and variety musicians.[18] Instead, inflation and sharply increased wage demands led managements of symphony concerts and opera into 'unavoidably high' costs.

The basic picture of orchestral concert-giving for the first ten years after the war differed little from before. It consisted primarily of concert series during the main season from October to May, presented by the usual organizations, including the Royal Philharmonic Society (RPS), the London Symphony Orchestra (LSO) and the Queen's Hall Orchestra (QHO). Experiments in new music, from the Continent and locally, were featured in annual visits of the Russian Ballet, under the management of Sergey Diaghilev, and in discrete concert series organized and conducted by young, enterprising British musicians who longed for musical change and novelty.[19]

The art of orchestral programme building depended on finding a balance of conductor, soloist and repertory that would prove both attractive and cost-effective. The postwar equation was skewed by inflation, which caused significant rises in artists' fees, musicians' wages and hall hire. In contrast, ticket prices were more or less fixed, limiting potential takings, so that it was feared that 'some drastic measures must be adopted or orchestral concerts will cease to exist'.[20] Of prime consideration was the question of whether to bring in foreign conductors and artists, exploiting long-held British attitudes that European artists were of better quality than their British counterparts, or whether to subscribe to the war-driven demand for 'British-owned' goods and services.[21] There was, after all, unprecedented support for British composers and new British works, even after recent German works and composers had been reintroduced into programmes.[22] Nevertheless, the box office was the bottom line, and audiences consistently used their buying power to vote for top European soloists and conductors, both before and after the war.

In 1924, as economic recovery was celebrated generally, the *Annual Register* recorded 'the same weary round of concerts and occasional opera in London and the provinces as before, a general level of mediocrity, and the changes were rung on much the same programmes'.[23] By 1926 orchestra managers, struggling under mounting costs, fought to remain in business, as did the concert halls. Facing a deficit of nearly £2,000, the shareholders of the Royal Albert Hall considered alternative uses for 'a faded relic of a bygone age'. Even the Queen's Hall was threatened with conversion into a cinema.[24]

Given the particular qualities of the early 1920s British social scene – obsessed with modernizing technology, afloat with inflation and over-stretched with concerts that did not pay – just how did an orchestral series like the Promenade Concerts *fit in*? In these economic circumstances, how did the post-World War I Proms fare in relation to its audiences, to musicians and to the charismatic public visage of the seasons, the conductor Sir Henry Wood?

Boosey's Postwar Proms

An argument about the Proms broke out in the pages of the *Daily Telegraph* in September 1918.[25] The complaints set up certain issues of programme balance – between novelties and traditional works, between British music and 'foreign' – that would characterize Proms discussions for the next twenty-five years and were recurrent focal points for press attention and dissension; in fact, the complaints became 'traditions' in themselves.

> What is the matter with the direction of these concerts? ... These people insist on the same old stuff we have heard for years and years. ... I am getting sick to death of hearing the eternal Tchaikovsky, Grieg, Mendelssohn, Liszt, Saint-Saëns, Handel –

the same old 'Peer Gynt', Hungarian Rhapsodies, Pathetic Symphony – and I protest vehemently it is playing down to the public.[26]

The 'eternal' works cited here are of interest: what music made up the remembered, the noticed, pattern woven by the Proms in 1918? Tchaikovsky led the way and would continue to do so until the end of the next world war. But Grieg's *Peer Gynt*, Liszt's Hungarian Rhapsodies and Saint-Saëns? With changing interwar tastes and less polarized political priorities – notice the non-Germanic origins – these iconic leaders would fade into the background, replaced by composers and works whose heyday was yet to come.

A contributor to the discussion complained that 'so little regard is paid to our own composers and their works. … Can anyone say a British night would be unreasonable[?]'.[27] The response from the Proms' managers articulated the crux of the debate:

> We would suggest that [he] should lease from us at cost price Queen's Hall, the Queen's Hall Orchestra, and the incidental expenses, and experiment upon a week of programmes of modern British music at the Promenade Concerts. We would willingly see him successful. We, as English publishers, have much more to gain by exploiting copyright works by modern composers rather than non-copyright works by the dead masters. Unfortunately, as we said before, the obstinate British public, who will not be dictated to, still stand in the way. They still prefer Beethoven to Joseph Holbrooke, and Tchaikovsky to Villiers Stanford and Granville Bantock.[28]

Decisions underlying Proms programming were ultimately dictated by the box office: the balance between old and new, and between Continental and British, were entirely dependent on previous successes, measured by profitability.

In contrast to other orchestral series, the postwar Promenade Concerts continued as ever before in the eyes of their audiences and in print. The seasons continued under the auspices of Chappell & Co., for which William Boosey was managing director,[29] and they were run by their creator, Robert Newman, until his unexpected death in November 1926. The twenty-fifth season in 1919 'continued with complete success for ten weeks',[30] and in 1920, when Richard Strauss was reinstated in the programmes and 'a new type of Wagner programme' was introduced, they were hailed as 'the most important concerts in London educationally, to which the seekers after musical novelty owed the largest debt'.[31] In 1921, the Proms 'were more than ever successful, and it is noteworthy in this connexion that the most popular evening of the week was Friday when a severely classical programme, usually of Bach and Beethoven, was offered'.[32] And between 1922 and 1925, their success and content were so entirely predictable that the series as an entity did not need to be mentioned in the *Annual Register*'s record of music events.[33] The idea of 'success' had apparently become just another Proms tradition, and the mid-1920s series receded into the tired fabric of London concert life.

There has been a similar tendency when the Proms story is told for Chappell's manager, William Boosey, to recede into the background, dismissed as an obstructive reactionary who could not adjust to changing times – particularly with respect to broadcasting. Reginald Pound, Wood's biographer, presented this precise view: Boosey 'remained implacably opposed to broadcasting in theory and practice. He refused to allow microphones in Queen's Hall. He "struck off" Chappell's list of instrumental soloists and singers any who took engagements with the B.B.C.'[34] Nevertheless, Boosey had worked hard before the war to adjust and redefine the opportunities by which musicians (and their publishers) might profit from their work. He was not unerring in his predictions, however, and had to reverse several political stances, particularly with respect to the new sound technologies.[35] He had initially dismissed their relevance;[36] but when technologically produced music, over which he as a publisher had no control, started to bite into sheet-music profits, Boosey understood the potential of the composer's performing rights and led the way towards the formation of the Performing Right Society in 1914.[37]

William Boosey, Managing Director of Chappell & Co., whose reluctant negotiations with John Reith eventually resulted in the Proms' alliance with the BBC.

When Boosey, on behalf of Chappell's, helped to save the Promenade Concerts in 1915, the privilege came with enormous responsibilities. Despite the formulaic reports of 'complete success' that appeared after the war, Chappell's ran the Proms at a loss, as it 'became evident that it was impossible for concerts, even when sold-out, to be profitable at the Queen's Hall'.[38] Like many in the entertainment business, Boosey saw the new competitor, the BBC, as an enormous threat to an already suffering industry;[39] the Company's financial set-up made it an unfair competitor. In April 1923, when BBC programmes had been aired for less than five months, the entertainment industry formally organized a representative committee,[40] and in May members agreed to stop accepting BBC contracts.[41] Thus Boosey refused to let Chappell artists – including conductor Sir Henry Wood – take part in broadcasts, and he denied permission for broadcasts to be given from the acoustically desirable Queen's Hall. He published a long, often-quoted article in the *Daily Telegraph* on 19 May 1923, stating his position in detail. He was not against the general idea of broadcasting, but 'against broadcasting under its present conditions. … The Broadcasting Company is a competitor of the entertainment industry, paying no entertainment taxes, but being absolutely subsidised by the Government.'[42] While traditional concert-givers were drowning financially, this modern, new 'concert-giver' was unhampered by box office or taxes,[43] and it was subject to a thoroughly modern concept of financing: subsidy by public funds.

The ban forced the BBC to find alternative performers; and its new Music Director, Wood's long-time friend Percy Pitt, began drawing up contracts with artists willing to work with them despite the ban – generally those without agency representation.[44] Moreover, the Company's Managing Director, John Reith, held urgent meetings with the British National Opera Company (BNOC), the only performance organization willing to broadcast. The BNOC 'decided to ignore the threat made by the wretched Boosey that any artist broadcasting would lose his Queen's Hall engagements'.[45] Yet although a BNOC solicitor had written to Robert Newman pointing out that 'the Artistes have nothing whatever to do with the Company's arrangements or the broadcasting of Opera',[46] four BNOC singers were not permitted to participate in the 1923 Proms because of the 'Boosey ban'.[47]

In 1924 the BBC decided to mount its own series of public concerts in direct competition with Boosey and his colleagues. Broadcasting large orchestras was not then possible from its studios, but the Company had the technology to air them, as 'Outside Broadcasts', from hired halls.[48] Selling tickets to these performances not only helped the BBC recoup costs, but transmissions from halls with full audiences were far more successful acoustically; ticket sales also provided a way of measuring audience popularity. Moreover, the BBC cautioned that 'the wireless listener should not confuse "tone" as broadcast, with its original',[49] frequently promoting the idea that listeners should go to concerts to hear music live.

The young Company also wished to be associated with public concerts for reasons of identity, image and prestige. For the BBC to establish a reputation for serious music-making, both at home and abroad, it had to achieve excellence in the realm of symphonic repertory, traditionally disseminated through concert performances, 'concert-quality' providing the standard by which it measured its music achievements. The Company thus inaugurated its public concerts amid huge amounts of self-generated hype and publicity by standards of the day – for which the BBC, unlike its competitors, had the necessary funds. And in 1926, in an arrogant gesture, the BBC launched its celebrated series of National Concerts, presented by an orchestra of 150 players.[50]

Reith did not limit his incursion into Boosey's sphere to public concerts. It is interesting to note that Wood met with Reith and Pitt as early as 1 July 1924; perhaps Pitt wished to sound Wood out about taking part in the second season of BBC public concerts, which featured internationally acclaimed conductors.[51] Reith noted in his diary: 'Interesting lunch with Sir Henry Wood and Pitt. Wood is very ready to broadcast, but is in Boosey's power till May.'[52] It is not clear whether there was any discussion of the Proms. A few days later, Reith attended a meeting at the Royal College of Music, at which was 'discussed all sorts of plans whereby the music profession might be

'The "Flying Squad" of the B.B.C.', from Radio Times (28 September 1928): the special Outside Broadcast van equipped with a miniature studio.

assisted and the schemes of Boosey and Powell frustrated'.[53] And finally, in October 1924 – shortly after the royal visit in honour of the Proms' thirtieth season – another meeting took place:

> Visited Percy Scholes in his flat and met Robert Newman, Boosey's Manager, who has been responsible for the Queen's Hall concerts for many years. He was fairly naturally afraid to be seen meeting me in any public place, but was quite amenable and I believe would like to work with us.[54]

Reith's description of Newman as 'responsible for the Queen's Hall concerts' gives a clue to his agenda, while Newman's interest, as Scholes later recalled, lay in the possibility of broadcasting Promenade Concerts.[55] Perhaps, despite Boosey's antagonism, Newman wisely recognized that the BBC had funds and potential: modernizing the Proms through broadcasting would be a means of ensuring the series' longevity within the difficult postwar economic climate. These meetings between astute businessmen were almost certainly linked to worrying news that had reached the newspapers: 'Rumours were rife in London earlier in the summer about possible changes at Queen's Hall and they reached their climax in the suggestion ... that there might be no Promenade Concerts this year.'[56] A subsequent notice clarified that 'there would have been no Promenade Concerts this year but for Sir Henry Wood's personal action'.[57]

But what circumstances had specifically threatened the Proms during that thirtieth anniversary season? The August *Times* article (almost certainly written by the *Times* critic H. C. Colles) explained a fundamental Proms illusion: 'We think of the Promenade Concerts as our best established music-making institution. But they are not really established at all and are not ours (that is, the music-loving public's), because they depend on private funds which may be withdrawn at any moment.' The fragility of the postwar financial climate led the author to question why the National Gallery, and even the plan then in the air for the foundation of 'national opera', should be considered in terms of public endowment, while there was no similar suggestion 'to establish the Promenade Concerts as a civic institution'. This idea would give the Proms its status as a national icon, not just in the sense of its cultural role and identity, but in solid, economic terms, bolstered by public subsidy. The author also wondered whether the lack of 'novelties' in the 1924 season might be explained by 'the fact that new works take a deal of rehearsing, and it is rehearsal time which costs money without bringing any adequate returns at the box-office'.

Thus 1924 was full of notable episodes, climaxing in the first royal visit to the Proms, perhaps as a stabilizing sign of support and approbation.[58] Viewed together, these events signalled that the Newman–Wood–Boosey–Proms alliance, never stable at the best of times, was deteriorating. Boosey had been restless about Chappell's assuming the burden of the Proms ever since he rescued the series in 1915. Newman's and Wood's powers of persuasion were perhaps no longer able to counterbalance the effects of the substantial losses incurred in running the New Queen's Hall Orchestra – estimated at something approaching £5,000 a year.[59] A further, surprisingly public, signal of declining relations appeared in a letter Boosey sent to the *Times* editor: 'You state that but for Sir Henry Wood there would have been no season of Promenade Concerts this summer. This is not correct. The Promenade Concerts are our enterprise, and are financed entirely by ourselves, and we alone have the right to decide whether there shall be a season or not, and under what conditions that season shall be given.'[60]

The waves were quelled publicly during 1925, suggesting a false sense of normality. As the theatres approached agreement with the BBC at last,[61] Boosey, too, seemed inclined towards reconciliation. Reith initially pursued the option to 'lease Covent Garden for a year to obviate our being frozen out of public concerts', but that idea faded, and in May a meeting left Reith with the impression that 'Boosey is actually agreeing to broadcasting from the Queen's Hall'. The idea progressed, Reith recording in July: 'lunch with W. Boosey at Savoy. Very affable. I saw Newman, his manager, later. Rice and Stanton Jefferies had lunch with Boosey two days earlier.'[62] However, Reith made no further reference to plans involving Boosey, Newman or Queen's Hall that year.

Nevertheless, economic realities led to the reopening of negotiations between Reith and Wood in early 1926. This time they both meant business, no doubt spurred on by Boosey's announcement that 'unless musical finance improved Queen's Hall would possibly be converted into a picture house'.[63] They met on 17 February, Reith concluding that

> [Wood's] desire for a three years contract arises largely from uncertainty as to what might happen if he were to take work from us, and although I imagine that his future is already very uncertain owing to the precarious position of the Queen's Hall, I expect his taking work from us might make it more so.[64]

Reith drafted an offer[65] – but then waited for financial assurance from the Post Office, which he did not receive until April.[66] In the meantime Wood had become impatient: 'Owing to the long time which elapsed ... it became necessary for me to make arrangements for the coming concert season ... in the concert world, it is essential to make arrangements some time in advance.'[67] Thus Wood rejected Reith's first offer – the first surprise move in the contractual games that Wood and the BBC would play for the duration of their interdependency. By spring 1926, coal stoppages had begun, and Reith was fully occupied preparing for what would become the General Strike (3–12 May 1926). Broadcasting's vital role during the emergency, communicating news, directives and public service announcements, enabled the Company to show its true power and capabilities for the first time, to Reith's satisfaction. At the same time, Wood left to tour North America, similarly solidifying his reputation, both abroad and at home, as a musician of international renown and consequence.

No further negotiations took place between Reith and Wood in 1926. But a far more profound event turned the course of the Proms irreversibly: Robert

Newman became ill and died in November. Wood was devastated: 'The Proms were Newman's creation and he was part of them; it was difficult to contemplate the Proms without him. But Percy [Pitt] persuaded me not to give them up.'[68] In contrast, Boosey barely mentioned Newman in his memoirs. Nevertheless, in the story of the Proms, the principal question now became: without this quiet man's expertise and focus, would Chappell's be willing to put in the effort to continue to manage, support and underwrite the Queen's Hall, the orchestra and the Promenade Concerts?

The BBC's Entrance

The year 1927 was remarkable in the history of modernism and mechanization. Charles Lindbergh completed the first solo flight across the Atlantic Ocean, guiding 'The Spirit of St Louis' from New York to Paris in 33½ hours. In San Francisco, Philo Taylor Farnsworth transmitted what might have been the first electronic television picture. And *The Jazz Singer*, starring Al Jolson, further modernized the already modern film industry, beginning the mass dissemination of talking pictures.[69] For the BBC, 1927 began with a celebration of its new status as an institution devoted to public service: on 1 January, the British Broadcasting Company, then in its fifth year, was reborn as a Corporation, established by royal charter valid for ten years. And in the music world, 1927 was the centenary of Beethoven's death. The BBC, like other concert organizations, planned grand celebrations to mark the event, devoting the week of 20 March to his life and music.[70] George Bernard Shaw commented:

> Thanks to broadcasting, millions of musical novices will hear the music of Beethoven this anniversary year for the first time with their expectations raised to an extraordinary pitch by hundreds of newspaper articles piling up all the conventional eulogies that are applied indiscriminately to all the great composers.[71]

From a less celebratory vantage, 1927 began for Chappell's and the Queen's Hall with the realization that Newman was no longer there to hold things together. For years financial circumstances had been pushing Chappell's towards a limit, and Newman's death, though not a catalyst, was perhaps the deciding factor. Rumours voiced a general fear that 'the glorious march of civilization [would turn] Beethoven out of Queen's Hall to make a home for newer deities',[72] and on 4 March the threat became very real. As *The Times* reported:

> Sir Henry Wood has received a letter from Mr. William Boosey informing him of the decision of Messrs. Chappell and Co. not to continue the concerts of the New Queen's Hall Orchestra after the present season. ... The orchestra ceases to exist from [19 March] ... [Chappell's] proposes to give no more symphony concerts and (what is even more serious) no more Promenade Concerts in the summer.[73]

A few days later, on 7 March, Chappell's made a formal announcement, blaming broadcasting to the last, as well as the crippling entertainment tax.[74]

Articles and rumours flew, and readers found the implications of 'no more Promenades' especially poignant. There was little blame: recognition was given to Chappell's for financing the orchestra for so long, 'never making, and often losing, money over the season'.[75] Nevertheless, the imminent loss of the Queen's Hall and the New Queen's Hall Orchestra to London concert life remained a fact, and the Promenade Concerts symbolized the crisis. In that Beethoven centenary month, a *Punch* cartoon of the 'Father of Modern Symphonic Music' shadowing Wood outside the Queen's Hall became a representative image: 'I cannot believe that this rich city, once so generous to me, will fail to find us a permanent home.'[76] There was urgent need to find a backer to replace Chappell's, and it was to the BBC that many – including, ironically, William Boosey – looked for resolution.

FOR THE HONOUR OF LONDON.

Shade of Beethoven (*Father of Modern Symphonic Music*) to Sir Henry Wood. "THIS IS INDEED TRAGIC, BUT I CANNOT BELIEVE THAT THIS RICH CITY, ONCE SO GENEROUS TO ME, WILL FAIL TO FIND US A PERMANENT HOME."

Cartoon by Partridge, from Punch *(16 March 1927): in the month celebrating the centenary of Beethoven's death, the eviction of Wood and the Proms from the Queen's Hall seemed imminent.*

Not surprisingly, Wood had already started the process. In February 1927, amid the rumours and uncertainties, he was ready to resume the contractual negotiations that had foundered the year before. But the BBC was now in the more commanding position, and the idea of having Wood contracted for twenty concerts a year seemed constricting: 'there is a very real interest in the different treatment accorded to different works by different conductors'.[77] Reith seemed willing 'to let the thing go, unless of course Sir Henry Wood's demands may have become less exacting'.[78] Nevertheless, when Chappell's stark announcements appeared, Reith wrote to Wood immediately, asking if he would 'be good enough to let us talk to you before you make arrangements for future work'.[79]

At that time, the BBC was airing its 1926–7 season of National Concerts from the Royal Albert Hall, but the inconsistent acoustics were not satisfactory.[80] The Corporation tried negotiating with Covent Garden,[81] but meetings culminated in frustration, Reith noting, 'it is all very complicated'.[82] Thus when Chappell's made its announcement in March, the BBC acted quickly. Its principal interest was not necessarily to save the orchestra or the Proms: it was simply highly desirable to have the Queen's Hall available for BBC concerts, broadcasts and recording agreements. And despite his public denouncements, Boosey seemed willing at least to consider whether BBC broadcasting fees might be what was needed to bolster the hall's books.

Reith worked quickly, meeting with BBC colleagues and advisors,[83] and on 7 March dined with Wood and Sir Walford Davies, having 'much [to] talk about the Queen's Hall and the orchestra there. Wood would like to work for us but is in the hands of old Boosey.'[84] Boosey's temper flared at an *Evening Standard* suggestion that Chappell's had been approached by the BBC.[85] But Boosey and Reith did meet, just days later, Reith noting with satisfaction: 'He was looking out for me on the pavement. He was very polite.'[86] They discussed several management options for the hall, and the part broadcasting might play. Boosey even admitted there was a possibility that he would continue with the hall and the Proms, for a time – though Reith knew (but did not say) that Wood was unlikely to agree to another Proms season with Chappell's, 'because he had had enough of Boosey's dictation in the matter of Chappell pianos, Chappell singers and Chappell songs'.[87] No agreement was reached at the meeting, and the ball was left in Boosey's court.[88]

Significantly, the discussions detailed specified costs associated with the 1926 Promenade concerts. The season was then ten weeks long, comprising sixty-one concerts. Orchestral costs were about £5,800 (76 players earning an average of 25s. per concert). Wood earned £250 per week, and the hall rental came to £350 per week. Thus the major costs for the season, 'excluding soloists and copyright but including rent', totalled around £12,000.[89] The orchestral estimate tied in with another major BBC concern at the time: in an effort to off-set its ever-increasing orchestral costs, the Corporation was investigating the idea of sharing a full-time orchestra with another organization.[90]

From Wood, Reith heard that Boosey considered running the concerts 'in connection with the BBC … in respect of one season only'.[91] But Wood's position was clear: 'if the B.B.C. cares to make a contract with me for three years I might be willing to conduct another season of Promenade Concerts at Queen's Hall as part of the engagement.'[92] Walford Davies' advice to Reith was unambiguous: 'I am quite as sure as it is possible to be that we ought to secure Wood's last lap of three years if it is within practical politics.'[93] But R. H. Eckersley, the Assistant Controller for Programmes, remained unconvinced: 'I still cannot see any practical point in the proposition at the present price.'[94] However, a developing financial dispute with the management of the Royal Albert Hall meant that the BBC were unable to plan the next season's public concerts, because it had no place to present them.[95] 'Perhaps', suggested Eckersley quite significantly, 'we should confine ourselves to Symphony Concerts of our own, merely for broadcasting and not for the public.'

John Reith as 'Prospero', cartoon by Essex, from Punch *(19 December 1934).*

Boosey at last responded to the BBC's suggestion of mutual cooperation: 'I am announcing that the Queen's Hall is going to be carried on for another year, but I am afraid I am not able to arrange any scheme of co-operation with you.'[96] The move prompted Reith to action:[97] he discussed with Wood once more the terms of a three-year contract, but when it was offered in what the BBC thought was an agreed form, Wood again turned it down: 'I am afraid my feeling is that the whole thing as now sketched out is much too all-embracing and binding as far as I am concerned.'[98] Boosey also wrote to Wood, suggesting they go ahead with a Promenade season:

> Mr. Thompson is familiar with Robert Newman's routine, and I think could put matters through for us if we could get a sufficient number of good artistes to make our venture worth while. Of course a great many of the artistes have already broad-casted, but I should not agree to their broadcasting during our season. No doubt you would agree with me.[99]

The letter was rife with significant issues: a possibility of the Promenades going ahead in 1927 against all odds; completely planned in just twelve weeks; for the first time without Newman; but with the aid of his trusty assistant, W. W. Thompson; but without broadcasting, as 'no doubt [Wood] would agree'. Persuasive stuff.

There's nothing like competition to focus attention: Reith immediately hurried the process of confirming Wood's contract, and on 12 May 1927 mutual agreement was reached at last.[100] It was quite a moment for British music: Sir Henry Wood, aged 57, a national icon linked with the Queen's Hall and Chappell's regime, had crossed over the line to become a BBC artist, a member of Corporation staff – under contract specifically 'to use your best influence … for the advancement of broadcasting'. The move of course put Boosey into check, and another proposal aimed to undermine him further. The Director-General 'met Sir Henry Wood and some of our staff … to go into the Promenade Concert prospects. We suggested we might run them in the Central Hall', Westminster.[101] So Reith proposed whisking the Proms conductor, the Proms orchestra and the Proms season away from the Queen's Hall. Boosey might plan a rival series, but what would be the point? What was, in fact, the essential identity of the Proms brand by 1927? And were aspects of that identity 'dispensable' now that its survival was so severely threatened?

When the BBC next met with Boosey to discuss terms for renting the Queen's Hall and obtaining microphone access,[102] Boosey proposed fees and arrangements that Eckersley deemed 'definitely preposterous … It puts any idea of *our* running the Proms on this figure definitely out of court.'[103] The BBC accepted the £100-a-night rate for individual concerts, but withdrew from further consideration of the Proms, 'generously' offering 'to remove any obstacle there might be, as far as we are concerned, to Sir Henry Wood's con-ducting the Promenade Concerts for you this year if you wished him to do so.'[104] This offer in effect represented the wishes of several BBC administrators, including Eckersley: to present public symphony concerts in the Queen's Hall, to agree microphone access at other times, and to have nothing at all to do with the Proms. But of course there was virtually no chance that Chappell's could run the Proms on its own, particularly with so little time remaining to plan and raise funds. Nevertheless, Boosey would accept none of the financial alternatives the BBC suggested. Suspecting there was no other option if the BBC was to get access to the hall, Reith sent Eckersley a telegram: 'Do you agree our running six weeks promenades plus twelve symphonies at his rental price … Estimate shows probable loss of three thousand … Pitt Nicolls and I on the whole recommend.' Eckersley agreed: 'worth while both from public viewpoint and getting into the hall'.[105] The essential BBC goals, there succinctly expressed, had at last been achieved.

In the end, the BBC effectively agreed to Boosey's terms and to a loss of £3,100 for the season. But Reith nevertheless felt he'd won the more important victory, noting with arrogant satisfaction in his diary:

> Queen's Hall matter settled to-night. I wrote a good letter to Boosey this morning which would have done for publication. … It is a complete capitulation on his part.[106]

In November 1927, the BBC were approached by an agent about the possibility of purchasing the Queen's Hall for £250,000, but the BBC 'were not interested in the purchase of this hall'; they were far more interested in 'obtain[ing] control of the bar'.[107]

Transition to the BBC Proms

An engineer 'with music qualifications' controlling the Queen's Hall amplifiers, from Modern Wireless (January 1933).

When I walked on to the platform on 13 August, 1927, for my first Promenade Concert under the British Broadcasting Corporation, I felt really elated. I realized that the work of such a large part of my life had been saved from an untimely death. I do not think I ever conducted Elgar's joyous *Cockaigne Overture* with greater spirit than on this occasion. I felt I was opening a book that, only a few months previously had seemed to be closed for ever.[108]

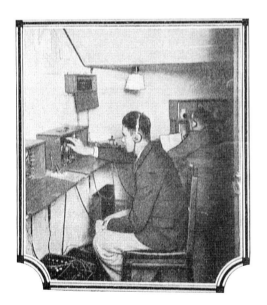

As Wood later recalled, the first night of the 1927 Promenade Concerts opened at the Queen's Hall as usual, just ten weeks after the formal BBC announcement circulated through the press: 'A six-weeks period of promenade concerts at the Queen's Hall … is to be given by the British Broadcasting Corporation under Sir Henry Wood. … The microphone is no longer banned from the Queen's Hall.'[109] The Proms had been rescued – for a year.

How was it possible for an entire Proms season to be put together in so short a time – programmes planned, publicity prepared, an orchestra and soloists contracted, rehearsals scheduled, the hall terms agreed, and the venue made ready?[110] Even Wood's Proms contract needed to be negotiated, since the recent agreement did not encompass the Proms – nor the hire of scores and parts from his

Interior of the Queen's Hall, August 1928, illuminating the sweep of the balcony opposite the organ.

extensive music library, indispensable owing to bowings and markings that saved precious rehearsal time and accounted 'for Sir Henry Wood's grip on the conductorship of the "Proms"'.[111] In fact, the Proms were brought to life for the 1927 season, as for each season that followed until after the Second World War, substantially due to the teamwork of Wood, who planned the basic programme content and rehearsal schedule, and W. W. Thompson, who contracted the orchestra and artists, and organized rehearsals, music hire, extra instrumentation, the tabulation of nightly ticket sales, etc. 'Tommy' had been Newman's assistant at Chappell's since 1916 and moved to the BBC during summer 1927; he eventually became the BBC Concerts Manager, remaining with the Corporation – as a primary player in the Proms team – until his retirement in December 1953. Thompson later remembered that in June 1927, Boosey 'telephoned to ask if I thought sufficient time was available to put on a series in August as usual. It took my breath away but without stopping to think of the difficulties I said immediately "Yes" … Within an hour the wheels were again in motion.'[112]

Opposite Covers of prospectuses for 1926 (top) and 1927 (middle) and of a 1927 programme (bottom) show the changing imagery from before and after the BBC's association with the Proms.

Despite the disarray and discontinuity of circumstances since Newman's death the previous December, in August 1927 the Proms appeared on the surface – to the Promenade audiences – very much as before. The *Times* critic was pleased that in the management change-over, 'nothing essential to the flavour of the true "Prom" had been lost'.[113] Following the war, Newman and Wood had worked hard to re-establish that familiar flavour, which in turn continued the successful festival formula they had honed between 1895 and 1914. Following on from the lively descriptions in *The Promenade Ticket* of the Proms

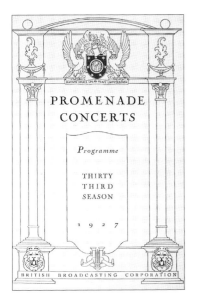

atmosphere before 1914,[114] surviving documents provide interesting clues to the inner workings and outer visages of the seasons under BBC management – and their costs.

The Queen's Hall was adorned, as before the war, with floral decorations, including groups of palms, ferns and flowering plants on stage, near the hall entrance and in the vestibule, the plants 'to be kept in good condition, changed when necessary' (11 guineas per week). Critically, the traditional fountain was missing that first BBC year – 'we might regret the pleasant pool, with its fountain, its flowers, and its fish'[115] – but returned in 1928 (constructed and maintained, £2. 10s. per week). Season success depended greatly on the 50,000 prospectuses of 16 pages that were printed and widely distributed, with a reprint of 5,000 at the end of August (total £126. 6s. 6d.). Posters, season and regular tickets, rehearsal cards and so on were ordered (£184. 8s. 2d.), newspaper advertisements placed (£806. 7s. 6d.), bill posting arranged (£307. 3s. 6d.) and press tickets organized, with particular critics, such as Edwin Evans and Eric Blom, invited personally. 'I doubt if any event in history has had the publicity accorded to the impending series of Promenade Concerts which the B.B.C. propose to sponsor', claimed one critic.[116] Most importantly, an orchestra of 77 players was hired at 'Symphony Concert terms … to include broadcasting', the principals at a rate of £14. 8s. per week, the sub-principals at £11. 5s., and rank-and-file players at £8. 14s., for a total weekly cost of £854. 17s. to include six concerts and four rehearsals. The total cost for the orchestra was £5,134 for six weeks, compared to £5,414 for ten weeks in 1926.[117]

Continuity with the past was maintained also in the prospectus, the guiding map of the season, its sixteen pages containing a chronological listing of repertory and soloists for each concert, with little variation in format or content from previous years.[118] But the cover immediately signalled change: the striking image on earlier prospectuses (and programmes) had been an ornately decorated Palladian portico framing the text; this not only beckoned the reader to the Promenade delights listed beyond, but had also evoked the familiar image of stately columns and pediment above the main entrance of the Queen's Hall, an authorizing symbol of the time-honoured values to be experienced within. In contrast, the clean, uncluttered look of 1927, with its elegant type, offered simply a small, modern emblem – a double circle encompassing 'BBC', the Corporation logo. 'Thirty-Third Season' was blazoned along the top – a reminder that the series was indeed part of a continuum – balanced across the bottom by the name of its new supporters, 'British

Broadcasting Corporation'. 'Sir Henry J. Wood and his Symphony Orchestra' appeared in place of the New Queen's Hall Orchestra.[119] 'Smoking permitted' was still an important feature, 'except in the portion of the Grand Circle reserved for non-smokers'. Interestingly, there was no reference within the prospectus to broadcasting, nor any indication of which concerts might be aired in whole or part, or on which wavelength – which remained true for Proms prospectuses throughout this period. Single ticket prices, 'including tax', remained the same as they had been since the First World War and – with the BBC able to stabilize pricing – would remain so until after the Second.[120] The Corporation also brought back the popular Season Tickets (withdrawn by financial necessity in 1915), at 25s. for the six-week series, transferable between listeners for the Promenade, but 'not transferable to higher-priced seating'.[121]

For the first time, the 1927 Proms had a nightly programme book in place of 'the old, large sheet'.[122] The cover of this book, intended for audiences at the hall, cleverly kept the traditional Palladian imagery of programmes past, but presented as a modernized line drawing. Each programme featured an introductory essay and descriptive notes by Rosa Newmarch (Proms' programme annotator since 1908), illustrated by head-shots of favourite Proms artists. The piano age was still going strong, the programmes carrying full-page illustrated advertisements for different kinds of pianos, often with endorsements from favourite Proms pianists. There was also advertising for two recording companies, that for Columbia endorsed by Wood and illustrated with his profile. Modern recording technology had already started to go hand-in-hand with modern Proms audiences.

The importance for the BBC of its association with the series was exemplified by its decision to commission, as an introduction to its first Proms, a particular telling of the Proms story that would appear every night of the season.[123] Newmarch's essay narrated, and thus helped to codify, the series' history, celebrating practices that were already cherished as traditions, and adding the BBC as a new chapter:

> Now, under the auspices of the B.B.C., the Promenade Concerts not only have the chance of a fresh spell of activity, but possibly the most potent phase of their influence on English music life is yet to come. The spirit of Broadcasting – its widespread democratic appeal – is in complete harmony with the spirit of the 'Proms'.[124]

It is significant that the Corporation chose to repeat Newmarch's essay in the first *BBC Handbook*,[125] its annual publication of information and propaganda, in which it proudly exhibited its organization, features, facilities and successes.

The New Dimension: Broadcasting the Proms

The BBC's impact on the new Proms was subtle, the main constructs of the concert experience undisturbed:

All the essentials were there: on the one side a fine orchestra, whose members were mostly familiar, though the number of women is smaller; and on the other the same enthusiastic and omnivorous audience. Most essential of all is Sir Henry Wood – to act as a conductor of the current between the two poles of orchestra and audience.[126]

Yet the new dimension of broadcasting was simply but directly represented right there in the hall: carbon microphones now hung above the orchestra (upgraded in the 1930s to ribbon microphones). Outside the hall, the impact of the BBC on the Proms was far more evident – and, more importantly, audible – on a national scale.

The BBC began introducing its first Proms season to radio audiences at the end of July 1927 with a leading *Radio Times* article by BBC music critic Percy Scholes. 'Britain and the adjacent parts of Europe are to become one great Queen's Hall. Sir Henry Wood's sceptre is to be waved not before a thousand subjects but before hundreds of thousands – perhaps millions.'[127] The connection between the 'two poles' – between Wood and his Queen's Hall audiences – had long characterized the Proms' particular energy, and it now stretched, via microphones, transmitters and receivers, to encompass an additional axis: one that included Europe and Empire. This modernized conception of 'concert-giving' no longer depended on direct exchange – visibility, audibility, focused concentration – between performers and audiences, but instead conveyed an audible semblance of concert intimacy to uncountable numbers.

The first page of the Radio Times *for 29 July 1927, announcing the BBC's broadcasting of the Proms, with a caricature of Sir Henry Wood drawn by Kapp in 1914.*

In parallel with the programme booklet, the *Radio Times* presentation for Saturday 13 August 1927 emphasized the importance of the occasion.

Unusually, the first Prom was preceded by a fifteen-minute broadcast talk by Dame Ethel Smyth,[128] an accomplished composer and friend of Wood, whose works were frequently performed in Proms of the 1920s and 30s. The concert began, as always in the interwar seasons, at 8 pm, the producer no doubt thrilled at Wood's well-known punctuality;[129] the first half was separated from the second by a fifteen-minute news broadcast at 9.40 pm. The concert was of course presented verbally, although presentation scripts at that time were normally minimal. 'Carriages at 10.30', as specified on the prospectus, was indeed borne out by the 10.30 pm radio finish (no encores!).[130] The Proms broadcast was usually followed by the nightly feature of late-night dance music – on this occasion the Havana Band at the Savoy Hotel. These elements were crucial to the new radio persona of the Proms. Unlike a concert experienced in the hall, at which carefully selected music was framed by the concert hall atmosphere, the radio concert was punctuated by the spoken word – introduction, announcement and presentation, continuity as necessary, the news (and anything else that might be sounding in the listener's local environment) – and followed by a lively coda of popular dance music.

The music presented in concerts, and its history and context, were almost never explained by radio presenters, BBC policy at that time adhering to the idea that music should speak for itself; any verbal explanation was aired at a time earlier in the week.[131] Instead, the BBC used print as the main medium through which to educate, inform and engage the interest of its audiences. In the *Radio Times*, the first broadcast Prom was accorded the special treatment given to major events: a special programme page firmly projected Reith's victory, with Wood's portrait flanked on either side by a woodcut of the Queen's Hall main entrance. This woodcut served as the Proms signifier in the *Radio Times*, the hall stamping its authority on Proms programme listings that would appear over the next few years.

That first concert in 1927 was broadcast on all BBC stations,[132] and during the following week, two further Proms were transmitted: from the London station in full on Tuesday (Mozart), and from Bournemouth and Plymouth on Thursday (mixed programme). The relative richness of three public concerts being aired in a week was possibly unprecedented, yet compared with the six concerts that took place in the Queen's Hall – subsidized by the nation's licence fees – the criticism that 'after all the fuss and talk from London as to the benefits listeners were to get from the Promenade Concerts, the apparent intention of the B.B.C. is to broadcast about one concert per week!' seemed justified.[133] The problem was scheduling. In 1927 the BBC boasted that 'eighty per cent. of the population ... [is] assured of an uninterrupted service of one programme';[134] thus the entire spectrum of programme offerings had to be available on each station each week in a balance determined by BBC policies and experience. It was simply not possible to offer a Prom every evening during peak broadcasting hours.

But a week after the Promenade season was launched, the BBC embarked on a highly important new initiative – perhaps of greater interest to the general population than the Queen's Hall coup: a new experimental wavelength, 5GB, began transmitting from Daventry, giving listeners in the Midland region who were within a hundred mile radius of the station a further choice of radio programmes. Despite its unstable nature,[135] Daventry 5GB gave the BBC the break it needed with respect to the Proms: an entirely unscheduled network on which it could 'experiment' with the glut of concerts that were now suddenly, and very publicly, its responsibility. For the remaining five weeks of the 1927 season, and during 1928 as well, on average three concerts were broadcast each week, one on 2LO, two on 5GB, and a few aired occasionally on other regional stations. By the 1929 season, five concerts were broadcast each week.

But even with programme alternatives, it was difficult to accommodate so many concert hours. In the late 1920s and the 1930s, good taste and focused listening were key promotional points,[136] the Corporation urging listeners to

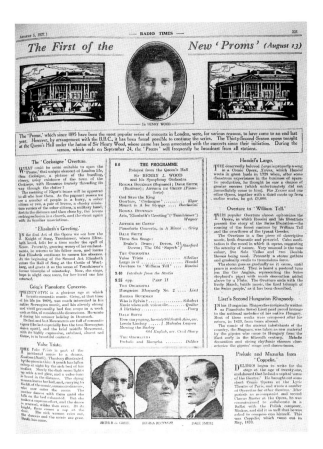

Programme of the first broadcast Prom on 13 August 1927, from Radio Times (5 August 1927), Wood's portrait flanked by woodcuts of the Queen's Hall.

tolerate programmes that addressed the tastes of others and encouraging 'good listening' habits. There were growing pressures to meet the full spectrum of tastes among the ever-increasing numbers of listeners, the 1928 Proms concert programme explaining, 'There are about 65,000 programme-hours to fill in a year. ... Disproportionate effort or expenditure on any one programme ingredient would seriously affect the whole service, and earn the dissatisfaction of the listening public.'[137] Thus the BBC had to base its decision about the Proms' continuation on public response – but Reith refused to permit formal research into the listening habits of radio audiences.[138] Therefore the Corporation chose to define the success of the 1927 Proms in the traditional terms of the concert hall, on the evidence of audience attendance and box office receipts. Since there had been 'no serious drop in attendance',[139] future concert programmes could proclaim: 'The unqualified success of the first B.B.C. Promenade season finally disposed of the legend that broadcasting is inimical to the prosperity of musical enterprises of that kind.'[140]

With growing confidence, the BBC decided to extend the Proms experiment. Both Wood and Boosey bargained for more money, without success, and in Wood's case also for a more favourable configuration of BBC conducting engagements, which he felt his stature deserved. This pattern of negotiation would continue for many years, with Wood often frustrated, feeling that the BBC was not specific enough, efficient enough, professional

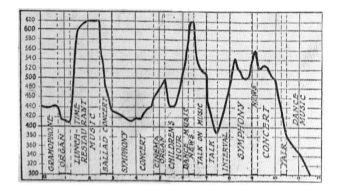

'Automatic Chart to Show Radio Listeners' Tastes', resulting from experiments to discover audience views of individual broadcast programmes, from Daily Mail *(1 May 1931).*

enough or appreciative enough, while the BBC often questioned among themselves whether it might be time for Wood to retire.[141] Although the conductor had Thompson to smooth the concert-organization process, the experience for Wood of bringing about the BBC-backed Proms was certainly not the balanced, efficient partnership that he had enjoyed for so many years when Robert Newman was at the management helm.

Of course, the BBC continued with the Proms well beyond those first experimental years. The transmitted concerts were aired in full in the late 1920s, and from the early 30s normally the first halves only were broadcast. In 1936 the BBC began the practice of 'dipping into Promenade Concerts from time to time instead of mechanically relaying the first half of each concert'.[142] The decision to broadcast selected works rather than concert programmes infuriated many listeners: 'Next week the new policy of itsy-bitsy symphony programmes comes into force at the expense of the Promenade Concerts.'[143] Nevertheless, the BBC found the policy convenient – especially as increasing political tensions in the late 1930s made the delivery of the 9.00 pm news a priority. Throughout the interwar period, first nights were greeted with anticipation, 'still the outstanding event of the ordinary music-lover's calendar'.[144] Last nights were also prominent: the entire concert was generally aired, the first half featuring a popular piano concerto and the second beginning with Wood's arrangement *Fantasia on British Sea Songs* and concluding with Elgar's *Pomp and Circumstance* March No. 1, according to tradition. 'At the end of the evening Sir Henry Wood received a tremendous ovation … and the audience showed that they could do some very good community singing in his honour and without the guidance of his beat.'[145]

The Corporation's interest in the Proms in the late 1920s was part of much larger decisions relating to its orchestral needs. What was finally negotiated in 1930 was the Corporation's own band, the BBC Symphony Orchestra (BBC SO) – a permanent, stable ensemble, with some of the best orchestral players in Britain, a significant number from Wood's orchestra. The Promenade Concerts contributed significantly to the new orchestra's performance profile.[146] The orchestra was launched on 22 October 1930, when Sir Adrian Boult, its Chief Conductor until 1950, conducted a high-profile concert at the Queen's Hall. However, the success and potential the BBC SO presented from this first concert was in part due to the summer of training the orchestra had experienced in rehearsing and performing a season of Promenade concerts under Sir Henry's exacting eyes and ears. The rigour of careful tuning, precise schedules, disciplined rehearsing and mounds of repertory, as well as the challenge and atmosphere of nightly performances, all contributed towards the intensive shaping of this group of exceptional players into a cohesive performing ensemble. The BBC SO soon joined the conductor, the Queen's Hall and broadcasting as one of the four essential elements that made up the identity of the BBC's Proms from that time until the end of the Second World War.

The Wood 'Formula'

A description by *Manchester Guardian* critic Neville Cardus of Wood's first Jubilee Season in 1938 tells of the pre-war Proms experience. In his view, the picture was not all bright and rosy:

> The Promenade Concerts go their remarkable and tumultuous ways. Each evening there is a large queue outside Queen's Hall … The ground floor is packed – until a space is made by somebody taken away unconscious. The congestion and the heat are often terrific. The applause is even more terrific. And the labours of Sir Henry Wood and the B.B.C. Orchestra every week for two months reduce those of the Augean stable to pampered indolence. A different programme nightly: all different schools of composition, Bach, Beethoven, Bax, Britten; Tallis, Tchaikovsky, Tcherepnin, and Tovey. … The orchestra plays [apparently in] the middle of a tropical jungle; palm-trees spread their luxuriance over the trombones. And all things considered, the execution is admirable. In the circumstances we cannot reasonably expect sensitive performances every time … Often we must content ourselves with a kind of broad map of the music.[147]

This 'broad map' conception could be extended to describe the series throughout this period. As Wood later recalled, Newman aimed for the Proms to 'educat[e] the public by interweaving novelties with the classics'.[148] Programming a long series of consecutive concerts on this basis – selecting worthy as well as engaging works from the standard repertory, contacting composers about recent creations, and auditioning and selecting solo artists who deserved a chance that year – Wood developed a seasonal pattern, which eventually gelled into a 'formula'. Wood's formula was not static; it evolved continuously over his five decades as prime programme-builder, in conjunction with changing circumstances and general developments in concert practices. Looking back when writing his autobiography, he acknowledged, 'Nowadays, far from being popular orchestral concerts for the people, the Promenades have become, many a night, very nearly Symphony concerts.'[149] The popular, lighter items – songs, ballads and opera excerpts – gradually waned, as the popularity and power of orchestral forces waxed.

By the time Wood's era ended in 1944, his Proms formula comprised seven basic elements: the season, the concerts, the artists, the programming of composer nights, classics and novelties, and finally the audiences.

An urban summer festival

After the First World War the Proms settled into a season of ten weeks (61 concerts), down to eight weeks (49 concerts) from 1928 until the beginning of the Second World War. The season began in mid-August and continued until early October, presented every night except Sundays. In the late 1890s there had been an average of eighteen items per evening, Wood's 'popular orchestral concerts' offering mixed programming with songs or instrumental numbers, accompanied by piano or organ, scheduled between orchestral works.[150] With each half-decade the average number of concert items decreased, to an average of thirteen in the years just before the First World War, eleven in the 1920s and eight in the 30s. Season prospectuses were produced from as early as 1902, and after the First World War were an annual feature that received much press attention.

A concert of two halves

Each concert consisted of two distinct halves, separated by the all-important interval, when audiences bought food, drink, cigarettes and cigars, raising valuable revenue for the hall.[151] Part I was more serious, often focusing on the music of a featured composer, and longer – from 1927 around an hour and forty minutes, timed to coincide with the news broadcast at 9.40 pm. In contrast, the second part was significantly shorter – just under forty minutes in the late 1920s and 1930s – and lighter in character, with a set of songs sand-wiched between orchestral numbers; until 1926 the sung portion presented ballads, a hangover from Chappell's old ballad concerts and almost certainly sung by Chappell artists from Chappell publications. Many cheered (while others of course complained) when the BBC firmly 'banned the ballad' in 1927 in favour of art songs: 'We need no longer … seek refuge in the vestibule from "platitunes" about June and little cottages, but can stay to enjoy songs by Schubert or Strauss or Parry.'[152] New works were often played in Part II, and in the 1930s second halves were usually not broadcast.

The artists

The practice of featuring solo artists each night at the Proms represented a smooth continuity, with little change in terms of planning or effect from what took place before 1927. A list of artists was prepared each season, which included vocalists and instrumentalists in almost equal numbers. For instance in 1934 there were 57 singers (female outnumbering male) and 60 instrumen-talists (27 pianists, 14 violinists, 3 cellists, 1 violist, 2 organists, 8 orchestral soloists and 5 composer-conductors). Favourite artists returned each year, the 1934 concerts presenting, among many others, the popular pianists Myra Hess, Moiseiwitsch and Frederic Lamond, violinists Antonio Brosa and Jelly D'Aranyi, cellists May Mukle and Beatrice Harrison, and singers Isobel Baillie, Astra Desmond, Oda Slobodskaya, Keith Falkner, Heddle Nash and Parry Jones.

A hierarchy of Proms soloists was evident from a financial point of view, each artist's pay revealing their place in the season's overall scheme. In 1934 the

BRITISH BROADCASTING CORPORATION

QUEEN'S HALL
W.1

Promenade
Concerts

NIGHTLY AT EIGHT
for eight weeks, beginning
SATURDAY, AUGUST 9th 1930

CONDUCTOR

SIR HENRY WOOD
AND THE
B.B.C. SYMPHONY ORCHESTRA
of 95 Players

SMOKING PERMITTED

TICKETS (including Tax)
PROMENADE, 2s.; BALCONY, 3s.; GRAND CIRCLE (——) 5s. & 7s. 6d.
SEASON TICKETS (PROMENADE) 35s. (a limited number)

*Flyer for the 1930
Proms season,
Sir Henry Wood
conducting the first
public appearance of
the BBC Symphony
Orchestra prior to
its official debut on
22 October 1930.*

total allocation for artists and choruses was increased to £3,100 for the season, which represented about 7 per cent of the entire estimated expenditure; total estimated costs of nearly £22,000 (including orchestra costs) aimed to reap profits of nearly £4,500.[153] In 1938 the season's budgetary allocation for soloists remained the same, but there survives a list showing the fees paid to each artist. The lowest rate, normally for local artists singing in the second halves of programmes, was 5 guineas, while local artists performing more prominent solos, such as Benjamin Britten giving the first performance of his Piano Concerto on 18 August, received 10 guineas. The highest fees went to big name pianists and sopranos on a scale shown in Table 1 (p. 100).

Many artists performed several times in a season, building audience support that sometimes belied the amount they were paid. For instance, there was particular loyalty to favourite soloists from the orchestra, such as Léon Goossens (oboe), Archie Camden (bassoon) and Frederick Thurston (clarinet), although they were paid only 8 to 10 guineas for their concerto appearances that year. At the same time Moiseiwitsch received one of the highest cumulative fees for his several appearances during the season, yet had one of the smallest audiences on his first appearance in the first week. Audience numbers had a pattern of their own from year to year, concerts in the first week often quite sluggish, Thursdays often sparse, and the final two weeks well attended, especially in 1938, Wood's Jubilee season. Hence on the first Thursday, the programmers almost certainly had hoped that Moiseiwitsch might help to pull in fans despite these annual trends, but even his lure was not strong enough.

Before 1945, although flyers included lists of artists, prospectuses did not promote them as particular features but simply listed the names each night without comment or distinction. Pre-season promotion included lists of soloists, singling out a few favourites, such as Myra Hess; but Wood, the Queen's Hall, the novelties and the overall programming scheme generally received greater attention. In contrast, for Proms that were broadcast, prominent attention was given to artists and their portraits in the *Radio Times*. The magazine followed popular marketing tends of the day, and glamorous photos and amusing drawings peppered the pages both to attract listeners' attention and to give a visual impetus to the sound medium.

How exactly were the artists chosen? In fact, how were any programming decisions made during this period? Although mounds of paper relating to the Proms are still held at the BBC Written Archives Centre, frustratingly little of substance survives that might illuminate Proms programme-building in the 1920s and 30s. There are hints at a planning meeting that took place each spring at the BBC, involving Wood, Thompson, the Director of Music (in the 1920s Percy Pitt, in the 30s Adrian Boult) and other BBC staff, but there are no minutes; only oblique references to what was actually discussed remain. A cosy photograph of a Proms 'programming team' sitting in Wood's garden – Wood, the composer Arnold Bax and Edward Clark, the BBC programme-builder then responsible for orchestral concerts – appeared in the *Musical Opinion* in August 1934 (see p. 103). Wood and Clark were certainly involved

TABLE 1 Scale of artists' fees in 1938 compared to ticket takings[154]

ARTIST	VOICE / INSTRUMENT	TOTAL SEASON FEE (GUINEAS)	SINGLE-TICKET TAKINGS (£ NET)	DAY	PROGRAMME TYPE
Moiseiwitsch	piano	157	184	Thurs 11 Aug	mixed
			374	Sat 3 Sept	Tchaikovsky
			348	Sat 24 Sept	Rachmaninoff
Myra Hess	piano	105	365	Fri 16 Sept	Beethoven
			320	Tues 27 Sept	Mozart
Eva Turner	soprano	105	233	Mon 19 Sept	Wagner
Solomon	piano	84	352	Wed 17 Aug	Brahms
			335	Tues 30 Aug	Mozart
Jelly D'Aranyi	violin	84	345	Tues 6 Sept	Schumann
			345	Wed 21 Sept	Bach-Handel
Elisabeth Schumann	soprano	78	316	Thurs 18 Aug	mixed
Parry Jones	tenor	78	163	Mon 8 Aug	Wagner
			297	Mon 22 Aug	Wagner
			261	Mon 5 Sept	Wagner
			345	Fri 30 Sept	Beethoven 9
Jo Vincent	soprano	73	345	Wed 21 Sept	Bach-Handel
			282	Mon 26 Sept	Wagner
Egon Petri	piano	63	334	Wed 14 Sept	Brahms
			368	Fri 23 Sept	Beethoven
Isobel Baillie	soprano	63	237	Mon 29 Aug	Wagner
			339	Wed 7 Sep	Bach
Oda Slobodskaya	soprano	63	261	Mon 5 Sept	Wagner
			348	Sat 24 Sept	Rachmaninoff
Keith Falkner	tenor	63	348	Wed 24 Aug	Bach
			237	Mon 29 Aug	Wagner
			337	Sat 10 Sept	mixed
Stiles-Allen	soprano	47	163	Mon 8 Aug	Wagner
			217	Mon 15 Aug	Wagner
			337	Sat 10 Sept	mixed
Roy Henderson	baritone	47	163	Mon 8 Aug	Wagner
			335	Tues 30 Aug	Mozart-Haydn
			312	Thurs 15 Sept	mixed
Harold Williams	baritone	47	217	Mon 15 Aug	Wagner
			345	Fri 30 Sept	Beethoven 9
Walter Widdop	tenor	47	233	Thurs 22 Sept	mixed
			282	Mon 26 Sept	Wagner
Lamond	piano	42	373	Sat 13 Aug	mixed
			331	Thurs 25 Aug	mixed
Muriel Brunskill	contralto	42	217	Mon 15 Aug	Wagner
			220	Tues 23 Aug	Sibelius
Lisa Perli	soprano	42	312	Thurs 15 Sept	mixed

in programming decisions, and it is intriguing to think of Bax taking part. There is no evidence for it, though as a friend of Wood's he may have given the conductor informal advice. It seems likely that much of Wood's programming of artists and new works came as the result of personal discussions held throughout the year.

The BBC staff involved in programming discussions were the programme-builders responsible for orchestral output: Clark, from 1936 Julian Herbage, their supervisor Kenneth Wright, and on occasion higher officials such as Basil Nicolls, who represented general broadcasting and matters of finance. The 1938 Jubilee season involved much correspondence between programmers and so gives a general sense of how things worked. Wood began the process by submitting a preliminary draft to the BBC as early as December of the year before, to try to get things moving and requesting a meeting,[155] but Wood's touring and the demanding schedules of all participants meant that the meeting was sometimes not held until April. Wood would present a detailed outline of the season at this meeting, and BBC staff would have issues and suggestions they would also bring to the table. The schedule was then refined and amended as needed, by letter and sometimes in subsequent meetings. Although many artists returned from previous seasons without audition, the BBC called for artists' auditions in May, almost always with Wood in attendance and making detailed recommendations. The programmes were finalized when Wood submitted his final draft for approval, usually in May or June, when a typed copy would be prepared and circulated throughout the BBC. The season prospectus was prepared for publication from this typed version and generally issued to the public in June, or early July at the latest. Artist contracts were negotiated and organized by Thompson, who was the primary BBC communicant with Wood throughout the process.[156] In June Wood submitted his famous, incredibly detailed rehearsal schedules (the one from 1944 survives intact),[157] Thompson's office sent notifications of rehearsals to all artists, composers and choruses, and hired orchestral extras and unusual instruments – and the forty-nine concerts began to materialize in the second week of August.

Composer nights
Although details naturally varied from season to season, Proms programmes followed a weekly structure aptly described in this newspaper preview to the 1938 season:

> The framework of the programmes is that of previous years, with Monday nights devoted principally to Wagner, Wednesdays to Bach and Brahms alternately, and Fridays to Beethoven. A feature of the Thursday night programmes will be the inclusion of important modern symphonic works ... Two evenings will be mainly devoted to Tchaikovsky, two to Sibelius, and one each to Handel, Mozart and Rachmaninoff. Then there will be two Haydn–Mozart programmes and one of Schubert–Schumann.[158]

Curiously Bach is not mentioned here, but his works – particularly his concertos – consistently made him among the most popular of composers in the 1930s, drawing capacity crowds from week to week. On occasion there were sorties into more exploratory evenings, for instance the Debussy–Stravinsky programme in the 1937 season, but such experiments usually failed as box office draws. An evening's focus on a particular composer was confined to the concert's first half.

The composer nights were originally adopted by Newman in the Proms' earliest years to encourage some predictable programming elements. By acknowledging competing tastes within the classical music market, he attempted to sustain the drawing power of the series by targeting different audience interests on different nights, rotating through each week of the summer season. From 1927, the BBC – charged by royal charter with accommodating a far wider spectrum of tastes – significantly did not change this system, but in fact etched its initially fluid outlines into defined patterns. Many found the 'too stern determination to divide the music into categories' to be restricting:

> The happiness of the old 'Proms' consisted largely in uniting people's special tastes, making them tolerant of each other and in the end become more catholic in their enthusiasms. That is a state of being which broadcasting does not favour. No doubt the listener by wireless is considered in the extension of evenings specially devoted to particular composers or types.[159]

In those formative years, when the BBC was actively introducing art music to a nation of listeners who were in large part unfamiliar with it, 'composer nights' in effect extended to concert-length the practice of its *Foundations of Music* series, in which audiences were systematically introduced to solo and chamber music repertory in fifteen-minute slots each evening, a different composer featured each week.[160] As a natural continuation of this established practice, the Corporation chose to characterize and market its interwar Proms by composer or composer 'type' (e.g. 'British composer' nights), concerts from 1927 involving fewer and fewer of the old mixed programmes. By September 1938 a critic noted, 'except for Saturdays, the Promenade programmes are nowadays devoted almost exclusively to one composer'.[161]

The 'classics'

A primary aim of the Proms from the beginning was educational, to enable general audiences from all kinds of backgrounds and levels of musical experience to become familiar with and be inspired by the sounds of full orchestras and orchestral music, especially in the days before gramophone recordings and radio increased access to orchestral performances. Wood remembered that Newman *wanted the public to come to love great music*. "I am going to run nightly concerts and train the public by easy stages", he said. "Popular at first, gradually raising the standard until I have *created* a public for classical and modern music".[162] This educative premise was not dissimilar to Reith's aims

for the infant BBC after the First World War: 'to entertain, to interest, to enlighten, in all these ways to bring the very best of everything and to spare no effort to do it, to the greatest possible number; to aim always at the highest standards in every line of achievement in whatever direction it may be'.[163]

But at the core of the Promenade Concerts always stood the conductor and his orchestra, and, to Wood, educative 'classics' meant core orchestral repertory. For each season from 1920 until after the war, there survive hand-lists of performed repertory, organized by genre, as recorded by Thompson's office.[164] Considering, for example, the symphony pages for 1926 (see p. 104), it is possible to see that the programming of classics involved logical patterns. The composer nights comprised the first level of the hierarchy. Symphonies were next, each composer's works systematically spread by week throughout the season, as here for Beethoven and Haydn. Then came the highly popular concertos, rousing overtures, featured arias and favourite Wagner excerpts (involving enlarged orchestras and specially hired instruments); and finally, the substantial 'Miscellaneous' section represented works from every other orchestral genre. These annual lists undoubtedly helped in the systematic process of slotting each type of work and composer into its appropriate place in both the nightly and seasonal programme formats.[165]

Programming decisions emerge from patterns of recurring composers and works in the annual lists. It is extremely fortunate that Thompson's records of nightly attendance and box office takings also survive from the same period. These bodies of data were interconnected, the programming of any BBC season based to varying degrees on the attendance patterns of the previous year. It is striking to trace patterns of popularity and observe how they changed over the pre-1945 period. The most dramatic shift is rather obvious: the immensely popular Wagner Mondays of the 1920s tail off throughout the 30s. Not surprisingly, by 1942 the basic pattern had so altered that 'Friday is still Beethoven night, but Wagner has now been dethroned from Mondays except for three half programmes'.[166] What is intriguing here is that Wagner and other canonic Germanic composers did not disappear from BBC programmes during the war, but were treated as cultural masterworks.[167]

Handlist of symphonies presented in the 1926 Proms season, listed alphabetically from Beethoven to Haydn, as prepared within W. W. Thompson's office.

Despite the increasing popularity of Sibelius, Tchaikovsky and Rachmaninoff during the interwar and wartime seasons, audience figures consistently reached their apex for concerts featuring Bach. It was not the large-scale solo vocal and choral works that drew in the crowds, as might be expected today, but principally the concertos and Wood's powerful arrangements of the organ works, from which the sounds and sections of the orchestra unfolded into full sonic glory. In fact, the drawing power of Bach's choral works were not at issue initially, for the simple reason that choral music itself was almost never performed during the Newman–Wood era; a notable exception was a 1923 Prom in which the Halifax Madrigal Society presented choral works from Palestrina through Byrd to Armstrong Gibbs.

An obvious manifestation of the choral music void came each year with the performance of Beethoven's Ninth Symphony, normally presented, following Proms 'tradition', on the penultimate night of the season and nearly always one of the biggest draws. Before the BBC, the symphony was performed 'excluding the Chorale Finale' – that is, without Beethoven's famous setting of Schiller's 'Ode to Joy', involving solo voices and choruses; the only exception was 1902, when Arthur Payne conducted a performance of the whole.[168] The 1927 Proms, that hastily thrown-together season, continued the tradition of omitting the final movement, causing *The Times* to criticize BBC stinginess:

> There is … a double expense, for to give the Choral Symphony would mean both engaging a choir and keeping seats in the orchestra for them which otherwise would be occupied (they always are on a Friday night) at three shillings a head. But what of that? The B.B.C. is a philanthropist. It can do what commercial managers may not be able to afford.[169]

Opposite London Underground poster, 'The Promenade Concerts', by Fred Taylor, 1920.

The entire symphony was presented the very next season, proudly utilizing the BBC's 'National Chorus'.[170] From then on, Beethoven's Ninth was performed complete at each annual Proms outing until the war. In addition, the BBC chorus took part in a few other Proms each year of the 1930s, for the most part avoiding the British oratorio tradition, the one performance of Elgar's

THE
PROMENADE CONCERTS
BY UNDERGROUND
TO OXFORD CIRCUS

The Dream of Gerontius (1930) outweighed by the frequent performances of Constant Lambert's *The Rio Grande* and Liszt's *Faust Symphony*.

What was the outcome of the pre-1945 Proms' approach to 'the classics'? Through its systematic presentation of core symphonic repertory, in effect the Proms made a substantial contribution towards defining twentieth-century conceptions of standard orchestral repertory. Although radio and gramophone recordings enabled even more frequent hearings of these works by mass audiences, it was that concept of familiarity through annual repetition that Newman and Wood formulated. That conception fitted in closely with the similarly educational one the BBC established for its music broadcasts – almost certainly influenced by the success of the Proms. Thus the Corporation was normally happy to follow Wood's lead in the programming of symphonic classics at the Proms.

Saturdays were 'Popular Nights', which presented lighter classics intended to draw in more festive weekend audiences. These mixed-programme nights were a concern in the late 1920s for, as the press frequently pointed out, the popular nights were that in name only. For example, the programme presented on Saturday 1 September 1928 featured two novelties, including the first English performance of Sibelius' *Tapiola*, yet the takings were only £190. 14s. 1d. for single-ticket sales, among the lowest of the season; ironically, the season high of £328. 18s. 11d. was achieved on a more 'serious' Bach Wednesday, which featured Myra Hess and the orchestra's leader, Charles

Advertisement for HMV's new All-World Armchair Radio, 1930s.

Woodhouse, as soloists – both audience favourites.[171] Thus 'popular' concerts as defined by the Saturday Proms of the late 1920s were no longer in step with popular, paying audiences. By 1935, the Saturday policy of 'engaging first class popular Artists' and the introduction of 'works of a rather more serious nature than hitherto' had been found to be 'successful and on the right lines'.[172] By changing the programmes to appeal to those who appreciated top artists performing serious repertory – that is, by programming more usual Proms fare and attracting more usual Proms audiences – the concerts grew in apprecia-tion in box office terms, rising from average takings of £208 per concert in 1929 to £256 in 1935.[173]

Two interesting points arise from this process of attracting audiences. First, nine seasons after the Proms had been allied with radio, success was still based solely on concert hall returns, the preferences of the many Proms radio listeners not yet part of the equation. Second, by the mid-1930s no one was interested in asking whether this approach to popular concerts counted as successful in terms of Newman's, and later Reith's, original models, which advocated using lighter programmes to draw in new audiences for serious music. As early as the mid-1930s, sound technologies and mass dissemination had begun to recast the nature of popular music and its reception,[174] so that the 'traditional' Saturday night Proms formula was no longer effective and had to evolve.

The boundaries between popular favourites and the serious 'classics' were also a consideration in the programming of the winter Proms, which were revived for three seasons in the mid-1930s. For two weeks starting around New Year, Wood and an orchestra of ninety players presented summer season highlights – though in rather different conditions, since the Queen's Hall in January offered a much colder prospect than in August, despite the tropical decorations. In the main, crowd-drawing classics were on display, including concertos with popular artists, a profile of symphonies and other orchestral favourites.[175] There was, however, a struggle to coordinate the winter Proms with the already congested broadcasting schedules. In 1935 it became BBC policy 'that part of each concert should be broadcast somewhere';[176] but fitting in winter programmes so that they ended before the national news at 9.30 pm was often problematic. Administrators finally determined that broadcasting the winter series was not viable, and they were discontinued after the 1935–6 season, not to be reinstated until after the war.

The performance of the standard classics at the Proms, summer or winter, was rarely discussed in any detail in contemporary print. Much press attention surrounded the Proms, of course, but interest in the classical performances was usually roused only when some discordant event took place, such as Daisy Kennedy's dramatic memory lapse during her performance of the Brahms Violin Concerto in 1927 ('she returned to the platform, held up her hand for silence, and then announced that owing to want of what she felt to be the necessary amount of rehearsal she was sorry she had not been able to do her-self full justice'),[177] or when the end of the first movement of Mahler's First

Symphony was disturbed in 1930 ('the silence … broken by a prolonged "Boo", which came from the grand or upper circle, and was repeated by the same person immediately afterwards').[178] Such exciting moments aside, press articles and reviews focused attention primarily on Wood, particularly his longevity as a conductor and the marathon nature of the series, on the artists and on the composer nights. Attention then swiftly turned – without fail, in direct contrast to the tacit 'tradition' of the classics – to the novelties.

Novelties

Time and again it is the novelties that have received most attention in writings about Proms programming. They were works that were presented at the Proms as some kind of first performance[179] and, as Wood explained, the aim from the start consisted of 'interweaving novelties with the classics'. They held such significance for Wood that he included in his autobiography an appendix listing the 'more important' novelties he had conducted year by year, a list that has appeared in expanded and extended form in several books on the Proms, most notably that by David Cox.[180] Season novelties were also listed annually in BBC publicity materials, and works and composers noted in previews and reviews in both the specialist music and the general press. Like solo artists, novelties represented an element of Proms programming that was actually given *notice*.

In the pre-1914 period, Proms novelties assumed a status that was not unlike that enjoyed by recent novels or films in our own day. As Rosa Newmarch recalled,

> There arose an audience, elementary and uncritical perhaps, but one which craved for living forms, energetic movement, colour and genius of race – in a word, the audience which discovered Tchaikovsky first and Bach afterwards. … It appeared that only gulps of what was then very modern orchestral music (Tchaikovsky and other Russians, Richard Strauss, Elgar and Sibelius) could appease this awakening hunger for a vital, secular art.[181]

But what happened just before the First World War, in the Proms as in other concerts, when the nature of more serious novelties and audience expectations for them began irreparably to grow apart and disengage? How could assimilation possibly keep up when the nature of new musical language changed so rapidly and fundamentally that there was often little for audiences to grasp and enjoy on first hearing? In 1944 Sacheverell Sitwell, looking back at fifty years of the Proms, encapsulated this essential discontinuity, the fundamental change in attitude that characterized audience responses to 'the modern' in art music throughout much of the twentieth century:

> When Sir Henry was a young man and the Proms began, it cannot be denied that the contemporary music had a greater vitality than now. So many great names in music were still living. Brahms and Dvořák; and among the lesser immortals, the deathless Johann Strauss. And was not Grieg among the masters? There were

Debussy and Albeniz too; Richard Strauss was a young genius then. Is it not the truth that these were the last waves of the great age of music, before it ebbed and died? Compared with them, what names has the whole of Europe to offer in 1944?[182]

Popular dismay and dismissal of the new was an intrinsic part of changing cultural history, but now both new music and audience responses to it turned a corner. Early twentieth-century distrust of the novelty began the process of audience disengagement, the new decentralized in evolving art appreciation. The process of assimilating new creations and ideologies into a body of received and acknowledged music slowed, and most listeners enjoyed the new luxury of repetition, often technology-aided, preferring the familiar tried and true to the increasingly inaccessible novelties on offer.

Was musical modernism of the time manifest in the interwar and wartime Proms? The nature of concert-giving was itself modernized in 1927, enabled by modern technologies, modern media and modern means of subsidy. In that sense, the 1930s Proms were perhaps as permeated with modernist effects as were William Glock's Proms of the 1960s; but such qualities, in that intense decade of political fervour, economic plunges and technological advances that modernized nearly every aspect of living, were smoothed over, the BBC gaining more from constructing an image of continuity with the past. Reference to the 'new' thus continued to focus, as tradition dictated, on the novelties and other recently composed music that Wood and the BBC programmers carefully selected for each season.

Thus as part of the annual Proms routine, novelty lists were circulated in internal memos and external publications, highlighting both first performances and works to be conducted by their composers, a practice instigated in 1902 with Elgar, and brought in more broadly as a promotional experiment in 1913. Throughout the First World War and into the 1920s, composer-conductors gained status as an annual Proms fixture, with frequent appearances by such figures as Frank Bridge, Eugene Goossens, Herbert Howells, Cecil Armstrong Gibbs, Arthur Bliss, Vaughan Williams and Malcolm Sargent – conducting at his first Prom in 1921 his orchestral poem *An Impression on a Windy Day*.

So what recent music was performed at the Proms? There is no meaningful way in which Proms novelties and recently composed works, British and foreign, performed over twenty-five years can be characterized briefly. 1927 marked a change in new music selection, the programmes featuring more established composers, often with one fairly accessible standard work given year on year. Thus Stravinsky's suite from *The Firebird* ballet, Hindemith's overture to his comic opera *Neues vom Tage*, Lambert's *The Rio Grande* for piano, chorus and orchestra, Debussy's *L'après-midi d'un faune* and *La mer*, Walton's *Façade* suites and Strauss's tone poems – these and other selected works by living composers appeared in nearly every Proms season in the late 1920s and the 1930s. As for the classics, the composer and idiom became familiar to audiences through repetition, their assimilation into Wood's core repertory securing them places in the Proms 'formula'.

The British works would often be listed and promoted separately from those of the Continent and elsewhere, and this practice became commonplace too in many press features on the Proms.[183] The division into British and foreign reflected political as well as nationalist trends of the time – the *British Broadcasting Corporation* should, as the Director of Entertainment put it, 'encourag[e] home products'.[184] Thus the BBC made a point of publicizing new British works as something 'other' than new music from Europe and North America in all its music programming, including the Proms. There were occasional campaigns to promote British music throughout an entire season, as happened in 1929 as part of a wider BBC initiative. British composers were featured on Thursday nights, which included first performances of works by Lambert, Berkeley, Bliss, Berners, Howells, Bax and Walton – along with non-first performances of pieces by Ethel Smyth, Goossens, Balfour Gardiner, Warlock, Ireland, Moeran, Boughton, Holbrooke, Bantock, Delius, Holst, Vaughan Williams and of course Elgar. This represented a fairly full deck of the established living composers of the day. Although ostensibly providing a solid platform for raising awareness of British music for the Proms and the still-new radio audiences, Thursdays were in fact found to have consistently low attendances and profits (the average net receipts for British Thursdays were £173, compared with £294 for Beethoven Fridays).[185] In subsequent seasons the BBC determined that British works should be mixed into Proms programmes rather than showcased on specific nights. Many critics and audience members expressed relief.

A *Musical Opinion* article of August 1934 pointed out a significant aspect of presenting novelties at the Proms – an oft-repeated Proms trope questioning 'whether the B.B.C. Symphony Orchestra, in its daily rehearsal of three hours, could be expected to devote much of its precious time to the preparation of new works, and, if it could, whether the results would be anything but unsatisfactory'.[186] That was almost certainly a problem throughout the Proms' first fifty years, given the minimal rehearsal time available for each concert. But from 1930 difficult works were often part of a bigger BBC strategy. For example, in August 1934 Wood conducted Berg's *Three Fragments from Wozzeck*,[187] a difficult work in a new idiom; yet it did not pose a problem for the BBC SO at the Proms. The orchestra had performed the entire opera the previous March, having undergone many hours of rigorous rehearsal, far more than could have been expected for a Prom. Arnold Bax challenged the article's negative view, which he thought was countered by Wood's meticulous working methods: 'In preparing the novelty [Wood] leaves nothing to chance. Sometimes almost every bar of the score is annotated in blue pencil with reminders and symbols of important points to be made – evidence of the most careful study before he goes to the conductor's stand.'[188] Given the limited rehearsal time, the Proms had to follow the BBC's trailblazing when it came to difficult, 'ultra-modern' music; but at the same time the Proms often led the

BBC in introducing music of somewhat less technically demanding styles, especially that of British composers. One critic nostalgically welcomed in 1943 'the revival of the old tradition by which the Promenades were the chief trying-out ground for new works'.[189]

Leading, following – in a way it did not matter; the fact was that Wood conducted novelties as an essential aspect of his musical contribution. In 1944 Bax offered an interesting estimate of its quantitative effect: 'I would hazard a guess that 75 per cent of all orchestral music by established native composers has been given under his direction, besides an immense quantity of works played once and since forgotten.'[190] By any reckoning, that is an astounding achievement.

Audiences: 1938, Wood's first Jubilee

The final, and perhaps most fundamental, element of the interwar Proms 'formula' was of course the audiences. The Proms could not have survived without the loyal, excited and curious audiences who eagerly purchased tickets time and again to gain entry to the Proms experience. And audiences, too, were most affected by the added dimension of broadcasting. It was necessary to acclimatize broadcast listeners, so that they might receive over their radio sets not just the music, but a sense of what it was that made the Proms concerts special and different for those in the hall – and why it was worthwhile for their licence fees to support an expensive London-based venture. In 1929 the BBC

Cartoon by E. H. Shepard, from Punch *(21 February 1934).*

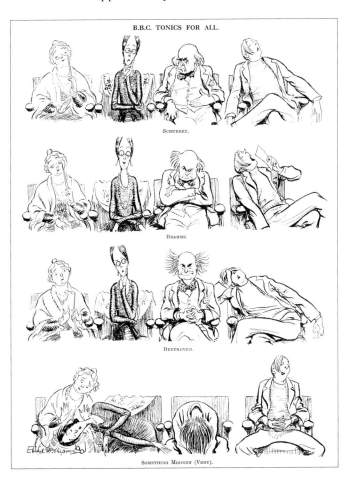

B.B.C. TONICS FOR ALL.

SCHUBERT.

BRAHMS.

BEETHOVEN.

SOMETHING MODERN (VERY).

pulled out the stops and heavily promoted the Proms season as a major feature of its summer calendar. Five concerts were broadcast in most weeks of the eight-week season, and there were major articles, full page or over two pages, in each *Radio Times*. The idea was to negate prevailing conceptions of concert hall formality:

> The Proms are, in fact, the 'Annual Festival of the Ordinary Listener', and we are – we congratulate ourselves – the most wonderful audience in the world. … It is a sign of only nascent musical culture to enjoy everything as much as we do. Because, we do enjoy music – tremendously, perhaps indiscriminately – and we are quite unashamed about it. We applaud everything uproariously. In fact we are the amateurs – in the old and great sense of the word: the lovers of music.[191]

What a message the BBC transmitted by such a statement! In a way it expressed an attitude that opposed what was becoming standard practice in the concert hall. Proms audiences in the 1920s and 30s had grown not only in size, but also in inclination, becoming more sophisticated perhaps due to Proms attendance, broadcasts, recordings and the plentiful information about classical music and artists in wide circulation, not least in BBC publications: 'Gradually it was found that a new generation of listeners was coming to the concerts – a generation that could do with less promenading, fewer drinks between the items, less match-striking during the music, and a diminishing proportion of commonplace ballads.'[192]

By 1938, this acclimatization of Proms listeners, both in the hall and over the air, had proven surprisingly successful. Popular radio was in large part a personality medium, and Wood's personality, in particular, had by then reached legendary proportions. Through his many broadcast Proms and Symphony Concerts, as well as special performances given in the regions and internationally, Wood had built up enormous loyal audiences well beyond the walls of the Queen's Hall – 'a great national figure, doubtless known throughout the empire'.[193] The BBC helped mark the fiftieth anniversary of Wood's first conducting engagement by supporting a celebratory Proms season and airing part of the special anniversary concert on 5 October 1938.[194] Wood used the publicity for the occasion to appeal for public support to fund hospital beds for orchestral musicians. The first night witnessed a broadcasting first: Wood, who had on principle 'never spoke[n] over the air and did not feel inclined to start now',[195] recognized the financial potential of an appeal, and so decided to transmit a short speech in the interval to encourage donations. 'My <u>mind</u> is full of the music we are playing to you to-night but my <u>heart</u> is full of the <u>needs</u> of my friends, the orchestral musicians.'[196] The appeal was heard not only by radio listeners, but also by those in the hall, a sound system set up specially since Wood did not speak from the stage.

Two days later another Proms first took place, building on an experiment that had taken place the previous May, when a series of concerts conducted by Toscanini was televised in sound to great success. It was decided that the first weeks of the 1938 Proms would similarly be relayed on the '7-metre television [sound] wavelength',[197] transmitted from Alexandra Palace nightly from 8 to 9.00 pm, before scheduled TV programmes began. The television broadcasts were not yet the audience-builders they would be for the Proms in the 1950s, since few among current BBC audiences yet owned television sets. Yet the experiment indicated the enormous pace at which both sound and vision technologies were advancing towards improving the quality of sound reproduction. The point of televising in sound only (and many non-audiophiles today would think that this *missed* the point entirely) was indeed audio quality, the 'exceptionally high standard of sound reproduction … obtainable on the ultra-short wave'.[198] Thus after forty-three years the Proms was still a player in exploring what was new, or even cutting-edge, in concert-giving and audience-building.

In addition to these innovations, there was an impressive list of Jubilee season novelties – first performances of works by composers with whom Wood

Sir Henry Wood at a rehearsal preparing for the 1938 season, his fiftieth as a conductor: the quality of Wood's pose portrayed half a century of musical passion, and perhaps the image was also seen to display iconic determination in response to growing European tensions.

had had close associations over the years, including Rachmaninoff, Lambert, Bliss, Walton and Milhaud. But however important these innovations were, the Jubilee was principally an occasion for looking back, an opportunity to recall Wood's long-time accomplishments in music-making. Thus the season celebrated also the novelties of Proms past, many concerts including one or more 'items which were first heard in London at a Promenade concert'.[199] The BBC promoted this retrospective also in print. In the season prospectus (110,000 copies printed), Wood's longstanding friend and chronicler Rosa Newmarch once again related her history of Wood and the Proms: 'I know of no other series that has gone on for forty-three years without interruption, always with the same style of programme, and under the paramount influence of one conductor.'[200] Tributes appeared in newspapers and music journals by leading critics and musicians; Vaughan Williams, for example, recorded his impressions as a Proms composer, conductor and audience member:

> In the present state of musical culture in this country it is more important that listeners should hear all Beethoven's symphonies played through reasonably well in eight weeks than to hear one of them superlatively given in eight years. At the Promenade Concerts the conductor goes boldly and frankly half-way to meet his audience; he determines that every piece played to them shall glow with his own exuberant vitality.[201]

And it was the audiences whose tributes to Wood especially resounded through the season, with record attendances and enthusiastic responses following their own time-honoured Proms formulas. Thus the opening night began

> with the traditional scenes of enthusiasm. The applause was already noble when Sidonie Goossens arrived, very early, to put her harp in order; and afterwards, a steady crescendo of acknowledgement greeted first the wind players and then the leaders of the strings, until Sir Henry arrived, as buoyant, as enthusiastic, and as punctual as ever.[202]

The crowd applause, crescendoing as players came on stage, the order of arrival, the climax with Wood's entrance at the stroke of eight – and the season was launched with the audience playing its expected part. The finale was similarly ritualistic:

> I have seen many a last night in the Queen's Hall, but never remember a promenade that looked so tight-packed. The applause all through the evening was terrific. No one item appeared to be liked either more or less than any other. Everything and everybody was greeted rapturously, and Sir Henry Wood got the lion's share.[203]

Again, the vociferousness of the applause, the crush of the arena, the rapturous excitement, even the lionization of Wood – as in a pre-written script, audiences played an essential part in this annual story and held an essential place within the Proms formula.

How is it possible to cut through the rhetoric, repetition and ritual to rediscover the audiences of that 1938 Jubilee season? Interestingly, 'the Proms audience' dissolved into individual audience members when it came to the many photographs that were published each year in conjunction with the Proms stories. And in 1938 such illustrations were especially abundant, the richness and significance of the occasion marked by large, dramatic images. A six-page section in the *Picture Post* is particularly relevant.[204] The first spread featured a pictorial sequence of Wood at the podium in his waistcoat, not looking tired or old after fifty years, but spry and intent, conducting, as noted in the piano-reduction excerpts running across the middle of the page, Beethoven's Sixth Symphony, complete with nightingale. The middle spread captured the orchestra in casual rehearsal dress and named each well-known player in the captions. The final spread depicted the third partner in the performance triangle, 'Promenaders' in various positions and with a variety of expressions, all listening intently in their own ways. It is a powerful sequence, characterizing the most fundamental reasons for Wood's decades of success:

Year after year, under all kinds of adverse circumstances, [Wood] has made first-rate music available in London – and he has made it available at a price ordinary people can afford to pay. Long hours spent standing – for many of his keenest admirers have never yet had a seat at one of his concerts – have meant nothing to them, if only they could be there and listen.[205]

War Interrupts

Owing to the special arrangements for broadcasting which are now in force, the BBC very much regrets that the symphony orchestra will no longer be available for these concerts in London. I am, therefore, very sorry to say that from to-night Promenade Concerts will close down until further notice. I must thank you, my dear friends for your loyal support and I hope we shall soon meet again.[206]

On Friday 1 September 1939, a Beethoven evening, amid the black-out 'decreed for the whole kingdom' as part of the 'full machinery of the civil defence of Great Britain' set in motion that day,[207] Wood conducted the Piano Concerto No. 2 with Harriet Cohen, the 'Pastoral' Symphony, and John Fullard singing 'An die ferne Geliebte'. He then 'broke his 45 years' silence from the platform' and announced the end of that season's Proms. The following day the BBC Symphony Orchestra, and many of the Music Department staff, were evacuated to Bristol.

The 1939 Proms had been planned in detail, building on the great success of the 1938 Jubilee season, which had reached record attendance and made record profits of £8,200.[208] The story of what happened next, between the abrupt end of the 1939 Proms and the changed circumstances of the following season, is complicated. A quick version might be gleaned from the newspaper spat that arose in April 1940, the *Times* first announcing:

The B.B.C. has decided not to continue to be responsible for the Promenade Concerts, but arrangements have been made to carry them on under the auspices of the Royal Philharmonic Society. They will begin on August 10. It will be Sir Henry Wood's farewell season so far as the conductorship of these concerts is concerned. … Sir Henry Wood, in making the announcement last night, said he was grieved that the BBC could not see their way to continue the concerts. … But Mr. Keith Douglas and Mr. Owen Mase had agreed with him that the concerts must go on, and all arrangements had been made within a few hours to carry out the project.[209]

The Corporation immediately countered with a statement in the *Daily Telegraph*: 'The B.B.C. was anxious, subject to certain emergency safeguards, to undertake a Promenade season in the coming summer … It was forced reluctantly to abandon the idea because it was informed by the lessors of the Queen's Hall that the Hall was already let and could not be made available in August.'[210] In his published response to this, Wood's politeness barely hid his annoyance: 'I sincerely hope that the full text of the negotiations which had ensued for many months past between the B.B.C. and the lessors of Queen's

Hall on the one hand, and the B.B.C. and myself on the other, will be given daylight.'[211] The story has been 'given daylight', with increasing detail at each telling, the most thorough by Arthur Jacobs in his biography of Wood.[212] But that version leaves out several factors.

When war was declared, all London theatres, including the Queen's Hall, were closed by government order. When the order was relaxed in mid-September, the BBC still had the hall booked, but the BBC SO was gone and the Corporation's attention was focused on war preparations. This is a well-known story, as is the heroic role of Sandy Macpherson at the cinema organ during the first month, playing the majority of music that was broadcast – while the BBC SO waited in Bristol with little to do.[213] Many in the performing arts, including Wood, wrote angry letters deploring the artistic standstill at a time when people needed exactly what the arts would offer to relieve anxiety and bolster courage. Remembering what had happened during 1914–18, Wood was anxious about musicians suddenly losing their livelihoods and made numerous suggestions to the BBC for morale-boosting concerts to keep London orchestras playing, but they mostly fell on deaf ears.[214]

The situation improved slowly, particularly from October as everyone settled into new routines. Myra Hess began her lunchtime concerts at the National Gallery, which were immediately popular, and the BBC resumed the broadcasting of orchestral music, though on a far more limited basis than before. Behind the scenes, BBC staff were involved with the complicated process of refunding or negotiating payments for public concerts that would not take place, the Proms a particularly challenging case. Wood found the process annoying, and the negotiations about payments dragged on into the new year.[215]

In November 1939, former BBC staff member Edward Clark and composer Elisabeth Lutyens, representing the recently formed Association of British Musicians, approached Wood about running a series of promenade concerts in the Queen's Hall with the LSO in January. Wood was interested, but the idea fizzled out, Wood telling Thompson, 'I have only recently suffered much anxiety and trouble discussing a series of Winter Promenade Concerts with a Committee, headed by Mr Edward Clark, and I have no hesitation in saying, I should not care to have to again consider allowing these Concerts to get into hands so inexperienced.'[216] Wood also had offers from others interested in managing the 1940 summer Proms, but he hoped the BBC would run them as usual. By January he was frantic for an answer: 'I look upon them as MY LIFE WORK and the Cradle of Music in England, and as such, I have no intention of allowing myself to be directed by amateurs, or by any organization that has another object in the background.'[217] Receiving unsatisfactory responses from the BBC, he astutely investigated other options.

Meanwhile, M. R. Ricketts, representing Chappell's, demanded from the BBC full compensation for loss of earnings for the 1939 season, which was eventually agreed.[218] As the Corporation then cancelled Queen's Hall bookings well into 1940 (the orchestra was no longer on hand to perform there) and avoided coming to a decision about the Proms, Ricketts became increasingly difficult. Chappell's tried various ploys to force the Corporation to a Proms decision,[219] but the BBC remained uncommitted, suggesting that if Chappell's had another organization willing to run the Proms, the BBC would offer broadcasts. At one stage the Corporation considered running a six-week series from Bristol, but Herbage objected: 'To start a Bristol series of Proms. at the same time as the Queen's Hall series would be a grave tactical error, giving the impression of personal animus by the BBC towards the organisers of the forthcoming series.'[220]

In fact, the BBC was unable to contract new Queen's Hall dates in early 1940 because it could not come to agreement with Chappell's over two fundamental issues. The first involved the upkeep of the hall, to which, in the circumstances, Chappell's felt the BBC should contribute more than the £600 per year agreed in 1937. The other point was contractual: the BBC required an additional 'war clause' that would absolve it of liability should the war prevent events from taking place. Having paid thousands in reparation for the 1939 season, the BBC regarded this as essential – but it was clearly not in Chappell's interest. After weeks of stalemate, the BBC offered a 'John Anderson' clause instead – the booking subject only to cancellation by order of the Home Secretary[221] – but Chappell's response was decisive: 'the Hall was no longer available as it had been let to a third party.' Basil Nicolls, the BBC Controller (Programmes), immediately

> wired Henry to say that we were unable to conduct a season … Henry wired back – a long rigmarole – saying that in view of our refusal he was reluctantly compelled to accept a last-minute offer from a third party (which, no doubt, he had had in his pocket for the last month or so).[222]

The newspaper exchanges began the next day, 5 April, and the public arguments led to very bad publicity for the BBC, which was blamed for letting the side down at a difficult time. Boult reported, 'Music Department has come in for a good deal of abuse. Unpleasant letters, strong anti-BBC conversations at lunch parties; it appears that Sir Henry Wood is avoiding all personal contact with BBC officials.'[223] And Chappell's had turned from obstinate to impossible, refusing permission for third parties to obtain broadcasting rights from the hall.[224] In response, the BBC decided to avoid seeking permission to take any broadcasts from the Proms,[225] but Boult warned, 'the question will inevitably be raised as to why we are not relaying these concerts.'[226] When Herbage analysed the season, he discovered that 'the programmes have been constructed without any regard to the "fixed points" of broadcasting. … We would obtain adequate programmes for broadcast, but not a proper cross-section of the Promenade repertoire.'[227] Nevertheless, the BBC tried to open negotiations for airing some Proms, offering also to pay additional subsidy toward the hall's upkeep.[228] But on 18 July, Herbage reported, 'Promenade negotiations have failed owing to completely impossible figure demanded by Chappells for minimum of twenty broadcasts.'[229] So the BBC was dissociated from managing and mounting the 1940 season, and no Proms were broadcast that year.

But as Boult asked above, why was this so? Indeed, why did the BBC negotiate at all, when it was not physically or financially viable for the Corporation to use the hall while the BBC SO was based in Bristol? One reason was contractual: the BBC had a crucial agreement with Chappell's dating from April 1937, which ensured an annual sum towards the hall's upkeep and promised that 'during the next seven years, all the major outside concerts in London of the Corporation will be given in Queen's Hall'.[230] The BBC also remained involved due to an unexpected phenomenon that emerged in the early months of the war: 'nearly every Concert that is given in London to-day is turning money away … the musical public in London are thirsting for the Concerts which they have had in the past years'.[231] The BBC wanted both to support the public's interest and to profit from it. But a third, and perhaps most important, answer to *why* related to the BBC's dependency on Chappell & Co. – not as manager of the Queen's Hall, but in its main function, as a music publisher:

> As [they] are probably the largest musical publishing house in London and hold about 60 per cent of musical grand rights of the popular sort they are in a position to make themselves extremely awkward and expensive to the B.B.C. … particularly of modern American musical numbers, Chappells control far and away the largest proportion. … There is a considerable use made of the Chappells repertory in the ordinary sound broadcasting programmes.[232]

Popular though the Proms were, when it came to arguing with 60 per cent of popular music – including musical comedies such as *Dear Love* and *No, No, Nanette*, and film music including *Top Hat* and *Shall We Dance* – the series was eclipsed. Songs and other excerpts from Chappell-controlled works lay at the centre of BBC daily programming. If relations with Chappell's broke down entirely, it could cripple their popular radio output. The BBC business manager astutely realized that it was as much in Chappell's interest to resolve the issues with the BBC as the other way around. After tempers had cooled the following autumn, Richard Howgill, then assistant to Nicolls, was able to report that Chappell's had authorized Keith Douglas, the sponsor and manager of the 1940 Proms, 'to agree with the BBC that they may broadcast any or all of your concerts for this [next] short season'.[233] There was a chance for the 1941 Proms to reach the wider radio public.

The Wartime Proms

The wartime Proms were perhaps the most vivid of those given during Wood's second quarter-century. The season once again meant more than an annual rendition of a pleasant summer music tradition, which it had threatened to slip into during the relatively comfortable years of financial and managerial stability since 1927. The very public disagreements that preceded the 1940 season certainly helped to bring the Proms to the forefront of public attention,

and there was a general determination for this cultural icon, so closely identified with the national figure of Henry Wood, to survive at a time when
national survival was the name of the game.

In effect, the Proms was among the music entertainments that seemed to
fulfil particular public needs of the time, like Myra Hess's National Gallery
concerts, and the events organized by the government-funded Council for the
Encouragement of Music and the Arts (CEMA), subsidizing events to raise
the spirits of those at home, and by the Entertainment National Service Association (ENSA), which entertained the troops at home and abroad.[234] CEMA
in particular brought soloists and touring orchestras to town halls all over the
UK, taking concerts out of the concert hall and bringing them to a general
public that soon demanded more.

Similarly, the Proms brought London audiences out of the black-out into
the Queen's Hall, where they could experience as a community the solid
British traditions for which they were undergoing such great disruption and
danger in their daily lives. The wartime Proms attracted many who had had
no interest in orchestral concerts before; servicemen and women on leave in
London found a congenial atmosphere in which to listen to music that caught
their interest. Like the cinema and other popular entertainments, the Proms
enabled them to be among people in an informal setting, a temporary escape
from the discipline and duties of their war work. C. S. Taylor, the Queen's
Hall manager of many years, described the variety of Proms audiences in 1941,
using language and images that were very much of their time:

> The Promenade is everybody – almost: the man in the street, the ordinary person,
> you, in fact; and from time to time you did things that the Symphony Concert
> audience would never do …
>
> They say that you applaud with considerable enthusiasm but no discrimination.
> I think that you exercise your discrimination before you come, because if you're not
> going to like it you don't come. Your numbers vary with the nature of the pro-
> gramme … On Fridays for Beethoven we never had enough room for you, on Bach
> Wednesdays you exhibited a strikingly large preponderance of young men (though
> the last two seasons have been different – the young men were elsewhere). If con-
> temporary music was being played you were not so numerous but were much more
> highly coloured, with a partiality for frantic ties and frenzied shirts, sandals, and no
> socks, and a tendency to argue solemnly about rhythmic impulse and whole-tone
> scales over lager at the bar.[235]

But the Proms was also about orchestras, and the war was indeed about
being called up, the young men 'elsewhere'. Orchestras found key players
missing and whole sections depleted as members were called to duty. A substantial amount of correspondence in BBC files of this period has to do with
the BBC SO – considering who would be available when, hiring replacements
and requesting those who seemed irreplaceable to be made available to the
BBC for its essential war work, lifting the spirits of the nation. But while
the BBC SO was subsidized, other London ensembles, such as the LSO and

the LPO, struggled hard to keep their organizations together and in work, and CEMA was literally a lifeline. Of course the quality of playing suffered with all the fluctuations, replacements, touring and difficult conditions for rehearsal and performance. The BBC SO moved from Bristol to Bedford in July 1941 when bombing became so dangerous in the coastal city that relocation was essential. And the LPO lost many instruments (but luckily no players) in the bombing that destroyed the Queen's Hall.

The five wartime Proms seasons were all planned, and performed at least in part, despite the often trying and frequently dangerous conditions. In fact, the story of the wartime Proms – managed without the BBC in 1940 and 1941 and with it again from 1942 through the Golden Jubilee of 1944 – has become so well known as to be legendary.[236] Briefly, the 1940 Proms – 'Sir Henry Wood's Forty-sixth and Farewell Season of Promenade Concerts'[237] – were run under the auspices of the Royal Philharmonic Society by Keith Douglas, Honorary Secretary of the Royal Philharmonic Society (RPS) and financial backer of the series (Wood was a guarantor), and Owen Mase, formerly of the BBC Music Department. Wood conducted the LSO in standard Proms fare, which was received by large audiences to enormous enthusiasm. The programming was noted 'in some respects [as] a reversion to former practice … the number and variety of novelties mak[ing] the forthcoming season like those of the pre-B.B.C. epoch'.[238] Wood took the opportunity to programme again as he liked, without committee input. There was an initial predilection for works by Allied composers, a visible and aural support of the war effort that increased year by year. Air-raid warnings frequently sounded during performances, but were in the main ignored by those within; one long Wagner night in 1940 was simply extended until the small hours of the morning:

> AN AIR-RAID WARNING HAS BEEN RECEIVED THE CONCERT WILL CONTINUE BUT THOSE WISHING TO LEAVE MAY DO SO

The Queen's Hall notice of an air-raid warning.

> The orchestra were prepared to carry on till the 'all clear' should sound, and did so under the direction of Mr. Basil Cameron … A five hours concert was given to which members of the London Symphony Orchestra contributed solos; then song-books were handed round, and there was a spell of community singing; then volunteers were called for, and members of the audience came to the platform and gave whatever they could give.[239]

However, heavy bombing eventually curtailed the season, which was suspended after the 7 September concert.

In an air raid on the night of 10–11 May 1941, over 300 bombs were dropped, damaging major London landmarks including the House of Commons, Westminster Abbey and the British Museum. The Queen's Hall was also hit and enormously damaged; the photographic image of Henry Wood

Below *Ruins of the Queen's Hall, gutted by a fire bomb during the night of 10–11 May 1941.*

Opposite *From the Albert Memorial, a view of the Royal Albert Hall, with towers of Imperial College beyond, 1951.*

standing in the ruins became a powerful symbol of defiant survival (see p. 31).[240] Despite this enormous loss, Wood met with Herbage shortly thereafter to continue discussions of the 1941 Proms season; although the BBC was not in a position to manage the series – Douglas would do that under the auspices of the RPS (with Wood again as guarantor) – the Corporation was involved in the programming to ensure suitable broadcasting material.[241]

The RPS quickly decided that the Proms should take place in the 'only likely hall', the Royal Albert Hall in Kensington Gore[242] – larger and potentially more profitable than the Queen's Hall, but far less satisfying from an acoustic point of view. Publicity was circulated to dispel the prejudices about the acoustics and to lure the Promenaders to the new location:

> For the Promenade Concerts the velarium [a huge sail cloth permanently suspended in the dome] has been lowered to intercept the echoes and also to reduce the apparent size of the hall. A strip of parquet floor has been placed in front of the platform to increase reflection and brighten tone and the rest of the arena will be used for the promenade. At the same time the platform has been surrounded with screens to reflect sound and localise the source.[243]

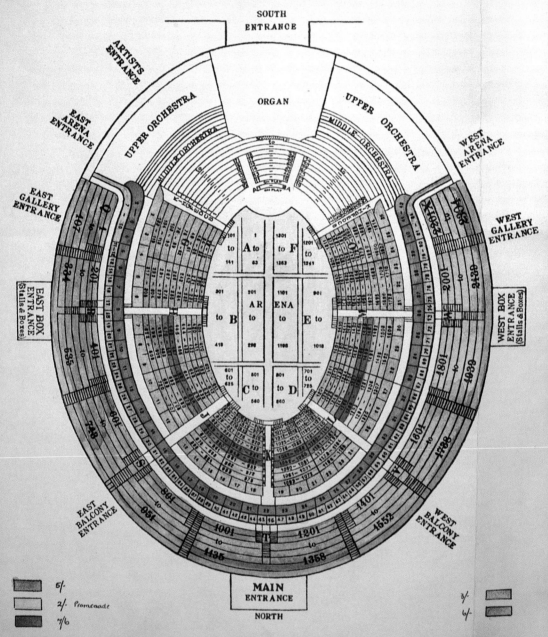

ROYAL
ALBERT HALL

Velarium hung under the dome of the Royal Albert Hall until 1949 to improve the hall's acoustics.

The six-week 1941 season – 'Sir Henry Wood's Forty-Seventh Season of Queen's Hall Promenade Concerts'[244] (Queen's Hall surviving in name and indicative of Wood's wish for quick rebuilding) – was brought forward in the summer, running from 12 July to 23 August, and was presented at the earlier start-time, 6.30 pm, to make the most of daylight while the black-out continued. Wood again conducted the LSO, and for the first time there was a named Associate Conductor for the series, Basil Cameron, who usually conducted the concerts' second halves. There was yet another difference that season, as critic William Glock pointed out in the *Observer*:

> The programmes have a noticeably different character. New works have been shunned, and since the traditional solos in Part Two would be simply lost in the Albert Hall, pianists and violinists will cling fast to the orchestra – a policy which reaches its climax on August 14 when Mr. Kentner will play both of the Chopin concertos.[245]

Opposite Royal Albert Hall seating plan, 1942, colour coded to show ticket prices (coding explained near the bottom).

Thus, with the move to the larger hall, the traditional songs in the second halves finally disappeared. The allied 'theme' was continued in an 'Anglo-American' concert on 5 August, in which a 'Symphony in One Movement' (i.e. Symphony No. 1) by Samuel Barber was played alongside Vaughan Williams' *Serenade to Music*. In a final break with tradition, but perhaps as a sign of relief that he had reached a season's end, Wood gave his first last night speech on 16 August 1941, thanking the sponsors – except Keith Douglas, with whom major tensions had developed.[246]

As early as April 1941, the BBC Home Board had agreed that it was 'desirable, in view of importance of Promenade Concerts to BBC's music position, for Corporation to resume control, (with London Symphony Orchestra and Thompson as manager), in the event of Keith Douglas being called up for military service'.[247] In the event, Douglas was not called up and the BBC did not need to take on the management of the 1941 Proms. But at the end of the season, discussions with Wood and the deteriorating relations with Douglas[248] led the BBC Home Board to extend that decision and eventually to agree to run the 1942 concerts. The new Albert Hall profits would sustain the cost, estimated at £4,800, of an additional orchestra sharing the season.[249] Many details needed to be worked out that autumn, not least the complicated issue of the acoustic screens and canopy, which were Douglas's personal property;[250] and in December the terms of the series' long-term continuation were raised as well as its name, the start of protracted discussions with Sir Henry and Lady Jessie, who were now wary of the BBC.[251] In mid-February 1942 the contract with the hall was signed, and agreements and rehearsal schedules were prepared for the LPO to perform the first four weeks,[252] with Cameron assisting Wood, and the BBC SO to perform the second four weeks, with Boult assisting. This plan, originally mooted as early as 1940, had the added benefit that one orchestra would not become fatigued by playing the full season. In fact, the scheme was found to be far kinder to the orchestra and resulted in better-rehearsed concerts, despite the costs involved with a second ensemble. No Proms season was ever again presented by a single orchestra.

The eight-week 1942 season – 'The BBC presents Sir Henry Wood's Forty-Eighth Season of Queen's Hall Promenade Concerts'[253] – ran from 27 June to 22 August, again with a start-time of 6.30 pm, changing to 6.00 pm for the final weeks in August. This hugely popular and successful season proceeded to the end without interruption. A featured work, presented on 29 June in a specially revised programme, was the first public performance of Shostakovich's Symphony No. 7, the 'Leningrad', exactly a week after Wood broadcast the first British performance with the LPO.[254] The series was also notable for rehearsals that were opened to school-children, four hundred at a time: 'While Sir Henry conducted, Sir Adrian Boult came and talked to them about each item before it began.'[255] Thus postwar schemes to make Prom concerts more accessible to younger audiences had wartime precedents. The last night was noted as such for the first time in a prospectus, and Wood gave another last-night speech – the practice, in its second year, speedily turned into a Proms 'tradition'.

The 1943 season was similarly constructed and similarly carried out. One important first related to the Bach–Brahms concert originally planned for 7 July. In the event, 'owing to the Royal Albert Hall being required by H.M. Government for a meeting in honour of China',[256] the Prom had to be postponed. The only option was to schedule it for 2.30 pm on Sunday 11 July – the first Sunday Prom in the history of the series. Another notable aspect of the 1943 Proms was not as revolutionary, but perhaps more prophetic. After Wood conducted the

first two Proms, he became ill and the doctors prescribed rest for the next three weeks. He was thus unable to conduct this first Sunday Prom, and instead watched from the audience – a well-known photograph of him in a loggia box records the unusual moment.

The 1944 Golden Jubilee was planned to celebrate the Proms' fiftieth season, not to mention Wood's seventy-fifth birthday, and the jolly staves, musical notes and trumpets bordering the prospectus cover represent a clear shift from the staid, plain look of the previous four years. The idea of celebration paralleled a wider social mood, which had already begun to look hopefully towards the end of hostilities, in fact still more than a year away. Elaborate planning and negotiation was needed to prepare a scheme involving three orchestras: the LPO would take the first two weeks, then the LSO, and the BBC SO would play the final four weeks, its schedule thus including Thursday 10 August 1944, the exact date of the fiftieth anniversary. In 'Sir Henry Wood's Jubilee Season Promenade Concerts',[257] first performances abounded, with works by Americans Samuel Barber and Roy Harris (who had become known through many wartime performances), by Russians Prokofiev, Stravinsky and Shostakovich (the first British performance of Symphony No. 8), by Hindemith, and by a varied group of British composers of the day – Granville Bantock, Vaughan Williams, Montague Phillips, Constant Lambert, Arnold Bax, Alan Bush and Elizabeth Maconchy. The season was given considerable press coverage (another sign that the war situation had changed), and enjoyed an auspicious start on 10 June with Wood conducting. However,

Wartime Promenaders listening to a concert in 1941, the first season at the Royal Albert Hall.

a new type of bombing started around the same time: with V-1 flying bombs the enemy executed a particularly vicious late stand, and after a near miss on 29 June the Proms were once again suspended. Some performances of works that had been planned as Prom broadcasts were given from Bedford by Boult and the BBC SO before invited audiences, but the season was an enormous disappointment for all – not least those hoping for record profits.

In a final twist, Wood's health had for a long time been declining, and he became terminally ill in late July. With a forceful and memorable broadcast of Beethoven's Seventh Symphony on the 28th, he conducted his final performance. He was too weak to listen to the Jubilee concert on 10 August even on the radio – and the final hero of this chapter died nine days later. Although a heroic season had been planned to celebrate the Proms' first fifty years, circumstances instead reduced the 1944 season to a mere shadow.

The Proms as Survivor

'When is a Prom not a Prom?' A BBC official asked that question as the 1940 negotiations with Chappell's foundered.[258] But it might well have applied at the end of the Golden Jubilee season in 1944. After fifty vibrant years, where did the Proms now stand and what were its essential qualities and identities? Its founders, Newman and Wood, were both dead; the concert hall at its core was destroyed; many of the concerts of recent seasons had gone unplayed; and some nights in 1944 had been performed out of the Proms' home city and without Proms audiences, a few works transmitted by radio, the Proms' sister-medium. How could the Proms as an entity survive with so many essential characteristics gone? And what then defined the nature of any 'Promenade Concerts' that might continue?

In fact, for all that seemed lost, the series had proved adaptable from the start. The Proms had already survived financial threats and the First World War, carried through by the determination and energy of both Newman and Wood. It had even survived Newman's death and the shaky conditions of Chappell's management, by accepting in 1927 association with the modern medium of broadcasting and new, mass audiences. Wood, Chappell's and the BBC chafed against each other, adjusting their expectations in a common willingness to maintain the tradition-based visage of the Promenade Concerts. In association with the Corporation, the Proms brand was defined and upheld by the Wood formula and by the firm guidance of Wood himself. In 1930 the Proms happily survived the formation of the BBC SO, the performance quality and stability adding a sheen to the Proms brand, which settled into a relatively durable groove for nine seasons, with Wood, the BBC, the hall and the audiences falling in with its somewhat predictable annual routine.

But with the return of war in 1939, the Proms' association with the BBC proved unreliable, the BBC SO shifted out of the picture with little warning; but the Proms managed once again to survive. Wood, perhaps precipitously, accepted the ready assistance of Douglas and the Royal Philharmonic Society to sustain the brand, and the absence of broadcasts, now found to be essential, was remedied in 1941. The destruction of the Queen's Hall was a vital blow, the Proms fundamentally part of the hall and its generations of audiences. Nevertheless, wartime circumstances and the enormous public demand for concerts undoubtedly aided a smooth transition to the Proms' new home in the Royal Albert Hall, the series surviving once again.

But in 1944 that home too was deemed unsafe; the season was truncated and the audiences dispersed. The celebration of the fiftieth anniversary concert was transmitted only, presenting merely an intangible shape of the Proms as programme, without its many other identifying elements. Even Wood, whose determination had carried the Proms through since Newman's death, lay on his death bed. As Marina Warner has noted, 'myths almost always deal with the reality of death. They travel to the land of the dead and bring back news of its arrangements. They dramatise the passage from life to after-life.'[259] Transition and reconstruction would lead the Proms to its postwar afterlife – but what would the series then be? For all that Wood and Lady Jessie tried to safeguard this legacy, what would fifty years of the Promenade Concerts become after Robert Newman, after the Queen's Hall and after Sir Henry Wood?

The BBC in Possession

1945–59

ALISON GARNHAM

IF EVER THE PHRASE 'THE END OF AN ERA' WERE APPROPRIATE, IT WAS NOW. Having led the Proms through half a century and two world wars, the Founding Father was dead, and the BBC, his publicly acknowledged and unchallenged heir, finally took possession of his legacy. Despite sixteen years of close collaboration, it was an anxious moment – even for W. W. Thompson, the BBC Concerts Manager, whose Proms experience went back nearly thirty years: 'To get matters in the right perspective', he advised Director of Music, Victor Hely-Hutchinson, 'we should regard the next Season as the first rather than the fifty-first Season.'[1]

Thompson's anxiety was caused not only by the loss of Sir Henry Wood. There were severe practical problems from which the end of the war brought no immediate relief. The BBC Symphony Orchestra was still evacuated to Bedford and currently locked in a bitter dispute with the BBC's management over the date of the players' return. Arrangements for readmitting players called up for military service were delayed by discussions over the size of the orchestra and imperilled by the alternative employment opportunities now available to musicians in postwar London. As well as competition for players, the BBC was facing renewed pressure from concert promoters and from a newly buoyant Musicians' Union over the right of its orchestras to give public concerts at all.

Despite the challenges faced by its Music Department, the BBC as a whole had undoubtedly emerged from the war in some triumph. Its war record had left it secure in the nation's esteem and widely admired in the rest of Europe, while the immense significance of broadcasting to almost all walks of life was now unquestioned. Wielding a monopoly that few doubted was in worthy hands, the BBC had already laid ambitious plans for its contribution to the reconstruction and re-education of Britain at peace. Music was to play a significant part in these plans, and so the opportunities for the Music Department – and consequently the pressures on it – were increased.

'The Proms –
"Possession of the
Whole Nation"':
this statement and
accompanying
photograph, of
Sir Henry Wood
conducting the
opening night of
the Jubilee Season
(10 June 1944),
introduced the 1945
Proms prospectus.

It was imperative that the 1945 Proms should be a success, both as a fitting tribute to Wood and proof that, in the hands of the BBC, the series could survive his death.

The Proms' long history notwithstanding, this success could not be taken for granted in the new musical world that emerged at the end of the war. Much had happened during six years of wartime to change both the BBC and the concert-going public. The Proms, which had originally filled a blank in London's concert diary, now had a greater potential audience, but also a more discriminating one, whose loyalty could not necessarily be relied on in the midst of increasing competition. The London Symphony and London Philharmonic Orchestras had both survived the war, if a little precariously, and were eager to re-establish themselves in postwar London concert life. Both had gained a foot in the door of the Proms when the BBC did not promote the concerts in 1940 and 1941, and they were not dislodged when the BBC Symphony Orchestra returned. Peacetime then brought two new orchestras to London: the Philharmonia, founded by Walter Legge of EMI in 1945, and the Royal Philharmonic, established by Sir Thomas Beecham in 1946. This meant that the BBC Symphony Orchestra,

which before the war had unquestionably set the standard for British orchestral music-making – attracting the finest players, performing exciting and innovative programmes and earning international recognition – now faced competition from four other independent symphony orchestras based in the capital. It was not surprising, therefore, that the best players might not automatically wish to work for the Corporation, despite the relative security of a BBC contract. As the BBC's Director-General reported to the Board of Governors at the beginning of 1947, 'since 1939, the Orchestra has lost 40 out of 119 players, many of them principals of outstanding ability … The majority of them can be attributed to players being tempted by outside market conditions.'[2]

These market conditions were remarkably good in the years following the war, when audiences for orchestral concerts grew rapidly. The 1940s saw an unprecedented surge of interest in the arts in Britain, despite postwar economic austerity – or perhaps partly because of it, since rationing still limited the ways in which one could spend one's money. Orchestral concerts, like cinemas and theatres, were packed, often with people who were eager for more than simple entertainment, and whose tastes had been expanded by the wartime work of CEMA (Council for the Encouragement of Music and the Arts) and ENSA (Entertainment National Service Association).[3] Cheaper gramophone recordings and the BBC's own broadcasts gradually increased the musical experience of these new audiences, whose appetite for 'good' music was further fuelled by the seriousness that the war had brought to all levels of society. The same postwar idealism that produced the 1945 Labour landslide, the National Health Service and universal secondary education also gave rise to the BBC Third Programme, the Arts Council and the abundance of new orchestras, festivals and other new arts organisations that sprang up all over the country in these years.

The Third Programme was the BBC's contribution to this idealistically educative mood, and it began broadcasting in September 1946. Although the idea of a cultural network had been mooted several times before, the Third as it went on air was really the brainchild of William Haley, the new Director-General, an energetic autodidact who arrived in 1944 with ambitious plans for the postwar education of the British people. Intended for 'persons of taste, of intelligence and of education',[4] the Third's schedules were full of music, plays, poetry, scientific lectures and philosophical discussions. This was not the only new choice for listeners, however. Persons not yet able to aspire to such heights were offered a new Light Programme, which in 1945 replaced the extremely popular wartime Forces Programme. Despite its lightness of tone, however, even the Light Programme was not just about simple entertainment. Haley's intention in creating these new alternatives to the Home Service was not to divide his audiences into classes (although that is ultimately what happened), but to unite them in a quest to make available to everyone 'the best that has been thought or said or composed in all the world'.[5] His three networks were to provide three parts of what was, essentially, the same service. As he explained to the BBC Governors in 1944:

> We do not intend that the three Programmes shall be rigidly stratified. Rather will they shade into each other, their differences being in approach and treatment rather than in range of content … The classical music in the Light Programme will, we hope, be attractive enough to lead listeners on to the Home Service; the Home Service should lead on to the Third Programme.[6]

To Haley, the listening audience was like a pyramid, 'with a lamentably broad base and a lamentably narrow tip', the shape of which the BBC's three main networks – Light Programme at the bottom, Home Service in the middle and Third Programme at the top – would together strive to change. 'My conception was of a BBC through the years – many years – which would slowly move listeners from one stratum of this pyramid to the next.'[7] The Promenade Concerts' unique mix of popularity and artistic innovation suited this educative mission very well. Here was material for all three networks united in one high-profile series of concerts. 'I hope it is clear we are not merely going to run this year's Proms', Haley told Lindsay Wellington, Controller of Programmes in 1945. 'They are to be a continuing BBC institution.'[8]

Cartoon by Hickey, from Punch *(6 November 1946).*

Of course this was not the only reason why the BBC wanted to retain control of the Proms. It was a very popular, successful and – since the move to the Royal Albert Hall – lucrative series of concerts, whose profits, according to Senior Controller Basil Nicolls, were 'a windfall for the BBC, which we normally put against the losses on other public concerts'.[9] These were the days, Wellington remembered later, 'when we looked to profits from the Proms to cover most of our public concert finance'.[10] Even during the war the Proms had made a profit – indeed, in 1944 it was estimated that the concerts would have made over £10,000 had the flying bombs not forced an early end to the season. In 1945, with the Albert Hall's gallery now freed from wartime restrictions, even bigger audiences could be accommodated, and the proceeds were more than £13,000. This figure was so high in part because the BBC did not include in its calculations the salaried BBC Symphony Orchestra, the costs of which were considered to be offset by the many hours of broadcasts the Proms provided.

The BBC's immunity to the risks borne by other orchestras and concert promoters continued to cause resentment after the war, with the Corporation still accused of operating at an unfair advantage when it came to public concerts. In 1946 the Musicians' Union (MU) renewed its attempts to force the BBC orchestras back into the studio, first asking the Corporation 'to amend the [players'] contracts to exclude public concerts upon the grounds that performances of the latter character by [BBC] Orchestras were unfairly competitive with outside orchestras'.[11] When this was unsuccessful, the MU informed BBC players that it 'intended to forbid public concerts by B.B.C. Orchestras', but this strategy foundered when the players would not cooperate in giving up such a satisfying part of their work. The union then changed tack somewhat, suggesting to the BBC in 1947 that 'the Corporation shall engage an outside orchestra to perform a studio engagement as a quid pro quo for every public concert played by a B.B.C. Concert Orchestra'.[12] This line of argument was also pursued by the National Association of Symphony Orchestras (NASO), formed during the war, and it led to a formal agreement between NASO and the BBC in 1949, which laid down the terms for such 'compensatory engagements'.[13] The Proms naturally featured prominently in these negotiations, and an agreement to share them with outside orchestras formed part of the final accord.

The establishment of the Corporation's ownership of the Proms was therefore an issue of some importance to the BBC's management in the years immediately following Wood's death. The circumstances of the BBC's withdrawal from the concerts in 1940 and 1941 had unsettled the succession somewhat, particularly in the eyes of Wood himself, who was reluctant to give his legacy freely to the Corporation unless he could be assured that such a situation could not be repeated. After much discussion, during which Wood even considered establishing a separate company to 'licence' the Proms to the BBC,[14] a formal and public exchange of letters between Wood and Haley took place during the Jubilee Season of 1944, when Wood bequeathed the Proms to the BBC, and the Corporation confirmed its commitment to the series and renamed it after Wood.[15] For the BBC's management this seems to have settled the issue, and it only remained to defend the control of the Proms, which it now considered the Corporation's undoubted right. In the Music Department, however, a certain hesitancy was detectable, emanating no doubt from a consciousness of the weight of responsibility laid upon it by such an inheritance. The Music Department's diffidence about taking command of the Proms was criticized by Nicolls, who seized on statements of Hely-Hutchinson's like 'We must regard ourselves in this case as Trustees for the present season at any rate of what has become a national institution'[16] as being insufficiently proprietorial:

> Although, to save possible complications, we went through the motions last summer of getting Sir Henry Wood to 'bequeath' the Proms to us, we must not forget that up till the suspension in 1940, for I think thirteen years, they were run in every way as 'BBC Promenade Concerts', were billed as such on posters, in the printed programmes and everywhere. We rescued the Proms in 1927 when otherwise they would have been abandoned, and while very properly admitting Sir Henry Wood's goodwill and founder interest in the Proms, there is no need for us to regard ourselves as trustees vis-à-vis any third party. I do think it is important in the long run that we should not adopt the attitude that we are doing the Proms on sufferance and that anyone else has just as good a right to do them.[17]

Prommers queueing for the penultimate concert of the 1945 season.

After fifty years, Wood's shadow over the Proms was long. There being no obvious successor to take his place, a definite view prevailed, at least initially, that no one should attempt to do so. In the Music Department, according to Hely-Hutchinson, there was 'the feeling that the series should be "de-personalised"'[18] – or rather, although this is not actually expressed, that there should be no new personality to compete with that of Wood. It was at this point, of course, that the Proms were rechristened 'The Henry Wood Promenade Concerts', and the preface to the newly expanded prospectus announcing the 1945 Proms – 'The Proms Go On' – explicitly invoked Wood's blessing: 'His spirit is in this new Season; his example and inspiration animate us all – orchestras, conductors, organizers, and the great public to whom he brought his art and whose love for music he so largely created.'

Still, despite this tribute, the tone of the 1945 preface as a whole was one of triumphant celebration of the BBC's coming into its inheritance. Much was made of the Corporation being the chosen heir of Sir Henry, who 'himself always had a vision that transcended personal achievement and association'. The BBC also allied itself quite explicitly with the new postwar spirit: the preface was full of wartime images of the 'loyalty and courage of the public' and the 'grave risks' they took in attending concerts during the bombardment, contrasting such difficult times with the 'happy consciousness of victory' in which the current season would take place. 'Another Epoch begins', in which the Proms were now a 'great institution', and Wood was brought in again to declare that 'the Promenade Concerts [are] more important than any one man'. Tribute was paid to the glories of the past, but especially highlighted were the BBC's 1927 rescue of the concerts 'for the nation', and the way in which broadcasting had made the Proms 'the possession of the whole nation and the admiration and envy of a listening world'. Even the curtailing of the Jubilee Season the previous year was presented as a triumph for the BBC: 'the broadcasts, which continued from Bedford, reached millions of homes nevertheless. The Proms would not give in.'

Sir Henry was dead, canonized and appropriated, but still very much alive was Lady Jessie Wood, who in the years immediately following Wood's death kept a watchful eye on the BBC's stewardship of the Proms. Lady Jessie was a forceful presence who kept in regular correspondence with everyone involved, from the Chairman of the Governors down, arguing vigorously against any perceived departure from Wood's 'mission to teach the younger generation'.[19] Innovations to which she objected included the use of more than one orchestra (to which, she insisted, Wood had acceded only as a wartime necessity); the use of any orchestra other than the BBC Symphony Orchestra ('these "outside" unsubsidized organisations ... are a law unto themselves'[20]); the increasingly symphonic programmes ('these stodgy academic programmes ... may well kill Henry Wood's great heritage'[21]); 'prima donna' conductors and programme planners 'who know nothing or little of the art of rehearsal';[22] the impact of the Third Programme ('the gravest danger to these concerts'[23]); the use of well-known soloists ('we should never forget the MISSION of his

Sir Henry Wood and Lady Jessie Wood arriving at the Royal Albert Hall to attend a Promenade Concert, 1 July 1943.

Promenade Concerts … to bring forward YOUNG UNKNOWN artists'[24]); and, finally, the use of the Royal Albert Hall itself:

> The Albert Hall is regrettably just the kind of building to propagate that evil of our time – mass hysteria – and in this hall, I am convinced the *mission* synonymous with the 'Henry Wood Promenade Concerts' is at stake. It is that spread-out amphitheatre which thrills and attracts the masses – (the war has taught them this in the factories etc;) – among which I fear, the majority come to 'have a good time' but less, to listen and learn, as was the case in those past years in Queen's Hall – that correctly designed hall for music, musicians, and of course – musicians in embryo.[25]

Lady Jessie may have been a voice from the past – and her letters increasingly illustrated the extent to which the Proms changed after the war – but she was a force to be reckoned with for some years to come. Many of her activities centred on raising money for the new concert hall that she hoped would be built in Wood's memory, and included several attempts to get the BBC to contribute some of its Proms 'windfall' to this cause. Her arguments naturally impinged on the BBC's right to the Proms, and specifically its use of the name of Henry Wood. The BBC's solicitor was of the opinion that, while anyone could mount promenade concerts, the 'Henry Wood' title was definitely vested in the BBC by Wood's and Haley's correspondence in 1944, and Lady Jessie's attempts to force a royalty payment failed.[26] Where she did succeed, however, was in compelling the BBC to restart the winter Proms in 1948, by threatening to run the series herself under the auspices of her newly formed Henry Wood Concert Society.[27]

The BBC never really wanted to resurrect the winter Proms, but the prospect of another organization running Henry Wood Promenade Concerts in the Royal Albert Hall was so alarming that the Corporation felt compelled to do it 'to stake a claim', as Haley put it.[28] Nevertheless, it came at the price of considerable criticism from other concert promoters, who resented any increase in the BBC's concert-giving activities during the main winter concert season: 'This is an incursion into the field of private enterprise', complained the impresario Harold Holt to Haley, explaining that while the long-established summer season did not interfere with other promoters' efforts, winter Proms most certainly would.[29] Ultimately, the interests of other promoters were saved by the fact that the postwar winter Proms were never very successful. As a basic survey of popular repertory for two weeks each January, they were less interesting musically than the summer series and, as *The Times* pointed out, gumboots and woollies in the drafty Albert Hall in January – especially in the bitterly cold winter of 1947 – were not quite in keeping with the Proms atmosphere:

> The distinctive character of the Promenade Concert depends on other things besides the programmes, of which an almost Mediterranean luxuriance in summer warmth is one.[30]

The BBC kept the winter Proms going from 1947 until 1952, by which time it was reasonably sure that the financial returns were so bad that no one else would want to do them. The Royal Festival Hall on the South Bank had opened the previous year, providing much warmer and more comfortable concert-going facilities for the public. After the BBC's withdrawal, however, the London Symphony Orchestra did step into the breach in 1953 to run a one-week winter series in the Royal Albert Hall, with a fanfare of approving headlines – 'Orchestra Saves the Proms'[31] – and at least one commendably innovative programme. This even included Humphrey Searle's *The Shadow of Cain*, with Dylan Thomas declaiming Edith Sitwell's text – a programme so 'desperately enterprising', in the words of the BBC official who attended the concert, that it all but emptied the hall.[32]

Refreshments for queueing Promenaders, 1948.

In all its dealings with the winter Proms, it is noteworthy that it was not just the fact of another promoter doing promenade concerts that the BBC feared, but another promoter doing them *badly*, and thus sullying the image of the BBC's own series. The BBC was concerned to preserve high standards at the Proms – and have them recognized as such – particularly after 1945 when the Corporation had assumed full responsibility. 'Whilst such a flop may not have any material repercussion on future series in the summer,' wrote W. W. Thompson after the London Symphony Orchestra's 1953 season, 'it certainly does not contribute towards maintaining the popularity of this particular type of musical entertainment.'[33]

'The BBC regards the Proms as a Trust', announced the 1945 *BBC Year-book*[34] – a statement that Hely-Hutchinson, who had been promoted to head the Music Department only the year before, seems to have taken at its face value and found a little overwhelming: 'It is very difficult, if not impossible, especially in these years immediately succeeding Sir Henry Wood's death, to see how best we may serve the interests of the national institution of which we are custodians.'[35] Basil Nicolls, as we have already seen, had little patience with what he called 'the Music Department's rather soft un-proprietorial attitude to the Proms',[36] but Hely-Hutchinson's instinct was to play for safety and change as little as possible. He appointed Sir Adrian Boult and Basil Cameron as Joint Principal Conductors of the 1945 Proms, because their names were both already associated with the concerts and would provide 'continuity of tradition'.[37] Programme-planning would be in the hands of a committee, consisting largely of those who had worked closely with Wood: programme-builder Julian Herbage, Concerts Manager W. W. Thompson, and Deputy Director of Music Kenneth Wright joined the two conductors.

Curiously, Hely-Hutchinson decided not to take any active role in proceedings, but to keep himself in reserve as 'the last "court of appeal"' in case of dispute between the others, and to act as 'the musical representative of the B.B.C. which is promoting the season'.[38] This would indeed appear to indicate an 'un-proprietorial' attitude on Hely-Hutchinson's part, and it also shows how far the Proms then were from the centre of the BBC's musical concerns. The situation was very different in 1959, when William Glock immediately identified the Proms as one of the 'most creative tasks in BBC music'[39] and personally took charge of their programming. In 1945, however, the rebuilding of the BBC Symphony Orchestra and the demands of the new radio services left the Director of Music little leisure to consider interfering with the Proms. In any case, the Proms were the Proms: a winning formula now hallowed by long tradition. Hely-Hutchinson was happy to let them be run simply 'in accordance with Sir Henry's known wish'.[40]

Sir Adrian Boult, as Chief Conductor of the BBC Symphony Orchestra practically since its foundation, and also Head of the BBC Music Department until 1942, could presumably have taken charge of the artistic direction of the Proms if he had wanted to. But he too seemed reluctant to step into Wood's shoes. Boult disliked conducting at the Proms, where the nightly concerts left him insufficient time to prepare. Promenade conductors, he told Wright, needed to be 'able to project themselves nightly into an entirely new artistic world'. He preferred to work at a less frenzied pace and professed himself unable to change. 'The fact that my machinery seems to be much slower than this is unfortunate perhaps, but personal, and I know that if I tried to speed it up it would mean a loss of standard.'[41] There was also a more commercial reason:

> The Chief Prom Conductor cannot be the Chief Conductor of the B.B.C. Symphony Orchestra. It simply does not make sense that an artist who is available at Prom prices during July and August, should expect to draw at the prices we charge for Symphony Concerts for the rest of the year.[42]

'I am quite ready to be either,' Boult assured Wright, 'but I naturally prefer what is I suppose still the more important of the two.' The winter Symphony Series, though consisting of ten concerts a year, was still where the BBC concentrated its efforts and resources, while the Proms, with five times the number of concerts, were run on a minimum of rehearsal. Boult was persuaded to remain in the Proms in 1946 and 1947 – 'for the sake of the Proms it is too early for his personality to be withdrawn'[43] – but he made it very clear that he was only doing so as a BBC duty, at least while the current schedule was in force.

There was thus something of a power vacuum. The BBC's Chief Conductor was eager to leave the Proms, and his colleague, Basil Cameron, was not sufficiently eminent to carry on alone. The BBC's Director of Music was deliberately keeping himself at arm's length – and in any case, it was soon evident that Hely-Hutchinson was a very sick man. 'He gradually got sleepier and more and more listless', according to Wright.[44] This illness was ascribed by some to 'a spinal bug he picked up in Italy when he went over to see Toscanini',[45] but whatever the cause, he died a sadly early death in 1947, after which the post of Director of Music changed hands with alarming rapidity. Wright held the reins until the beginning of 1948, when Sir Steuart Wilson was appointed to take over the Department. Wilson had worked briefly for the BBC before, as Overseas Music Director during the war, but he was basically an outsider, a well-known tenor who returned to the BBC from his previous position as Music Director of the recently formed Arts Council. He was a rather abrasive character, whose most significant decision during his tenure was to remove Boult (to whom Wilson's first wife was now married). Boult was forced to retire in 1950; Wilson himself left the BBC in the same year, to be succeeded by his deputy, Herbert Murrill, a more sympathetic and musically thoughtful character. Unfortunately, Murrill too fell ill after only a few months in the post, and he also died in office, leaving Eric Warr as Acting Head in 1952. The following year Richard Howgill, who as Controller of Entertainment had had the oversight of the Department throughout this period, was appointed to head it. Commensurate with his seniority, and perhaps also with the number of broadcasting hours that Music now provided, he was given the new title of 'Controller, Music', and the Department became a Division. This brought managerial stability, due to Howgill's superb administrative ability, but not musical leadership. Howgill was not a professional musician – indeed, he once admitted frankly, 'as far as I am concerned, only a sense of duty gets me to any one of the Proms'.[46]

The Proms therefore began their 'New Epoch' without a musical leader, and effectively stayed in that condition for the next fifteen years. Although a new figurehead did emerge, it was not one who could command the whole series as Wood had done for so long. Yet the Proms remained coherent and controlled, and this was largely due to the dedicated work of Julian Herbage, who planned the series from the background throughout this time. His official title was 'programme builder', but Herbage did much more than this. He took over from Wood the huge task of designing the overall pattern of each season and overseeing every detail of the complex broadcast arrangements. He attended soloists' auditions, was present at every concert in the capacity of overall producer, and at the end of each series he wrote a formal report to advise the Corporation on future policy. What is surprising, given the size of the job, is that he did all this as a freelance, for an annual fee of £500 (which rose to £700 by the end of the 1950s). Although he had been on the BBC's staff since 1927, Herbage had elected to leave in 1946 – but the Corporation quickly decided that it could not do without him. As Lindsey Wellington ruefully admitted to Hely-Hutchinson:

> We learnt a useful lesson last year and this about the abominably difficult problem of building and running Promenade Concerts in a way which fitted in with broadcast requirements without spoiling their character as public concerts. Herbage discussed broadcasting requirements with planners, built programmes accordingly and then attended each concert in the capacity of producer and stage manager. By this means he reduced the disasters attendant upon variable timings to a minimum. This year all went remarkably well until Herbage took a well-earned holiday. We promptly suffered several disasters and acid memoranda began to circulate which effected nothing at all.
>
> May I suggest that we book Herbage to plan, build and run next year's Proms in close collaboration with Home Service and Third Programme Planners?[47]

Despite successive Directors of Music feeling that the planning of the Proms really ought to be taken back 'in house', Herbage remained indispensable, receiving a separate contract for the planning and running of the Proms each year until 1961. He was not alone in his co-ordinating role, however, since W. W. Thompson, Wood's concert manager since 1916, remained on the BBC's staff until 1954. Hely-Hutchinson's original Proms planning committee soon dwindled effectively to a partnership of Herbage and Thompson, who would draft out the season together (Herbage specialising in repertory, Thompson in artists) before discussions with the conductors and the rest of the Music Department began. Once the season was under way, they would jointly be responsible for every detail of its organization.

This backstage nature of Proms planning explains the rather reactive character of the Proms' development over the next few years. The series changed decisively from what it had been in Wood's day, but this was less a result of BBC managerial enterprise or artistic vision than simply because the Proms inhabited a rapidly changing world. One of the most important changes of all – a radically new orchestral schedule – took place in 1947, and this was made in response to the new orchestral world in which the BBC found itself as it considered the state of its own Symphony Orchestra after the war.

For Sir Adrian Boult, the first year of peace was a desperately frustrating time. He was well aware of the strain on his players' loyalty, as the BBC's management prevaricated over their return from their wartime evacuation at Bedford, vacillated over the future size and role of the BBC Symphony Orchestra, and, humiliatingly, appeared to overlook the orchestra completely in its programming for the celebration of Victory in Europe. Boult and his musicians felt taken for granted as they saw their former status dwindling almost by default, because there appeared to be no understanding of the problem or will to address it among senior executives. The first year after the war ended saw the resignation of thirty players, many of whom the orchestra could ill afford to lose; they included, for example, all the principals in the wind section.

The 1946 season of Promenade Concerts brought matters to a head, when the nightly performances put the state of the orchestra under a harsh spotlight. Boult, whose protests had not been much furthered by the ailing Hely-Hutchinson, then received the more effective support of Dr Ernest Whitfield, a BBC Governor, who was shocked by how tired and underrehearsed the orchestra seemed at those Proms he attended. At the end of the season, Boult wrote a frank report on the orchestra and the Proms, and the Corporation at last paid attention.

Put bluntly, does the Corporation wish me to try and bring the Orchestra up to its 1939 standard or would it prefer to have a useful and efficient working body that will accede to all the demands of the various Services? There is naturally in planning circles a strong bias in the latter direction, and the corporation's apparent agreement to the assumption both at home and abroad by various British orchestras of the premier position in this country, makes me feel that it might perhaps be simpler to yield to all planning demands, work our schedule on a minimum of rehearsal, and a minimum of public appearance, and give up inviting our Toscaninis and Menuhins, or at any rate acquiesce in their refusal to visit us when they discover what is happening.[48]

There was also the question of the increasingly ambitious programmes that Boult found himself being asked to conduct on one rehearsal. The BBC seemed to want to raise the status of the Proms to a level that Boult insisted was unsustainable without major changes:

I would ask for a fundamental overhaul of our attitude to the Proms, which seem to have over-reached themselves to a dangerous degree. On paper, we are giving

programmes of identical calibre with our Symphony Concerts, at greater length and at half the price. Even the artists are now on the same plane. This is not only an absurd situation: it is dishonest, for the slipshod nature of our performances cannot be understood by most of that young audience, and even our professional critics seem to assume that we have three rehearsals for every concert.[49]

Stimulated by an interview with Boult that was published in the *Daily Telegraph* on 23 September 1946, Lady Jessie joined the debate, writing first to William Haley and then to the BBC Chairman, with whom she had a meeting at the beginning of October. Her solution to the crisis over performance standards was, not surprisingly, to return to Wood's model: one conductor, with one orchestra, performing nightly on one rehearsal, with the programmes limited accordingly. Novelties and young artists should continue to be an important feature, but the scope of the programmes would be constrained by the nightly schedule – she even proposed bringing back instrumental solos into the second half of the concerts to limit the number of orchestral items that needed to be rehearsed. While concurring on the importance of keeping Proms programmes popular, the BBC otherwise disagreed with Lady Jessie, and made a very significant decision: it resolved to bring the Proms performances up to Symphony Concert standard, employing the London Philharmonic Orchestra (LPO) and London Symphony Orchestra (LSO) alongside the BBC Symphony Orchestra (BBC SO) in a nightly alternation that was designed to give each concert a full nine hours' rehearsal. This was not originally intended to be a permanent decision, but it proved to be the beginning of a lasting concern for high performance standards at the Proms, which increasingly took precedence over the traditions of promoting new artists and new works.

The orchestral scheme thus introduced in 1947 increased the available rehearsal time while preserving the nightly concerts by employing the orchestras in parallel, one rehearsing while another was performing. This added £1,500 a week to the cost of the Proms, in addition to the fees due to the third chief conductor. The scheme was originally suggested to the BBC by Thomas Russell of the LPO[50] – who, as he admitted later, had never expected the BBC to accept it, and was 'both surprised and delighted' when it did.[51] As Wellington, now Controller of the Home Service, warned Nicolls:

> This will involve expenditure which will wipe out Proms profits, which in past years have constituted a large and important contribution to Programme Reserve. The counter-balancing and decisive advantage is the lessening of the burden on the BBC Orchestra which is particularly necessary while it is being remodelled and repolished.[52]

This huge expenditure was thus intended as a temporary measure to help the postwar recovery of the BBC SO: the use of outside orchestras on this scale was initially approved by the Board for the 1947 season only, and the uneven performance and poor discipline of the LPO reduced the orchestras to two again the following year.[53] In the event, that 1948 reduction proved to be only a brief setback, and the LPO was back in 1949, the BBC Opera Orchestra was added in 1950, the Royal Philharmonic Orchestra came in regularly from 1952, the Hallé Orchestra of Manchester every year from 1953, the National Youth Orchestra and the Bournemouth Symphony Orchestra in 1955 and the Liverpool Philharmonic in 1956. The Proms were moving towards becoming a national festival of orchestral music. The beginning of this process was marked by Herbage in his foreword to the 1947 prospectus:

> It is at least tempting to describe this Season as a Festival. Could even Salzburg, in the palmy interwar years, offer us three orchestras, three principal conductors, to say nothing of an associate conductor and composers directing their own works? An eight weeks' orchestral season in which the nightly concerts are allotted an average of three rehearsals each? It can safely be asserted that no such musical enterprise has previously been conceived.[54]

This was a decisive step away from the past, and it was made in response to the enormous changes that were happening in the musical world outside the BBC. The increasing accessibility of orchestral music through the capital's burgeoning concert life, the availability and affordability of gramophone recordings, and the BBC's own broadcasting efforts had created a public that was markedly more discriminating than before the war. The BBC was forced to face facts: 'The Proms are a survival from the days when the standards of orchestral playing and the expectations of the public in this respect were infinitely lower than they are today', wrote Hely-Hutchinson to Howgill.[55] Rather than risk the relative decline of the 'great institution' whose future had been so proudly trumpeted only the year before, the BBC was prepared to invest significant amounts of money. The five-figure profits that the Corporation had been enjoying as a result of the move to the Royal Albert Hall were never seen again.

Lady Jessie had a point when she identified programme-planning and rehearsal techniques as part of the problem. For the first time in the Proms' history, the series was not being planned primarily by its conductor – a conductor, moreover, whose 'unique technical efficiency', in Herbage's words, had 'reduced advance study and preparation to a fine art'.[56] The main role in the planning of the Proms now fell to Herbage, who had worked with Wood as a programme-builder for most of the decade before the latter's death. This experience offered some continuity, but Herbage was now planning for different conductors, none of whom quite had Wood's overview of the series or his extraordinarily effective rehearsal skills. Inevitably, too, this separation of planning from performance meant that other concerns became more prominent, such as the increasingly complicated broadcasting arrangements. Herbage was a fine administrator with long experience of preparing concerts for broadcast, a clear mind and a meticulous eye for detail. He was also something of an academic musician, specializing particularly in music of the seventeenth and eighteenth centuries, to whom the intellectual challenge of building such an enormous series of concerts must have appealed.

Herbage cautiously began to try out new thematic programme schemes. In 1945, mindful of the consistent success of 'composer nights' – as Hely-Hutchinson put it, 'the Promenade audience … likes its favourite composers in large doses'[57] – Herbage tried a complete series of Sibelius symphonies. 'It cannot be said that this was loudly acclaimed by the public', admitted Hely-Hutchinson, although he concluded that the welcome was warm enough to allow the experiment to be repeated, in the hope that 'in a year or two it will become an essential part of the scheme'.[58] A complete cycle of Vaughan Williams's symphonies (which numbered five at that date) was added to those of Sibelius in the 1946 season, with Vaughan Williams himself conducting *A London Symphony* on Wednesday 31 July – also thereby inaugurating a new series of Wednesday programmes specially featuring 'the music of our time'. Herbage seems to have been particularly proud of this Wednesday series, announcing that 'on the planning of the Wednesday programmes alone this season's Proms can claim to have changed in character and to have kept abreast of the times in enterprising music-making.'[59]

It is interesting to compare these Wednesday concerts with another series aiming to 'keep abreast of the times' that Herbage planned in 1959, at the end of his time with the Proms. 'Masters of the Twentieth Century' comprised only four concerts, in which all the works programmed had been composed within the last sixty years. There was nothing remotely avant-garde, however; indeed, many of these works – such as Debussy's *La mer*, Ravel's *La valse*,

Opposite *Prospectus
covers for the 1945,
1947 and 1951 seasons,
with designs by
Michael Ayrton
(1945), Joan Hassall
(1947) and Victor
Reinganum (1951).*

Prokofiev's 'Classical' Symphony, Holst's *Perfect Fool*, or Vaughan Williams'
symphonies – were already Proms staples. None of the premières listed as
'novelties' that year was included. This conservatism notwithstanding, the
audience figures for all four programmes were the lowest of that season's concerts – by a very long way. By contrast, the box office receipts for Herbage's
1946 Wednesday series almost matched the average for the season as a whole;
indeed, the figures for the whole of the 1946 season were remarkably consistent. The programming principle was very different from that of 'Masters of
the Twentieth Century': Herbage's 1946 series generally placed one substantial
twentieth-century work – such as Walton's (First) Symphony, Rawsthorne's
(First) Piano Concerto, Bartók's Violin Concerto, and the first English performance of Prokofiev's Fifth Symphony – safely in the middle of a popular
programme; and apart from their mention in the prospectus Preface, the concerts were not highlighted by being given a specific title. Four of the season's
fourteen novelties were placed in these concerts, including both world premières. Wednesday 28 August went a little further, putting the première of
Lennox Berkeley's Nocturne together with Poulenc's Concerto for Two Pianos
and Vaughan Williams' *A Sea Symphony*, but again this was managed without
any noticeable effect on takings.

Another innovation in 1946 was a new presentation of Wagner, whose popularity with British audiences had declined sharply during the previous
decade. Wagner was to be a recurring problem, as the BBC Music Department continued to feel some responsibility to present his music in the concert
hall – at least, wrote Hely-Hutchinson, 'until Covent Garden gets going on
Wagner as part of its repertoire'.[60] The Proms, with their long tradition of
Wagner concerts on Monday nights, were the obvious place to discharge this.
By contrast, the BBC's winter Symphony Concerts in this period abandoned
Wagner completely, and not a note of his music was heard there between 1946
and 1953. How Wagner should be represented at the Proms, however, was a
matter for repeated discussion, as the audiences on Monday nights dwindled
and the traditional 'bleeding chunks' were increasingly considered 'grossly
inartistic'.[61] After moving Wagner away from Monday nights in 1945, Herbage
tried the experiment in 1946 of a linked series presenting much larger excerpts.
Four Wagner half-concerts were given, each presenting substantial scenes
from one of the operas of the *Ring* cycle. As Herbage said, 'The day when
Wagner merely titillated the ear has gone for ever, and Wagner must now be
displayed as a dramatic symphonist.'[62]

This idea of Wagner as a 'dramatic symphonist' betrays another of Herbage's
themes. Lady Jessie was not alone in complaining about 'the excess of heavy
symphonic music' that characterized the 1946 Proms.[63] Hely-Hutchinson was
persuaded by a weary Boult that 'the symphonic aspect of the programmes
was rather overdone this year',[64] and the Director-General agreed, issuing via
Nicolls an instruction that 'this tendency should be corrected'.[65] The BBC's
senior management repeatedly stressed the need to 'keep [the] Proms to their
basic objective of being popular'.[66] Yet symphonies were extremely popular

with London concert audiences at this time, and also – not coincidentally – with British composers. A reason for limiting their appearance at the Proms may have been to preserve the distinction between Promenade concerts and the winter Symphony Series, Prom programmes having traditionally been composed of a greater number of smaller works. This was certainly the reason for another directive issued after the 1946 Proms: 'Major international artists of the Menuhin type not to be used.'[67] This instruction seems to have come as a surprise to Herbage, who had written excitedly in his Preface to the 1946 Proms prospectus that Menuhin's appearance that year, playing the Elgar Concerto, 'brings to mind the list of distinguished artists who, now that wartime barriers are broken down, will help us once again to make music an international art'.

The question of the Proms' special identity, now that Wood was no more, clearly exercised the BBC at the start of its 'New Epoch'. Hely-Hutchinson's view in 1946 that 'the thing which should differentiate the Proms from Symphony Concerts is the presence in the latter of great international artists'[68] was unlikely to be sustained for long in the face of the pressure to raise performance standards. A clearer distinction could be seen in the programming. The Proms was still primarily an orchestral series, and many of the major choral works that figured prominently in the Symphony series were to be conspicuous by their absence from the Proms for another ten years. Still fundamental to Proms programming, despite the increasing availability of music from other sources, was the mission to bring music to 'new concert-goers, and lead them on to an appreciation of the classics of the orchestral repertoire'[69] – classics that were drawn overwhelmingly from the nineteenth century and were predominantly Germanic. Balancing this choice of repertory was the duty 'to encourage British music [and] perform new works',[70] which was clearly considered to be an essential part of the Proms at all levels of the BBC but was not much in evidence in its Symphony series. A difference could also be seen in the programmes' shape, as Proms programmes continued to be longer and more varied. Symphony concerts were moving towards either a standard overture–concerto–symphony pattern or a large choral work standing alone, while Promenade concerts remained more flexible. Traces of former traditions, such as having the weight of the programme in the first half, or novelties in the second, still lingered in the programming patterns, and when works like Elgar's *Dream of Gerontius* and Verdi's *Requiem* finally made their appearance in the later 1950s, they accounted for only part of a concert.

Cartoon by Lee, from the London Evening News *(21 July 1947).*

"See what I mean, Mum? NOW do you want me to go on with those flipping five-finger exercises?"

'Sir Henry Wood, I am sure, was so secure in the affections of the Prom audience that he never worried how he was going to "go down" with them – he knew that what he gave them they would accept … It was this sense of mutual trust that built up the Proms', wrote Julian Herbage in 1951.[71] When the BBC asked Wood's audience to transfer its trust to the Corporation, there was a risk that without the personal guarantee of their familiar conductor, people would no longer identify with the concerts. The BBC was aware that the Proms audience was a rather special one: 'the Prom-audience will either come to the Proms or will stay at home: it will not easily be attracted elsewhere.'[72] After the 1947 'Festival', therefore, doubts began to be expressed about the wisdom of the 'de-personalising' policy. Would more orchestras – and particularly more conductors – dilute that intimate relationship between platform and Promenaders that had been one of the Proms' most important distinguishing features? Thompson seems to have thought so: the nightly alternation of orchestras and conductors that year had been 'altogether too disruptive', he told Wright:

By reason of the constant change the audience were never given a chance to settle down and engender the true warm-hearted Prom spirit. In the past this has been a main-spring of the success of these concerts and for which they are justly famous. If this spirit is lost the whole fabric will be destroyed leaving nothing more than a series of nightly Symphony Concerts.[73]

Wright agreed, and concluded that the conductor was the crucial element: 'Multiplicity of conductors is contrary to the spirit of the Proms. People have talked glibly about making the Proms steadily more impersonal, but I believe this to be wrong.'[74] Nicolls thought the same: 'we don't want the Proms under their multiple conductors to lose the human touch which was one of the chief ingredients in the building up of them by Henry Wood.'[75]

The BBC really needed a conductor of stature to lead the Proms, a personality who could channel and preserve the famous 'warm-hearted Prom spirit'. He had to be British, of course – even in 1960, Glock's first attempt to introduce a foreign guest conductor would be greeted with consternation, and aborted.[76] The person the BBC most wanted for the Proms (and, later, for the BBC Symphony Orchestra) was Sir John Barbirolli, but he was not to be prised away from the Hallé Orchestra in Manchester. There was, however, an alternative already on the scene. The 1947 expansion to three orchestras, and hence three conductors, had brought a very well-known figure into the Proms, whose performance convinced the BBC that here was a second choice whom they could not afford to lose. 'When we find a man of ideal characteristics like Sargent, we should make the most of him', thought Wright, who wrote to Howgill half-way through the 1947 season, describing his 'brilliant debut'[77] and urging that he should quickly be secured for the future. Both conductor and BBC saw their chance, and Malcolm Sargent became the Proms' new figurehead for the next twenty years.

Sargent, in 1947, was already a most celebrated conductor, and his identification with the Proms made his fame even more durable. As one of his biographers has pointed out, some conductors working in America, notably Toscanini and Stokowski, had by then made the transition to mass-market fame, while in Britain efforts made during the war to popularize classical music had created a gap in the market-place for someone who could combine musicianship with an unfailing common touch.[78] Sargent's wartime work made him an ideal candidate. His 'Blitz Tour' with the LPO, bringing orchestral music to the music halls and variety theatres of major provincial cities then suffering heavily under the bombings, had been a tremendously popular contribution to the war effort – and, incidentally, to the survival of the LPO, whom their founder, Sir Thomas Beecham, had abandoned for America. Sargent's ensuing tours for the British Council, as 'the ambassador with a baton', showing the flag of British culture often under difficult and even perilous conditions, had raised his already high profile abroad as well as at home.

Even more significant, however, was the way in which radio had recently made him a household name to millions of people who had never heard his

Sir John Barbirolli rehearsing the Hallé Orchestra for a Prom, 24 August 1953.

concerts. Sargent had been a successful radio speaker since 1929, but it was his regular wartime participation in the *Brains Trust* that turned him into a radio celebrity. The *Brains Trust* (originally known as *Any Questions?*) was a simple idea – a radio panel discussing questions sent in by listeners – but it became a national phenomenon. It was listened to by almost thirty percent of the population, who, at the programme's height, sent it over 4,000 letters a week.[79] As Asa Briggs has put it, this programme 'was to take its place in every social history of the war … the term "Brains Trust" would soon become a household word and would be applied to Army Brains Trusts and Rotary Brains Trusts alike.'[80] Sargent joined the programme in 1941 and was consistently one of its most popular panellists – in 1943, BBC Listener Research voted him second only to founder-member Julian Huxley.[81] One of Sargent's biographies includes a large selection of quotations from the programme, which show the conductor speaking with a lively charm and homespun common sense to which people naturally warmed. He was unafraid to disagree with his fellow panellists, thereby carving out a distinctive niche for himself, as the following example shows:

QUESTIONER If you were a fairy godfather at the christening of a baby girl, what five attributes would you bestow on her in the hope of insuring her a full and happy life?

DR CYRIL JOAD Well, number one, good health.

JULIAN HUXLEY I put health and energy at the top.

COMMANDER CAMPBELL I should put health first most decidedly.

SARGENT Health? I've known many people who were healthy and extremely selfish and unsympathetic. I'm not sure we haven't all seen people much improved by certain bouts of illness. I would not be brave enough to wish that any godchild of mine should be, throughout life, healthy. The child might miss something that is learned only through some sort of affliction.[82]

Such sentiments (which had particular private resonance for Sargent, whose own daughter was suffering from polio) obviously struck a chord with wartime audiences and did much to increase the affection in which he was held by many members of the public. By musicians, however, he was less loved, since his forthright opinions on the subject of pensions for orchestral players had caused a storm in 1936. 'As soon as a man thinks he is in his orchestral job for life, with a pension waiting for him at the end of it, he tends to lose something of his supreme fire', he was reported to have said in an interview in the *Daily Telegraph*.[83] By some he was never forgiven – notably the LPO, which had suffered the removal of several players by Beecham only the year before. Sargent unwisely made reference to those sackings in the *Telegraph* interview, giving it as his opinion that an orchestral musician ought to be expected 'to give of his lifeblood with every bar he plays. Directly a man gets blasé or does not give of his very best he ought to go. It sounds cruel, but it is for the good of

the orchestra.' The lifeline provided later by the Blitz Tour notwithstanding, when Sargent came into the Proms in 1947 the LPO made a particular request that he should not conduct them.[84]

Colin Davis, who was later to take over from Sargent at the Proms – and who conducted the famous Last Night in 1967 during which Sargent literally dragged himself from his deathbed to say farewell to his beloved Promenaders – was of the opinion that 'the affection granted him by the public made up for that which was denied him by professional colleagues'.[85] There is certainly no doubt that Sargent thrived on public acclaim, and the close relationship between conductor and audience at the Proms obviously suited him. After the 1947 season, he wrote to Thompson: 'I shall always remember it as one of the happiest seasons of music that I have been fortunate enough to take part in.'[86] The Promenaders were to remain of enormous emotional significance to Sargent, their central place in his affections symbolized at his death when at the memorial service held for him at Westminster Abbey 'the entire nave was set aside for Proms season ticket holders'.[87]

In many ways, Sargent's fame in 1947 was a product of the times. His pre-war success with regional choral societies, his wartime conducting in provincial cities and his willingness to travel widely had prepared him for the less exclusively metropolitan character of English musical life after the war.

His successful social climbing and access to aristocratic circles, while he still retained his popularity with ordinary people, were products of the increasing mobility of British society. His eager embracing and skilful use of new technologies – gramophone recordings, radio, and then his huge success with the Proms on television – made him more recognizable than any conductor before him. By his side, Sir Adrian Boult looked more and more like a figure from the past, as can be seen in this vivid description of him by the writer Alan Bennett – whose own musical education, through radio and the founding in 1948 of the Yorkshire Symphony Orchestra, was typical of that time. Having grown up in a 'desperately provincial and unexciting' Leeds, Bennett recalled,

> So famished was I for fame I must be one of the few boys who could have seen Sir Adrian Boult as in any sense an exotic and even a glamorous figure. Not quite an Edwardian, which he certainly looked, Boult seemed of another age entirely, a contemporary (though he wasn't) of Elgar, whom with his walrus moustache he also resembled. Though what he also looked like was one of those inflexible generals (Sir Hubert Gough comes to mind) who had conducted the First War. [He] eschewed any emotion on the podium, his impassive beat varied only by the occasional clenched fist.[88]

In adopting Sargent ('urbane, Brylcreemed, and always with a carnation in his buttonhole and a wolfish smile'[89]) the BBC had taken another step towards moving the Proms firmly into the new postwar world. The speed at which the world has moved on since that time, however, has perhaps made it difficult for us now to see Sargent as a modern figure. By the time he died twenty years later, he was already something of an anachronism in Glock's new Proms, the great choral performances for which he had been most acclaimed outmoded by the new interest in authenticity, and the Englishness that had been such an important part of his wartime popularity by then deeply unfashionable. But in 1947 his status as a media celebrity was something new, smacking more of the film than the concert world. When T. W. Chalmers, Controller of the BBC's Light Programme, described the 'near hysteria' with which the Promenaders greeted Sargent at the Last Night a couple of years later, he remarked that he 'could not help noticing the similarity to Sinatra's recent audiences at the Palladium'.[90]

Television arrived at the Proms in the same year as Sargent – and he was one of the few involved who welcomed it with open arms. The broadcast of part of the 1947 Last Night was very much an experiment, being the first visual television broadcast of an orchestral concert ever attempted in this country.[91] Such a broadcast had been contemplated by the television service for some time, but it had not been easy to persuade a reluctant Music Department that it could be done 'without upsetting the Orchestra or the conductor'.[92] The first tentative suggestion to televise the Last Night of the 1947 Proms was put to the Music Department in July that year, after the season was already underway, and final agreement was reached only at the end of August. The programme was nearly cancelled at one point because of the limited resources that television then had at its disposal, which meant that expensive outside broadcasts were no easy undertaking.[93] The postwar resurrection of television was still only a year old, and the vast majority of the BBC's time and money remained firmly concentrated in Sound. This broadcast was managed with only two cameras, one of which had to be rushed to the Royal Albert Hall at the end of the afternoon from the Oval, where it had been televising a cricket match between the newly crowned county champions (Middlesex) and the Rest of England.[94] Maurice Gorham, Head of the Television Service, was naturally anxious about attempting such a ground-breaking programme unless he could be reasonably confident that it would be a success – but in the end it was, despite a couple of technical hitches and a 'simply awful' commentator.[95] According to the intense and energetic new Television Programme Director, Cecil McGivern, 'The Prom. was something of a victory for Television',[96] and there was a self-congratulatory mood in Alexandra Palace after the event. 'I have spoken to dozens of people inside and outside the BBC', McGivern told a rather unimpressed Basil Nicolls. 'They were unanimous in their praise of this transmission … [and] P.C.S. [Programme Correspondence Section] say that the correspondence for the Prom. is the biggest viewer response they've had for any one television programme.'[97]

Nicolls and other senior executives at Broadcasting House thought rather less of the broadcast and did not rush to support McGivern's eagerness to televise more concerts. 'I find Television's keenness to go after such material rather disturbing', Nicolls told him, saying that he personally considered concerts 'third-rate visual material'.[98] McGivern was not to be put off: 'I regret I must strongly disagree with your views on the televising of the Prom.' Nevertheless, Howgill explained (rather more gently) that 'we feel we cannot over-ride the objections of the musicians themselves',[99] whose feelings Kenneth Wright had summed up as follows: 'Television of last concert made it more of a picnic than ever. Orchestra in general unhappy because of the glare and heat.'[100] McGivern was still unwilling to give up, telling Nicolls that, while the musicians' attitude 'must be taken into consideration … it is, from one point of view, just another of the difficulties Television continually experiences and which we must try to get over somehow'.[101] Indeed, it was true that television in the 1940s was fighting a very similar battle for acceptance to that fought by radio in the 1920s – except that this time there was additional opposition from within the ranks of the BBC itself, some of whose members had evidently forgotten the struggles of their youth.

It seems that television was also thought to be too frivolous a medium to be allowed into a serious concert, to judge by Howgill's explanation to McGivern when turning down his next request to televise the orchestra – in a concert to celebrate the BBC's Silver Jubilee in December 1947: 'In view of the seriousness of a symphony concert, as opposed to the light-heartedness of the last night of the Proms, it is undesirable that television should be attempted.'[102] McGivern therefore turned his attention to the last night of the Winter Proms in January 1948, when presumably conditions in the Royal Albert Hall would be cold enough to make the hot lights almost welcome. Permission for this was reluctantly granted, although the Music Department was not exactly eager to cooperate. When the department's Head, Herbert Murrill, met Ian Orr-Ewing, television's Outside Broadcast Manager, to discuss practicalities, 'as a true lover of music he was quite at a loss to understand why we wanted to televise a Promenade Concert and at least 45 minutes was spent in arguing the case.'[103]

As before, the Television department's straitened circumstances produced difficulties. The musicians had to endure hot lights again, as 'it now seems improbable that we will have the new sensitive cameras'.[104] Once more, sporting commitments on the same day (this time rugby from Twickenham) meant that some of the camera equipment was unavailable for rehearsal, giving the television producer 'nine minutes in which to set up three cameras, give them limits and focus'.[105] This broadcast was less successful than that of the previous summer, even in the view of the TV people – but, said the indefatigable McGivern afterwards, 'as we have insinuated ourselves, we shouldn't drop out of the battle with the music people'.[106] Despite his determination, it was the Musicians' Union that finally rendered the battle unwinnable for the time being. Having woken up to the new medium, the Union decided to insist on treating it as a 'completely separate field of employment from sound broadcasting',[107] and there were no televised concerts for another five years.

When television returned to the Proms in 1953, it was to a new world, in which the balance had shifted decisively in its favour. In 1947, television had been available only to viewers in the London area, of whom 14,500 had licences. By 1953, television was approaching nationwide coverage, and the number of licences in force exceeded two million. In 1947, television cameras (as opposed to film cameras) had been kept determinedly out of Westminster Abbey on the occasion of the royal wedding, but in 1953 live television was allowed to show the young Queen Elizabeth's Coronation to the world. The success of that broadcast led to it being described as 'Television's Coronation'[108] – the moment when the new medium finally 'came of age'.[109] Another difference in 1953 was that Kenneth Wright, who had been a stalwart of the Music Department since 1926 and had led it through two interregnums, was now Head of Music Programmes, Television. The delicate business of getting musicians in front of the cameras was now in the hands of someone who knew them well.

As in 1947, the first orchestral occasion that the BBC chose to televise was the Last Night of the Proms, described by McGivern as '*excellent* for us'.[110] McGivern and Wright decided to try for a broadcast in 1953 because in January that year an industrial tribunal, arbitrating in one of the many disputes between the BBC and the Musicians' Union, had ruled in favour of the Corporation using its own orchestras on television.[111] Having regained the right to televise, and having been reassured by Wright that 'Yalding [i.e. Music Division] is out to *help us*',[112] McGivern decided to broadcast from the first night as well as the last. All did not go as smoothly as might have been hoped,

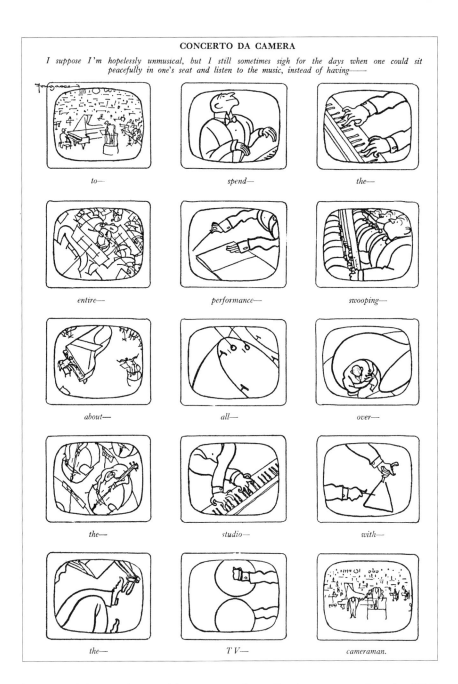

Cartoon by Fougasse,
from Punch
(19 August 1953).

however. More union problems came from Equity, representing the BBC Chorus; like the Musicians' Union, it had decided on a 'policy of regarding sound and television as completely distinct'.[113] Equity demanded the enormous additional sum of three guineas per singer for the privilege of showing the chorus singing along with the audience in *Jerusalem*, which was obviously out of the question when the members of the orchestra were getting only 4s. 6d. After considering changing the programme, or engaging an amateur choir – which was ultimately deemed too provocative – the BBC settled for having the BBC Chorus leave the platform early, filling their empty seats with Promenaders for the benefit of the cameras.

Frustrating as this no doubt was, more fundamental problems came from within the BBC itself and were caused by the inevitable tension between the needs of the different audiences now served by the Proms. For over twenty years, BBC radio had been balancing broadcasting requirements against its obligations to audiences in the hall – a balancing act rendered more complicated by the fact that the postwar structure of radio had divided the Proms between three very different networks. The Controllers of the Light Programme and the Third in particular exerted considerable and contradictory pressures on concert planning, which sometimes made it difficult to construct a coherent series. In 1949 the Director-General, convinced that 'the Proms are in danger of being pulled out of true under the demands of the programme planners', had given the Music Department 'plenary powers' over the programming of the Proms and firmly asserted their primary purpose as public concerts.[114] Now television had arrived, bringing with it a host of new technical demands and yet another audience to stake its claim to the series. A dispute between Antony Craxton of television's Outside Broadcast department and W. W. Thompson, supported by Royal Albert Hall manager C. S. Taylor, over the positioning of the cameras at the 1953 First Night provides a good illustration of the conflict between the interests of the Promenaders and the viewers, while the huge row that erupted between Craxton and Herbage just before the concert went on air shows up the difficulties in the relationship between Vision and Sound.

'As the B.B.C. run these concerts I cannot see why we have to consider the view of a few members of the audience in the hall before that of our vast viewing public.'[115] Craxton's statement, after he was refused permission to put a camera in the middle of the arena, marks the beginning of an argument that was still current twenty years later, when Robert Ponsonby was doing his utmost to defend the Promenaders from the cameras in their midst.[116] Ponsonby lost his battle, but in 1953 the BBC's position was different: 'the ticket-holders must have first consideration … [because] if future availability of Proms. via Television must be associated with distraction and discomfort within the Hall, the audience may prefer to stay at home.'[117]

This prioritizing of the audience in the hall shows the continuing importance to the BBC of the Proms ticket income. In 1945 the BBC had begun its Proms ownership making a profit of over £13,000, which its subsequent efforts to raise performance standards had obliterated. Losses in 1947, 1949 and 1951 were balanced by small profits in other years, but the Proms were no longer providing sums that the BBC could 'put against the losses on other public concerts'.[118] Faced with a situation in which its most popular and successful series of concerts, instead of subsidizing other concerts, would itself require support, Nicolls issued the instruction in 1952 that 'every effort must be made to make the Proms pay'.[119] Ironically, the Corporation's overall income was about to rise beyond all precedent, as the sale of television licences accelerated. Revenue from sound-only licences began to fall in 1951, and as the decade progressed, the balance between the two media quickly changed. In 1956, the chairman of

On II September 1965, Sir Malcolm Sargent conducts the Last Night of the Proms – an occasion transformed from the Last Nights of the pre-television age.

the 'Future of Sound Broadcasting in the Domestic Services Working Party' was already writing that one of the purposes of radio would henceforth be 'to serve TV'.[120] The beginnings of commercial competition, after the launch of independent television in 1955, had focused attention firmly on television, and it now seemed that this was going to be the medium on which 'the BBC's reputation and possibly its very existence are going to depend'.[121]

At the time of the 1953 First Night – only a month after the broadcasting of the Coronation – television's star was most definitely in the ascendant, and Malcolm Sargent, with his unerring showman's instinct, knew exactly what the new medium needed from him. 'Sir Malcolm Sargent', wrote Antony Craxton afterwards, 'had some definite ideas of his own', which Craxton found contributed greatly to the visual impact of the concert:

He conducted the Promenade
Concerts from 1895 to 1944.

Sir Malcolm suggested that we should bring on the orchestra section by section, our commentator identifying each group as they made their way to their seats. I thought this an excellent idea, but I explained that this might take longer than we had allowed and might delay the start of the concert until about 7.32 p.m. Sir Malcolm then stated emphatically that he considered that this was Television's night and he wished to take his cues from us for as long as we were on the air.[122]

It can probably be imagined what the reaction to that was from Radio. The Light Programme was also broadcasting the concert, but its staff were not even informed, let alone consulted, about the new arrangement. 'It was too late to argue so we accepted the cold fact that Television were running the Prom', said the Light Programme producer, adding, 'perhaps we should have expected it knowing the musical knight'.[123] This was all the more irritating for them because Sargent was already famous among sound producers and announcers for ignoring radio requirements in his public concerts. 'The Chief Conductor gave Television carte-blanche to do exactly what he refuses to allow the Sound services to do',[124] complained the Music Department afterwards, and Herbage gave vent on the night itself to a quite uncharacteristic 'tirade' in the Artists' Room (where Moisewitsch, the soloist, was trying to prepare himself for the concert) when he found out what was happening, minutes before they went on air. According to Craxton's report the next day, 'he demanded what right Television had to interfere even in the smallest way with the running of the concerts, which Sound had been broadcasting for umpteen years.'[125]

The vehemence of this protest was doubtless greater because of the part played by Sargent, whose relationship with the Music Department was deteriorating rapidly. Sargent had been appointed as Chief Conductor of the BBC Symphony Orchestra in succession to Boult in 1950, but within months the Music Department was having regrets. Despite Sargent's enormous popular success at the Proms, he had neither the breadth of repertory nor the commitment to orchestral training that the larger job required. Not only did he spend a significant proportion of his time conducting elsewhere, but he appeared to be averse to studio work, preferring always the atmosphere of a public occasion. He also disliked accommodating himself to the requirements of an institution – not for Sargent the tedium of working from his office, attending auditions or negotiating with administrators. 'On joining [the B.B.C.] I thought that the Music Department existed for the use of the Chief Conductor to assist him in his music making,' he wrote soon after his appointment, 'but in actual fact the Chief Conductor seems to exist solely for the use of the Music Department, if and when they want him.'[126] This description of the crux of the problem contained some truth, to judge by the Controller of Music's picture of Sargent's 'perpetual failure to see himself in the correct perspective as an instrument of BBC policy'.[127] Or, in the words of Herbage's 'tirade', as reported by Craxton, 'Sir Malcolm … was only the paid servant of the Corporation.'

In truth, it was clear from the start – indeed before the start – that Sargent would never see himself in that light, and as the years went on matters got

Memorial window to Sir Henry Wood, by G. E. R. Smith, c. 1944, at St Sepulchre-without-Newgate, London.

worse. 'His despotic and personal approach to everything makes it very difficult,' complained Maurice Johnstone, the Head of Music Programmes, Sound, during the 1953 Proms: 'I am both amazed and dismayed to discover to what an extent Sargent expects both staff and resources to be wholly at his disposal.'[128] Later on in the same season, the Controller of Music wrote to the Director-General to criticize Sargent's 'ingenious and somewhat deceitful manipulation of our machine' – designed, Howgill thought, to 'enable the BBC Symphony Orchestra to be a vehicle for his own personal vanity'.[129] Naturally, Sargent's critics attributed his enthusiasm for television to vanity, but there is no doubt that he had an instinctive sense of what would look well on the screen. It is noteworthy that Sargent arrived at his new formula for the Last Night immediately after television started broadcasting it again – moreover, he seems to have designed it with the viewers very much in mind, as the increased audience participation in the hall gave television some marvellous pictures of singing and cheering Promenaders. Certainly the new format was very much better suited to television than to radio, as Wright told Howgill in the first year of the finalized formula:

> Did you notice that the V.R. [Viewer Research] on this relay is the highest ever: – 48 % of the audience and 76 index. It seems to show that the worse it becomes as a Sound only programme, the better 'entertainment' it becomes for Television! Will it end up with television only taking over the last night each Season???[130]

The Last Night of the Proms had been something of a headache for some time, as the postwar Promenaders seemed to have become noticeably more exuberant than their predecessors. As Associate Conductor Stanford Robinson said to Wilson in 1948,

> I cannot help feeling whilst thinking of the last night of the Proms last summer that it is time we dropped the 'Fantasia on British Sea Songs'. It seemed to me that it has now got beyond a joke – the good humour of previous generations of Prom-goers seems to have degenerated into hooliganism to a marked degree.[131]

Thompson agreed: 'The hysterical outburst on the part of the audience when [Wood's *Sea Songs*] is performed is now beyond human control.'[132] Even Lady Jessie thought that a change was needed, in order to avoid 'the deplorable exhibition which turned the 1947 season into a music-hall rabble … I am certain Sir Henry would say that the time has come.'[133] Director-General William Haley was less sure – as Nicolls reported to Howgill, 'D.G. feels that it would be a great mistake if we went too far in robbing the Proms of their traditional features and in particular their traditional fun on the last night'[134] – but he nevertheless allowed the BBC to experiment with a more sober Last Night in 1949, in which Boult conducted a rather more substantial programme than usual, including Bax's *Overture to a Picaresque Comedy* and Sibelius's Symphony No. 7 – despite a warning from Tom Chalmers, Controller of the Light Programme, that 'Sibelius is still a frightening composer' for his listeners.[135] It was not a success. The restraint of the programme apparently left the

Promenaders 'puzzled', according to Chalmers, and Boult's reserved manner contrasted unhappily with Sargent's exuberance the year before: 'Boult is clearly the wrong man; never have I seen anyone look more unhappy when greeted by the audience.'[136]

After this failure, Chalmers advised that the BBC should 'really go to town' and present an unashamedly popular concert on the Last Night, since that was evidently what the audience wanted.[137] He had in mind Tchaikovsky's *1812* overture and Dvořák's Symphony 'From the New World', but Sargent, who this year would conduct the whole concert for the first time, had other ideas. Wood's arrangement of *Fantasia on British Sea Songs* was preceded by Elgar's *Pomp and Circumstance* March No. 1 (which had appeared in the 1945 Last Night, as part of the victory celebrations), and this was in turn preceded by Johann Strauss's *Blue Danube* waltz and Britten's *Young Person's Guide to the Orchestra*, which by then had become a very popular Proms staple. After a first half that had opened with a Suppé overture and included Tchaikovsky's *Nutcracker* suite instead of a symphony, the effect was to make the audience even more excitable than ever. Chalmers was dismayed at the 'frightening emotional orgy' that resulted: 'For the first time, I realized the full extent of the dangers that attend the popularising of music. Plato knew what he was doing when he proposed to banish music and poetry from his Republic.'[138] Kenneth Adam, who was about to succeed Chalmers as Light Programme Controller, was equally appalled: 'nobody could possibly claim that the last night in 1950 made anything but execrable broadcasting.'[139]

Queue for the Last Night of the Proms, 17 September 1949.

This 'unworthy programme', to quote Nicolls's opinion,[140] was condemned on all sides, as were Sargent's alterations to the programme of the last night of the next Winter Proms. Nevertheless, somewhat surprisingly, the BBC allowed him to do pretty much the same the following summer, ending up once again with *Blue Danube*, *Young Person's Guide*, *Pomp and Circumstance* and then the *Sea Songs*, by which time the audience was in very much the same state as the previous year. 'It was Bedlam', moaned Adam. 'The whole effect was much worse than last year.'[141] A halt was therefore called in 1952, Sargent was made to share the conducting of the last night, and the programme was toned down. Then, with television cameras looming in 1953, the BBC finally made the contentious decision to drop the *Sea Songs*, replacing them with Hubert Parry's *Jerusalem* and Thomas Arne's *Rule, Britannia*, justified to some by the fact that this was Coronation Year. The Promenaders were immediately up in arms:

> All regular attenders of the Henry Wood Promenade Concerts are asked to be present at a meeting on the steps of the 'Little Albert' behind the Royal Albert Hall at 5.30 P.M. to discuss the removal of the *Sea Songs* from the last night Prom. and determine how we may best bring our dissatisfaction at this move to the notice of the BBC's programme Planners, the Press, Musicians and people of influence, in particular with the BBC.[142]

This call, circulated among the audience by 'Three Arena Members', was the climax of weeks of pro-*Sea Songs* lobbying, which had, unsurprisingly, 'given the Chief Conductor cold feet'.[143] Despite Maurice Johnstone's impatient assurances that all would be well '*provided* he [Sargent] identifies himself with his employers for once',[144] a more sympathetic Howgill settled for the compromise of having the *Sea Songs* performed as an encore but not broadcast. Once again there was friction between radio and television, and some confusion as to quite when the broadcast was supposed to end. McGivern was furious at not being consulted over a decision that forced him to 'watch impotently, while a Television O.B. Producer, under orders, faded out a programme at a moment which was bound to result in criticism of the Television Service', and indeed his switchboards were 'jammed immediately with protests from 97 bitterly angry viewers'.[145] 'Off the record, I hope that this is the last time the B.B.C. make such a foolish decision', wrote Craxton to Sargent afterwards, and indeed it was. Despite Howgill's touchingly naive wish that 'we may reasonably hope that next year they may be completely forgotten', the *Sea Songs* were back in 1954, in a new version by Sargent, ending with his own arrangement of *Rule, Britannia* in full. Also back were *Jerusalem* and Elgar's *Pomp and Circumstance* March No. 1 ('Land of Hope and Glory'), which have likewise been fixtures ever since.

It is interesting to speculate on the extent to which television contributed to the ossifying of the Last Night of the Proms. Although the lasting formula arrived at in 1954 was primarily Sargent's – his handling of the audiences' community singing reminiscent of his legendary control over amateur choral

Televising the Last Night of the Proms, 17 September 1955. Seated (right) is Robert Beatty, 'The Man with the Mike', who in 'Saturday Night Out' invited viewers to join him at the Royal Albert Hall.

societies in days gone by – the speed with which *Land of Hope and Glory*, *Rule, Britannia* and *Jerusalem* also became hardy annuals probably owes even more to the expectations of viewers, who knew little of the rest of the series. To the frustration of many in Music Division, for whom 'the finale of the Proms [should] more worthily reflect the BBC's musical ideals and national responsibilities',[146] television detached the Last Night from the rest of the season, turning it into something of a national institution in its own right. 'I very much wish that Television could drop in for once … on a night other than the first or last', complained George Willoughby, Thompson's successor as Concerts Manager, in 1958. 'The emphasis given to balloons and banners, high-jinks and hysteria, is giving a completely false idea of the real nature of the Prom audience to millions who have never been to a Promenade Concert.'[147]

To Sargent, however, the Last Night each year was the climax of his intense relationship with the Promenaders. Much as Music Division may have preferred to dispense with his demanding presence, it is true that the affection in which Sargent was held by the audience was crucial to the maintenance of the Proms' identity as the series moved away from its exclusive association with Wood towards its new incarnation as a major international festival, in which an ever-increasing variety of conductors and orchestras would share. Sargent's highly visible personality formed a bridge between Wood and a future in which the Proms as a great music festival could survive without such a figurehead. The fact that Sargent continued as chief conductor of the Proms well into Glock's era undoubtedly eased the acceptance of the more radical changes that the new Controller introduced.

Sargent seems to have had a very protective view of his beloved Promenaders, to which may be attributed in part his reluctance to confront them with new and challenging repertory. 'This special young audience should be carefully nursed', he told Howgill, 'and not used as a trial ground for music in which we have no faith ourselves, or abused in order to give us "distinguished" (!) press prestige.'[148] 'He must have a very low opinion of the Promenaders' was apparently the sharp response of Peter Racine Fricker and Ralph Vaughan Williams to this sort of remark[149] – which may have been the case, to judge by the rather patronizing and sentimental preface Sargent wrote to *The Story of the Proms*, published by the BBC in 1955, in which he described the Promenader's 'child-like exultation … pure and saintly in its unqualified gratitude for loveliness received'.

'My own feeling is that it is more important to get new music lovers than new musical works', wrote Sargent when trying to dissuade the BBC from including 'difficult' repertory in the Proms. 'I think it is unlikely that we shall find sixteen good new works each year.'[150] This was a very different attitude from that of Wood, in whose day, according to Vaughan Williams, 'the Promenade audience had to endure the thousand failures so as to be sure not to miss the thousand and first'.[151] Throughout the 1950s, the caution displayed in the Proms programmes with regard to new works received a good deal of press criticism, in which 'Sir Henry's name was thrown about freely'.[152] It was in 1950 that the critics began to be particularly vociferous about the small number of 'novelties', as the BBC was still calling them, of which the Elisabeth Lutyens Viola Concerto was the only actual première. Ticket sales, on the other hand, set a new record that year, and even with the added expense of its new rehearsal schedule, the BBC made a healthy profit of over £3,000. Some of this criticism about the BBC's lack of enterprise was 'less than disinterested', as Herbert Murrill pointed out in 1950, a description that might also have been applied to the short book on the Proms that the LPO's manager, Thomas Russell, had brought out the previous year:

> More attention is given to the problem of attracting a steady audience of five thousand a night than to leading that audience along the new paths of music. If this gives more credit to those who looked ahead even under the perpetual threat of insolvency, it can only condemn those who are responsible for the present policy, supported safely as it is by public money.[153]

'If it is [said] that Sir Henry Wood always gave every chance to a young artist or a new piece of music,' replied Herbage, 'the answer is that he cut his musical cloth according to the prevailing musical conditions and standards.'[154] Conditions and standards were of course now very different – although, as Thompson put it, 'Few seem able to appreciate that the higher standard of programme and execution must bring in its wake greater selectivity in the choice of new works.'[155] Nevertheless, it might have been thought that the more generous rehearsal allowance now in force would have allowed the inclusion of many works that were impossible to prepare adequately within the confines of Wood's punishing schedule.

Much more significant in the 1950s was the competition that the Proms experienced from the many new provincial festivals that had come into being since the war. The Cheltenham Festival of British Contemporary Music began in 1945, the Edinburgh Festival in 1947, and the Bath Festival in 1948, which was also the year in which Benjamin Britten founded the Aldeburgh Festival. Herbage repeatedly urged the BBC towards a more active seeking out of new work – citing the 'hours, days, weeks' that Wood spent 'reading new scores and auditioning new artists'[156] – as the BBC began to lose more and more eye-catching premières to the new festivals. In 1945, for example, although the Proms gave the first London performance of the 'Four Sea Interludes' from *Peter Grimes*, it was the newborn Cheltenham Festival that secured their first concert performance, only a week after the new opera's astoundingly successful première at Sadler's Wells.[157] 'The young composer of today is spoiled by first performances, which musical festivals now scramble to obtain', wrote Herbage in 1956, adding that composers 'still [seem] to have the idea that a Prom performance will not be sufficiently rehearsed'. Even in 1958 *The Times* could write of Bartók's *Music for Strings, Percussion and Celesta* that it was 'too difficult to be played at a Prom',[158] which must have been dispiriting for BBC staff to read after a decade of stress on performance standards. More telling was the fact that even the BBC's own Third Programme increasingly preferred to broadcast from the festivals rather than the Proms. 'The alternative attractions of the Edinburgh Festival, etc. are well known, but was every omission justified?', asked Herbage in 1952, pointing out that of the sixteen programmes he had planned for the Third, 'not a note was broadcast from nine of these concerts, and only on three occasions was the concert broadcast in full'.[159]

A rather graphic illustration of the BBC's sluggishness about new music can be found in the first draft of the 1952 Proms that Herbage and Thompson sent to Murrill in January that year, in which the only reference to likely premières is the word 'novelty' inserted in brackets into programmes 'of which the box-office appeal is considered sufficiently strong'.[160] After complaining that 'no list of suitable Novelties has as yet been selected for this season', and that the BBC's method of doing this was currently 'unsatisfactory', Herbage and Thompson suggested that 'a well-known composer be commissioned to write a suitable Novelty for the opening night'. This suggestion was not taken up, and there were in fact no actual premières at all that year, which saw the BBC instead launching a new policy of 'second hearings'. This was indeed a worthy aim, second performances being notoriously difficult for young composers to obtain; but reading the files of the period, it is hard to escape the conclusion that it came about primarily as a way of justifying the fact that (in the words of Herbage's report), 'with the competition from Cheltenham and other festivals the Proms. have fallen sadly behind in the presentation of novelties.'[161] Indeed, the BBC of the 1950s seems to have decided to take its lead from the

EMI advertisement, from a 1959 Proms programme.

Cheltenham Festival, dispatching Herbage there each year to find new works for the Proms, 'in which', said Howgill in 1955, 'we like to include works that have gone well at Cheltenham'.[162] The 'novelty' issue was not the only sign of corporate inactivity when it came to modern music, however. For example, both the sixtieth birthday concert for Stravinsky and the memorial concert for Schoenberg (repeating the Five Orchestral Pieces premièred so memorably by Wood) that Herbage and Thompson presented in their original draft were deleted from the final scheme 'in favour of less enterprising concerts that turned out to have little box-office value', as Herbage bitterly noted later.[163]

Herbage must have found his position most aggravating. Planning the Proms from the background, on an annual contract, his position weakened by his freelance status, he kept successive series together against enormous odds – aware, as Directors of Music came and went, and the years of acrimony with Sargent took their toll, that he was almost the only source of a consistent artistic policy.

Unfortunately every Prom conductor thinks he is a Henry Wood, imposing his ideas on the small part of the scheme that he has to direct. Yet actually Henry Wood never did do this, and was the most amenable conductor with whom I have ever built programmes. The only alternative to the conductor who, like Wood, was prepared to direct every work in the repertoire, is the conductor who can be placed in the programme scheme with his own speciality.[164]

Herbage's frustrations burst out in his annual report of 1953, in which, he noted apologetically, 'the typewriter seems to have taken everything into its own hands, and doubtless most of what has been written should be expunged from an official report'. It is, however, a most interesting document, which shows Herbage's awareness of the way in which the Proms' environment had changed, and projects a vision for the future that has striking similarities to what the Proms were to become a decade later:

> In the first thirty years of this century the Proms could be effectively served by one orchestra and one conductor, provided the latter had the capacity for work and the catholicity of musical taste of Sir Henry Wood, and the former had little competition from non-deputy orchestras, or visiting orchestras from abroad. Already, before the 1939 war, the Proms had to face the danger of becoming an anachronism; today values have to be completely adjusted to the present musical scene. The Third Programme, the Long-playing record, numerous Festivals, both specialised and comprehensive, have altered the whole scope and style of music-making, and while all this has not affected the basic purpose of the Proms, it has completely altered the method by which this purpose can be effectively implemented.
>
> The Proms today have to cover a much wider range of music than ever previously; this wide range of music has also to be covered from a completely different stylistic angle. A 'symphony orchestra', as it was called, could do it all in the old days, but today the expression 'symphony orchestra' means very little. It has been disrupted at the modern end by works such as Schönberg's Kammersymphonie, Stravinsky's 'Histoire du Soldat' and Britten's Chamber Operas. At the earlier end we are at last realising that Bach's Brandenburg concertos really were concertos, planned for soli and ripieni ... Let us use [the] specialities of Sargent and Cameron to the utmost, but let us not pretend that they can cover what today should be the complete Prom repertoire, nor that orchestras such as the BBC, London Symphony, London Philharmonic and Royal Philharmonic are specialists enough to give ideal interpretations of every masterpiece of music written between 1700 and 1950.
>
> I do not think the Proms should aim at anything less than a survey of the greatest music written during these 250 years, each work being given an artistically faithful performance by specialists.

'On re-reading these last few words', Herbage concluded modestly, 'I find them a little elementary – but would it not be good to get down to something elementary at the Proms? They have been leaderless for too many years.'[165]

Herbage wrote his last report in 1960, by which time the Proms had a new leader – not a conductor, but William Glock, the new Controller of Music, who at last had the power to do what Herbage could not and the artistic will to make the most of it. 'I have in the past referred to the Proms as Music Division's dustbin', admitted Herbage wryly – but reviewing the new Controller's first season, he could see already that this was at an end: 'The Proms are clearly in for a new lease of life.'

Reinventing the Proms

THE GLOCK AND PONSONBY ERAS, 1959–85

DAVID WRIGHT

> What Glock did was to ruthlessly propagate modernism – thank God that era's all over – which left us with a gap between composers and audiences.
>
> DAVID POUNTNEY, 2002[1]

> Under Glock the Proms have been revitalized and restored to the quality they had in Sir Henry's best years.
>
> *SPECTATOR,* 1963[2]

THE SEASONS BETWEEN 1960 AND 1985 MARK A TURNING POINT IN THE HISTORY of the Proms that sees them transformed into an international music festival of the first rank. Now we take it for granted that each and every Prom season will make a distinctive impact, presenting its own, individual mix of the familiar, the recondite and the newly composed. And part of the fun of the Proms comes from looking at the year's new Proms Guide (as the prospectus is called) to see how cunningly all this music has been programmed, and marking down concerts not to be missed. Then, appetites whetted, we confidently await their realization by some of the world's greatest musicians. These are, after all, 'The Proms'.

Yet this version of the Proms, with their reputation for distinctive programming and first-class playing, is a comparatively modern invention. And the person most responsible is someone usually represented as music's bogeyman: Sir William Glock, BBC Controller of Music from 1959 to 1972. Glock directed the 1960 to 1973 Proms seasons, and his artistic goals were shared by his successor, Robert Ponsonby, Controller of Music from 1972 to 1985, who directed the 1974 to 1985 Proms seasons (and outlined much of 1986).

The transformation of the Proms' range and standards during those twenty-five years involved more than innovative programming. It was bound up with the BBC's own attitudes to the concerts. As Glock's success made the Proms a source of international prestige, so the Corporation came to value them more. Although this new and hitherto unexpected level of esteem – the cultural dividend, as it were – came at an ever-increasing cost, it was a price the BBC was essentially willing to pay. Glock played this situation with considerable skill, planning for an approximate break-even at the box office, but safe in the knowledge that shortfalls would be covered. His guiding belief was that, as a public service broadcaster, 'the BBC's job is to put on programmes that others can't'.[3]

Blind Man's Buff, *by*
Peter Maxwell Davies,
at the Roundhouse,
7 August 1972. The
flexible performance
space and informal
atmosphere of the
Roundhouse made it
an ideal late-night
venue for contemporary
music Proms.

But from the late 1960s the BBC was immersed in a difficult economic
and political climate; thus Ponsonby inherited Glock's dauntingly impressive
achievement at a time of tough financial pressure on radio (where the Proms
continued to sit as part of Music Division). It was television, newly enhanced
by the opportunities of colour technology, that now called the shots, corner-
ing BBC resources in the battle for viewer ratings against Independent TV.
The Proms offered television an ideal opportunity to expand its coverage of
prestigious popular culture, but the radio-centric Ponsonby resisted this, feeling that television was an intrusion into the concert occasion. He stubbornly
held his ground against attempts to make the First Night a television spectacular, which gave the BBC's management the sense of important chances being
wasted. Yet the BBC owed much to Ponsonby's imaginative and substantial
programming. His seasons were especially important in restoring the reputation of the Proms after the disastrous Musicians' Union strike in 1980, which
badly damaged the Corporation's image as champion of the nation's music.

Glock

William Glock (1908–2000) had an unusual musical background that helps
to explain his approach to the Proms. Formative were three years of private
study with the great pianist Artur Schnabel in early 1930s Berlin. The city's
vibrant musical environment – with concerts by Klemperer, Furtwängler, and
the Busch and Rosé Quartets, as well as opera – gave Glock a thorough knowledge of the standard Austro-Germanic repertory. He absorbed a European
cultural outlook that, as music critic for the *Daily Telegraph* and the *Observer*
(1934–45), made him impatient with the limitations and insularity of much
musical life in Britain. Glock's contacts were further broadened by a 1947
tour of major European music centres that he undertook for the BBC Third

Programme (always more international in its cultural perspectives), reporting on recent developments and new music.

Then, at Schnabel's suggestion, Glock was approached in 1948 to direct a new Summer School for Music, which later became the Dartington Summer School. As the School's Director from its inception until 1979, he attracted an astonishing range of teachers and composers, including Stravinsky, Hindemith, Elliott Carter, Georges Enescu, Luigi Nono and Nadia Boulanger. These figures, and British students such as Harrison Birtwistle and Maxwell Davies who were drawn to study with them, made Dartington something of a counter-cultural powerhouse. In addition, Glock established *The Score* as a journal for serious debate about modern music (published 1949–61) and chaired the music section of the Institute of Contemporary Arts (1954–8). He also ran the International Musical Association, which offered a London refuge, with rehearsal and recital space, to Pierre Boulez and pianists such as Yvonne Loriod (Messiaen's wife) and David Tudor, the American pianist who championed avant-garde and experimental works. Glock also maintained his piano playing at a high level and performed Mozart's Piano Quartet in E♭ Major, K. 493, with members of the Lindsay Quartet at the Proms in 1974, after his BBC retirement.

Newly arrived at the BBC, Glock took personal charge of the Proms. Proms programming thus returned to the hands of a single person, as it had been at earlier times in its history, but now under very different circumstances.[4] In particular, Glock was in a position to conceive each season as a whole in a different way from Sir Henry Wood, who had programmed the concerts with an eye on what was practical to deliver with a single orchestra playing to a reasonable standard. As BBC Controller of Music, Glock was positioned to influence the degree of Corporation subsidy to the Proms. Thus Glock – and also his successor, Ponsonby – could plan their seasons in an integrated way, balancing potential losses on innovative and adventurous programmes with fuller houses for core repertory concerts so as to secure reasonable box office returns overall. On this basis they could mount individual concerts that no commercial promoter in Britain had the resources to present. Certainly there were financial pressures on particular seasons, but under Glock and Ponsonby the Proms effectively achieved a degree of leverage over the BBC; by 1985 the Proms genie was well and truly out of its bottle, boasting an enhanced profile which the BBC was anxious to capitalize on but could not afford to diminish.

What did the Proms seem like in Glock's time? Glock himself has often since been portrayed as a musical extremist, an avant-garde hardliner with a self-appointed mission to feed Proms audiences a diet of wilful dissonance. But this image tells us more about commentators' attitudes to modernist music than it does about Glock's period of Proms history. The two comments heading this chapter illustrate these contradictory perspectives. David Pountney, writing in 2002, blamed Glock for creating a situation that encouraged composers to write without regard for their audiences, a burden for subsequent festival directors. Yet, from the 1960 season, the *Spectator*'s critic, David Cairns, had been making very much the opposite point in his wholehearted support for Glock's reforms. While the comment at the head of this chapter, about the Proms being revitalized by Glock, is not by Cairns[5] (it is taken from the *Spectator*'s topical 'Notebook' column), it is typical of his tone. As we shall see, Cairns spoke for many who wanted more up-to-date musical experiences from the Proms, closer to the modernity and the increasingly cosmopolitan outlook of their lives. Glock's innovations made the Proms symptomatic of the new vitality of the 1960s, and so opened the doors to a new generation of Prommers.

Swinging the Proms into the Sixties

Looking back on his experiences of the Proms in the late 1950s, Stephen Plaistow, a radio producer appointed early in Glock's time, had the impression that they were not for the young.[6] And many shared his opinion. Commenting on Glock's first season, in 1960, the critic for the *Daily Herald* – the Labour paper later relaunched as the *Sun* – noted that 'a tussle is developing between youth and age in the future of the Promenade Concerts'; that season, 'there was a drop of about 4 percent in the total attendance *although the number of young promenaders and galleryites increased*'.[7] The *Herald*'s diagnosis was that the BBC had a choice:

> attract the old faithfuls and the better-off in the stalls with more old music, or go out to capture youth with still more adventurous programmes. The second course would probably pay. And Mr Glock is all for it.[8]

Glock's radicalization of the Proms resonated with the adventurousness of the new cultural and social attitudes of the 1960s. We see a strong counter-challenge to prevailing attitudes in *Declaration*, a 1957 collection of essays edited by Tom Maschler.[9] In 'Get Out and Push!', filmmaker Lindsay Anderson created one of the most evocative images of this time. He lambasted the British cinema industry in terms that captured a sense of British postwar provincialism and insularity – the same insularity that Glock was so determined to change in British music:

Audience at the Last Night of the Proms, 16 September 1967, in a photograph that captures the fun of the Last Night atmosphere.

It is six years since a British feature won a prize at Cannes. … It is a fair reflection of the way our films have fallen out of the running. …What sort of a cinema have we got in Britain? First of all it is necessary to point out that it is an *English* cinema (and Southern English at that), metropolitan in attitude and entirely middle-class. … It must also be said that it is snobbish, anti-intelligent, emotionally inhibited, wilfully blind to the conditions and problems of the present, dedicated to an out-of-date national ideal.[10]

Anderson made explicit his sense of Britain adrift from its European neighbours. He remarked that returning to England from the Continent was something of an ordeal, not just because of British food and the saying good-bye to wine and sunshine, but because:

coming back to Britain is also, in many respects, like going back to the nursery. The outside world, the dangerous world, is shut away: its sounds are muffled … Nanny lights the fire, and sits herself down with a nice cup of tea and yesterday's *Daily Express*; but she keeps half an eye on us too.[11]

There is a good illustration of such cultural nannying in the Introduction to the 1959 Proms prospectus: 'The Proms are always "up-to-date" to the extent which tradition, purpose, and a confident assessment of public taste permit' – good taste, naturally.[12] The new departure of devoting four concerts in the season to 'Masters of the Twentieth Century' was deemed a 'perhaps repeatable feature'.[13] Their fare, which included a Sibelius tone poem, Shostakovich's Fifth Symphony and Ravel's Piano Concerto in G major, would hardly have raised Nanny's blood pressure. By contrast, Glock's inclusion of electro-acoustic music, Webern, Ives and Schoenberg the following season represented a completely different interpretation of the BBC's obligation to its musical public.

The reality was that until Glock's arrival, the BBC Music Department had done much to keep pre-war modernist works and those of the postwar avant-garde well at bay. But this situation contrasted with developments elsewhere in the British cultural experience of the late 1950s and 1960s – not least on the BBC's Third Programme. For example, modernist theatre, influenced by French surrealist Antonin Artaud, presented works such as Samuel Beckett's *Waiting for Godot* (1955) and *Endgame* (1957), Eugène Ionesco's *Rhinoceros* (1960) and Peter Brook's *Marat/Sade* (1964). Similarly cinema was influenced by producers such as Federico Fellini, and writers by Jean-Paul Sartre, Roland Barthes and William Burroughs, especially his novel *The Naked Lunch* (published complete in 1964). Modernism shaped the visual art of Elizabeth Frink, Bridget Riley and David Hockney. In a wider context, developments in the reinvigorated BBC of Hugh Greene, the new Director-General, brought fresh outlooks to television audiences, who experienced the effect of Greene's wish to make the Corporation a place where talent, however unconventional, could flourish. In that climate, many felt that changes Glock brought to BBC music and to the Proms – exposing audiences to whole new ranges of music, early as well as contemporary – were an essential stimulus to British musical creativity, in performance as well as composition. At last, adventurousness in music was on a par with that which had been taking place in the other arts.

Youth culture was the force that generated the counter-cultural attitudes characterized by the 'Swinging Sixties'. Pop music and pop fashion produced a new commonality across class boundaries, assisted by technologies such as the electric guitar, the personal gramophone, the transistor radio and tape recorder, which increasingly empowered individual tastes. With the crossover of technologies between the avant-garde and pop, it was not such a contradiction as it may have seemed to discover Stockhausen appearing in the cover montage of The Beatles' *Sergeant Pepper* album. The new *mores* in matters of individual freedom and sexual behaviour had musical counterparts in the questioning of the 'accepted canon' and of conventional notions of idiom and taste. At the same time, new universities were opening, and exposure to the thinking of radical European and American philosophers encouraged a larger student population to overturn received wisdom and the Establishment status quo.

The 1960s brought conspicuously stylish consumption, which became one means of throwing over the perceived dreariness of the 1950s. Fellini's film *La dolce vita* (1960) helped stimulate a craze for Italian modishness, in suits, espressos and on vespas. Terence Conran's Habitat shop brought style to everyday living, and in Chelsea's King's Road, Mary Quant's shop Bazaar introduced the mini-skirt. The boutiques of Carnaby Street changed the British view of fashion, assisted by a new plethora of glossy fashion magazines. As Roy Porter observed, 'after decades of aesthetic barrenness, London acquired some flair.'[14] Add to this mix the impact of the beginnings of mass tourism, with some two million people holidaying in Europe by 1958, and it is easy to see why the French and Italian experience had become such a potent counter to British austerity – and brought with it a strong impetus to recreate it in England. Elizabeth David's *French Provincial Cooking* became a best-seller on its publication in 1960, helped by the new availability of such exotics as garlic, olives and aubergines. The American influence was also a vitalizing and important element, thanks to Hollywood.

The ability to absorb all of this was fuelled by a boom in personal affluence. Disposable income had grown as weekly wages increased at nearly double the rate of prices, and this sense of economic ebullience, underpinned by very high employment, generated a social extroversion that transformed the nature of London's life and the entertainment it sought. Dowdy Proms were an anachronism in this febrile atmosphere.[15]

Glock himself remarked on the changing nature of potential Proms audiences, as a rising generation was made more knowledgeable and sophisticated by BBC music broadcasting and the widening of the LP repertory. But Glock was also shrewd in harnessing the popular spirit of rebellion and the 'wish to hear something adventurous' as legitimizing elements of his reforms.[16] This is clear from his decision to programme Stockhausen's electronic music piece *Gesang der Jünglinge* in his first season. This innovation was ultimately thwarted, because the technology to play the four-channel tape could not be found in the UK. Berio's two-channel *Perspectives*, for which the technology was available, had to be substituted. According to critic Desmond Shawe-Taylor:

> The audience treated it as a great lark, broke into mirth when sudden pops and gurgles broke an ominous silence, and perhaps genuinely enjoyed some of the prettier and more fantastic jingling sequences. There was no booing, much good-humoured applause.[17]

Glock had originally programmed the Stockhausen with Mozart's overture to *Idomeneo* and Piano Concerto in C Minor, K. 491, Stravinsky's Symphony in C and a scene from *The Rake's Progress*, concluding with Ravel's *Bolero*. It was an early example of how eclectic Glock's mixed programming could be, and Shawe-Taylor remarked that although the traditional top-tier element was a little thin, audiences 'responded with marked enthusiasm to Mr Glock's New Deal'. The term 'new deal' – with its allusion to Franklin D. Roosevelt's measures to counteract the effects of the Great Depression in 1930s America, and their democratizing benefits – is striking in this context. To Charles Reid, writing in the Liberal daily newspaper the *News Chronicle*, Glock's first year was 'turning out to be the most exciting Proms season since their formative years under Henry Wood'.[18] This sense of a new adventurousness in audience response to Glock's programming was often echoed in *The Times*, which noted that though most of the audience had presumably been drawn by a popular work in the first half, many stayed for a demanding modern work in the second:

> On Thursday an audience much of which, one presumes, had come to hear Tchaikovsky in B flat minor stayed to be thrilled by *The Rite of Spring*. Last night again the Albert Hall was nearly as full for Roberto Gerhard's Violin Concerto after the interval as it had been for Sir Malcolm Sargent's dispensation of Beethoven before it.[19]

Laying the Foundations, 1960–65

Glock's ambition was that the Proms should harness the creative achievements of the new, offer a fresh representation of the past and be invigorated through the stimulus of an international perspective. His first season (1960) had 49 concerts using 4 orchestras and 11 conductors. In his last (1973), the roster had expanded to 55 concerts, with 25 symphony and chamber orchestras, 3 opera companies, several specialist early music and contemporary ensembles, a string quartet and 34 conductors. That final season included complete concert performances of Beethoven's *Fidelio*, Mozart's *Magic Flute* and Britten's *Gloriana*, as well as extracts from a further seven operas (including Gilbert and Sullivan). And among the mainstream repertory that Glock introduced to the Proms during his tenure were important works by Bach, Handel, Haydn, Mozart, Beethoven, Schumann, Berlioz, Bruckner, Tchaikovsky and Mahler. This roll-call hardly suggests the attitude of someone whose vision was 'to ruthlessly propagate modernism'. Instead, someone looking back at Glock's

Promenade Concerts is more likely to be astonished by the sheer breadth and vitality of what was programmed. They were truly exploratory in scope and inclusive in spirit; importantly, they placed the central musical repertory in a fresh context, revivified by its contact and juxtaposition with older and newer repertories of different kinds.

Glock's programming decisions focused on mixed programming, high performance standards and the strong representation of contemporary music. This gave him a coherent basis that enabled him to build seasons of great variety and character. Using the principle of mixed programming, Glock expanded the Proms' repertory well beyond its traditional orchestral base while retaining orchestral music as the main foundation. Glock's approach to programming was analogous to the act of authorship. He was obsessive about it, endlessly playing around with combinations of works and taking the plans away with him on holiday. He thought mixed planning worked best with few works arranged in clear patterns: 'arch-like (old-new-old), crescent-shaped (new-old-new), and an ascending curve, as it were, from old to new. I think I was very aware of these patterns, so that the programme-planning had an aspect of geometry to it.'[20]

Glock's concern with high standards of performance for all music was fundamental to his Proms leadership. He realized that there was no point in presenting new contemporary music unless the quality of the performance (regardless of idiom) could be taken on trust as a faithful representation of the composer's intentions. Bringing specialist early and new music ensembles to the Proms was a natural consequence of this 'fiduciary', or trustable, principle of performance, as was his determination to raise the standards of the BBC Symphony Orchestra and to boost the standing of the Proms by inviting the world's best orchestras and conductors to participate. In new music, Glock was proactive, commissioning through the BBC works from composers in whom he believed, and he used the Proms to secure the widest hearing for these and other contemporary scores. This represented a change of the BBC's musical focus – a move away from commissioning works for the Cheltenham Festival, that 'Festival of British Contemporary Music' which had gained a reputation during the 1950s for neo-romantic conservatism, as in the unflattering epithet 'the Cheltenham Symphony'.[21]

Glock's reforms faced a significant hurdle in the shape of Sir Malcolm Sargent, whom he inherited as Conductor-in-Chief of the Proms for the 1960–67 seasons. With his restricted repertory and generally work-a-day standards, Sargent focused on buttressing his reputation as darling of the Prommers. In retrospect, Sargent was a useful brake on Glock in those early seasons, easing the way by ensuring a process of gradual innovation (rather than abrupt change). And certainly Glock recognized Sargent's positive contribution to the season in his own preferred repertory. In a diary entry, written in light of the conductor's terminal illness, Glock considered that without Sargent, 'the representation of British works such as those of Delius and Vaughan Williams will be a difficulty; perhaps Sibelius, too'.[22]

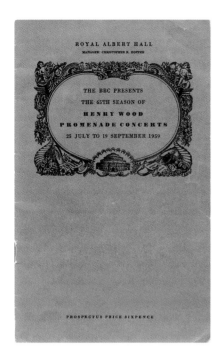

Prospectus covers for the 1959 and 1960 Proms seasons, signalling a move from the primly classical to the boldly modern.

Something that would immediately have struck audiences in 1960 was the modern look of the redesigned prospectus, its faux-classical cover replaced with a modernist silhouette of the Royal Albert Hall and a sans-serif font. It symbolized a conscious attempt to refashion the Proms, to make the 1960 season a 'landmark' in their history by giving them a 'bolder purpose', 'at the highest possible standards'.[23] To achieve this Glock made a preliminary assault on established Proms programming, by introducing more radical concert patterns. The *Times* critic commented:

> A glance shows that no revolution has taken place, though the concerts are more varied and enterprising than they have been for some years – memory says since 1945. The new syllabus [*sic*] … has successfully returned to the spirit of the Proms as they were in Henry Wood's day.[24]

Before the establishment of Radio 3, Proms concerts were shared out across the BBC Home, Light and Third radio networks and any fixed points in their respective schedules had an impact on the design of the concert programmes. The main evening news on the Home Service was fixed at 9.00 pm, and so, with the Proms beginning at 7.30 pm, Glock had to pattern an extended first half for concerts aired on that network. This constraint on programme structures eased the following year when the news was moved to 10.00 pm.

Glock's mixed programming followed the long-time practice of balancing the box office by offsetting the effects of a modern work with a popular one. For example, a 1960 programme praised by the *Times* critic for its sophistication and value for money[25] mixed Haydn's Symphony No. 98 with Schoenberg's Variations, Op. 31, and balanced them with Mendelssohn's Violin Concerto and Ravel's *Alborada del gracioso*, before concluding with Dvořák's Symphony No. 8 in G. Over the season, the guaranteed takings from perennial favourites such as Gilbert and Sullivan or Viennese evenings would be set against programmes dominated by modernist works that attracted smaller audiences. Like Newman long before him, Glock quickly learned that the Proms could be made to attract multiple types of audiences with different tastes, and that concerts sold better if a minimum of two works were likely to appeal to the same 'kind' of audience member.

Glock brought in new conductors, including Colin Davis, for works outside Sargent's usual repertory. More choral music appeared, with Beethoven's *Missa solemnis* and the *Grande messe des morts* by Berlioz receiving their first Proms performances, as did Stravinsky's *Œdipus rex*, Symphony in C and Symphony in Three Movements. Surprisingly, 1960 featured the first Proms performance of Mozart's Piano Concerto in C Major, K. 503, reflecting the tendency then for a narrower Mozartian repertory. Glock often encouraged the best possible performance by programming into the Proms a work previously prepared in another context; the 'thrilling' performance of *Œdipus rex* had been given by Colin Davis and the same forces at Sadler's Wells earlier that year.[26] Similarly, the Proms premières of Webern's Six Pieces, Op. 6, and Schoenberg's Variations, Op. 31, were played not by the BBC Symphony Orchestra, but by the Liverpool Philharmonic conducted by John Pritchard, reflecting the success of Liverpool's contemporary Musica Viva series. The year 1960 was also a vintage one for first appearances by artists, such as singers Janet Baker and Elisabeth Söderström, pianists Charles Rosen and avant-garde specialists Alfons and Aloys Kontarsky, and string players Henryk Szeryng, Norbert Brainin and Peter Schidlof, the latter two of the Amadeus Quartet.

An issue for Glock during his early seasons was the traditional Beethoven focus of the Friday night concert, which contradicted the principle of mixed programming. Treading carefully in 1961, Glock continued the changes began by Julian Herbage in the late 1950s, not omitting Beethoven but recontextualizing him. In Glock's hands, however, the recontextualization was radical. One Friday concert featured the Piano Concerto No. 5 (the 'Emperor'), and the *Leonora* Overture No. 3; Haydn's Symphony No. 93 took the place of an initial overture; and the programme concluded with the first Proms performance of Stravinsky's *Les noces*. On two later successive Friday evenings, Glock programmed Schoenberg's Violin Concerto and Piano Concerto, the first in the company of Beethoven's Romance in G for violin and orchestra, the second with his Piano Concerto No. 2. Each concert included a Beethoven overture and symphony; the first also added Debussy's *La mer* and *Marche écossaise*, the second finished with extracts from Wagner's *Die Meistersinger*. This effectively established mixed programming throughout the season, and with some pride Glock noted in the 1962 prospectus that the concert containing the Schoenberg Violin Concerto had 'the largest attendance of the whole season'.[27] Aware of the irony, Glock programmed three all-Beethoven programmes into his final season over a decade later, but they were unconventionally patterned. One began with Roger Woodward playing the Piano Sonata, Op. 111 (the 'Hammerklavier'), and another prefaced the Ninth Symphony with two sonatas for cello and piano (Pierre Fournier in the event substituting for Jacqueline du Pré).

The 1961 season also featured the first semi-staged presentation in the Proms of a complete opera, importing Glyndebourne's production of Mozart's *Don Giovanni*. Early music also began to make an impact, with the performance of Thomas Tallis's *Spem in alium* and two Canzonas by Giovanni Gabrieli. In all, the season contained some sixty works that were heard at the Proms for the first time; the fact that Schumann's Symphony No. 2 and Mendelssohn's Symphony No. 5 (the 'Reformation') fall in this category again highlights the limited repertory of past decades. Glock had enormous enthusiasm for Haydn, then generally known (before complete recorded sets were available) mainly for his later symphonies, especially those composed at the end of his life for London concerts (Nos. 93–104). Four Haydn symphonies (Nos. 67, 91, 93 and 95) had their first appearance at the Proms in 1961, three of which were programmed as curtain-raisers, in place of an overture. Glock's championship of Haydn was something he shared with Henry Wood, who had programmed a range of Haydn's symphonies in the 1920s (the 1927 season featured No. 7 'le Midi', No. 22 'The Philosopher', and No. 88, as well as the overture *L'isola disabitata*).

The 1961 season also saw the Proms becoming the platform for BBC commissions, with works by Elisabeth Lutyens, Malcolm Williamson and Anthony Milner receiving their premières. This practice was confirmed in 1962 by commissions from the younger generation – Maxwell Davies's *Fantasia on an In nomine of John Taverner* and Nicholas Maw's *Scenes and Arias* – as well as from Thea Musgrave and Alan Rawsthorne. Thus in these first three seasons (1960–62) Glock tested the water and their success laid the basis for developments in the three that followed.

The next year, 1963, was the first season since Edouard Colonne appeared as Wood's deputy in 1908 that a foreign conductor directed a Prom. Glock had intended the Italian Nino Sanzogno to conduct in 1960, following successful appearances earlier that year with the BBC Symphony Orchestra, but Lady Jessie Wood (as redoubtable guardian of Prom traditions) created such a fuss about the introduction of a non-British conductor that Glock temporarily shelved the idea. Three years later, and more firmly in the saddle, Glock programmed an irresistible galaxy of international stars such as to trump any traditionalist objections. The schedule included Georg Solti conducting the company of the Royal Opera House in the entire third act of *Götterdämmerung*, marking the 150th anniversary of Wagner's birth; Stokowski with the BBC and London Symphony orchestras; Carlo Maria Giulini directing Verdi's Requiem in celebration of the composer's 150th anniversary, as well as a second concert, both with the Philharmonia; and Silvio Varviso conducting Glyndebourne's production of Mozart's *Marriage of Figaro*. When later asked about the criteria he used to select operas for the Proms, Glock replied that because the Proms' focus was on orchestral repertory, he made it a rule to programme only operas in which the orchestra played a primary role in the musical process.[28]

Only in the late 1950s and 1960s did Mahler and Bruckner begin to feature regularly in London concert programmes. The 1963 season included the Proms premières of Mahler's Second and Sixth Symphonies – the Second in a legendary performance with Stokowski – as well as Bruckner's Third Symphony. Early music that season included Monteverdi's *L'Incoronazione di Poppea*, the significance of which event was underlined by David Cairns's observation that the Royal Albert Hall audience alone far exceeded the number of people in Britain who had heard *Poppea* before.[29] Britten's *War Requiem* was performed, conducted by the composer, to a full house on 1 August 1963 and then repeated the following year with essentially the same performers. The *War Requiem* had received great critical acclaim since its first performance in Coventry Cathedral in May 1962, and Decca's famous recording, with Britten conducting, sold in unprecedented quantities for a contemporary work. The repetition of the *War Requiem* in two successive Proms seasons is more indicative of Glock's responsiveness to the mood of his times – the anti-war sentiment, for example, generated by the Campaign for Nuclear Disarmament (CND), with its Aldermaston Marches and other rallies – than of his own feelings about the work.[30]

The 1964 season was characterized by the inclusion of chamber music, with the Octets by Stravinsky and Mendelssohn, and Haydn's String Quartet, Op. 76, No. 3 (the 'Emperor'). This quartet began an all-Haydn concert on 4 September, and there was another featuring *The Seasons* on 31 July. Both were Fridays – truly a substitute for the traditional Beethoven evenings! Yet, except for the First, all Beethoven's symphonies were heard, spread across the season, with only the Ninth retaining its traditional place in the penultimate concert. Chamber orchestras, such as the English Chamber Orchestra and the London Mozart Players, with their new style of reduced-scale performances of the classical repertory, were another of that season's innovations, and prepared the way for small specialist early and contemporary music groups. More ensemble music was programmed in the 1965 season, including Walton's *Façade* and Mozart's Wind Serenade in B♭ Major, K. 361; and Glock included more organ music, sometimes to conclude a concert, giving exposure to several younger players, including Peter Hurford and Gillian Weir. Pierre Boulez made his Proms conducting début, as did Antal Dorati, Istvan Kertesz and Gennadi Rozhdestvensky. An extended opera sequence also appeared in 1965, with Purcell's *Indian Queen*, Mozart's *Marriage of Figaro*, Verdi's *Macbeth* and Schoenberg's *Moses und Aron*. The Purcell concert was completed with Bach's last three Brandenburg Concertos, performed by the English Chamber Orchestra and Charles Mackerras – a move away from Sargent's large-scale orchestral performances of Baroque music. BBC commissions for that season were Iain Hamilton's *Cantos* for orchestra, Elizabeth Maconchy's *Variazioni concertante*, Malcolm Williamson's *Concerto grosso* and Hugh Wood's *Scenes from Comus*. Glock also capitalized on the increasing variety of Prommers' tastes by offering a 'Special Season' ticket that gave a free choice of twenty-five concerts on the basis of a small premium, pricing the ticket at 87s. 6d. (the price of the half-season ticket was 75s.).

Winning Through, or 'Nous avons changé tout cela'

How had all this change been received? Glock received a significantly generous tribute for his planning of the 1960 Proms from the planner he displaced, Julian Herbage, who commented:

> In the past I have at times referred to the Proms as Music Division's dustbin: this year musical garbage has been conspicuous through its absence. ... The Proms are

clearly in for a new lease of life, with a very slight loss of audience which may indeed be only temporary.[31]

Herbage remarked on changes in attendance patterns. Noting that the seating audience (assumed as the older element) were more cautious about new repertory than the Promenaders, he observed that the evening with the largest advance booking for seats (the Gilbert and Sullivan evening) did not sell out the gallery promming space. Herbage also recorded a significant reduction in the number of British compositions played; there had been an average of 43 during the previous two seasons, as against 29 in 1960. Similarly, foreign artists had increased from 17 in 1959 to 32 in 1960.

An audience survey of the 1965 season was undertaken by the *Spectator* in collaboration with the BBC. Questionnaires were distributed at the Royal Albert Hall, but Charles Reid, who published the results, did not specify the number of respondents, only commenting that 'many' were returned.[32] Although a self-selecting rather than a scientifically run opinion poll, replies to the open-ended questions appeared to reinforce a widening enthusiasm for unfamiliar twentieth-century works. Asked 'Which was the most important programme from the viewpoint of the work or works performed?', the two favourites were 19 July, the concert version of Schoenberg's *Moses und Aron*, voted the 'season's most important novelty'; and, on 7 September, Boulez's Proms début with Stravinsky's Symphonies of Wind Instruments and Four Studies, Berg's Three Fragments from *Wozzeck*, Webern's Six Pieces, Op. 6, Boulez's *Le Soleil des eaux* and Debussy's *Images*. Malcolm Sargent came first in the question, 'Who was the best conductor and on what occasion?', but interestingly Boulez came second. Jacqueline du Pré was voted the 'best solo instrumentalist' for her performance of Elgar's Cello Concerto at Sargent's 70th birthday concert. Respondents were very enthusiastic in their support of Glock's '"expansionist" programme policy', though reservations were expressed about the principle of mixed programming: poor audience behaviour in more challenging works led some respondents to think that specialist programmes might be preferable. Most respondents called for more foreign conductors (requesting Klemperer and Karajan in particular), suggesting that the move to internationalize the Proms reflected the heightened expectations of an audience influenced by recording and broadcasting. Most felt that chamber music did not work well in the Royal Albert Hall itself but came across on air. There was concern at the massive increase in the price of season tickets (discussed below) and anxiety that reduced attendance might force the BBC to popularize the programmes. The survey captured an interesting age profile: 39% were 18–25; 27% were 26–35; and 11% were 36–45. Men outnumbered women by three to one. Students formed the biggest single group, followed by office workers, then lecturers and teachers. This survey suggests how well Glock had in many respects caught the mood of Proms audiences and was harnessing, and in turn shaping, their tastes for new repertory and new performance practices. As Reid expresses it, the poll

'certainly reflects the widening enthusiasm of the new-type Prom-goer for unfamiliar or newly familiar twentieth-century music in a wider range of forms or media'.[33]

While the daily ticket sales fell by some 7% in 1960, this was countered by a steady increase in Promenade season-ticket holders, from nearly 31,000 in 1959 to above 34,000 in 1964. However, in 1965 the price of season tickets nearly doubled, and purchases fell by half. Glock was indeed attracting a younger, promming audience to the Proms, as the *Spectator* survey showed, but ironically this was the very constituency most vulnerable to the significant rise in season ticket prices. That year the cost of daily Prom tickets also rose, by 43% – but seat prices only increased by a relatively small margin, the top price by 16% and the lower by 4.5%.

The wider context for these increases was the economic disarray of the Wilson government during 1964 and 1965 (when balance of payment and sterling crises prompted attempts to stave off devaluation, with income tax raised to 8s. 3d. in the pound, or 41.25%). More specific to the Proms, increased ticket prices were a corrective for the exceptionally heavy loss of over £13,000 for the 1964 Proms season.[34] The pricing strategy worked in that the 1965 season produced a financial profit of over £1,000, despite a 2% fall in overall attendance, but at substantial expense to the Prommers themselves.

Heavy investment was needed to transform the Proms into a first-rank international festival. As Glock drove up standards, so the respective budgets for orchestras and artists more than doubled between 1959 and 1965. This doubling of costs was caused by Glock expanding the number of orchestras involved in each season (this reduced the strain on individual orchestras and so boosted the quality of their performances), and by his insistence on using the best possible artists in each repertory. Glock's assumption of direct responsibility for the Proms meant, in terms of the Corporation's structure, a shift of level from Herbage as external consultant planner to the Controller of Music; the Proms thus moved from the periphery of BBC music operations to its centre. And Glock ran the Proms as a quasi-autonomous operation, with an independent budget agreed within the radio hierarchy. Howard Newby, as Controller, Third Programme, recalled that Glock spent most of his time on the Proms and other BBC public concert series and never attended a Third Programme Music Meeting, even though he was responsible for the Third's music output.[35]

The BBC Governors signalled their support for Glock's policy, acknowledging that his 'contribution on Music was highly encouraging' and remarking on the success of the 1960 Proms.[36] But the mounting expenses of the series prompted an internal debate within Radio about just how much represented an appropriate level of loss – that is, subsidy from BBC radio resources – in a season. A memo from M. F. C. Standing, the Controller, Programme Organisation, Radio, asked whether the Proms should attempt to break even by programming concerts that were good for box office, 'or should we take the line that the programme policy is pretty well right and worth a deficit of £5/6000?'.[37] The framing of this question in a way that entertains a £5–6000 deficit as a viable option is significant. It represents an important shift in attitude away from the Proms being viewed as a revenue source to support other BBC public concerts[38] to their recognition as a cultural investment that it was acceptable for radio to support. But Glock could be practical, too, as when he was asked by Richard Marriott, the Assistant Director of Sound Broadcasting, to ensure that Saturday evenings were good box office nights with programmes suitable for airing on the Light Programme. Far from dismissing this suggestion, and no doubt understanding it as a price for central Corporation support, Glock replied, 'You will be asking me for a tight-rope act, but it's the kind of challenge I enjoy.'[39] This comment also indicates Glock's concern for a particular type of Prom audience and his sensitivity to what would appeal at different levels, even if the result had only limited interest for him personally. Although Glock is frequently portrayed by detractors as a desiccated ideologue, the Proms testify to the catholicity of his taste, as well as the pragmatism and skilful diplomacy by which he achieved his goals.

In retrospect, it is clear that Glock was given very privileged treatment by the BBC, as a second memo from Standing indicates. Contributions to the Proms by BBC music services and the orchestras were not generally assessed in terms of real market costs. Thus Proms accounts of that time gave only an approximate picture of overall Proms finances. In early 1968, Standing attempted to indicate something of these 'concealed costs'. He concluded –

while taking into account the free provision of the BBC orchestras' services to the Proms – that the 1967 Proms season cost the BBC, in box office terms, well over £20,000 more than it received. But as Standing made clear, the Proms were to be judged on rather different terms than direct market costs:

> I have to talk in terms of these rather depressing figures, though I am well aware that the season was a great success from the point of view of prestige and of larger attendance. I also understand something of the difficulties in working to a very precise budget in so large an operation. But the fact is that last year expenditure exceeded the *estimate* by some £14,000 and though nearly half of this was retrieved at the box office, the outstanding sum is still very large.[40]

One development during Glock's tenure – and a justification for increasing financial support from the central BBC administration – was an expansion in the broadcasting of the Proms. In Glock's first season, only some three-quarters of the concerts were aired on radio, and only the opening half of the First Night and the second half of the Last Night were televised. Yet, as Glock pointed out, the radio coverage represented an increase of some 20% from the previous year, and for the first time every Saturday Prom would be broadcast in its entirety by the Light Programme.[41] The 1961 prospectus set out the normal broadcasting schedule for the concerts: Mondays, Wednesdays and Fridays on the Home Service, Tuesdays and Thursdays on the Third Programme and Saturdays on the Light Programme. Individual concerts would sometimes be split, with the first half on the Home Service and a more adventurous second half on the Third. But in these early Glock years it is interesting how often pride of place went to relays from the Edinburgh International Festival – highlighted by a decorative bordered insert in the *Radio Times* – rather as though the BBC could not quite believe in the quality of its own Proms. For example, four 1961 Prom concerts (one of which featured Stravinsky's Symphony in Three Movements) ceded their place to broadcasts from Edinburgh, two by the Berlin Philharmonic with Jascha Horenstein. It was in 1964 that Proms coverage increased significantly, with radio relays for all concerts. That year's launch of BBC2 as an arts and education television channel was a strong impetus for television to develop its coverage of music programmes. And, introducing the season, Glock announced an increased television presence, with BBC1 broadcasting four concerts and BBC2 airing six: 'this dramatic development in the diffusion of the Proms means that they will probably have a total audience, in the hall and over the radio and on television, of about fifty millions during the course of the season.'[42] In particular, televising the Proms beyond the traditional Last Night had huge implications for the dissemination of the series. The greater involvement of television meant that the Proms became much more important to the BBC's cultural identity.[43] In addition, the tide of public response finally turned; the overall number of tickets sold in 1967 was, for the first time, higher than in 1959, the last season before Glock took over planning. It had been a long haul, but it was evident that with Glock's Proms the BBC had a success on their hands.

Broadcasting raised interesting issues of presentation, and a Miss Helen Cook, concerned at the tone used by radio announcers for Proms in the 1969 season, set out the problems as she saw them in an internal memo. She identified the need to

> welcome a listening audience in a way which suggests that they are going to enjoy it. He [the announcer, then all male] should sound involved, because, for the duration of the concert he *is* the BBC, speaking on behalf of other staff who mounted the concert and are actually transmitting it. It is when his method jars with their intentions that something has gone wrong.

Among instances she cited are:

> Personal remarks about artists and their apparel, a relic perhaps of the Eileen Joyce days of quick changes backstage. [About] Jacqueline du Pré: 'the audience is applauding this blond, fair-haired, tallish figure; twenty-four, married, as we know to Daniel Barenboim, the conductor … a long-haired, Alice-in-Wonderland figure …' (her, not him). This, after an excessively extravagant performance by the lady herself, is, I submit, too much of a good thing.[44]

The World Service too were experiencing difficulties in giving their audiences sufficient sense of the context of the Proms they broadcast. The system in place was that the External Services Organizer (then David Cox) proposed certain Proms to the World Service and provided appropriate continuity material (notes about the artists and music for the announcer to use). The World Service felt that broadcasting a selection of Proms was an important part of their remit, and received more letters about them than about any other concerts they transmitted. Feeling themselves the 'poor relation' of the Proms operation, the World Service Presentation Organiser felt that the material they were given was 'aimed at the denizens of Kensington Gore not the World Service audience … Radio 3 can assume its audience is fairly familiar with Beethoven's Fifth; World Service can't.' Together, these two examples illustrate something of the perennial difficulty felt within radio in achieving the appropriate presentational tone. As is discussed later, the television professionals felt that it was their medium that was most able to convey a sense of what it was really like to be in the Royal Albert Hall, and so to make the external audience truly feel part of the event.[45]

Another interesting issue debated at the time was whether radio audiences or audiences in the hall had a better experience of the music. As we have seen, some of Glock's innovations, such as chamber music, were felt to work better as broadcasts, not least because the acoustics of the Royal Albert Hall remained unsatisfactory. The hall's notorious echo was a persistent problem for many audience members, and there had been several attempts to improve it. A flat-surfaced orchestral canopy had previously cured the problem for radio audiences. But the most concerted effort was made in 1968, when a series of large convex plastic discs – the 'flying saucers' – were attached to the inner roof area to break up the sound and so prevent the echo forming. Some, however, remained critical of the acoustic. To Michael Nyman, 'everything

tends to sound the same – thin and undernourished, and the BBC Symphony Orchestra has sounded dessicated [*sic*] to within an inch of coherence'.[46] Some felt the best results for home audiences came from 'simulcasts', in which stereo sound from radio accompanied television pictures, which audiences would watch with the TV volume turned completely down.

The Festival in Place, 1966–73

Ironically, the seventy-second season in 1966, in which Sargent as 'Conductor-in-Chief' celebrated his 500th Proms appearance, was the series whose style and content would have seemed least familiar to him. The reassuring certainties of the repertory he had long valued and performed were being endangered by new music whose idioms he resented. His reported remark to the agent Howard Hartog, 'I intend to get the intellectuals out of music', was prompted by a work no more threatening than Tippett's *Fantasia on a Theme of Corelli*.[47] Where once Sargent had held centre stage in a restricted field, he was now overshadowed at the Proms by a different breed of international star conductor, from Stokowski, Solti and Horenstein to Boulez, Haitink and Davis.

Proms repertory and standards of performance had changed beyond recognition from the homely, essentially national enterprise of the 1950s. For what Glock had realized in shaping his strategy was that in the age of the LP the only way in which Proms concerts could continue to draw public audiences was if they matched the standards of recorded performance. Also they had to offer the bonus of being an opportunity (at a ticket price well below that of

With typical passion
Paul Tortelier sorts out
a string while Sir
Adrian Boult looks
calmly on, 1972.

most festivals) to witness star artists making music. But the artists had to be convinced of the value of the Proms as a platform before they would agree to appear, as Julian Herbage noted in his report on the 1960 season:

> There still remains the problem of how to attract and engage the top-line artists for these concerts. It has been said that agents do not like their artists appearing at the cheaper Proms prices.[48]

Glock's success in engaging such performers for the 1966 season marked the arrival of the Proms on the international festival circuit. He reinforced the festival atmosphere of the Proms by planning within each year a series of 'massive events that surpassed anything in previous seasons'.[49] These concerts were made especially distinctive by the quality and reputation of the performers, their repertory, or both; they effectively went beyond the scope of commercial concert promoters and as a result increased the perceived significance of the Proms as a series.

But planning truly international seasons brought other types of perils, too, such as those caused by the use of the arts as a political pawn in Cold War diplomacy. There was always uncertainty as to whether an unexpected worsening in the political situation, or the defection of a high-profile artist, would result in Eastern Bloc authorities prohibiting their musicians from fulfilling long-planned engagements. It could also make for a hostile context, as in 1968, when the sell-out first Prom by the USSR State Orchestra on 20 August coincided with the Soviet-led invasion of Czechoslovakia by troops of the

Warsaw Pact. The concert went ahead despite anti-Russian demonstrations and, by a tellingly poignant coincidence, Mstislav Rostropovich was the soloist in Dvořák's Cello Concerto.

In retrospect, the new internationalism that characterized the 1966 season was, in an ironic sense, apposite. For Sargent's regime was ending. Illness prevented him from conducting his eighteen scheduled programmes the following year, although he managed to make an emotional *adieu* at the Last Night, which Colin Davis had taken over. As Glock recalled in his diary:

> The last night of the Proms – the first time I've attended it, I think, for 33 years. … A quarter of an hour before the end Sargent arrived, and watched the proceedings on a small television set. Then he walked onto the platform – having had a six-hour injection of glucose – and made a short speech, which had made me (as an idea) rather angry when I heard about it this morning, but in the light of subsequent knowledge was quite justified on the part of his doctors. … Colin and I joined about 100 prommers at a pub near Queen's Gate.[50]

Sargent died shortly afterwards, and a Memorial Prom was held on the Friday preceding the First Night of the 1968 season. This also proved to be the inauguration of a new structure for the Proms – subsequent seasons have commenced on the Friday instead of the Saturday, freeing the opening night from having to conform to the more popular Saturday pattern.

The faces show that the Prommers are as involved as Colin Davis and Alfred Brendel in this performance of Mozart's Piano Concerto No. 17, K. 453, 27 August 1971.

For his remaining seasons as Proms director (1969–73), Glock continued to develop his expansion of the Proms repertory and to establish new types of concert patterning, tending to programme fewer works in a concert, so giving them a sharper focus. Sargent's death had severed the remaining tie to traditional 'orchestral' Proms and removed complications caused by his personality cult. Now with more latitude to structure the season, Glock planned First Nights that made spectacular curtain-raisers for the season. From 1969 these included Berlioz's *Grand messe des morts*, Messiaen's *La transfiguration de notre Seigneur Jésus Christ*, Mahler's Eighth Symphony, Beethoven's *Missa Solemnis* and, in 1973, Stravinsky's *Symphony of Psalms* and Brahms's *A German Requiem*.

Without doubt, the Proms played a part in generating a new British market for historical repertories. This encouraged the development of a plethora of specialist early music performance ensembles, such as Musica Reservata, the Accademia Monteverdiana, the Philip Jones Brass Ensemble, David Munrow's Early Music Consort of London, the Steinitz Bach Players and the Monteverdi and Schütz Choirs. Exposure at the Proms often helped to affirm a work's canonic status, as with Monteverdi's 1610 *Vespers* (which Glock

A quintessential Proms image: Sir Malcolm Sargent's adieu to 'his beloved' Promenaders at the Last Night of the Proms, 16 September 1967.

programmed several times either entire or in sections), Bach's *St Matthew Passion* and *St John Passion*, and his B Minor Mass. More people became aware of what the music of composers such as Machaut, Dufay and Dunstable actually *sounded* like, and one extraordinary piece of mixed programming in 1979 offered a spectrum of British music from Dunstable to Byrd, Purcell, Elgar, Vaughan Williams and Alan Bush.

'Late Night' Proms began in 1970. Two concerts were scheduled in an evening: the main concert, in the Royal Albert Hall, was followed by a 'specialist' concert that started at 10.00 pm, from 1971 often held in a different location, such as the Round House in Camden Town or in Westminster Cathedral. The intention was to provide a more sympathetic architectural context for early and contemporary music. The Round House, originally an engine turntable shed, became a favourite theatre and performance space in the 1960s. It was particularly favoured by Boulez, who wanted a more informal and interactive setting for contemporary music, and to many it became synonymous with the Boulez avant-garde Proms that ran from 1971 to 1982. In 1971 the Proms made its first and only visit to the Royal Opera House in Covent Garden, for Musorgsky's *Boris Godunov*, with the stalls seats removed to create a promenade area. The cost was prohibitive, as the BBC's Chief Accountant for radio sniffily remarked:

> The Promenade Concert to be staged at Covent Garden is anticipated to show a net loss of £7,000 which has to be carried by the season as a whole. This seems to be a high price for one concert, but presumably is desirable from a programme point of view.[51]

And, signalling continued innovation, the prospectus was redesigned in 1971, the entire text appearing in an aggressively modern sans serif font.

Depending on the commentator's perspective, Glock was either famous or notorious for his advocacy of twentieth-century and contemporary music. Stockhausen's *Gesang der Jünglinge*, having been thwarted in Glock's first season, finally arrived at the Proms in 1969 in its full, four-channel glory, in company with Berio's *Sinfonia* (the composer's iconoclastic reworking of Mahler), Messiaen's *Turangalîla-symphonie* and Boulez's *Pli selon pli*. These works are, in their different ways, highpoints of postwar modernist composition. Yet, extraordinary as it may seem now, the 1969 Proms were accused of being both too didactic and too conformist. This charge came from Michael Nyman, the new critic of the *Spectator*, and someone very familiar with earlier as well as contemporary repertories, who grumpily opined, 'The Proms this year seem more than ever to have been planned as a kind of metropolitan vacation course in practical, but fairly conventional, "musical appreciation".'[52]

But Glock remained conscious of the Proms' role as a showcase for contemporary British compositions; planning statistics for 1968 gave a percentage of some 17% of hours devoted to British music for the whole season, representing 38 works, 22 of which were by 12 composers.[53] Interestingly, British first performances at Glock's Proms, including commissions, covered a wider

Ballot paper, 12 August 1968, inviting the audience to choose which of three new pieces by Don Banks, Thea Musgrave or John Tavener should be repeated (Tavener won by a landslide).

range of compositional idioms than is now generally remembered. They range from William Alwyn's overture *Derby Day*, Malcolm Arnold's *Peterloo Overture*, Harrison Birtwistle's *Nomos*, Lennox Berkeley's *Sinfonia concertante* for oboe and chamber orchestra and Arnold Cooke's *Variations on a Theme of Dufay*, across Elisabeth Lutyens' *The Essence of our Happinesses*, Thea Musgrave's Viola Concerto and Alan Rawsthorne's Concerto for Two Pianos, to Roger Smalley's *Beat Music*, Tim Souster's *Triple Music II*, Ronald Stevenson's Second Piano Concerto, John Tavener's *In alium* and Hugh Wood's Cello Concerto.

Perhaps the most controversial British commission was for Peter Maxwell Davies's *Worldes Blis* in 1969. Many audience members walked out of the performance, and it prompted a tirade from Robert Simpson (a senior BBC producer) in rebuke to Glock, which began, 'What kind of composer is it that can miscalculate the length of his own work by some 45 per cent?' (the composer had given the work's running time as 23 minutes, but it in fact lasted 37 minutes in performance), and concluded, 'I would suggest that in future we do not encourage Davies to attempt what is so patently beyond him.'[54] Simpson also complained that the music sounded like 'an almost featureless mass of squashed Schoenberg' and argued that people had walked out of the performance not 'because of the "bizarre effects" mentioned in the South-East News, but because there were indeed no effects, bizarre or otherwise'. The situation was exacerbated by Davies's programme notes, which the Head of Presentation, Radio, described as 'almost incomprehensible'.[55] P. H. Newby, the Controller, Third Programme, stepped in to calm matters:

The Pied Piper's magic: David Munrow and members of the Early Music Consort of London, 29 August 1974.

> The difficulty of presenting new work by an avant-garde composer is clearly very great even when the audience is sympathetically interested in new music …

Authenticities: a Prom concert of Venetian music in the recreated Byzantine splendours of Westminster Cathedral, 31 July 1975, with Jill Gomez (left), Jennifer Smith, and Robert Spencer (lute) in the pulpit.

When they are a more general audience, I do think the fact should be recognised by presentation that will help to put them into the appropriate frame of mind for listening. This, I suggest, is rarely achieved by a close description of the work expressed in private language. In an ideal world Peter Maxwell Davies would have been warned the audience for this particular concert were a bit conservative and been invited to consider what he wd like the announcer to say that would meet them half way.[56]

What Newby recognized was the traditional purpose of the Proms in educating audiences, and the need, however gently expressed, to ensure that the presentation of the music, regardless of idiom, fulfilled that purpose.

As we have seen, Glock gave a broader representation of British music at the Proms than his critics allowed; nevertheless, he was always clear about his own likes and dislikes. A diary entry for 21 August 1967 – two years before *Worldes Blis* – reads:

> The last week of commuting between Dartington [Summer School] and London. Went to the Monteverdi rehearsal of Denis Stevens and his group at the Albert Hall, p.m; but couldn't face the prospect of [Robert] Simpson's 3rd Symphony and of [Andor] Foldes playing Beethoven [Piano Concerto] No 2 in the evening, and went instead to see West Ham beat Burnley 4–2.

Another example may be seen in an exchange of memos between Glock and Christopher Samuelson (the Concerts Manager, who effectively ran the practical organization of the Proms), which also shows how they worked. Samuelson's responses to Glock's text are in *italics*.

28/4

Chris,

(1) It now looks as though the Walton Ov. on Aug 20 will be a <u>first</u> pfce – it won't be ready for N. York (see D. Telegraph, 27/4/68)

(2) do the J. Strauss items on Aug. 10 really amount to 37 mins?? *Yes, I am afraid so. J. B[arbirolli] is consistently slower than M. S[argent].*

(3) Sept.9: I think we shd [sic] say J. Strauss for the last item. *Yes, will do*

(4) July 27: the timing of the 1st half is very 'tight'. *Yes, but we can't change the Ov. [overture] because of Enigma.*

(5) July 31: has Nielson No.1 been played in this country before? *Yes, it has*

W.G.

On the left-hand margin going down the page, Samuelson has added the following:

Have spoken <u>to Alan Frank</u> [Walton's publisher]. First perf. due in N.Y. on June 18. Of course, if work is not ready for New York, we cannot give first perf. as it has been commissioned by New York. Walton is intending to start again next week-end. I will be in touch with Frank. If W. fails to write the work he would like to conduct his Johannesburg Ov.

Glock circled 'Johannesburg Ov.' and commented[57]

Heaven help us.

W.G.

PROMS 1895
PROMS 1905
PROMS 1915
PROMS 1925
PROMS 1935
PROMS 1945
PROMS 1955
PROMS 1965
PROMS 1972

Prospectus for the 78th season of Henry Wood Promenade Concerts, 15p

£1

Bernard Levin *Proms Preview*
Hugh Macdonald *The Trojans*
Peter Heyworth *Boulez*
Hugo Cole *Premières*

The BBC presents the
88th Season of Henry Wood Promenade Concerts
16 July to 11 September 1982

From austerity to approachability (certainly the Trojan Horse has the Royal Albert Hall firmly in its sights): prospectus covers for the 1972 and 1982 Proms seasons, with designs by Malcolm Johnston (1972) and Roger Kennedy (1982).

Glock continued to widen the representation of contemporary music at the Proms with works in more experimental compositional idioms: examples included *Keyboard Studies* by the American minimalist Terry Riley (1970), John Cage's *HPSCHD* – performed in the Round House as part of the 'International Carnival of Experimental Sound' and involving seven harpsichordists, 52 tape recorders and 16 film projectors – and Cornelius Cardew's *The Great Learning, Paragraph One*. The Cardew piece, performed by the Scratch Orchestra, a politically motivated experimental ensemble, caused concern because the BBC feared that the Maoist slogans it contained would precipitate a political demonstration in the hall. Eventually, Cardew agreed that the performance could go ahead without the slogans, on the basis of the disclaimer that 'By agreement between the composer and the BBC, the political content has been removed from this note by the Scratch Orchestra Ideological Group and from this performance.'[58]

The first appearance of world music at the Proms came in 1971. As an imaginative pairing to Stockhausen's *Mantra* (a piece for two pianos and live electronics), the renowned sitar player Imrat Khan gave two late-evening rāgs. Despite the practical difficulties of presenting Stockhausen's *Gruppen* for three orchestras in 1967 – which had required around 35 hours of rehearsal time[59] – the composer's *Carré* for four orchestras and choirs was performed twice in a late night Prom in 1972, with the four orchestras sited in the arena and with the composer talking about the work between performances. It was an extraordinary evening, beginning at 7.30 pm with David Munrow's Consort playing music from the court of Maximilian I, followed by a second half of Tallis and Schütz motets and a Bach organ Prelude and Fugue, and finally, at 10.00 pm, by *Carré*.

Despite accusations of imbalance – often levelled by those with strong memories of difficult, avant-garde works – Glock never neglected the central classics, which remained at the core of his planning of the Proms, albeit sometimes in unlikely company. His final season, in 1973, once again made a particular case for Haydn. In the first of two Haydn evenings, Glock shaped an imaginative sequence, interspersing Bartók's *Two Portraits* and Third Piano Concerto between three Haydn symphonies. The second evening began with the String Quartet, Op 77, No. 2, followed by the Symphony No. 101, the 'Clock', and ending with the *Nelson Mass*. Such evenings demonstrate that one of Glock's innovative approaches to programming was to blow away the familiar pattern of overture-concerto-symphony and to assert programme-making as a creative art.

Attempts to change the Last Night tradition met with less success. To celebrate the centenary of Wood's birth, in 1969 the Last Night presented his *Fantasia on British Sea Songs* in full, omitting the cuts Sargent had instituted. But following protests about its removal, Elgar's *Pomp and Circumstance* March No. 1 made a conciliatory but unscheduled eleventh-hour appearance, slipped in 'so surreptitiously that not until the arrival of the big tune itself did the audience fully realize their battle was won'.[60] Glock tried another tack, responding to a challenge expressed by the secretary of the Proms Circle that 'the last concert is not a musical night. We do not expect it to be.'[61] He commissioned works with audience participation as a specific component: Malcolm Arnold's *Fantasy for Audience and Orchestra* (1970), Malcolm Williamson's mini-opera *The Stone Wall* (1971) (given as the *Stern Wall* in the prospectus) and *Celebration* by Gordon Crosse (1972). But Boulez, who had taken over as Chief Conductor of the BBC SO (1971), did not want to conduct the Last Night, and Colin Davis (having done the Last Night from 1967 to 1972) did not want to conduct another. So in 1973 Glock gave in. He invited Norman Del Mar to guest conduct a 'traditional' last night, tacitly acknowledging the Last Night's independence from the rest of the Proms' activities.

Ponsonby's Seasons, 1974–85

Robert Ponsonby succeeded Glock as Controller of Music in December 1972, and the first Proms season that he planned was presented in 1974. Like Glock, Ponsonby had been an Oxbridge organ scholar, but he moved directly into arts administration, first with Glyndebourne Festival Opera and then as Director of the Edinburgh Festival (1956–60). While he was at Edinburgh, his programmes had included the La Scala Opera with Maria Callas, the Hamburg State Opera, the Royal Ballet, the Jerome Robbins and the Jean Babilée ballet companies, Beecham with the Royal Philharmonic Orchestra, Klemperer with the Philharmonia, and the Leningrad Philharmonic. After a period with the Independent Television Authority (ITA), Ponsonby became General Administrator of the Scottish National Orchestra, collaborating with Glasgow University to present the first 'Musica Nova' festival in 1971, which highlighted the work of contemporary composers. He therefore not only had practical

Top *Sultan Khan (sarangi) and Irshad Khan (surbahar) at the first all-night Prom, 28–29 August 1981.*

Above *'England expects': the* Evening Standard *celebrates the unheralded return of 'Land of Hope And Glory' in 1969.*

experience of orchestra management, he had also programmed a high-profile arts festival and had a serious interest in contemporary composition.

Ponsonby had enormous admiration for Glock's ground-breaking achievements and was determined to build on them with his own ideas. In a 1984 interview, he distinguished three criteria as the basis of his programming: music of importance, very great music (as opposed to minor pieces) and music of very great promise. As he expressed it:

> You have to have faith and confidence in certain composers. If we cannot make up our minds here, subjectively, about who we think is good then we're not doing our job properly. Posterity will prove us wrong – in most cases![62]

Ponsonby also commented on the challenges of music selection, especially

> when there is no really clear profile to contemporary music. I don't think I'm alone in finding it difficult to perceive a mainstream of new music. There is immense variety. I don't go along with the so-called neo-romantic school, if it can be called that, but I'm glad these composers are doing their own thing. We must have confidence in our own taste.[63]

Those who had hoped that Glock's successor would be more compromising in his approach were to be disappointed.

Ponsonby felt it was important to find a way of engaging more directly with Proms audiences. An early initiative was the 'Pre-Prom' talk, which he began in 1974 as an informal introduction to music that was to be played that evening. These talks quickly became an important feature of the series – not least because of Boulez's support and generous collaboration in the first year, when, as Chief Conductor of the BBC Symphony Orchestra, he gave five of the sixteen talks. Ponsonby made a point of introducing the talks himself, and though in some ways he regretted that they were not broadcast, this exclusivity made them a real bonus for members of the Royal Albert Hall audience, without the added tension of being aired on radio.

A second development Ponsonby's tenure introduced was to exploit the potential of the Proms prospectus to whet the reader's appetite for what was to come. As we have seen, the prospectus was redesigned in 1960 when Glock took over. In 1971 and 1972 further changes were made: the prospectus adopted a starker look, which included a new cover graphic designed to symbolize the Proms as history, with the current season emphasized as the latest of a long succession. In 1976 the effect was softened, and the prospectus became both more visually appealing, with coloured paper and photos, and more enticing, carrying descriptions of the contemporary composers featured in the season.

In 1979 a completely new type of prospectus began to take shape. Articles introduced the season's main works and performers; for example, a feature on the Gamelan music of Indonesia was matched with details of Britten's gamelan-inspired ballet *The Prince of the Pagodas*. (The price had risen too – 60p, as against 20p for the 1974 prospectus.) The cover of the 1981 prospectus, which cost £1, was the first of a succession of informal sketches of the Royal Albert

Hall. The 1982 cover had an amusing reference to Berlioz's *The Trojans*, showing Prommers hauling a wooden horse into the Royal Albert Hall. The emphasis had clearly shifted to give the publication visual appeal and an attractive prose style. The articles themselves had clear, didactic purposes, and some retained their interest beyond the functional period of the Proms season. For many Prommers, the annual prospectus would have provided the clearest explanations of what was meant by 'authentic' early music performance, or the cultural contexts for music from Indonesia (1979), India and Thailand (1981), and Korea (1984), or the mysterious processes by which the Proms were broadcast. At the same time, the new-format prospectus was profitable: in 1981 the publication attracted extensive advertising revenue – the £40,000 target was met – and it turned a profit of around £29,000.[64]

Ponsonby's achievements as Director of the Proms have been less celebrated inside and outside the BBC than they deserve. His period is sometimes unfairly thought of as a Glockian half-life, a slightly grey period – especially by comparison with the blustery manner of John Drummond, his exuberant, publicity-conscious successor. Certainly Ponsonby instinctively supported continuation of the radio-based, high-art culture that typified Glock's BBC. Thus while he continued to provide Proms audiences with seasons of the highest quality, Ponsonby's reluctance to conceive these in ways that would more wholeheartedly exploit the potential of television dissemination caused tension with other members of the BBC hierarchy. In 1972 Stephen Hearst was appointed from television to become Controller of Radio 3, and that same year helped to pioneer the idea of the 'simulcast', a concert broadcast simultaneously on television and radio. The involvement of television pushed up audience numbers, while the radio transmissions meant that listeners could experience good sound in stereo. Ponsonby resisted the increase in simulcasts of the Proms because a central camera would take up the space of fifty Prommers, a concern that to him overrode Hearst's estimate of an additional three million viewers. To Hearst, this 'was the difference between someone who thought of concert-going and someone who cared about broadcasting'.[65] It is certainly indicative that the man chosen as Ponsonby's successor was a former BBC television professional.

Television's Advance

From 1979 the Thatcher government's programme of economic liberalism threatened the BBC with further extensions to broadcasting competition. This came after the Annan Committee's recommendation in 1977 of a fourth, independent television channel. It was made clear that the Corporation needed to dispel suspicions that its public funding base had created an ethos that was inherently elitist and anti-competitive. In this climate, the Proms – with its long-standing historical identity and now, under the aegis of the BBC, a household name – represented an asset that could be exploited to justify the BBC's position. The Proms' democratic cultural image, with appealing middle-brow as well as high-brow content, was something that could be packaged and covered in different ways on BBC1 and BBC2 (now established as the serious arts channel) and enhanced by the wonders of colour technology. Thus increasingly sophisticated television coverage of the Proms developed, anchored by popular TV personalities such as the newsreader Richard Baker (who presented many Last Nights between 1960 and 1995) and Esther Rantzen.

The situation was given a new edge by the appointment in 1978 of a television executive, Aubrey Singer, as Managing Director for Radio. Singer, later described by Drummond as 'a dangerous bundle of undirected energy',[66] was keen to involve himself with Proms' planning, especially of First Night occasions, which he felt were natural television events. His essentially populist approach, based on what might deliver high television ratings, clashed head on with Ponsonby's conception of the Proms as concerts for radio. He – and the Prommers – believed that the processes involved in televising concerts were intrusive and therefore distracting to audiences.

Ponsonby's attitude was especially uncomfortable in view of the Peacock committee's minatory scrutiny of television's treatment of music in 1970. Unimpressed by the evidence submitted by both television providers of the time, the BBC and the ITA, the Peacock Report commented on their obligations to achieve a more adequate representation of orchestras as an aspect of cultural life significant to a substantial minority of viewers. Highlighting the success enjoyed by serious television dramas such as *The Forsyte Saga*, the Committee was sure 'that television has a predominant role to play in awakening the interest of new audiences (just as radio did when it was the dominant medium)', concluding: 'We believe that too little thought has been given to the role of television in music, which should be a social art thriving on communication.'[67] Relays of Viennese Nights at the Proms were evidence of television's ability to secure mass audiences for the series: figures grew from 3.7 million in 1976 to 5.8 million in 1979, when Rantzen introduced it.[68] Ponsonby's decision to drop a Viennese Night in favour of an Offenbach operetta thus bemused those on the television side. In 1984 the Brahms Violin Concerto with Ida Haendel as soloist attracted 3.5 million viewers, and the Last Night that year 6.9 million.

Given such figures, Ponsonby's resistance to television seemed anachronistic. The need to rebuild audiences after the 1980 Musicians' Union strike, which forced the cancellation of the first twenty concerts of that year's Proms,[69] raised the stakes for a successful First Night in 1981. Singer reacted with alarm to Ponsonby's programming of Britten's *Spring Symphony*, asking whether 'it is powerful enough when compared with previous years. A Verdi Requiem, a Beethoven's Ninth is one thing; Britten's *Spring Symphony* – wonder work though it is – is another.'[70]

Matters erupted again the following year, in disagreements about the 1982 First Night, a spectacular undertaking of the complete presentation of Berlioz's mammoth opera *The Trojans*. Enormous in terms of forces as well as musical scale, it was to be spread over two evenings, Act I on Friday's First Night, and the rest the following Sunday.[71] Problems began when the television programmers refused to take the Friday performance of the Berlioz – that is, they refused to televise the First Night. In an aggressive memo, Singer stated 'that unless the First Night of the Proms is televised the season will not have the success it deserves', and proposed beginning the season on the Thursday, with a programme acceptable for television.[72] Ponsonby expressed astonishment that Singer could even think of pre-empting what promised to be a sensational performance of *The Trojans*, featuring the renowned soprano Jessye Norman, just so that television would take the First Night.[73] Nothing could have made their conflicting priorities clearer. Later that year Singer disbanded the BBC Music Division and moved Ponsonby aside, away from radio programming responsibilities – though he retained the Proms together with responsibility for the house orchestras. Meanwhile a new music department was established (reporting to the Controller of Radio 3, Ian McIntyre) to fulfil the radio programming role.

For the next five seasons, from 1983 to 1988, the Proms were planned from outside the newly structured 'Radio 3 Music Department', but clashes between Ponsonby and the television producers continued. The performance of Elgar's *The Dream of Gerontius* with Janet Baker, planned for the 1984 First Night, had to be abandoned because the Television Division had already contracted to broadcast the work from the Three Choirs Festival; moreover, the Last Night had to have an extended interval to accommodate the popular TV soap *Dynasty*.[74] In another expression of mutual incomprehension, in 1985 the television team tried to prevent the First Night programming of Mozart's version of Handel's *Messiah*, on the grounds that it would 'pose problems of expectancy from a television audience perhaps more tuned to the traditional British *Messiah*'. Ponsonby's reply – 'what Mozart (a great genius) did with Handel (another great genius) *must* be of absorbing interest' – may have had less impact than his *coup de grâce*: it would be sung in German, the language of the text Mozart had set.[75] Ponsonby did concede that a more representative selection of concerts was televised in 1985 than in previous seasons; but, as the post-mortem meeting observed, televising more adventurous programmes led to marginally lower viewing figures.[76] The Prommers (quite as much as Ponsonby) continued to resent the intrusion of television and its disruption of the concert atmosphere, complaining about the noise of cue cards and the cooling lights, and about obstructed views caused by cameras and cameramen trying for close-up shots.[77] But change was inevitable. The accepted view that radio was the most appropriate medium for broadcasting concerts and that television could be tolerated only as an occasional visitor (most viable for popular occasions) was to be overturned. For the need to be seen to be democratizing classical music was now a BBC priority. Television – with its additional visual appeal – had now become the medium to open up the Proms as a lived experience witnessed by a global audience.

The BBC's Investment

The increase of the BBC's investment in the Proms raised a new marketing issue. What would be the best way of emphasizing the concerts as 'traditional' Proms while signalling the extent of the BBC's financial stake in the series? The BBC's Board of Management discussed the issue of Proms branding in 1979, agreeing new wording for the prospectus to express the relationship between the two institutions: 'The Henry Wood Proms presented by the BBC'. Ponsonby stood firm against subsequent attempts to label them the 'BBC Proms':

> Whether we like it or not, the proms were created, not by the BBC, but by Henry Wood. … We inherited them from [him]. … We must honour that fact.[78]

An important consequence of television's increased involvement was that it reinforced the identification of the Proms as a BBC brand, with the display of the BBC logo in the background acting as a constant visual prompt. But developing the Proms under the BBC imprint also necessitated constant investment in the series' quality as part of the message that the truly special Proms events were things that only the BBC could do.

Ponsonby certainly achieved some spectacular and prestigious Proms concerts that emphasized the benefits of BBC ownership. For audiences interested in the avant-garde, there was the Proms evening at Westminster's Royal Horticultural Hall in 1982 that presented two performances of Boulez's *Répons* by the Ensemble InterContemporain of Paris; the concert required a complex technological set-up that was projected to cost £25,340.[79] The early music audience was treated to a late-night concert of Charpentier's *L'Enfers* and *Actéon*, performed by the Parisian ensemble Les Arts Florissants, at a cost of £10,800. And costs were rising inexorably as mainstream audiences were treated to a parade of world-class orchestras. In a memo contemplating the financial consequences of engaging three of them in a single season, Ponsonby explicitly expressed a sense of competition: 'M.D.R. [Managing Director,

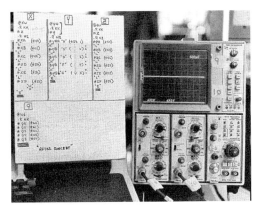

Stylish chapeaux and technological spaghetti: IRCAM members setting up for Boulez's Répons, *Royal Horticultural Hall, 6 September 1982.*

Radio] is anxious that we maximize the use of world class orchestras in order to compete vigorously with Capital Radio and the commercial promoters of concerts.'[80] In 1982 a visit by the Philadelphia Orchestra under Muti cost £19,000 for each of their two concerts. In 1984 the two concerts by the Vienna Philharmonic under Abbado cost £29,000 each. To help cope with such fees, the BBC set aside a £50,000 contingency fund against possible losses in 1979–81, and in 1983 the Director General approved a corporate fund to support the Proms, which covered the costs of hiring venues. From £132,000 in 1983, the fund reached nearly £169,000 in 1985.[81]

These subventions were vital. Ponsonby's arrival at the BBC coincided with the 1973–4 oil crisis and a period of economic 'stop-go' as successive governments wrestled with inflation, which by 1975 rose to over 25%. The recession that followed meant financial cutbacks in both the public and private sectors, which in 1981 hit advertising badly. Although inflation fell to below 5% in 1983, unemployment by then had risen to some 3 million. These economic factors had obvious effects on Proms box office returns, and ticket prices had to be carefully managed. This was emphasized in a memo from Singer to Ponsonby about prices for the 1980 season:

You are going to have to put the price up Robert. There is no question about this. And I think the thing should be operated on a strictly commercial basis, especially with the cold wind that is about to blow through from outside.[82]

In 1974 a single Prom ticket cost 50p and a full season ticket was £12.00. In 1980 a differential between arena (90p) and gallery (at 75p) was introduced, with seasons at £30 and £25 respectively. In 1986 these prices had become £1.50 (arena) and £1.20 (gallery), with season tickets at £50 and £36. A stalls seat that in 1974 cost either £2.00 or £2.50, in 1986 was set at £8.00 (normal price), £11.50 (special price) and £27.00 for the Last Night. The introduction of more sharply differentiated pricing showed a new determination to make the most of expected rises in demand for particular occasions.

The 1980 Musicians' Union Strike

The 1980 Musicians' Union strike and its aftermath, although part of wider BBC history, are very much part of the Proms' story. The fact that the Proms could become the flashpoint for the larger issue of the BBC's employment of musicians indicates how close had become the identification of these concerts with the interests of the Corporation; there was no doubt that, in targeting the Proms, the strikers knew that they were directly harming the BBC's interests. The BBC's timing of the announcement that triggered the strike (with the new Proms season in the offing) had handed the Musicians' Union a trump card, which they played to greatest effect.

The strike centred on the BBC's plan to reduce the number of orchestral musicians it employed, and twenty Proms were lost that year before a settlement was reached. The strike and its fallout impaired the Proms as a BBC enterprise and resulted in reduced attendances for several years – partly because the Corporation's clumsy handling of the strike and treatment of its musicians caused much anti-BBC sentiment. Bitterness across the music profession provided a focus for the resentment that was felt by many composers whose music had not been included in the Proms since Glock's time. Thus a secondary consequence of the strike lay in attempts to diminish the role played by the BBC's Controller of Music, by presenting the programming process as high-handed and inherently unfair.

The strike grew out of developments to the socio-economic context of BBC music provision in the 1960s and 1970s. The BBC's historian, Asa Briggs, pithily captured the core issue: 'The BBC was both taste-maker and patron. This carried with it financial burdens, and the main problems that lay ahead in the mid-1960s concerned finance, not music-making.'[83] But terms like 'taste-maker' and 'patron' had, by the late 1970s, gathered significant negative connotations in a new British social environment with more variegated cultural preferences.

Glock was lucky to have directed the Proms when he did: the scope for an increase in the scale of the series in the 1960s reflected a general expansion of BBC operations, generated by continuing growth of the television market and the fact that greater numbers needed to buy the more expensive combined television and radio licence. However, when the market for black-and-white television became saturated (it peaked in 1970), BBC income levelled out. The Corporation then relied for supplementary income on governments agreeing to increase the licence fee, a dangerous situation when inflationary pressures and escalating costs made such rises politically unpopular. As Briggs has pointed out, the 25% increase in licence fee granted by the Wilson-led Labour governments of the 1960s compared with a threefold (i.e. 300%) increase in the government funding of other public services.[84] In 1969 the government upped the combined licence fee to £6.00, which the BBC claimed was too little, too late, and the Corporation was thus forced to raise money by borrowing. The government then imposed conditions on agreeing a further rise in the fee to £7.00 in 1971, one being the abolition of the radio licence, effectively a reduction in BBC income. Fortunately for BBC finances, this happened at the start of a new technological cycle, in which volume sales of colour television sets, which attracted a substantial licence fee premium, were beginning to take off.[85] Seizing the opportunity, the BBC ploughed considerable investment into programmes that would exploit the potential of this new colour market.

These developments in television placed greater economic pressures on radio and especially on BBC plans to set up local radio networks. In 1968 the BBC – prompted by an estimate that by 1974 radio would be running a deficit of £4.5 million – began a large-scale review of its structure and use of resources.[86] One result was the policy pamphlet *Broadcasting in the Seventies*, which recommended savings of around £1.5 million in classical music output, as well as increased 'needletime' (broadcasting of records) and the disbanding of several BBC orchestras.[87] Predictably, these plans prompted an outcry,[88] and the embattled Wilson government (anxious to avoid antagonizing the trade unions) added as a further condition of the 1971 licence-fee increase that the BBC should aim to 'maintain the employment of musicians at about the

Protest by the Musicians' Union outside Broadcasting House, 3 July 1980: the strength of the public's support for the musicians caught the BBC management by surprise.

current scale'.[89] This meant no savings on music after all, and the Director General, Charles Curran, remarked that the condition 'had in effect insisted that the BBC should continue to be a considerable patron of the music profession beyond its broadcasting requirements'.[90] It effectively represented a clear and unwelcome intrusion by government into the BBC's allocation of its resources. In 1976 Howard Newby, the Managing Director of BBC Radio, reasserted the Corporation's view that the maintenance of all the house orchestras was a disproportionate burden, arguing that BBC expenditure represented employment, not patronage.[91] The implication was that in light of financial stringency the BBC should be able to reduce its workforce to the level required for the needs of broadcasting, and not be held to act out of 'a disinterested commitment to art'.

These economic and political contexts set the scene for the Musicians' Union strike in 1980, and it was triggered by a proposal to axe five of the BBC's twelve house orchestras (involving some 172 redundancies) as part of a scheme to save 8% of BBC music expenditure.[92] The strike began on 1 June, which made the Proms an immediate focus. Ponsonby was put in an extremely difficult position: Aubrey Singer, as Managing Director for Radio, carried out the negotiations, and Ponsonby, as Controller of Music, found himself in the middle. In the build-up to the strike, Ponsonby spelled out his position to Singer:

> I believe we have a clear moral obligation to try to secure the Proms *as public concerts*. It is extremely unlikely that they can be broadcast, but we hold the concerts in trust and would rightly be blamed if we did not make every effort to save them for the concert-goer.[93]

Ponsonby cited the precedent of the Second World War, whereby the Royal Philharmonic Society promoted the Proms.[94] He suggested that a similar promoter might be found for the 1980 season and showed how such an arrangement might work. Singer's reply was brusque:

> It would be a great pity if a desire to please the London concert goer were to upset our national orchestral aspirations. Therefore, no approaches must be made on this matter to any outside body without my express permission.[95]

Ponsonby's honourable position with regard to the Proms would have further confirmed him as 'not one of us' in BBC terms.

Sir Adrian Boult also made a move to try to save the season. He proposed that the Proms should go ahead as concerts, with the BBC recording them but not broadcasting them or paying performers' fees until the strike was over. Following a House of Commons debate about the BBC's music costs on 27 June, the Arts Council offered 'to do what it can to preserve at leas[t] part of what has become a national institution' in promoting the series.[96] On 18 July, the House of Commons' Education, Science and Arts Select Committee heard evidence about the cancellation of the Proms and rushed to publish its report – an indication of the degree of urgency that was felt. The Committee recommended that Lord Goodman (former chairman of the Arts Council) mediate between the parties. Meanwhile, the Musicians' Union arranged for 'alternative' Proms to be given at Wembley Stadium. It was very clear not only that musicians were solidly behind the strike, but that the audience was too – all united against the BBC, the Proms provider. The strike was a public relations disaster for the BBC. Under Lord Goodman agreement was finally reached, and the Proms commenced, twenty days late, on 7 August. The Press release giving news of the season's start also announced a week-long offer to ticket holders of a free ticket for each one held, and offered to new purchasers two tickets for the price of one.

The 1980 season had an overall deficit of some £148,000, most of which was due to the cost of cancelled concerts and compensation. But the damage to the Proms brand continued to be felt for several years. Applications for the 1981 Last Night ballot were down by a third, and poor attendance in the early part of that season resulted in a projected deficit of around £40,000.[97] In an attempt to counter this downturn and re-establish public esteem, from 1982 to 1984 the BBC ran an attractive Proms travel promotion as part of their publicity campaign – offering up to a 50% reduction on travel costs. Only in 1984 did the Proms again make a profit at the box office.

Although the strike itself had ended, the process had compromised the BBC's image as a disinterested guardian of the nation's music. This opened the door to a sustained attack on the right of the BBC, through its Controller of Music, to impose its taste on the music programming of the Proms. These accusations were the central focus of Robert Simpson's contentious booklet *The Proms and Natural Justice*.[98] Simpson had earned a reputation both as a composer of symphonies and string quartets and as a writer on music, whose studies of Bruckner and Nielsen in particular had helped establish those composers' reputations in Britain. He had also been a senior member of the BBC Music Division until he resigned in protest at the Corporation's handling of the Musicians' Union strike. Now free to express his own views on the organization of the Proms, Simpson published this brief, but trenchant, polemic, the impact of which was considerably strengthened by the author's former position within the BBC music hierarchy.

In the pamphlet, Simpson questioned the morality of an authority that allowed Proms programming to be the prerogative of a single person for an indeterminate period. To rectify the situation, he proposed a complicated system of governance that would, in his opinion, ensure a balanced outcome of composer representation. To support his argument, he provided a detailed analysis of featured composers, whose inclusion or omission from the Proms represented a political decision of who was 'in' or who was 'out'.[99] The significance of enjoying BBC patronage or not was directly related to the influence of broadcasting, which had since the 1930s made the BBC the nation's dominant musical establishment. For a composer to have his or her work taken up by the BBC not only carried prestige, it also had wider implications in terms of professional development and economic independence. Being signed by a reputable publisher was an important indication that a composer was making a mark; but being invited to compose a Proms commission suggested that the composer had 'arrived', and represented considerable career advancement. It strengthened the position of the composers concerned by increasing their opportunities for other prestigious commissions and prizes, as well as their potential to be taken up internationally by orchestras, opera houses and specialist performance ensembles. Inevitably, therefore, composers who were 'neglected' – Simpson's term for excluded – were resentful and indignant, often complaining of unjust treatment.

Glock's own commitment to twentieth-century music polarized perceptions. His focus on modernist contemporary music was a reversal of prevailing BBC attitudes of the 1950s, in which 'difficult' avant-garde composers were almost entirely ignored. Accordingly, many British composers found their broadcast representation suddenly cut. They felt that the BBC was not fulfilling its obligations to British music because of the new attention being given to modernist works. They accused the BBC of exercising censorship, because their music fitted neither with Glock's musical values nor with those of the producers he appointed. This abrupt change of musical climate meant that some composers were, in a very real sense, winners and others losers, because artistic and economic considerations were inextricably enmeshed. And Ponsonby's subsequent period as Controller brought no relaxation of attitude: 'There are many British composers whose music is not worthless or uninteresting, but it just does not fit with the criteria of showing great promise, and there simply isn't room for it [in the Proms] with all the other pressures.'[100]

Although it was Glock (as much as Ponsonby) who was the intended object of Simpson's home-spun logic, inevitably it was Ponsonby who suffered more from the fallout. Ponsonby's approach to Proms planning had been discussed and supported at a meeting of the Central Music Advisory Committee (CMAC) in October 1978.[101] In light of the furore caused by Simpson's pamphlet, Ponsonby and the BBC Chairman, George Howard, were interviewed on the radio arts programme *Kaleidoscope*; the BBC weekly publication the *Listener* also featured a series of articles and letters debating the future of the Proms' planning.[102] These letters included remonstrances by several composers, including Carey Blyton, who presented the standard anti-Glock arguments:

> Mr Ponsonby says that the BBC Music Division is 'deeply committed to the support of living composers', yet he omits to add that they must write the 'right' sort of music for him and his colleagues; namely, music of, and derived from, the Second Viennese School. … In 1959, when William Glock became Controller of Music, with Hans Keller as his Chief Assistant, [of] New Music, the BBC Music Division began a rigorous championing of the more extreme forms of avant-garde music to the virtual exclusion of any new music which had an immediate appeal. ('Schoenberg is the One True God and Pierre Boulez is His prophet' became the faith that all had to live by, whether composer or BBC producer.) Sadly, this policy has continued under Mr Ponsonby. …
>
> He [Ponsonby] has it in his power to start to undo the great harm done to our musical culture over the past 20 years by the Glock–Keller regime, which … still

favours … music of Continental origin and music written by a small faction of British composers thoroughly indoctrinated in this 'foreign musical policy' to the great detriment of the vast majority of our own composers.[103]

Quite apart from the harshly xenophobic tone of this letter, its central accusation is not borne out by the range of British composers awarded Proms commissions. As we have seen above, Glock included a range of non-avant-garde composers such as William Alwyn, Malcolm Arnold, Arnold Cooke and Thea Musgrave. Despite difficult economic circumstances during his Controllership, Ponsonby was successful in persuading the BBC to increase the fund available for the commissioning of new music, which rose from about £3,000 to £30,000.[104] He was also concerned to extend BBC patronage by continuing the Proms as a traditional venue for British composers, and his period saw steady support being given either by commissions or by giving a Proms' platform to new, non-commissioned works. Commissions went to several of the younger generation whose musical outlook had been very much shaped by Glock's programming, such as Oliver Knussen, Dominic Muldowney, Robert Saxton and Brian Elias. But Ponsonby's commissions reached across the generations, from Robin Holloway and Colin Matthews through Richard Rodney Bennett, Jonathan Harvey, John Buller and Gordon Crosse to Arnold Cook, Edmund Rubbra and Elizabeth Maconchy.

After the *Listener* debate, CMAC again discussed the issue, drawing on a position paper in which Ponsonby explained his planning strategy.[105] His original idea had been to plan the Proms in association with a different composer each year; however, the idea foundered when Michael Tippett, the first composer he approached, was prevented from accepting by compositional commitments.[106] Instead, Ponsonby formed a consultative 'Proms Group' of colleagues to discuss his plans and receive ideas. Significantly, Simpson was offered membership of this group, but declined. After explaining a variety of influences that shaped the content of Proms programmes, Ponsonby described his role as that of 'a single editorial mind … [which] naturally and unavoidably has the final say'.

Conclusion: The Proms Audiences

One of the most striking characteristics of the Proms of this period was the way they acted as a musical forcefield, affecting much that went on around them. Partly this is explained by the fact that each series represented a concentrated season generating many exciting performances and new discoveries. But do these Proms compare well with other London concert events? A broad indication is given by two published analyses of Royal Festival Hall audiences, one dating from the beginning of Glock's period and the other from the end of Ponsonby's.[107] In the first, we learn that from a total of 629 orchestral concerts spread over three seasons, 1961–2, 1962–3 and 1963–4, more than half (355) were 'Popular' concerts, defined as programmes of 'familiar or frequently played works in the standard orchestral repertoire'. Each of these popular events sold on average between 2,020 and 2,292 seats out of a capacity of 2,900 (between 70% and 79% respectively). In contrast, each of the 274 'Adventurous' programmes – containing one or more works outside the 'popular' category, i.e. nearly all twentieth-century music – averaged sales of between 1,160 and 1,711 seats (between 40% and 59% respectively).[108] Compare this with an assessment of the average attendance of 4,346 per concert in the Proms seasons of 1961–3.[109]

The second survey estimated the average Proms attendance in 1983 at 72%, measured in terms of *seating* capacity, that is to say not including the Prommers themselves. This compared with 66% of seats sold for the Royal Festival Hall 'classical concerts' of the 1983–4 season.[110] Of course seating capacity in the Royal Albert Hall is much greater than in the Festival Hall, so the comparison is not like-for-like: it takes far more people to fill 75% of the Albert Hall.[111] But what is interesting is that even when this imbalance is taken into consideration a projected comparison shows significant growth in Proms attendances to 1992 (to 84%) against a steady decline at the Festival Hall (to 61%).[112] In the 1984 prospectus Ponsonby wrote that in 1983 (when the Proms were still suffering the effect of the 1980 strike) the average attendance per concert over a season of 57 concerts was 3,000: 'we filled the Festival Hall every night and the Barbican 1½ times every night'.[113]

Even more interesting are attendance figures that indicate audience taste. In 1973 – Glock's final season, with audiences averaging around 5,000 per concert – an all-Stravinsky concert on 20 August, including *Agon*, *Les noces*, *Renard* and *The Rite of Spring*, attracted nearly as many people as an all-Beethoven programme on 30 July, and indeed more than an all-Mozart concert on 28 August. A concert on 27 July that presented Birtwistle's *The Triumph of Time*, Berio's Two-Piano Concerto and Berlioz's *Symphonie fantastique* drew a greater audience than the programme on 3 August, which featured Britten's *Four Sea Interludes*, Lennox Berkeley's *Sinfonia concertante* for oboe and chamber orchestra, Berkeley's Third Symphony and Tchaikovsky's Sixth Symphony. But a Renaissance choral and brass concert on 24 August outsold all of these.

As was noted above, as a result of the 1980 controversies the 1981 season began with a marked drop in attendance. Accordingly, a Listening Report was undertaken in the last week.[114] Compared with a Listening Report of 1973,[115] the age profile of the two audiences showed little change: 10% were 19 or under, 51% were 20–34 (the 1973 survey had 70% for ages up to 34 years), 29% were 35–54 (21% in 1973), and 10% were 55 or above (8% in 1973). There was a slight drop in women attending, down 6% to 39% in 1981, and audiences were predominantly white collar, at 80%. In 1981, 57% lived in 'Inner and Greater London', with 24% from the Home Counties (in 1973 London and the Home Counties were grouped together and a total of 85% was given). There had been a slight increase in those attending from across the UK – from 9% in 1973 to 13% in 1981 – and 5% of audiences came from abroad. Thus the Proms remained an essentially London festival, not surprisingly given the cost of transport: in 1981 most paid £1–3 to travel to concerts, though 11% paid above £5. Many drove to the Royal Albert Hall (39%), with the primary transport for others being the train (21%), tube (15%) and bus (10%).

The 1981 survey shows that those who came either more or less frequently to the Proms did so owing to busyness, time availability and geographical proximity, which made it either easier or more difficult for them to attend. Cost was often given as a reason for less frequent attendance, while those who came more often did so for social reasons and to hear appealing programmes. However, only one in ten of the less frequent attendees said they listened to more Proms on the radio, which emphasizes the importance of the actual concert experience for them. Of those who listened to eleven Proms or more on the radio, 16% attended one or two concerts, while 33% attended between six and ten. Interestingly, 22% of those attending did not listen to a single Prom on the radio. But it was good news for Ponsonby: when asked how the 1981 season compared with previous ones, 22% said that it was more appealing, 16% found it less appealing, 41% said it was the same and the rest seemingly didn't know! The major source of information about the Proms for 70% of attendees was the prospectus, while for 17% it was other people spreading the word. Only 7% gained their information from the radio, and 2% from television. Reasons given for not attending highlighted such issues as the accessibility of the Royal Albert Hall (including parking), as well as its acoustics and its amenities. Some attendees wanted less mixed programming and more separation of contemporary from 'traditional' programmes.

The 1981 Listener Report reinforced the extent to which Proms audiences were not necessarily confirmed Radio 3 listeners. It also underlined the distinction between audiences for whom the Proms existed primarily as broadcast events and those for whom attending the Proms was likely to be a special feature of their year, with occasional concerts carefully selected – enhanced, or even determined, by a perceived sense of community. The characteristics of this community also emerged: when asked why they liked the Proms, reasons included 'atmosphere', explained also as 'informality', 'joie de vivre' and 'excitement'.

But what this 1981 Listener Report reinforces was the extent to which the Glock and Ponsonby reforms had been embedded within the continuously evolving Proms traditions. During the quarter-century between 1960 and 1985, the Proms had changed in important ways. They had become an inescapable point of reference within the concert calendar, whether audiences were interested in hearing the world's greatest performers, in discovering early or new music, or in hearing the mainstream orchestral repertory in interesting, fresh contexts. The variety of musical experiences on offer fuelled different sorts of debates across the range of Proms audiences: anecdotal reminiscence, discussion of the finer points of interpretation, issues of performance practice or new music aesthetics. But above all, what Glock and Ponsonby had achieved was to make their Proms musical events that really *mattered*.

Joining the Queue: The Proms Audiences

IVAN HEWETT

HAZEL, SOUTH WALES, 84 *The Proms has changed and yet it hasn't – there's a oneness about it ... We learn things from each other.*

THAT COMMENT – ONE OF HUNDREDS MADE TO ME BY PROMMERS I INTERVIEWED during the 2004 and 2005 seasons – points to the special nature of Proms audiences. The members know that despite their arguments (and how they *love* to argue about the season, or what they heard back in 1963), as a nightly audience they're much more than an accumulation of individuals – which makes them interestingly different from audiences at the Barbican Hall or Royal Festival Hall in London.

In terms of bare statistical fact, Proms audiences today as a whole are not unlike classical audiences anywhere: weighted towards older, white, middle-class people. But there are small differences. The Prommers are slightly younger, with a greater preponderance of lower socio-economic categories and a larger out-of-town membership. Such minor statistical deviations may only hint at the audiences' character, but when viewed *in situ* the statistics' meaning jumps into focus. The tradition of Promming – standing in the arena or in the gallery for just a few pounds, or less if one buys a season ticket –

Prommers queueing for the Last Night, 12 September 1981.

Royal Albert Hall arena during the Last Night, 14 September 1991, conducted by Andrew Davis.

means that the moneyed element is not so visible. At the Festival Hall you are aware of the highest-paying members of the audience occupying the best seats, whereas the Royal Albert Hall, despite its red curtains and upholstery, feels much more democratic. There are expensive boxes round the perimeter, but they are not at the highest point: they are looked down on by the circle, which in turn is looked down on by the balcony audiences – who, along with the Prommers in the arena, have paid the least. The effect is a gratifying one of 'levelling up' and of 'enveloping'. Everyone partakes in the grandeur.

The Prommers constitute only a fraction of the whole audience – 1,400 out of a maximum capacity of 5,909 – yet they embody much of the meaning of the Proms, not just for themselves but in the gaze of the world. This bias has been sharpened by televised coverage of the Proms, which likes nothing better than images of fresh-faced Prommers. This points to the fact that Proms audiences are as much an imagined construct as a social reality. Or, to be more exact, there are two sorts of constructs. One is the product of the audience members themselves, revealed by the fact that when they are asked about their tastes and opinions, they so often say '*we* think such-and-such'. But just as important are the constructs made by onlookers – the organisers, critics, BBC mandarins and cultural commentators – for whom the character of 'the Proms audience' is a peculiarly important topic. The tone of their observations is never neutral; on the contrary, they're anxious for Prommers to conform or live up to a certain image. That image is an aspirational one, and this persistent tendency to see Proms audiences as aspirational goes back to the beginning of the series – right back, in fact, to the gleam in founder Robert Newman's eye in 1894. Half a century later, Henry Wood recalled Newman's words:

> I am going to run nightly concerts and train the public by easy stages … Popular at first, gradually raising the standard until I have created a public for classical and modern music.[1]

James Loughran conducting the Last Night of the Proms, 1981.

Even allowing for Wood's possibly rose-tinted memory, the cultural confidence of the Proms' founder is breathtaking. And, as if by magic, reality followed the vision. By the Proms' thirtieth anniversary in 1925, the *Daily Telegraph*'s music critic could note the result with satisfaction:

Nowadays it is Wagner, Beethoven and the accepted classics – Mozart, Haydn, Bach – who are the safest draw.[2]

It wasn't just the fact that thousands of people were cramming into the Queen's Hall to hear 'good' music that pleased the critic. It was the fact that their enjoyment had a special kind of inclusiveness and sincerity that couldn't be discerned at the more select gatherings of the Royal Philharmonic Society.

> Flattery has always been the last charge that could be levelled at a Proms audience, and snobs – who like the poor we always have with us – are ever overwhelmed by the simpleheartedness and sincerity of *habitues* who love everything regardless of cliques and claques.[3]

The idea that Proms audiences' lack of knowledge was a sign of sincerity is a tenacious one. We find it again thirty years later in Malcolm Sargent's introduction to the BBC's *The Story of the Proms*:

> Dear 'Promenaders',
>   I rejoice in this opportunity of greeting you and singing your praises.
>   Too often I have heard and read that the 'Promenader' is 'uncritical', 'fanatical', 'hysterical', 'uneducated musically', 'lacking in discrimination'. … But one can judge affection, love, in other people, only by seeing how much they are willing to suffer or deny themselves in favour of that which they adore …
>   The 'Promenader' comes to his concert, not to judge between this performance or that; not to listen for slight defects in the playing, not that he may be able to discourse learnedly on some small point of interpretation – he comes to 'enjoy' the music. And the 'Promenader' is right.[4]

It's hard not to feel that Sargent was patronizing Proms audiences as much as praising them; and of course, by praising them in these terms, he forestalled any urge that audiences might have had to be critical. Compton Mackenzie, writing in 1946, was blunter, noting that in his early Promming days at the Queen's Hall audiences were more restrained:

> Undoubtedly almost every member of the audience had come there to listen to the music, and there was never the exaggerated applause which a contemporary Promenade audience affects. I say 'affects' because I have not yet heard the slightest discrimination between the good and the mediocre, or even between the good and the definitely bad performance. Therefore I suspect that the contemporary audience is applauding itself as much as the musicians.[5]

The alleged lack of discrimination of Proms audiences is a perennial topic, about which present-day Prommers themselves have differing opinions:

JOHN TOMLINSON, MID-70s *I do think people are a bit indiscriminate … I heard a broadcast recently of a recording made in 1936 or 37 and the applause was very, very polite, but by [Malcolm] Sargent's day the audience went absolutely mad whenever anything finished. It was really over the top.*

Violinist Iona Brown receiving a bouquet after performing Vaughan Williams' The Lark Ascending *at the Last Night, 12 September 1981.*

TOM BAKER, PITTSBURGH *Yes, but would you really want to control this? You can't put 'don't applaud' in the programme. Really, I think the Proms audience is the most appreciative in the world.*

WOMAN, SOUTH WALES, MID-50S *Any composer who can get a Prom performance is lucky, because we really listen, and I don't think I've ever heard a boo.*
Q. But isn't that a sign the Proms audience is undiscriminating?
A. *Well, it's more to do with applauding honest effort … but if we really think something is not very good, we won't get him back on stage more than once … we won't throw eggs, we won't boo, it's more 'thanks and goodbye'.*

The idea of applauding honest effort seems a peculiarly British notion, akin to 'it's more important to play than to win'. It certainly helps to explain another long-observed feature of the Proms' audience: its friendly responsiveness to new music. It also raises the topic of the alleged 'Britishness' or perhaps Englishness of the Proms, to which we'll return.

Mackenzie's tart 1946 view of the Proms does at least point to the peculiar quality of 'togetherness' observed by audience-watchers. For those who share it, that togetherness has quite a different and almost mystical significance. The publisher Victor Gollancz stood for a performance of Monteverdi's *Coronation of Poppea* in 1963 and compared the experience to 'a Christian love-feast':

> The music, the people, the performers, the conductor, oneself – we were all merged in a sort of perfection of living: I would even dare to say that we all loved one another. And what a joy it has been, night after night, suddenly to find oneself young again, if only by a kind of adoption! They are *heaven,* these young people, with their honesty, their eagerness, what I can only call, in the spiritual sense, their courtesy and grace.[6]

Was Gollancz, down among the Promenaders, any closer to the reality than the *Daily Telegraph* critic looking down from the stalls? The question is a slippery one because feelings of transcendence by their nature become detached from their circumstances, and when described tend to sound the same. But in amongst the effusions about being 'transported and overwhelmed' there is a recurring theme: these feelings begin with a 'conversion'. C. B. Rees, a jovial Welshman, had such an experience himself before the wars:

> If a young and lonely individual, thrown on slender resources in London, chooses on a wet night to wander into Queen's Hall, largely because it is the only place he can afford to enter, and finds, in a mood of mingled curiosity and obtuse ignorance, that something goes on there which has on him the effect of a kind of 'conversion', he cannot be expected to forget it. This experience is not unique. Indeed, Henry Wood made it general. But it shakes you. It shook me.[7]

Mingled in with the sense of the sublime is an intimation of hidden mysteries that only longer acquaintance would reveal:

> I paid my first shilling for the Proms in order to hear the Queen's Hall Orchestra play the *Pinafore* selection. I shall never forget the chill that stole over me as the first half of the programme proceeded. Slowly the realisation forced itself upon me that here was music, bigger, on a loftier scale, of infinitely greater significance, than any I was acquainted with. It did not exhilarate me or charm my sense in the way the music I cared for did. But something within me *knew* that it was splendid, that its beauty must be clear and magnificent to ears more sensitive than mine. I began to go often to the Proms. Soon, I began the regular attendance that I have kept up ever since.[8]

Promenaders singing 'Auld Lang Syne' at the Last Night, 20 September 1952.

This is an example of a commonly expressed phenomenon: being tempted to a Prom by the promise of one sort of experience, and finding oneself pleasurably ambushed by another. This can happen in any concert hall, of course, but it seems to be unusually prevalent at the Proms. One reason is that in the early days many people were attracted to the hall by the more populist programming of the second half, and found to their surprise that they enjoyed the more serious first half too. That contrast between the two halves has long since vanished, but that sense of being 'surprised by music' still happens today, perhaps because the range of motives for attending is so wide: the lure of a powerful brand name, fondness for the venue, or wanting to be part of a national institution, to name just a few. Here's an example of a motive that no sociologist could have anticipated:

WOMAN, READING, 77 *It was funny how it started ... I was always brought up with light music, I always loved those old 78s. My family used to listen to the Palm Court Orchestras ... Then one day, when I was about 14, my friend said, 'Ooh, look, that pianist in the Prom brochure looks just like James Mason', so we went along just to see if he really did look like James Mason ... He didn't, but once I was in there, I didn't care, I was hooked, it just got me. It was Chopin, I remember.*

This sounds very like the 'oceanic' feeling characteristic of religious states, and both Proms venues – the Queen's Hall and, later, the Royal Albert Hall – had the peculiar combination of informality, close intimacy and space needed to generate it. They were not quite the same: the Queen's Hall was more of a friendly, even sweaty, crush:

> One little group consisting of four men and a girl being so closely packed together that the girl was literally unable to blow her nose. One of the men had to manipulate a handkerchief and do it for her.[9]

By contrast, the Royal Albert Hall seemed at first almost too spacious. One early journalist spoke of its 'vast wastes' and doubted whether any feeling of intimacy could be engendered. But its virtues soon became apparent. When packed with Prommers, there was an intimacy in the centre and a sense of space all around. To which is added, these days, a feeling of a noble history:

BRONGWYN, CANADA, 26 *It's great being in the Royal Albert Hall ... especially coming from Canada, where we don't have much architectural history.*

DICK BUTLER, 70 *The size of the building is so wonderful, and it suits certain kinds of music so well. We just heard Strauss's Alpine Symphony, which has 16 horns ... That just wouldn't sound good in a normal hall.*

MR COBB, THAME, 64 *I've heard many good halls like the Concertgebouw in Amsterdam, but there's nothing to touch the sound of a big orchestra in here ... I love Gustav Mahler, and if I want to hear Mahler I wouldn't go anywhere else. I come here to hear the vastness, the bigness. If the strings are in good form and the conductor knows how to restrain the brass, you can get a magical effect.*

MAN, 37 *I heard Mahler's Sixth here at a Prom … Three people next to me, all unknown to each other, were all in tears. I said to the middle-aged lady next to me, 'It's strange, why do we come here to be made miserable?' 'Yes', she said, 'isn't it wonderful?'*

The shock of transcendence, the sense of scale – this is the groundswell of audience reaction, something that persists from year to year pretty well unchanged. What has changed, naturally enough, are the feelings aroused by the choice of music and performers, since these things mutate over time. In the early days of the Proms, the focus of audience enthusiasm was as much loyalty to individual performers as to the music. Unlike today, this enthusiasm extended to players in the orchestra, whom they would see night after night, and of course to Henry Wood himself:

> Presently the members of the orchestra began to appear in groups of twos and threes, and as individuals were recognised so they were cheered; amongst them Mr. Crabbe, head of the cellists; Mr. Kiddle as he appeared at the head of the organ; Mr. Woodhouse, the leader, as he took his place at the first desk of the first violins. At eight o'clock there was a decided hush – for Sir Henry Wood's punctuality is proverbial, and reliable as Greenwich herself; and when he appeared, flower in buttonhole, there was a prolonged crescendo of applause that meant far more than a mere greeting of the popular conductor on his return from California.[10]

It wasn't just orchestral players who were treated like personal friends; there were a handful of especially favoured soloists.

> One of my earliest memories is of the genial, white-haired Belgian pianist, Arthur de Greef, who came season after season and usually played the Grieg concerto. I never hear the concerto, even today, without thinking of him … Two other great pianists stood out in my early Proms – Moiseiwitsch and Myra Hess. All three are, happily, still packing the Albert Hall as they used to cram the Queen's Hall with their devoted followers.[11]

But as the unique place of the Queen's Hall Orchestra gave way to the BBC Symphony Orchestra, and then, after the Second World War, as the pool of orchestras and soloists grew wider, so there was a transference of loyalty away from the specific – this operetta aria, that cornet soloist – to something loftier and more abstract: the idea of 'classical music'. It was a massive change, which could not happen suddenly in one leap; and there was an intermediate stage, a curious amalgam of the popular and the classical, described by social historian Ross McKibbin:

> There developed throughout the period [1918–51] not a big demand for 'serious' music, but a canon of 'middlebrow' music which was established before the First World War. This had its origin in both religious and secular music, was enormously reinforced and extended by the cinema and radio, and further reinforced by certain wartime varieties of 'serious' music. … By the early 1950s the middlebrow classical canon was fixed and probably will remain fixed.[12]

The programming of the Proms in its early days reflected this middlebrow canon faithfully, and its traces linger still in the second half of the Last Night. But this was only a strategic concession, because in its heart of hearts the Proms has been hostile to the middlebrow. The middlebrow is comfortable and unchanging – complacent would be the severe description of it – whereas the Proms is aspirational and restless. This is in part a reflection of a wider cultural phenomenon, the adoption of the cultural preferences of the upper classes by the wider population of listeners from the middle and lower-middle classes. It was a process massively reinforced by the democratizing power of radio, and the use of serious classical music was to boost the morale of radio listeners during the Second World War. As Lady Colefax wrote to Bernard Berenson:

> The war has proved my pet thesis – In spite of our dear Kenneth [Clark], Eddy Sackville West, the intelligentzia [sic] – the enthusiasm of the English for music has been proved up to the hilt – hitherto the music was too expensive and either by day when the workers could not go or by night when they were too tired or it was too dear – All through the war there have been concerts in the lunch hours in factories by people like Thibaut (who can't get over the audiences he has in the circumstances) Myra Hess – in fact first rate music – has all been received with touching enthusiasm.[13]

This wasn't just a matter of 'middlebrows' aping the tastes of the highbrows. The value system that lay behind those tastes had been thoroughly internalized, and had become 'second nature'. During the 1940s the BBC monitored the response of radio audiences to the Proms through its 'Listener Research Reports'. They make fascinating reading, because they show how eager listeners were to aspire upwards with the Proms. Anything outside the proper classical 'canon' was suspect; for example Liszt's *Hungarian Fantasia* was described by one listener as 'vulgarly showy'.[14]

The clearest way of signalling that one wasn't middlebrow was to take an interest in new music. Liking it wasn't necessary – in fact a certain dislike was all to the good, as it showed one's motives weren't sullied by anything as vulgar as appetite. There is often a sense that the listener has delegated his or her taste to the Proms itself, especially when its authority was vastly augmented by association with the BBC. The following Listener Research Report on a 1942 concert, which included the première of Britten's *Sinfonia da Requiem*, captures all these attitudes in one fascinating paragraph:

> The most commonly given special reason for listening to this concert was 'curiosity about the new works' (80 per cent of respondents) ... Respondents were 'anxious to give modern music a trial, even if they did not particularly care for it', the most important reason was 'liking for the Proms'. As for the experience of listening to the Britten, around a quarter of the respondents said they enjoyed it, though only 'moderately', while more than half of them did not like the work at all, while the rest did not like it much. One comment was 'I enjoyed the Sinfonia because for me it symbolised the death of the BBC crooner, and his well-deserved punishment in Hell.'[15]

ЕНАДИЙ ♥
ПОЖАЛОВАТО СНОВА НА НАШИХ PROMS !!

The first Proms appearance by a foreign orchestra: the Moscow Radio Orchestra, August 1966.

Sometimes the embrace of the Proms' aspirational ethos feels a little strained, as in a comment made by one listener on the British première of Copland's *Billy the Kid*: 'I believe I shall like it very much on future hearings.'[16] One wonders whether responses like these were singled out for quotation in the reports because they fitted so well with the improving mission of the Proms.

Imagined Proms audiences – those created by commentators and critics – loom large up to the Second World War and beyond, but references to them become scarcer in the 1960s and 70s. In the age of Harold Wilson's 'white-heat of technological revolution', of political satire and anti-Vietnam protest, the peculiar ethos of Proms audiences must have seemed a hangover from a bygone era – particularly as the programming itself underwent a kind of 'white-heat of revolution' thanks to William Glock.[17] In the 1980s and 90s, as nostalgia and historicism became intellectually respectable and questions of national identity started to become more urgent, Proms audiences once again became objects of interest; in the series' 100th season, this historicizing mindset was reflected in the programming, which focused on the Proms' own history.

But what of those other imagined Proms audiences – the ones created by audience members themselves? On this subject the records are almost silent. The only clues come from the BBC Listener Research Reports, which feel very remote from the contradictions and exuberant variety of the audiences you encounter outside the Royal Albert Hall or in the bars in the interval.

That variety is likely to be more pronounced now than it was in the past, given the notorious fragmentation of cultural practices and tastes in contemporary society. Along with the fragmentation there has been an ebbing away of the idea of deference to 'the classics' and cultural authority generally. All this might lead you to think that the very idea of 'Proms audiences' is a fiction, and that all we can expect to find now is a set of individual preferences. One finds those, certainly, but alongside them – or rather, underlying them – are shared sets of values, whose expression varies according to the age of the interviewee.

Among the older ones, they are expressed with confidence, even vehemence. Among the younger ones, there is a diffidence; you can tell that the process of acculturation into the Proms mindset is not yet complete.

One of those shared values is a commitment to the new.

DONNA HALL, 23 *I don't tend to come to Proms with new music … unless it's stuff I'm pretty sure I'm going to like.*

JOHN, AUDIENCE MEMBER SINCE 1941
Q. Are you looking forward to the première of Thomas Adès's Violin Concerto?
A. *Oh yes, I've got a CD at home with other pieces by Adès, which I'm working hard at … it's only 17 minutes after all [laughs].*
Q. What makes you feel classical contemporary music deserves that kind of effort?
A. *Well, it can pay off over time. I go back to 1946 when Menuhin brought out a recording of Bartók's Violin Concerto. I couldn't make head or tail of it, but I thought if Menuhin's prepared to spend time on it, so will I, and now it's one of my favourite violin concertos.*

But John's friend Jacqui disagrees:

I've heard some terrible things … We have a good laugh about those words 'BBC Commission'. 'Look out,' we say, 'here comes another turkey.'

ANDREW, MID-30s, PROMENADER FOR 16 YEARS *Well, what we often ask ourselves is, 'Whatever happens to these new works … frankly the good ones are rare. I did like John Tavener's Protecting Veil, but that was a one-off.*
Q. Have you learned from the Proms?
A. *Oh yes, I didn't know much about Schoenberg, but he is tonal after all, and I do like it now … but not the 13-note [sic] Schoenberg stuff. Where's the tune, I say to myself.*

MR COBB, THAME, 64 *I tend to watch the Proms as an indicator of something new. Tonight's new work was very impressive [The Immortal by Zhou Long]. I use the Proms as a reminder of what I haven't heard or what I want to hear.*
Q. So the prominence of new music is something you value?
A. *Oh very much, it's terribly important. It's a reminder to me that there is twentieth century music.*
Q. Were you scandalized by Harrison Birtwistle's Panic?
A. *No, I thought that was great … you can take classical music too seriously. On the other hand, you sometimes can't take it seriously enough.*

WOMAN, 43 *I think it's good that they pop one modern work in. I wouldn't come to a concert that was all modern … hearing one in a mix is good and sometimes you're pleasantly surprised. We heard a piece by that Finn, what's his name … Salonen … it was ok, yeah, it was quite exciting, but if someone said, just as we still listen to Brahms and Beethoven now, will we still be listening to Salonen in two or three hundred years time, well I'm not so sure about that.*

Notice how the old criterion of 'passing the test of time' persists as tenaciously as ever.

Does all this show that the mindsets of Proms audiences are simply the faithful reproduction of mindsets the cultural mandarins and critics always wanted them to have? No, because the confidence of each individual in his or her own judgment appears so much greater than before. A Prommer will, in the same breath, assert the value of difficult music and dismiss the latest commission as rubbish.

Alongside the 'test of time', we find the idea of the pursuit of 'the best', which could be said to be the overriding value for Proms audiences. Anything that goes against it gets short shrift:

Q. Do you think British composers and British music should be highlighted at the Proms?

WOMAN STUDENT, 23 *Well, it's nice to support British composers, but only if they're as good as the foreigners. Personally I'd be happier if nationality wasn't an issue at all.*

MAN, 66 *Well, the Proms used to do that, didn't they, in the days of Henry Wood? I think we hear a lot of British music, especially at the Last Night, and that's probably enough. I think it's a very good thing the Proms have become more international.*

The attachment to the highest quality – of music and performance – is expressed partly through a shared perception of a 'canon' – a body of exemplary works that ought to be at the heart of Proms programming. Which composers and which pieces are allowed into the canon has of course changed over time. Liszt, as we saw, was rejected in 1942; these days he is let in, although perhaps on probation. Certain composers have always been there: Handel, Mozart, Haydn, the three B's, Wagner and Mendelssohn (long a British favourite). In the last thirty or forty years or so, several more composers have been admitted to the top table, as is revealed by these remarks.

Q. Who's in your top rank of composers?

ANDREW, MID-30s, PROMENADER FOR 16 YEARS *Oh Beethoven has to be the tops, followed closely by Shostakovich and Mahler. I quite like Mozart, too, though it can be a bit twiddly.*
Q. How about Wagner?
A. *Oh yes, he's up there …*
Q. And Stravinsky, Schoenberg, Bartók?
A. *Well, it depends on the piece. The Rite of Spring I can get on with …*
Q. What about early music?
A. *Oh yes, give me that any day. The Sixteen were here the other day, that was wonderful.*

WOMAN, TWICKENHAM, 44 *When I was young we just didn't get Mahler … then suddenly they started playing him and I loved it.*

MAN, 45 *Gunter Wand conducting Bruckner … that's my favourite Proms memory. And you know before that, I didn't really listen to Bruckner at all.*

MAN, ENFIELD, 54 *I remember years ago I came here to hear Shostakovich's Tenth Symphony, and it was fantastic, I was knocked out. Since then I think I must have heard all the symphonies in that space, which is just right for it.*

Prommers in the arena of the Royal Albert Hall, 2002.

HAZEL, SOUTH WALES, 84 *I remember I heard that piece by Berlioz, the one with all the brass playing up there in the balconies. I'd never heard Berlioz before, but I thought it was wonderful.*

Mahler, Bruckner, Shostakovich, possibly Berlioz – these are the composers who have truly entered the Proms canon. This isn't solely due to the advocacy of the Proms; since the war these composers have been on the rise everywhere. But a combination of the awe-inspiring venue – so apt for Berlioz's colossal choral works and Mahler symphonies – affection for the Proms, and the internalizing of its improving mission, must have created fertile ground.

One striking aspect of Proms audiences, young and old, is how tolerant, even welcoming, they are of the Proms' educative mission:

DICK BUTLER, 70 *We've tried to broaden our taste, not entirely successfully ... people at the Proms are generally crazy about Bruckner and Mahler, who we still haven't quite come to terms with. I like the composer of the year idea. I don't like the Birtwistle and Ligeti ... I'm floored by that so I tend not to come.*

CHRISTOPHER, AUSTRALIA, 47 *This year I decided to hear more contemporary music. I've been to Birtwistle and Messiaen ... You can't know too much, and here it's so easy, it's right under your nose. I thought I'd surf the wave ... especially if you subscribe, only £4 ... I went to lots last year.*

STUDENT, 20 *Yes, the Proms are a big part of my life, I see forty or fifty a year. It's handy being a music student ... It's nice to be able to see so many pieces here you don't see elsewhere, like that Messiaen piece that was 95 minutes long [Éclairs sur l'au-delà].*

DOWNIE FAMILY, BRIDGEND
DAD: *I've dragged my two daughters along today, kicking and screaming [laughs].*
TWO DAUGHTERS: *[protesting] Dad, we're having a lovely time, we just don't have the knowledge you have.*
Q. So what made you want to come?
A. *It's an occasion, isn't it? And Dad's enthusiasm has rubbed off on us, we want to learn more.*

TWO STUDENTS, HUDDERSFIELD UNIVERSITY
MALE: *I tend to stick to the things I know.*
FEMALE: *Oh no, it's made me want to just learn everything.*
MALE: *That's rubbish, the first Prom you came to, it was all old stuff.*
FEMALE: *Yeah, but what about last week's Prom with that new piece by that Finnish man, what's his name ... Salonen ... I wanted to find out more about him.*

If all this sounds implausibly high-minded, it should be remembered that the lofty sentiments are kept aloft partly by the accumulated excitement of a long series:

URSULA SCHULTZ, BREMEN, 'NOT SO YOUNG' *In every concert there's always something to find out ... Really it's like a drug, I just have to keep going.*

Q. Is it difficult to come back down to earth when it's all over?
A. *Oh it's really* miserable *[says Ursula's friend Sheila from Eastcote]. I just don't know what to do with myself.*

For some people the Proms becomes a way of life for two months of the year, a fanatical devotion that never fails to attract some gentle mockery from the newspapers. Here's an example:

> Andrew Campbell … didn't miss a single night for three consecutive seasons. His life remains on hold. After late-night Proms and when the trains are on strike, Andrew sleeps at work. 'I'd always wanted to go to a Proms Season' he said. 'Three years ago my parents bought me a season ticket, and I've been going ever since. It costs £70 for a gallery season ticket – that's £1.03 a concert' … Computer program-mer Dai Lowe, 41, met his partner Lucy Perry, 31, [there] eight years ago. Her parents met there too. On 8 August each year Dai toasts Lucy with champagne and presents her with roses on the steps of the Albert Hall. But he admits the limita-tions of 'Promenerding' as a way of life. 'On the whole, the men are not that prepossessing – a bit nerdish really. For some people it's their only way of finding a partner. Recently I heard someone remark 'Oh my God, it's nearly the last night! What on earth am I going to do for the rest of the year?'[18]

The Arena Season Ticket queue, 2002.

It is devotees like this who are invariably put forward by the media as typical of all season-ticker holders, but in fact very few of them go to every concert.

Again, exaltation and disappointment seem to have remained much the same, whether they appear in reports from 1925 or 2005. What has changed are revealing little details of behaviour. One thing the early days of the Proms had in common with football in its mass heyday was the audiences' stoical endurance of discomfort. This was especially true of the Queen's Hall, recalled here by Rosa Newmarch:

> One could not move for the crush … but it was an inspiring sight to see the floor of Queen's Hall packed with an audience who will stand patiently through the longest concerto or symphony. To stand motionless for 55 minutes is a trial that might well extinguish all but the most impassioned ardour.[19]

Like football, the discomfort of the event was for many people preceded and followed by an equally uncomfortable train journey, as one audience member reminisced in a Listener Research Report of 27 June 1942:

> In peace time I took parties up to London … we started from Leicester in the after-noon and returned on Sunday morning about 5.30 am, and it was worth it.[20]

Twenty years later, Eugene Goossens noted admiringly in his memoirs that

> The stamina required for a person to remain standing during the performance of three hours of music (and that, in the case of many enthusiasts, every night except Sundays for ten weeks) is in itself no small matter. Add a knowledge of the orches-tral repertory which would put many musicians to shame, plus again the fact that most of the audience at the promenades are engaged in strenuous professional

activities, and you have a picture of a music-lover who makes the average listless, condescending patron of our concert halls look what the Americans call a 'piker' in comparison.[21]

Informality in dress has been the watchword of the Proms from the very beginning, but, as we've seen, this goes hand with utmost seriousness with regard to the musical experience itself. This is why informality of behaviour is frowned on. Dick Maidment, a Prommer since 1938, recalled that 'in the old days, one wasn't even allowed to sit down; stewards used to come round and make people stand up.'[22] Certain aspects of concert behaviour become flash-points for arguments about what is acceptable. One of them is applause between movements. In 1951 a Mr Burston Armagh wrote to the *Daily Telegraph* to say:

> I have just listened to a performance of Tchaikovsky's Fifth Symphony broadcast in the Home Service from the Royal Albert Hall. I was surprised to hear applause after the second movement, but when applause broke out again towards the end of the last movement, I was astonished. Can it be that the Promenaders are so musically ignorant these days that they do not know one of the most popular and indeed greatest symphonies of all time?[23]

But letters such as this are often challenged by replies that plead for the rights of 'impetuous youth'. In the last ten years or so, the applause rule has slackened noticeably, but even so you can feel in the hall a certain resistance when applause breaks out between movements. This isn't just to do with the applause 'breaking the spell' of the piece: it's a failure to 'tune in' with the Proms' civilizing mission, of which discomfort and restraint were (and are) such potent symbols. One 19-year-old student from Huddersfield University interviewed in 2005 expressed his irritation at the 'clappers' in just the same disdainful tones as Mr Burston Armagh in 1951.

But by and large, today's audiences agree that casualness of behaviour is now acceptable:

DONNA HALL, 23 *I like the informality, and the fact that we were able to lie on the floor … It was great, there was loads of space.*

URSULA SCHULTZ, BREMEN *I was so impressed by my first Prom season in 1996, so now I book a half-season … I liked the way people are in the gallery, just sitting, lying down. One year there was a lady doing some quilting. For contemporary music it's wonderful to see it and hear it. Now I've become part of the Gallery Bay 6 friendship.*

One thing people agree is a crucial factor is the peculiar physical characteristics of the Royal Albert Hall, whose gallery provides flat spaces to lie down in, and little nooks and crannies where one can knit undisturbed. Perhaps one reason for the Proms' continued health is the cultural malleability of its venue. It can simultaneously give expression to the grandeur and

confidence of the nineteenth century and the casualness of the twenty-first.

Another aspect of the Proms audience allowed for by the venue is eccentricity, its most visible quality. It's difficult to wear silly hats and blow whistles in the serried seats of the Barbican; at the Albert Hall promenading space it's easy, however – all too easy, some might say. It takes various forms, from mild quaintness to out-and-out loopiness:

Q. Does the Proms attract eccentrics?

MAN, RETIRED SCIENCE TEACHER, 59 *Oh yes ... You get little groups of season ticket holders who stick together. There's one who goes around handing out aniseed balls, and another one who hands out jelly babies. He's in his mid-60s ... he's really quite charming.*

Q. Are there certain 'characters' you look out for?

JOHN DAVIS, 69, ATTENDING PROMS SINCE 1946 *Oh yes, there's a guy who lives in Kingston been coming for years, known affectionately as Ken [now deceased]. He would bring a baton and wear evening dress and conduct the orchestra along with the real conductor.*

MAN, LATE 30S, PROMMER FOR 13 YEARS *There's a group of us who get together for a regular Proms breakfast ... We tend to get on better with the regulars than the day-trippers, or 'trippers' as we call them.*

Q. Do they not get on?

A. *No, they're two different camps ... and believe me there is a lot of Bette Davis-type campery. It's quite a palaver you know, keeping your place in the line. You have to sign in at 3.00 and again at 4.15 ... it's like the bread queue in the Soviet Union. Some people try to cheat by getting their friends to write their names on the list. I imagine you know what we Prom audiences are like. We're a funny lot, but really when it begins we're deadly serious ... When the orchestra is really going 'con belto' I'm so excited I can't even describe it. You think I'm mad, don't you?*

That last interviewee typifies the way in which deep emotion and eccentricity run side by side; or, to be more exact, the eccentricity is a cover for the emotion and keeps it private. This emotional ambivalence, if anything, is what gives the audience a very English flavour; as Alan Bennett once said, 'the English are serious and not serious'.

Perhaps this is why the Proms directors, however much they may wince at the silliness, have put up with it – with one exception. In 1995 John Drummond made two radical moves towards making the Last Night a more serious occasion. The first was to commission Harrison Birtwistle to compose a new piece, which turned out to be an obstreperous saxophone concerto called *Panic*. Its appearance at the beginning of the second half seemed deliberately provocative, and it reached mass television audiences on BBC1.[24] The other was a clampdown on balloons, for reasons Drummond explained in the *Independent*:

Some girl pushed 200 of them off the balcony and of course everybody popped them and [conductor] Andrew Davis ended up abandoning his speech. Well, what was this girl thinking about? Balloons are a bloody nuisance. …

There's a man who comes every year with an inflatable parrot on a string. He comes up and says 'I've got my parrot'. And I think 'Oh yes, of course you've got your bloody parrot'. And all through the thing he's bobbing up and down with his bloody parrot … Me, me, me, me, me! That's what it's all about![25]

Were the Prommers abashed by this curtailment of their ancient rights and privileges? Not exactly:

WOMAN WITH PEARL EARRINGS, WALES, MID-50S *Mr Drummond said we weren't allowed to make loud noises, so instead of sounding loud we dressed loud. My friend came in a jester's cap and uniform. Really he deserved it, because it was a bad idea to put that in the Last Night. We do have a sense of mischief … and we like it when performers don't take themselves too seriously.*

Drummond's desire to rein in the Last Night audience was not shared by his successor, Nicholas Kenyon. 'I am a "let joy be unconfined" man myself', he declared to the press, and actually expanded the Last Night by relaying it on screens in Hyde Park for the thousands who couldn't get into the Hall.

The eccentricity of the Prommers is one thing that exasperates high-minded music-lovers. Even more vexing to them is the Prommers' appetite for the full-throated rendition of patriotic hymns on the Last Night. On an admittedly unscientific sampling, general Proms audiences seem to be divided three ways on this mingling of silliness, nostalgia and flag-waving. There are those who approve of it, those who are embarrassed by it and – the largest group – those who enjoy the Last Night, but with a twinge of guilt:

HELEN HEWITT, STUDENT, **19** *I listened to them at home with family. I've grown up with them, they're a tradition … but I do find the Last Night a bit embarrassing.*

JAMES MATTHESON, **47** *I love the atmosphere but the Last Night, it all gets a bit too much. I'd prefer to see it change, and I really applaud Mark Elder for what he did all those years ago.[26]*
Q. What do you think about Birtwistle's *Panic*?
A. *Oh, fantastic … I enjoyed the upset as much as the piece.*

John Parsonage of Devizes has been to three Last Nights. 'It's all about having fun, waving the flag, being proud of being British without feeling a complete prat', he explained.[27]

ALEX CASE, **27**, HIS FIRST VISIT TO THE PROMS *I came because my girlfriend persuaded me, though I did know about the Proms because we used to watch them on TV at home.*
Q. What did you think of the Last Night?
A. *Oh, I used to like it. I grew up in North Yorkshire and it was like the outdoor concerts at Castle Howard. It just seemed a normal thing to do.*

Q. What do you feel about the Union Jacks and *Land of Hope and Glory*?
A. *Well, I suppose the songs could be seen as racist. But it depends how it's done. I think you can tell that at the Last Night it's just good fun … There's nothing wrong with a bit of flag waving, is there? Oh dear, is that politically incorrect?*

Thus it's a peculiar fact about the Proms that the Last Night – its climactic event – is an embarrassment for a sizeable proportion of many of its most ardent patrons. It's hard to think of any other festival for which this is true, and it points to the almost incorrigible tendency of the Last Night to become a separate event, hardly connected to the main body of the Proms at all. It is something every director makes strenuous efforts to overcome, by insinuating some serious music and some quiet reflective moments into the party. And it should warn us against treating Last Night audiences as symptomatic or typical of the whole. Above all, it should warn us against the notion expressed by some commentators that Proms audiences are essentially backward-looking and nostalgic.[28]

The one thing on which you can get Proms audiences to agree is that things are better now than they were.

Q. Do you think the changes in the Proms have been for the better?

MR COBB, THAME, 64 *Yes, I would say on the whole I do, I'm not keen for people to think that nothing changes … things do change. I like the way the Proms can adapt … you remember how the last night was altered for Lady Diana and 9/11.*

GIANCARLO, MILAN, PROMS ATTENDER SINCE 1964 *Yes, the Proms is better. I like the idea of a theme … last year Spanish, this year Czech. Performances also are much better now.*

JOHN TOMLINSON, MID-70s *I first came in 1941, when it was still Henry Wood. Later I didn't come so often because the concerts were mainly conducted by Sir Malcolm Sargent, and weren't so attractive as they have since become.*

DICK BUTLER, 70 *In the early days they played standard repertoire, which made sense because it wasn't easy to hear it in those days … just three orchestras played and three conductors, there wasn't the variety there is now. Mind you, the concerts were longer, they went from 7.30 to 10.15 … so by the standards of yesteryear we get very short measure.*
Q. Do you regret that?
A. *Well, a bit, but I know I'm being old-fashioned. The truth is things weren't well rehearsed.*

GEOFF, 63 *I Prommed back in the 70s and again since we came back to London five years ago. The music is much more adventurous now … you can hear the standard stuff on the radio, so you're really looking for something special these days.*

Although one encounters complaints – not enough choral music, not enough early music, too much new music – they're remarkably rare, and nearly always accompanied by the sense that these imbalances have a rationale and are done for the overall good of the festival.

Last Night of the Proms, 13 September 1980.

You would expect such an outlook from a body of people who are so devoted to the institution. What counts for them is that the vitality of the festival is demonstrated anew each year, and a certain friction between the content of the festival and their own individual tastes is taken as evidence that the thing they cherish is in rude health. Another symptom of that rude health is of course the Proms audiences themselves – their coherence, their camaraderie, their disputatiousness, their constant self-renewal. It's here that many of the older Proms audience members see cause for concern.

DEREK, **65,** AND HIS FRIENDS MABEL AND ARTHUR
Q. How has the audience changed?
A. *[Derek] There are fewer young people, not so many students … It's not a good sign. [Mabel] Yes, we don't just want old fogies like us coming along.*

Q. Do you get many tourists?

A. *Yes, and some of them are not so nice.*

Q. How do you mean?

A. *[Derek] Well, they don't always understand what it's all about. They get their lap-tops out and start typing. They always think it's going to be the same as the Last Night … Last year somebody took their shoes and socks off and started to put their foot medication on. [Arthur] I often sit with my back against the railing, but often I wish I hadn't. One time I saw this couple necking, and I said to them, 'if you want to do that why not stay in your hotel?' [Derek] It's the Classic FM syndrome I think. They think they're listening to single chunks of music … A lot of people pick up their shopping bags and go after one movement, because they think it's all over.*

ANDREW, MID-30s, PROMENADER FOR 16 YEARS *The queues are much shorter than they used to be. This year on the first night I saw someone buy a season ticket, now a few years ago you couldn't have done that, they would have been sold out.*

Q. Do you find the other people in the queue are regulars or casual?

A. *That's another change, these days quite a large fraction is casual. At one time we were all regulars.*

The declining number of young people is a lament one hears constantly from the older audience members. But equally significant is a vague sense that the nature of audiences is changing. The Proms cannot be immune to certain dispiriting trends in modern life, particularly the erosion of the sense of a public space, and the notion of commitment to cultural values at the cost of inconvenience or discomfort. The casual listener who

Opposite above
*Harpist Sidonie
Goossens signing
autographs, 28 August
1988.*

Opposite centre
*Mature Prommers
enjoying an interval
ice cream, August
1999.*

Opposite below
*The Prommers' queue
extending down the
steps towards the
Royal College of
Music, 2002.*

leaves after one movement, or who goes to the loo mid-movement, is just like the channel-hopper sprawled on the sofa at home – not really an audience member in the old sense. This casualization of audiences is most evident at the satellite events like the Proms in the Park, or the simulcast of the First Night on large screens in Trafalgar Square. Audiences for the latter consist mostly of passers-by, and the commonest answer to the question 'Is this your first encounter with the Proms?' is 'What's that?' (The second most common reply is a blank look.)

With that level of comprehension, it's debatable whether the hundreds of people in Trafalgar Square really count as Proms audiences at all. With the Proms in the Park, it's a different matter. Among the picnics and fractious infants in buggies, the music gets a bit lost, but there's no doubt that people are there because they intend to be there, and they agree that they're having a wonderful time. And there's a dim perception that this one event is part of something vaster and grander. Distance from the Proms – in the sense of being unfamiliar with it – can cut two ways. It can produce indifference, but it can also lend enchantment. 'The Proms, they go back to 1400, right?' was the awed opinion of one American visitor to the Last Night in 2005.

That power to create enchantment at a distance is a tribute to the continuing myth of the Proms, and to its enormous cultural weight. But that weight itself springs from the fact that the Proms has always been culturally alive, an arena in which disputes about cultural values and hierarchies have been played out. The most visible and tangible evidence of that vitality is of course the programming, with all its tensions between tradition and innovation, nationalism and internationalism, high-mindedness and populism. Those tensions are mirrored in the audiences, which complete and in a sense make real the cultural conversation, of which the programming forms the opening gambit. You could, with only a touch of hyperbole, describe the audiences as the truest and best cultural achievement of the Proms: it is their presence, in those patient queues and noisy bars, that gives the institution a profound human value beyond the aesthetic. Just how strong that value can be was captured for me by one remark:

WOMAN, READING, 77 *In my kitchen I've got the centenary poster of the Proms, and a picture of Henry Wood ... The Proms really is one of the best things that has ever happened to me. I love it, and everything about it. I've told my girls, I want my ashes scattered here ... don't let anyone see you do it, just scatter them in the bushes ...*

Branding the Postmodern Proms, 1986–2007

REFLECTING ON THREE LAST NIGHTS

TOM SERVICE

IF YOU ATTENDED ANY OF THE PROMS AT THE ROYAL ALBERT HALL DURING THE 2006 season, you could not have been in any doubt at all as to who was promoting the series. You would probably have heard the trailers on any of the BBC's radio stations, or seen them on the BBC's terrestrial or digital channels, or you may have bought your ticket online through the Proms website. Once you pitched up at the Albert Hall, you could not have missed the posters and banners that decorated the outside of the building, an expression of self-confi-

dent promotion proclaiming the importance of the 'BBC Proms'. Those two words have become an instantly and internationally recognizable brand, provoking a collection of images, sounds and ideas associated with 'the world's greatest music festival'.[1] Inside the foyer, hoardings and posters outlined the themes, premières and progress of the season. Such visual bombardment continued even within the auditorium itself, with its projected logos and specially coordinated lighting – and all of this before the music had even started.

How might the story of the Proms in the years from 1986 to the present day, under the stewardship of John Drummond (1986–95) and Nicholas Kenyon (1996 onwards),[2] explain these developments?

Above *The BBC Proms Website, 2006.*

Left *A Proms-branded London taxi, 2005.*

Above *The Royal
Albert Hall displaying
BBC Proms branding,
2002.*

Left *Foyer of the
Royal Albert Hall,
with BBC Proms
exhibition, 2002.*

There was of course the Proms' consolidation within popular, public consciousness and the cementing of its position within the BBC's internal structure. As Kenyon has said, 'the Proms now have a fixed, unquestioned place within the cultural activities of the BBC.'[3] In Drummond's time, however, that wasn't always true. The Proms had to weather a storm of pressures within the BBC, especially when John Birt was Director-General (1992–2000) and instituted an era of 'Producer Choice' from 1993, in which each BBC department had, essentially, to compete against every other department for its resources. In part, the differences between 1987[4] and 2006 can be explained by the different personalities of the two controllers: Drummond, notoriously bullish and strong-minded, as opposed to the more conciliatory and politically astute Kenyon.

So what do I mean by the 'postmodern Proms'? It's a phrase that encapsulates how the values of classical music were perceived to change since the mid-1980s. Instead of art music having an assumed, absolute value as a privileged musical art form, it was increasingly seen as one musical style among many, no more or less culturally significant than pop, rock or jazz – an attitude shared by many arts policies of the New Labour government that came to power in 1997. In terms of the Proms, this viewpoint resulted in a growing emphasis on inclusivity of musical styles, not just those of the Western classical tradition. In addition, the audiences became increasingly diverse, reached through an ever-multiplying variety of performance sites and broadcast media – digital television channels, the internet and the open-air spaces of Proms in the Park, as well as the listeners in the Royal Albert Hall itself and those who tuned in to Radio 3 or watched BBC 1, 2 or 4. The creation and dissemination of the Proms as a brand as well as a concert experience joins all these various issues to underscore what follows in this chapter.

But there are, of course, more obvious ways in which the 'postmodern Proms' simply continued the tradition of previous seasons and regimes. Given the orchestra's naturally pivotal role in the Proms season, our story from 1987 is also a narrative of changing batons at the helm of the BBC Symphony Orchestra: in 1987 Sir John Pritchard was still the Chief Conductor of the orchestra, but after his death in 1989, Drummond announced the appointment of Andrew Davis, who steered the BBC SO from 1989 to 2000. The BBC SO then appointed the American conductor Leonard Slatkin to succeed him, and the contrast between Davis and Slatkin was not just between two different nationalities and personalities, but also a matter of different attitudes to repertories: Davis was seen as an all-rounder, as comfortable in programmes of Boulez and Messiaen as Elgar and Vaughan Williams; in contrast, Slatkin espoused American as well as British repertory and was valued for his media-friendly persona and ability to communicate with audiences. Slatkin's was never an easy relationship with the orchestra, however, or with the critics, and his contract was not extended beyond 2004; the Czech conductor Jiří Bělohlávek took over the post at the start of the 2006 Proms season.

Opposite above
Last Night of the Proms, 14 September 1991, conducted by Andrew Davis.

Opposite below
Radio 3 presenter Susan Sharpe in the Royal Albert Hall announcer's box, 1988.

What has happened in the last twenty years of Proms history has reflected the shifting priorities within the cultural politics of the BBC and in the commercial world at large, as the Proms has responded to often seismic changes in the classical music environment. The conception of Proms' audiences is key to all this. During the initial BBC stewardship in the interwar years, audiences were treated as massed groups to be educated and fed diets of good music in order to 'improve' the cultural knowledge of the country as a whole; at the beginning of the twenty-first century, this was replaced by a climate that encouraged self-conscious analysis of audience figures and the changing approach towards the growing diversity of those audiences. The Proms' audiences were not just made up of those inside the Royal Albert Hall – they also comprised those listening to Radio 3's live broadcasts (on the night, or repeated the following afternoon or later in the season), those watching television relays on BBC1, BBC2 or BBC4,[5] those accessing the concert as streamed on

*Proms Director
Nicholas Kenyon
speaking at the
launch of the 2006
Proms season.*

the internet, or the hundreds of thousands who attended the Proms in the Park events that were part of Kenyon's directorial approach since his first year. Drummond himself signalled that change: in the foreword to the 1989 season Guide, he talked of the Proms as being about 'further enjoyment' rather than 'further education'. Kenyon has outlined his ethos and his vision for the future of the Proms as follows: 'to be as inclusive as possible and to create as wide an audience as possible for the sort of the music that the Proms encompasses'.[6]

Thus the Proms have changed from being an agent for the patrician provision of culture for the masses to a postmodern part of people's lives, from a conception of culture in which the audiences are passive recipients to one in which they contribute to the identity of the Proms as a brand and as a collection of concerts. The issues that faced Drummond, Kenyon and their Proms teams are, in one sense, only amplified versions of the concerns surrounding balancing box-office numbers, the provision of a public service, audience and critical approval, and BBC support that Wood, Glock, Ponsonby and every other Proms Director has also faced. However, the necessity of promoting the Proms as a brand as well as concert experience has arguably never been more urgent than in the last two decades, when the competitive noise outside has been deafening. That is the flipside of the 'postmodern Proms': the efforts of the Proms marketing department, the festival's online presence, Proms education work and, since 1996, the Proms in the Park events are directed towards affirming an indelible Proms brand as much as they are about introducing programmes to the public.

The Proms as high-value brand is a theme that underscores the debates about the function, relevance and integrity of the Proms seasons considered in this chapter. And, strictly speaking, we should now be speaking of the 'BBC Proms' rather than the 'Proms' or the 'Henry Wood Proms'. This is because since 1993, during a period of financial pressure and following an aborted attempt to secure commercial sponsorship for the Proms (something John Birt perhaps surprisingly opposed when he took over as Director-General), the series was eventually designated a BBC brand. Drummond strenuously resisted this branding, as he said in his autobiography:

> I was … totally opposed to the Henry Wood Proms becoming the BP Proms or the Royal Insurance Proms or whatever. I was in due course strongly resistant to their being renamed the BBC Proms, since this clearly contravened the agreement with Wood's heirs that his name should feature in perpetuity in the title. Yet this decision was taken without consultation with me, as part of the 'branding' of the BBC imposed on the organization by public-relations people like Tim Bell [a Birt consultant], who was paid huge sums for the deep originality of telling us we should say not 'Radio 3' but 'BBC Radio 3'.[7]

This was a move also resisted by Robert Ponsonby, Drummond's predecessor.[8] Drummond's opposition to the branding exercise exemplified what for him were the insidious changes brought about by Birt, which impinged on Drummond's control of the series towards the end of his tenure; they reflected the growing power of the BBC's marketing department, which in Kenyon's time was regarded as a close and valuable ally in making the Proms part of popular consciousness.

I have focused this chapter on accounts of three moments that reveal the buffeting forces to which the Proms and its management teams were subjected. These three flashpoints surrounded Last Nights, so often the point in the season when issues of musical and political identity have been amplified. We start in Drummond's final season – indeed, the final evening of his stewardship – with the Last Night of the 1995 Proms, and an auspicious commission.

Panic to Don't Panic: New Music at the Proms, 1987–2005

It all started innocuously enough. In a planning document for the 1995 Proms, a draft programme for the Last Night lists the following pieces in the first half: the overture to Berlioz's *Le Corsaire*; songs from Mahler's *Des Knaben Wunderhorn*; and waltzes from Strauss's *Der Rosenkavalier*. Sandwiched between the Berlioz and Mahler was the world première of a BBC commission by Sir Harrison Birtwistle, to be called 'The Piper at the Gates of Dawn'.

It is important to remember that 1995 was the Proms centenary, and as Drummond explained, his original plan had been to retire earlier: 'I was not expecting to stay more than six or seven years with the Proms, but coming up on the horizon, in 1995, was a very special anniversary – the Proms' centenary – and I was tempted to stay on to oversee that.'[9]

Drummond made the 1994 and 1995 seasons a double centennial celebration – 1994 being the hundredth Proms season, and 1995 the centenary of the very first season in 1895. The concerts in 1994 celebrated the history of the Proms, with programmes reflecting the older traditions of Wood and Sargent, as well as an ambitious, three-part concert to celebrate Glock's achievement. This particular event gave Drummond much anxiety: 'it was hard to find any single programme to do justice to William's programming because of the range of things he did, from early music to the avant-garde. So we came up with this tripartite programme.'[10] The concert featured the Nash Ensemble conducted by Martyn Brabbins, the New London Consort with Philip Pickett, and the BBC Symphony Orchestra conducted by Colin Davis, George Benjamin and Pierre Boulez, one of Glock's closest collaborators, who conducted his own *cummings ist der dichter* and Stravinsky's *Symphony of Psalms*.

There was only one new piece in the 1994 series, but the 1995 season in contrast looked forward, featuring a dozen new commissions, including Birtwistle's piece for the last night. It was a double celebration that perplexed some, including Michael Checkland, who was Director-General in 1990. 'I understand there is some confusion in the thinking for this event', Drummond wrote to Checkland. 'The Proms began in 1895, the centenary therefore falls in 1995. However, each year we publicize which season it is and 1994 will be the hundredth season. Both these facts seem inescapable … In 1994 … we should reflect what the Proms have achieved over a hundred years of music making in this country … In 1995 … we would commission from major living composers and plan a programme which looks ahead to the next century.'[11]

Drummond's uncompromising send-off season included new pieces from Kaija Saariaho (a violin concerto, *Graal théâtre*), Benedict Mason (a clarinet concerto that required only the soloist to be on stage, with the rest of the players promenading in the gallery of the Royal Albert Hall), Elliott Carter and Steve Reich. There was also the British première of Henze's Eighth Symphony, given by Simon Rattle and the City of Birmingham Symphony Orchestra; the London première of Thomas Adès' Chamber Symphony; and a concert suite from Thea Musgrave's *Simon Bolivar*. There were also new pieces from John Casken, Judith Weir, Peter Maxwell Davies and Tan Dun – although the world première of Tan Dun's *Orchestral Theatre 2* had to be cancelled due to a power cut that took out all of the hall's lighting. The penultimate night featured the infamous non-première from Luciano Berio. According to Drummond's autobiography, Berio was asked for a new piece, but simply added forty seconds to a work that had just been performed for the first time in Germany. The commission fee was eventually returned to Kenyon after Drummond had left his post.[12]

Whatever the adventure of these and other commissions, it was the Birtwistle that would cause by far the greatest reaction. By the time of the Last Night, 'The Piper at the Gates of Dawn' – a reference to a chapter in *The Wind in the Willows* by Kenneth Grahame – had become *Panic*, a concerto for solo saxophone and orchestra, to be performed by John Harle with the BBC Symphony Orchestra conducted by Andrew Davis. In a typical piece of Birtwistlean punnery, the title of the piece was to be taken as both noun and adjective: a state of high anxiety and pan-ic, 'of the Greek god Pan', suggesting the elemental power of the music that Birtwistle eventually wrote. Drummond thought the piece appropriate for the Last Night festivities, due in part to Harle's audience-friendly qualities. But when he saw what Birtwistle had written, he was shocked to discover that a ten-minute commission had grown to eighteen minutes with such a complicated instrumental set-up that it could no longer be accommodated within the first half. There was an inevitable solution: *Panic* should start the second half.

And that's where the problems began. The full Last Night of the Proms was broadcast on Radio 3, of course, as were all the concerts of the season. However, the Last Night 'traditionally' received television attention as well. By 1987, and for the next two decades, a familiar pattern had been established: the first half was aired on BBC2, known as the 'cultural' channel, whereas the second half was broadcast on BBC1, the BBC's most popular and mainstream television channel. This split reflected the different musical constitution of each half. The first half presented a concert in miniature, with a pot-pourri of popular classics, leavened over the decade since 1997 with the annual inclusion

Saxophonist John Harle, conductor Andrew Davis and members of the BBC Symphony Orchestra in Harrison Birtwistle's Panic, *at the Last Night of the Proms, 16 September 1995.*

of a contemporary piece. The start of the second half featured a different, high-profile soloist every year, and another collection of short, usually familiar works, but it ended with what had become a standardized sequence of British triumphalist music: Elgar's *Pomp and Circumstance* March No. 1, Henry Wood's *Fantasia on British Sea Songs* and Hubert Parry's *Jerusalem*.[13] The iconic status of this collection of pieces had been cemented, year after year, through sheer repetition: only in 2001 was the make-up and character of the end of the second half significantly altered (see below). For many listeners, these pieces became key signifiers of Britishness and Englishness, and the annual ritual of experiencing the Last Night, whether in the hall or through broadcasts, was the most important musical expression of British patriotism. BBC2 and BBC1 attracted wildly different audience figures: where the second half regularly pulled in millions of viewers, the first half was lucky to achieve one million.

The contrast was between different audience expectations as well as different musical priorities. Whereas BBC2 audiences might well have tolerated the Birtwistle, to have such an uncompromising piece as *Panic* opening BBC1's coverage would risk shocking not only a significant percentage of listeners in the hall, but millions of viewers all over the world tempted to tune in to hear *Land of Hope and Glory* rather than a hard-hitting piece of contemporary music. Stylistically, *Panic* lived up to its name: the piece shows Birtwistle's music at its most violent, energetic and dissonant. Given that this was the first time a new commission had been presented at the Last Night, it looked like a quasi-heroic gesture of Drummond's intractability, a refusal to be swayed by the contingencies of television broadcasting or to pander to the desires of Last Night audiences. But the positioning of *Panic* was not the self-conscious gesture of Drummond's authority that it might have seemed at the time. Not only had he originally planned *Panic* less controversially for the first half, he had also asked Birtwistle if there was any way to accommodate a different stage set-up, only to receive the answer, 'Well, it's the only idea I've got, and the only one you're going to get.'[14]

Drummond's distaste for the rituals of the Last Night had grown throughout his tenure, as had his intolerance for the behaviour of Proms audiences in general. In the foreword to the 1992 Guide, he had admonished listeners in the hall for the 'storms of coughing' that had blemished performances of the previous season, although he was careful to say that the Prommers themselves were free of these bronchial disturbances. And in 1995, at Drummond's request, balloons and party poppers were banned from the auditorium, in the interests of giving the Last Night greater musical integrity. For all his feelings of negativity about the Last Night – in his autobiography he remembered that he 'moved from tolerant enjoyment to almost physical revulsion as the behaviour of the audience inexorably took over from the music'[15] – he never went as far as Ponsonby who, after hearing the first half, reportedly actually left the hall to escape what he saw as the undignified spectacle of the second half.

BBC Director-General John Birt and Prime Minister John Major share a box on the last night of John Drummond's Proms directorship, 16 September 1995.

Panic lived up to its name both in the muted response within the hall and the complaints received by the BBC's audience line. Drummond reported that the switchboard was 'swamped with several thousand protesting calls'[16] – in fact, the BBC's records suggest complaints in the low hundreds. But as Drummond said, 'tributes to my "courage" have always embarrassed me', since he had hesitated over including the work in the second half. But he is proud of *Panic*, and cheerfully commented, in a typically colourful piece of self-assessment (not to say self-aggrandizement), that 'my successor running the Proms [Kenyon] has programmed several new pieces on the final night – though none, I may say, as powerful.'[17]

Many of the complaints to the BBC switchboard reflected the idea that a notional national pride represented by the Last Night had been tarnished by Birtwistle's music and, by extension, Drummond's programming. A Mr Potter of Epsom wanted to know 'what proportion of his licence fee would have been spent on commissioning the Birtwistle piece', Mr Prosser in London thought 'the Harrison Birtwistle piece was a disgrace and an insult to the British public', and Mr Fountain 'complained that a wonderful nationalistic occasion had been turned into a terrible nothing'.[18] Others who called that night felt that the constraints placed upon the Prommers, owing to the ban on party poppers and balloons, turned the whole evening into a damp squib, especially since 'they would sound better than that piece by Birtwistle'. Drummond is intransigent about what *Panic* represented. 'If the mummified corpse of the Last Night ever experiences any sort of reanimation, Birtwistle's *Panic* may have played its part.'[19]

The *cause célèbre* of *Panic* focused debates about the purpose of the Last Night and the centrality – or otherwise – of new music to the Proms agenda. It's ironic that the musical idiom of a composer who was, even in 1995, one of the elder statesmen of British music, and as such an Establishment figure (although not yet a knight of the realm, as he is today) should have caused the furore that it did. The lesson from the whole episode must have seemed clear to Kenyon, or to anyone else coming into the Proms job in the wake of the *Panic* panic: mess with the Last Night and you risk scuppering a big part of audiences' sense of what the Last Night of the Proms means and, wider still, what it means to be British (or at least English), given the patriotic fervour that many in Britain experienced through the predictable Last Night rituals. So Kenyon went in a fundamentally different direction: aiming not to shock existing audiences, but to draw in new ones.

The controversies of presenting new music can be as much about circumstance as about occasion; for instance, new music in late-night Proms has often resulted in halls less than a quarter full, something that concerned both Drummond and Kenyon. Perhaps it's almost inevitable that a 5,909-capacity hall would not be filled for most concerts of new music that began at 10.00 pm. Like Glock and Ponsonby before him, Drummond tackled this issue by experimenting with different venues for late-night concerts of new music and early repertories. St Paul's Church, Knightsbridge, was used for this purpose during his first four seasons, followed by Kensington Town Hall.

> This could seat 500 and, although acoustically very dry, answered well to the requirements of contemporary music. But it never caught on with the promenaders, on one occasion producing the smallest audience in the history of the Proms – less than 100.[20]

After the relative failure of this venue, Drummond looked around for other suitable halls but came to the conclusion that 'The Proms were synonymous with the Royal Albert Hall, so why not do everything there? It meant that some very small ensembles might be excluded, but the Albert Hall is surprisingly

The Royal Albert Hall,
1990.

flexible in its acoustics and kind to the human voice, so many possibilities were still available.'[21] Kenyon has never lost faith in the Royal Albert Hall; having increased the number of late-night concerts dramatically from Drummond's time, he has staged every evening concert there. The only exceptions have been the lunchtime Proms Chamber Music concerts, established in the early 1990s in the Victoria & Albert Museum; the series moved in 2005 to the sumptuous surroundings of Cadogan Hall, just off Sloane Square, substantially increasing audiences. A new Saturday afternoon matinee series of chamber orchestras was added there in 2006.

For Kenyon, renewal of the repertory has been as much about performance as about works, a shift of emphasis from the grand gestures of programming, like Drummond's commissioning of *Panic*, towards different ways in which the Proms might be delivered to new, previously untapped audiences. An important symbol of this latter goal was introduced right from Kenyon's very first season in 1996: the inaugural 'Proms in the Park'.

Inclusivity and Proms in the Park

The idea of staging a simultaneous concert in Hyde Park for the Last Night was not a new one when Kenyon took over the Proms after the 1995 season. Meetings in the early 1990s between the Proms and the BBC Marketing Department, when Kenyon was Controller of Radio 3, reveal that with his support plans were mooted for such an event during the 1994 season. But according to a letter from Sue Brealey of Radio 3 Marketing to the Head of Marketing and Publicity for Network Radio in February 1994, Drummond had misgivings – 'A live relay of this sort would reduce demands for tickets for the main event in the Royal Albert Hall', and it would detract from what was actually happening in the 'proper' Last Night. In her letter, Brealey counters these concerns with the example of the Royal Opera House, whose productions were relayed in the Covent Garden piazza with no loss of ticket sales.

> Nothing can beat the live atmosphere in the Royal Albert Hall on the Last Night. The event in the Park would aim to let a greater number of people share that experience and, if anything, I believe that is would add to the exclusivity of being in the Hall.[22]

In fact, Drummond's reservations were more personal, as he reveals in his autobiography, written in the late 1990s:

> I would feel much more involved sitting at home watching my television rather than sitting in a damp park hearing the BBC Concert Orchestra playing something completely different, or watching Michael Flatley of *Riverdance*.[23]

Ouch. Drummond's resistance to the idea of Proms in the Park was based on his long-standing feud with what, for him, were the dark forces of Birtism within the Corporation, and he opposed having 'the essence of mindless populism imposed on an event which is already dangerously rabble-rousing'.[24]

Buying Prom tickets for the arena, 2002.

One significant new development between 1994 and 1996 was a clear desire within the BBC for the Proms to prove itself as a brand, to use its power as an institution to reach new audiences and a different demographic in order to confirm the Corporation's vision of what the festival should be: an opportunity to involve as many people as possible in music. Another factor was Kenyon's strong desire to put to one side the arguments about nationalism that had bedevilled the Last Night over the years. This is how Kenyon viewed the adoption of the Proms in the Park format in 1996: 'The importance of Proms in the Park is its inclusivity; the Last Night is not about nationalism, it has become totally inclusive for everybody.' Kenyon has said that he gained very strong support from within the BBC for the idea of expanding the scope of the Last Night. In giving the final go-ahead for the Proms in the Park concert in 1996, for instance, Sue Farr, then Head of Marketing and Publicity for Network Radio, stated the mantra of the event's significance: 'The rationale is a familiar one – access/accountability. Let more people share in that marvellous institution "The Last Night of the Proms".'[25] Thus Kenyon saw the Proms in the Park as part of a wider conceptual shift concerning what the Proms are and who they are for: 'The Proms as a brand is not completely for connoisseurs. We're also out there for everyone who pays the licence fee, on the internet, [on] radio, on TV, and in the Parks.' And what if the Proms in the Park phenomenon had not materialized, and he had continued Drummond's line of resistance? According to Kenyon,

> I think we could have had a big problem with the Last Night if things hadn't changed. If Proms in the Park had never happened, the Proms might have been the target for the criticism that classical music was cut off from the majority of people. But because we took that bold step, the Proms have become part of popular consciousness in a new way.[26]

Proms in the Park was a reaction to this cultural climate, to the perceived inaccessibility of classical music. It was not simply a case, however, of presenting the main substance of the Proms, the conventional orchestral concerts, to new audiences in Hyde Park. Rather, to prove both within the BBC and externally just how inclusive classical music and the Proms could be, Proms in the Park – ironically – had to include types of music and performers who would never normally be considered to represent either classical music or the Proms, as we will discover.[27]

In 1996, Proms in the Park began as a single concert in Hyde Park alongside the concert in the Royal Albert Hall. Thanks to big-screen technology, there was a live link-up with the hall for the second half, so that the thousands in the park could join in with the traditional audience-participation numbers of *Land of Hope and Glory*, *Rule Britannia* and *Jerusalem*. The first half in the hall featured a London première by Poul Ruders. The park offered its own programme during the first half, but instead of a self-contained, classical concert, classical artists performed alongside names drawn from the worlds of popular and light entertainment. The whole event was hosted by Radio 2 presenter

Sheridan Morley. The people who attended the event numbered 28,000, and the entire concert was broadcast on Radio 2 as well as Radio 3. In addition, the first half as performed in the hall was televised on BBC2, and BBC1 coverage of the second half included not only what was happening in the hall, but also excerpts from the park event.

This diversity of broadcasting media reflected the new audiences for the Proms brand that the park events had sought to create. In the late 1990s and early years of the new century, Radio 2 was the network with the highest listening figures in the UK, and as with all BBC networks, massive potential international audiences due to its availability online. Radio 2 sought to appeal to the widest demographic of any of the BBC Radio networks, carrying a combination of everything from mainstream pop to easy listening and popular classics; in effect, the first half of the Proms in the Park events, from 1996 onwards, reflected in microcosm the breadth of Radio 2's remit. Building on the popularity of the Last Night, the partnership between the Proms and Radio 2 tried to maximize the reach and influence of the Proms; such was the success of the evening in 1996 that the Proms in the Park as a distinct brand and as an annual event was born.[28]

Proms in the Park had still other audiences that it was trying to attract. In 1992, classical music on commercial radio was launched in the UK in the form of Classic FM, a station of unashamed populism that boldly created classical music playlists, excised individual movements from pieces and encouraged the commodification and appreciation of classical music along the lines of popular music culture. This was a successful formula: Classic FM's audience gradually rose to a weekly reach of about six million compared with two million for Radio 3. Cheekily, Classic FM tried to piggyback on the Proms' achievements in the early years of the twenty-first century, handing out leaflets and posters to audiences as they left the Royal Albert Hall. Ironically, it was the popular success of the Proms, and its instantly recognizable identity, that made Classic FM see an opportunity in approaching audiences in this way. But in its initial seasons, was Proms in the Park similarly trying to tap into Classic FM audiences through its more popular formats?

Audience research undertaken after the 1997 season revealed just who the new Proms in the Park audiences were and what they expected from their evening of alfresco music-making. They were more likely to be Radio 2 listeners than Radio 3 or Radio 4 regulars, it was revealed.[29] The majority thought the 1997 programme, with its emphasis on popular acts rather than classical musicians, better conceived than that of the first year. Those who enjoyed the 1997 line-up said there was 'more variety' and a 'better atmosphere', while those who preferred the 1996 programme appreciated 'more traditional/classical music' and 'more of a connection with the Royal Albert Hall'.[30] Only 11 per cent of the attendees who were asked thought future Proms in the Park events should include only classical musicians, while just one per cent thought they should only include popular artists; an overwhelming 87 per cent thought the event should continue with its mixture of classical and popular artists.

Fast-forward to 2005, and Proms in the Park had become a firmly established event within the framework of the BBC Proms. Instead of a single concert alongside what went on in the Royal Albert Hall, there were multiple, simultaneous outdoor events in Belfast, Swansea, Manchester and Glasgow, as well as in Hyde Park, each involving BBC orchestras with a starry line-up of presenters and performers. The move to incorporate big names from popular music accelerated each year: the 2005 programme for Hyde Park included Mick Hucknall, ex-frontman of Simply Red, and a performance by the four-piece boy-band G4, finalists of the first series of ITV's reality show *The X Factor*. They provided support for the leading artist, the internationally renowned tenor Andrea Bocelli; the BBC Young Musician of the Year for 2004, violinist Nicola Benedetti, was also prominent. Terry Wogan – one of the most popular chat-show hosts on BBC television, an iconic figure in British broadcasting since the early 1980s and the most popular broadcaster on the whole of Radio 2 – was now established as the ever-present and evergreen host. What began as Kenyon's idea to create multiple Proms in the Park events had become an interactive extravaganza: in 2004, new vocal additions to one of the crown jewels of the second half of the Last Night – Henry Wood's *Fantasia on British Sea Songs* – were performed, reflecting different British regional identities. The performances by choirs in Belfast and Manchester were beamed to radios and television sets around the world, so that – thanks to the wonders of satellite technology – the four corners of the British Isles came together in the playing of the Wood *Fantasia* in a celebration of the Welsh, Scottish, Irish and English national identities. In 2005 there was a follow-up to this collegiate performance: as well as Bob Chilcott's arrangements of regional tunes as part of the *Fantasia*, bugle calls from naval tradition, which appear in Wood's original score of the *Fantasia* but which had not been played at the Proms in recent years, were assigned to different Park events, and knitted together in another paean to the participatory potential of new technology. A further index of the growing middle-of-the-road profile of the Last Night for the seasons since 2004 has been its television presentation by Alan Titchmarsh, more familiar as an expert on gardening and natural history than classical music, but one of the most recognizable faces on the box at the time.

Proms in the Park has been a highly significant part of the BBC's vision for the modern-day Proms, offering new approaches to the question of how the Proms might reach out to other audiences, and consequently how the Proms could demonstrate their centrality to the musical life of the nation. It is ironic that responsibility for programming these events, so important for the Proms' image, has not come solely under the remit of the Director of the Proms. Instead, Proms in the Park has been organized by the BBC Live Events department, also run by Kenyon, with the regional events co-funded by local councils. Thus the programmes have been arrived at collaboratively, with the involvement of all the producers in the national centres, albeit under the guidance of the Proms Director. Nevertheless, for the first time in Proms history, a regular Proms concert has not been directly programmed by the Director of

Fireworks at the BBC Children's Prom in the Park, Hyde Park, 12 September 2004.

the Proms: a loss of control that previous Directors (Drummond certainly, and possibly his predecessors) would have found intolerable. Proms in the Park as a brand has achieved huge recognition for the Proms, and unquestionably broadened the appeal and brand-awareness of the concerts. The event has also attracted considerable attention from within the highest echelons of BBC management: as long as Proms in the Park is around, the BBC believes that no one can accuse the Proms as a whole of elitism or narrow-minded, exclusivist focusing on classical repertories.

There are historical precedents for the 'new audiences' attracted by Proms in the Park. In terms of both programming style – short bursts of music, many soloists, line-ups that bridge the gap between classical repertories and the popular vernacular – and the profiles of those who attend, it is possible to argue that Proms in the Park has reverted to a style of event and concert-planning that the Proms developed in its earliest seasons. When you cast your eye over the character of music in any Proms in the Park running order, there is a striking resemblance to Wood's and Newman's early programmes. Even if you see Charlotte Church singing a Welsh hymn rather than Dame Clara Butt singing Elgar, the ethos of creating a programme as a compilation of greatest hits as well as populist 'novelties' has more closely resembled the Proms of 1900 than anything in post-1945 Proms' seasons.

But has the development of Proms in the Park come at a cost? It is clear that Drummond's concerns have not been borne out. There has been no let-up in the insatiable demand for Last Night tickets within the Royal Albert Hall in the last decade – if anything, people are even more inspired to go to the hall's Last Night after attending a Proms in the Park concert.[31] It's a clever way to side-step the debates about how to treat what some see as the musical and programmatic anachronisms of the Last Night: without sacrificing any sacred cows of the concert, the experience has been made available to thousands more people around the country – and to audiences that are definitely different from those that come to the hall or listen to concerts on Radio 3 regularly during the season. The park events have offered a solution that moves the Last Night away from associations of exclusively English nationalism, the 'rabble-rousing populism' that Drummond and Ponsonby so abhorred.

BBC Prom in the Park in Hyde Park: view from the stage during the 2004 Last Night.

However, there could be a more problematic underside to all this. The experience of the Proms in the Park has been associated so far only with the Last Night, although there have been more modest big-screen relays of the First Night in Trafalgar Square.[32] The Last Night itself has become the most immediately identifiable commodity for the Proms' national and international identity, and Proms in the Park has reinforced the idea that the whole season is embodied by the festivities of the final evening. What is more, thanks to the necessarily diffuse programming of Proms in the Park events, where the agenda has been to create as palatable a programme as possible for a majority audience rather than to shape a coherent artistic experience, the Proms brand has become associated with a different set of priorities from those that guide the rest of the season. Mick Hucknall would never appear in any other context at the Proms except on stage in Hyde Park; if he or G4 had been scheduled at any other time in the season, the core audiences would likely be up in arms. (It is interesting to recognize that the situation is the exact opposite of the *Panic* furore: *Panic* scared Last Night audiences; G4 would have a not dissimilar effect on audiences for any other Prom, were they to be included.) Research generated by the Proms Office has acknowledged that Proms in the Park audiences have not been the same as those who attended the hall – as in 1997, the majority have remained Radio 2 listeners. As yet, no evidence has suggested that individual members of the audience who have been to a Proms in the Park event would be more likely to come to the Royal Albert Hall during the rest of the season or to listen to broadcasts on Radio 3.

However, a key benefit of the Proms in the Park has been the leeway it gave to planners to include more adventurous elements in any given season. If the park events have not actually subsidized the rest of the programmes, they have allowed any season to contain any number of new commissions, twentieth-century classics or more obscure parts of the repertory thanks to the certain popular success of the season's final night. All this has ensured the 'untouchability' of the Proms within the BBC. As Kenyon put it, 'the pressure from the BBC is for the Proms to be as successful as possible. It's especially worth doing Proms in the Park because quite apart from its own success it enables us to keep doing the core of what the Proms are about.'[33]

The Last Night of the 2001 Season: The Proms as Tragic Pageant

The rituals of the Last Night have seemed as immutable as any musical tradition. Yet even within these constraints, there have been times when things had to change, proving that the modern-day Proms could still be reactive to world events and intensifying the issues of national identity and musical universality that the Proms have come to represent. There has been no more powerful example of these issues than the Last Night of the 2001 season.

The Last Night fell that year on 15 September, four days after the 9/11 attacks on New York and Washington, DC, in which hijacked planes were flown into the twin towers of the World Trade Centre and into the Pentagon, killing over three thousand people – an atrocity that shook the world. On the day of the attacks, a Tuesday evening, the Orchestre de Paris conducted by Christoph Eschenbach substituted the funeral march from Beethoven's 'Eroica' Symphony for the *Prometheus Overture* with which they had originally planned to open their concert. As the week progressed, it was recognized that the national and international mood had been so radically affected that the atmosphere of the traditional Last Night would not be appropriate. As Kenyon recalled, 'when we were making decisions about what to do, on the Wednesday of that week, at that stage there could have been anything up to five thousand British people involved in the Twin Towers tragedy, so it was absolutely clear that we couldn't do the triumphal bits of the Last Night. But we wanted to do something very positive instead.'[34]

This was the second time since 1996 that the end of a season had to be altered substantially. In 1997, after the death of Diana, Princess of Wales, the plan had been to include in the Last Night a performance of John Adams's *Short Ride in a Fast Machine* – a glorious orchestral showpiece but somewhat unfortunately titled, given the circumstances of Diana's death. The Adams piece was replaced by Copland's *Fanfare for the Common Man*, and *Jupiter* from Holst's *Planets* was also programmed because it contained Diana's favourite hymn tune, 'I vow to thee my country'. The 1997 season had other changes, too: with the death of Sir Georg Solti, Colin Davis stepped in to conduct Verdi's *Requiem* in early September, a concert that became a double memorial since the *Requiem* was one of the princess's favourite pieces.

But the situation in 2001 demanded something more than the simple substitution of works within the conventional framework of the traditional Last Night. In the event, the centrepiece of the second half was no longer Henry Wood but Beethoven: the finale of his Ninth Symphony. This is a piece that is regarded, as Esteban Buch has shown,[35] as an emblem of internationalism, an ode to a universalized 'joy' that has become virtually synonymous with 'freedom'. The often convoluted history of the work's reception has arisen from its long-held status as the *ne plus ultra* of the classical and romantic traditions. The rich fund of meanings that the work has accrued derives also from performances in recent decades, such as that given by Leonard Bernstein in Berlin in 1989 to celebrate the fall of the Berlin Wall, in which Schiller's 'Freude' ('joy') was substituted with 'Freiheit' ('freedom'). The melody of the *Ode to Joy* has also been adopted as the anthem of the European Union. With its inclusion in the Last Night of 2001, the shift in the concert's significance was clear: it moved from being the celebration of a narrowly British nationalism to a universal musical experience, a symbol of classical music's unique power to transcend and transfigure experiences of grief, disbelief and horror.

Kenyon described the process of changing the Last Night as

> very collegial. Mark Thompson, who was then Director of Television, Jenny Abramsky as Director of Radio, Roger Wright [Controller of Radio 3], Edward Blakeman [Editor, Radio 3] and colleagues discussed what the mood should be,

and then they left it up to me to decide with conductor Leonard Slatkin what the programme should be. On one side, there was the idea that we should leave out *Land of Hope and Glory* and the *Fantasia on Sea Songs* and *Jerusalem*. But I felt pretty strongly that there should be a link to the traditional Last Night programme, which was why we included *Jerusalem* at the end of the programme.[36]

The issues were not just to do with British national identity, or the commemoration of the then unknown number of British casualties. There were American sensibilities to consider. Within the BBC, American feelings assumed special importance, especially after that week's edition of *Question Time*, in which the atmosphere was felt to be 'virulently anti-American', in Kenyon's words. The BBC's flagship political discussion show, *Question Time* features a panel of politicians and commentators who are asked questions by the audience; in the course of the programme broadcast immediately after 9/11, comments were made from the floor about the imperialism of American foreign policy and the inequities of America's attitude towards the Middle East, especially its perceived close relationship with Israel and distancing from Islamic states in the region. 'As a result of that', Kenyon said, 'Greg Dyke [then the BBC Director-General] became involved, because he wanted to make sure that what was done on the Saturday was sufficiently respectful of American feeling. That was part of the reason why he suggested we included the American national anthem as well as the British national anthem, and of course that immediately resonated with Leonard, though I remember it being very difficult to decide where in the concert to include it.'[37]

Conductor Leonard Slatkin was the other key American element of the programme; the BBC Symphony Orchestra's Principal Conductor, he was in charge of his first Proms season. On the evening of Monday 10 September, he had led the orchestra in Vaughan Williams' *Sea Symphony*, celebrating the end of his inaugural season. In retrospect, Slatkin's performance of the new programme for the Last Night was to be the highpoint of his time with the orchestra. 'Leonard was incredibly flexible about the programme', Kenyon remembered. It was his idea to play John Adams' *Tromba Lontana*, the partner piece to *Short Ride in a Fast Machine*. (Adams' *Short Ride* must be one of most ill-fated pieces ever to have been programmed at the Proms: the piece was on the original billing for the Last Night 2001, due to receive a Proms performance at last following its cancellation in 1997. Once again it was pulled on account of its inappropriate title, finally receiving a performance in a Proms season in 2004.) Kenyon described the 2001 Last Night as 'Leonard's moment. His performance of Barber's Adagio for Strings was remarkable.'[38] The choice of the Barber was perhaps predictable: given its performance at state funerals the world over and its use in films like Oliver Stone's *Platoon*, where the music laments the futility of war and all of its victims, the Adagio had achieved iconic status as the music of mourning.[39] The Adagio for Strings was beamed around the country, to the parks in Gateshead and Liverpool, and to the Eden Project in Cornwall.

The choice of programme made the Last Night of the 2001 season a part of the worldwide process of coming to terms with the terrorist atrocities, as well as a part of political debate. The change of programme was widely reported on BBC television news, leaving no one in doubt of its importance. Not only did the transformation of the programme resound forcefully for those used to the traditional Last Night format; it also became meaningful in a wider sense, as a musical and human experience. It was an evening that revealed the relevance of the festival internationally – and not just its meaning for the national psyche.

The success of the 2001 programme – which, broadly speaking, received huge critical plaudits[40] – also offered an opportunity to change the established pattern of the Last Night for the future. In the event, however, subsequent seasons reverted to tradition, conforming to the post-1995 format of presenting a piece of contemporary music alongside more conventional repertory in the first half, and including the familiar participatory hits of the second, updated by the technological sophistication of link-ups with the parks and the internet. Those who regard the Last Night as an outmoded vestige of an older, even offensive, conception of Britishness think of this as a missed opportunity. However, sticking to the familiar pattern of the Last Night allowed for the diffusion of the Proms brand in new ways – and that goal has arguably been both the cornerstone of Kenyon's stewardship of the Proms and the BBC's vision of the festival in the future.

Evelyn Glennie performing Tan Dun's Concerto for Water Percussion, *2 August 2004.*

The Proms in the Twenty-First Century

In a video made about the Proms for an internal BBC presentation in 2003, the following message appears on screen: 'The Proms go "Wider still and wider" using the best of broadcasting and new technology to bring Henry Wood's vision of quality classical music for all into a new century.'[41] This ethos has lain at the heart of the development of the brand for the last decade, amplifying Wood's ambitions that the Proms should present the highest quality music to as many people as possible. Alongside these technological innovations, plans have also evolved to expand the Proms' educational activities, reaching out to new generations of potential listeners. One of the flagship events that signalled the importance of outreach work was a concert at the Brixton Academy in 2002 for an audience of schoolchildren, with the BBC Symphony Orchestra conducted by John Adams – an occasion featured on the 2003 video.

During the 2005 season, outreach work moved centre stage: in a day full of concerts celebrating young people and music-making, talented schoolchildren played alongside the BBC Symphony Orchestra in a performance of Respighi's *Pini di Roma*. In workshops run by the ensemble Between the Notes, children also created a new piece that was performed as part of the evening concert, on a stage in the centre of the Prommers' Arena. This piece was an energetic and exciting fusion of 1970s funk and contemporary idioms. Played by the young people themselves and a handful of players from the orchestra, the performance was a powerful symbol of how education work has not simply stood on the fringes of the Proms' activities, but has been a crucial part of its ethos. There are other ways in which this connection with young people has been made: the *Blue Peter* Proms, featuring presenters from the long-running popular BBC children's television show, have been annual events since 1999. In fact, in 2005 the *Blue Peter* Proms was given on two occasions, the only programme to be repeated that season. From 1998 to 2004, for the 'Nation's Favourite Prom', listeners could vote for the pieces they most wanted to hear online or by phone. All of this involvement of audiences with the fabric of the Proms has led to a dissolution of the boundaries between programmers, performers and listeners. It is a natural progression in terms of the Proms experience: the sense of audience involvement and investment in the concert experience is, after all, one of the unique attractions of the Proms, both for those who attend them – especially in the Prommers' arena – and for those who play at them.

The result of such innovations has been the creation of a new set of priorities for the Proms: a continuing move from a top-down model of programming and decision-making to a vision that has resembled a network of connections – between the Director of the Proms, the Proms team, the artists and the Proms marketing and education teams. It is a move towards postmodern diffusion: the way the Proms are disseminated – on radio, on television, online, in the Albert Hall and in the parks – has been considered an inherent part of the season's identity and of the Proms brand. The series now

Children in the audience at the Blue Peter *Prom, 25 July 2004.*

occupies a markedly different position from the one it did when Kenyon became Director in 1996.

What have been the consequences of the ongoing process of rebranding? How will the Proms sustain themselves in the future? One area in which Kenyon has moved in new directions has been the programming of world music, jazz and folk traditions: such events have included the Prom hosted by Julian Joseph that featured Jools Holland and his Rhythm and Blues Orchestra in 2001, concerts of Cuban music and Irish folk music, evenings featuring Baaba Maal from Senegal and Russian traditional choirs, to say nothing of the popular idioms encompassed by the Proms in the Park. This sort of cross-cultural exposure happened in earlier eras too – think of Glock's and Ponsonby's evenings of Indian music, or the brass bands that Drummond programmed in the early 1990s – but there has been a difference in emphasis in the years since 1996. A key sentence in the 2005 marketing states: 'the greatest music festival in the world'. Not 'classical music', still less 'serious music' or 'art music', just an unqualified 'music'. If the consequences of that promise were genuinely to be fulfilled, the Proms would become a totally different festival: however you dress it up, the Proms has in fact always been a celebration of mainstream classical, orchestral music.

The sprinkling of world music concerts into the programmes since 1996 embodies precisely the West's fascinated gaze on the exotic, and is arguably an opportunistic, not to say tokenistic, approach to the practices and repertories of world music performers. In reality, the thread that runs through the programmes compiled under Kenyon's directorship has been one of a reinterpretation and expansion of the existing canon rather than the replacement of orchestral music with an alternative musical culture. The questions for the future are simple yet profound: how long can the rehearsal of canonical

The Senegalese
singer-songwriter
Baaba Maal gives a
late-night Prom,
13 August 2005.

Below *Singer
from the Silk
Road Ensemble,
15 August 2004.*

orchestral works go on? And are there limits to the brave new world of technology? The real test will be how the Proms negotiates the tortuous cultural politics of early twenty-first-century Britain, both within the wider world of classical music, and, after more than eighty years of association with them, within the corridors of the BBC. For the festival's relationship with the national broadcaster has required the Proms to assume a chameleon-like identity, representing the best of serious, classical music at the same time as incarnating the most popular and populist event in the musical calendar. The institutional identities surrounding today's Proms have multiplied – the Promenade Concerts, the BBC, the Last Night of the Proms, the Proms in Park – and yet they coexist. The question is whether the differing entities that now exist under the Proms umbrella can overcome the insecurities that have afflicted many other classical music organizations, and proclaim precisely those values – ultimately, an uncompromising focus on classical music – that are resisted in today's cultural climate. Only then can the Proms continue to stimulate the adventurousness of its audiences for new music and new repertories[42] alongside an enthusiasm for downloads and link-ups between, say, Hyde Park and the Royal Albert Hall. Only then will the Proms live up to the spirit of novelty and experimentation – as well as populism – in which they were conceived.

Planning the Proms Yesterday, Today, Tomorrow

NICHOLAS KENYON

Meticulous preparation: Sir Henry Wood's annotated conducting score of Beethoven's Seventh Symphony.

AS THIS BOOK HAS VIVIDLY DEMONSTRATED, THE Proms represents one of the most thorough and consistent attempts to democratize classical music and to make it part of the mainstream of British cultural life. In mounting an orchestral series of the highest quality and the widest repertory, which was presented in a radically new listening situation in the Queen's Hall and attracted unusually mixed audiences, the founders of the Proms created something very rare: an artistically adventurous yet genuinely popular festival. When the BBC and the Proms came together in 1927, adding to that potent mixture the free availability of the concerts to everyone through broadcasting, they extended the Proms concept, in ways that could not have been foreseen, into something utterly unique, with powerful and far-reaching effects on the development of music in this country.

It is easy to take the success of that century-long process for granted, and this book has shown that many aspects of the conventional story of the Proms need to be re-evaluated and reinterpreted. Much has changed along the way – even the meaning of some of the words that describe the Proms. For Henry Wood, 'quality' would have implied his meticulous preparation of his scores and parts, his efforts to improve the performance standards of his over-worked orchestra, and the highly efficient use he made of every moment of his very limited rehearsal time. Today, 'quality' implies the ability to choose the greatest orchestras of the BBC, Britain and the world to perform at the peak of their powers the music that each of them plays best, in widely varying interpretations. For Henry Wood, 'repertory' meant pushing the boundaries ever outwards, from the popular miniatures with which he started, towards the great symphonies and concertos, and the 'novelties' whose introduction he so prized each season. Today, 'repertory' involves responding to a huge expansion in audience tastes that would have amazed Wood. It encompasses early music, contemporary music, non-Western musics, commissions and new works from around the world, as well as representing a realigned central repertory – in which the pieces that are significant to the various Proms audiences today are not necessarily the same as those that were important in Wood's day. To take one clear generic example, great choral music is now central to the season, whereas in the beginning the emphasis of the Proms was on orchestral music. Even when the BBC first became involved in the Proms, an introductory article (by Rosa Newmarch, reprinted in the 1928 *BBC Handbook*) characterized its audience as wanting 'something more adventurous and sensational in music than oratorio', an audience 'that craved for living forms, energetic movement, colour … this awakening hunger for a vital, secular art' as represented by orchestral music.

Which partner benefited more in the coming together of the Proms and the BBC in 1927 is perhaps open to discussion.[1] But it is because the musical aims of the founders of the Proms on the one hand, and the cultural aims of the nascent BBC on the other, matched so precisely and so naturally that the Proms have continued to develop so dynamically. Of course there have been a few bumpy moments, times when the planning of the Proms felt out of harmony with the tastes of the times and lost touch with its audience, or when the commitment to the Proms was less valued by the BBC (even, during the 1980 Musicians' Union strike, when the Proms was sacrificed to other agendas within the BBC). It is fascinating, though, how secure in the public mind are the guiding principles of the Proms, and how quickly any deviation has been spotted. When Sir Malcolm Sargent told Thomas Russell that 'he no longer regarded it as a responsibility of this series of concerts [the Proms] to present new works', which should instead 'present a balanced series of accepted works', Russell objected in his book *Philharmonic Project*: 'If Sir Malcolm will forgive me, I must say that this discloses a complete failure to understand the meaning of the Proms in relation to our music today.'[2] He might well have referred to the principle enunciated much earlier in the 1913 prospectus: 'Fortunately the Promenade audience has now been educated to such sound and liberal tastes that it is possible to organise programmes of a very high order and to include a good many novelties, provided the experimental note is not over-emphasised.' The ability of the Proms to be renewed without abandoning any of its central principles has been decisively aided by the series' increasingly secure place within the BBC, as well as its ability immediately to call on and take advantage of technological innovation – first radio, then television, the internet, audio-on-demand, big screens and free-to-air digital services. Thus the Proms tradition has been reinterpreted at the same time as the BBC's continuing role as a cultural patron has been developed.

BBC studio manager Philip Burwell in the old BBC control room on the balcony level of the Royal Albert Hall, c. 1988.

It may seem (at best) inappropriate or (at worst) a conflict of interest for the present Director of the Proms to reflect on the themes of this book. But it is striking how common the problems and the challenges have been across the years. Wood's strongly educative intention to broaden the repertory[3] involved a very deliberate placing of innovation in context – new works heard against the background of those symphonic masterpieces that enabled the audience to accept what was unusual. Pierre Boulez's supremely characterful Prom programmes of the later 1960s and 1970s did exactly the same for a different generation, except that the new was now placed against a completely different 'core' repertory, not of the nineteenth century – Beethoven, Brahms and Tchaikovsky – but of the 'classic' twentieth century – Stravinsky, Schoenberg, Debussy, Ravel and Bartók.[4] And so our understanding of the centre of gravity in the orchestral repertory subtly shifted (as indeed did Boulez's personal repertory: some decades later it now includes Janáček, although still no Shostakovich). Every Proms director must work with an acute sense of the history that underlies the series, and of the traditions that are valuable; but equally every director must respond to the imperative for development and change. Every director who has begun to change elements of the mixture does so with a sense of conviction mixed with caution, but is alert to the fact that potential audiences are certainly changing even faster.

Those remarkable audiences, originally drawn together by Newman and Wood and somehow recreating themselves from generation to generation in

Precision and power: Pierre Boulez, rehearsing the National Youth Orchestra for its Prom, 23 August 1971.

Cultural synthesis: Daniel Barenboim applauds members of the West-Eastern Divan Orchestra, 22 August 2003.

the unforgettable arena of the Royal Albert Hall, are the Proms' most valuable asset; it is vital to stay engaged with them, as the original promoters of the series did, leading and developing their listening habits while responding to their changing tastes. The planners of the Proms have never ignored audiences, never imposed repertory in a wholly top-down manner. As the story of programme-building traced through this book makes abundantly clear, Wood was acutely conscious of what worked and what did not, what could be repeated and what (Bruckner was an example) should not be risked again. William Glock always considered how the adventurous music he programmed could attract an audience and make sense for them, placing Schoenberg with Beethoven, Carter with Bach. The role of the artistic director is to sense the taste of the times and push it imaginatively forward, venturing further out to sea, as Glock once put it, than their own personal preferences might take them.

* * * *

The Proms' planning process is in some ways not so different now from in the past. My favourite recipe remains that of W. W. Thompson, working with Edward Clark for Wood in the 1920s: the first day was spent sharpening pencils, followed by a visit to Prado's for a bottle of Châteauneuf-du-Pape.[5] Glock still planned in pencil ('he has two big sheets on which he begins to fill in all the details, but they become so threadbare with rubbings-out that he may run through several sets', reported *Music and Musicians* in 1967), whereas we now plan on the computer (and do it many times before arriving at the final version, as the annual pile of printouts of the Proms planning drafts demonstrates); but his aims were very similar to ours. Like Wood and his successors, we mix the current central repertory with new works and rarities in an ever-changing balance that aims to move, stimulate, educate and inspire. Each concert must work on its own, but must also add up to a season that is greater than the sum of its parts and which offers some thematic, conceptual coherence. There must be a balance of repertory, although the available range is now so very great that there will inevitably be omissions each season. 'Creative unbalance' was a principle espoused by Glock; we recently shocked some by having one season without any Vaughan Williams (though his anniversary would be celebrated in 2008), and rather shocked ourselves by ending up with a season devoid of any Schubert a year after his bicentenary celebrations.

The balance between popularity and innovation in the story of the Proms is a continually fluctuating one: because of the support of the BBC, the Proms have usually (in fact always, perhaps apart from the early 1920s and the 1950s) been more adventurous than commercially-based concert series; but equally the BBC has had a continuing desire for the Proms to be successful and serve a large public. This was demonstrated especially when the concerts moved to the larger Royal Albert Hall during the war and ticket income initially soared; nevertheless, this short-term financial success was immediately sacrificed by the BBC to the challenge of improving the quality of the concerts by employing more orchestras and providing more rehearsal.[6] The financial equation changed immediately, and as the range of orchestras and complex repertory has continued to expand, so too has the call on the BBC's licence fee. The Proms benefits from being within the BBC because of the extensive and ever-increasing broadcasting opportunities that result from the season; in return, the Proms plays a key part in the BBC's public service role as a cultural patron. In all decades, directors have had to argue the case of the Proms as a financial need within the BBC, but with consistent audience success and international profile has come a recognition of the Proms' crucial value to the Corporation.

How much does success in audience numbers matter? As every concert promoter knows, there is short-term success and there is long-term success in developing audiences, and the two do not necessarily match. ('I have been to various Promenade concerts,' wrote Philip Heseltine wearily to Delius in 1914, 'but as a whole the programmes have been worse than usual and the audiences as a result proportionately larger.'[7]) While a desire for only short-term audience numbers would inevitably lead to a narrowing of the repertory, as has happened with some financially less well-supported organizations, the Proms has always taken the longer view, believing that real audience development involves expanding rather than contracting the available range of music. Still, the Proms is a popular series of concerts in a huge hall for a mixed audience, many of whom are encountering the music for the first time. So the BBC always insisted, from the 1930s onwards, that the Proms, as a leading festival of orchestral music, should be rather more mainstream in outlook than the BBC

Symphony Orchestra's own winter season of symphony concerts. I personally envy festivals such as Aldeburgh and Cheltenham their ability to experiment and take risks for an audience that trusts their taste.[8] Fortunately today, because of the consistent support of the BBC, the Proms can have it both ways – including challenging repertory, new works, leading artists and big occasions while remaining, because of its extraordinary reach and visibility through broadcasting, an overwhelmingly popular series of concerts that brings wide audiences to music they might not have thought of encountering.

In the past, BBC programmers perhaps collaborated less than we do today. 'The first 18 concerts are easy enough, and I put them down with a wild flourish in September. Then the problems begin', said Glock in the *Music and Musicians* article quoted above. I could not do that today. Whereas in the past planners might simply write down the pieces they wanted and hand out the programmes to hopefully servile orchestras, now everything is a matter of conversation and debate, suiting the themes and the works that are in our mind to conductors, soloists and orchestras. We plan much further in advance than the September after the season ends: two or three seasons in advance as far as major projects, conductors and touring orchestras are concerned, rather later for finalized programmes, soloists and late-night concerts. I keep a small alphabetical notebook of works we might want to programme (it currently starts with Adams *El Niño*, Arne *Alfred* … and it ends with Zelenka and Zemlinsky), and our artistic administrator makes copious lists of thematic works and other priorities. But seasons may go by before exactly the right occasion arises for including a particular work, and there are many questions to be asked. Is the piece already prominent in the previous London season? Do we have the right artists available? Is there a programme that provides the right context? Can we afford the necessary rehearsal? Balancing the repertory across a season is one huge challenge; balancing it across different seasons is an equally important task these days, when the idea of a 'Proms repertory' is embedded in both our minds and those of the audience. Only Beethoven's Ninth and the end of the Last Night are canonical, fixed each season; there are some classic concertos that recur frequently; and these days we expect a twentieth-century classic such as *The Rite of Spring* to occur most seasons. But how often should we programme the Verdi Requiem or Mahler's Second Symphony, great pieces that artists always wish to perform and audiences to hear? The question of repertory cannot be considered on its own: the critical matter of suiting the right performers to the right music is always at the top of our minds. There is no virtue in forcing artists to perform music with which they are not in sympathy: we can suggest and persuade, but the greatest experiences result from a fusion of artist, work and performance.

It is easy to forget that the international nature of the Proms is a development of the last forty years, becoming a main feature really only in the last two decades, during which the Berlin and Vienna Philharmonics and the major American orchestras have become regular visitors; as a result the programmes for the big touring orchestras need to be coordinated with other summer

festivals such as Salzburg, Lucerne and Edinburgh. In a complete change from the Proms half a century ago, we are inundated with offers from visiting orchestras and ensembles to appear, since the Proms is such a visible platform internationally and its audiences warmly welcome new and rare music. Another striking difference in recent years is that with changes in the economic climate, the oft-remarked dominance of the record companies in determining orchestras' programming plans has completely disappeared; the live event is becoming once more the focus of their artistic attention, and ensembles are generously keen to suit their ideas to the Proms' plans.

Freedom in planning and collaboration in the devising of themes is greatest with the BBC's own performing groups, of which the BBC Symphony Orchestra is the backbone of the Proms season; it is a wonderful artistic resource, but one that it is important not to overuse, since all its concerts must also be events

in their own right. Thematic planning has been an adventure of recent years, simply to energize and focus the organization of what might otherwise be a dizzyingly diverse repertory each season. The themes often arise as a development of existing plans: a collection of pieces to do with the interaction of music and politics, the influence of folk music on Western repertory, fairy tales in music, the sea, Bohemian music, or focuses on individual composers like Haydn, Bartók, Mozart or Shostakovich – all simply help to draw audiences through the season, linking concert-going with radio listening and television viewing, so as to give each season of the Proms a strong, differentiated character.

* * * *

The ever-changing balance of the Proms repertory, highlighted throughout this book, is a vast and fascinating subject worthy of a full-scale study. As Chapter 1 brilliantly makes clear, cultural and economic change, consumer behaviour and musical developments intersect in this process with the individual tastes of conductors, soloists and administrators, creating a very complex pattern of influences that it would be unwise to oversimplify. It is worth looking briefly at two different aspects of programme-building: the first table tracks a single musical form across the whole history of the Proms, while the second takes four equally spaced seasons to illustrate developments in the repertory.[9]

First is an examination of symphonies across the years, partly provoked by Adrian Boult's waspish complaint in 1946 that 'the symphonic aspect of the programmes was rather overdone this year'. Table 1 (pp. 266–7) shows an intriguing illustration of related phenomena: the rise and fall of the symphony itself as an ingredient in the Proms repertory, and the rise and fall of the reputations of various composers of symphonies throughout the same period. The trajectories are not the same. Symphonies were not especially important in the earliest repertory of the Proms, and like so much else, the educative nature of their introduction has become somewhat novelized over time. 'It was a bold venture in 1895 ... it meant years of hard work, and I quite admit, a certain amount of cunning ... We had to go slow at first, cornet solos, that sort of thing', said Henry Wood with a chuckle in a late BBC interview.[10] But that is exactly how popular concerts were then; Wood moved with the times and with his audiences to increase the quotient of serious pieces.

Thus from very slow beginnings, when the repertory was dominated by Wagner's bleeding chunks and countless smaller items, Beethoven, Tchaikovsky and Schubert became significant as symphonists. The symphony quickly became increasingly important to the Proms as the musical substance of the programmes grew. As early as 1902, with a change in promoter for the Proms to the German-born financier and serious music-lover Edgar Speyer,[11] a new approach led to the inclusion of more symphonies, and their number grew strongly in the following decades, as Table 1 shows (Beethoven symphonies never had fewer than forty performances in any five-year period – until 1965–70). Wood experimented with Mahler, introducing the First and Fourth Symphonies to the Proms but they did not establish themselves; in the 1920s, he systematically explored many symphonies of Haydn and Mozart (that was an individual enthusiasm rather than a general trend, however). Brahms gradually became a staple at this time, with a rise to a regular twenty performances every five years (all four symphonies every year), followed by Sibelius during 1935–40 – an example of a composer whose symphonies, like those of Vaughan Williams, joined the Proms repertory as they were actually being written.

The peak for symphonic repertory in the Proms came after Wood, in the comparatively atrophied programmes of the late 1940s and the 1950s, which religiously featured complete Beethoven and Brahms cycles, alongside plenty of Dvořák, Tchaikovsky and Sibelius. This was the heyday of the conservative Malcolm Sargent, who did however espouse some of the emerging symphonies of Shostakovich. Then in the 1960s, when William Glock took over, the whole repertory expanded hugely and many more choral and non-standard works were included: the list of 'First Performances at the Proms' in the annual prospectuses for those years,[12] ranging from Bach Passions and the Mozart Requiem to Schoenberg, Varèse and Messiaen, makes almost unbelievable reading. The symphony as an element in the programmes began to level off; Sibelius and Tchaikovsky were marginalized. From 1960 Bruckner, whose Seventh Symphony Wood had performed once and never again, and Mahler, whom the BBC had championed on the radio after the war but was slow to gain acceptance in the concert hall, became increasingly important: surprisingly, the very first appearance at the Proms of Mahler's Second Symphony was the incandescent performance under Stokowski in 1963.[13] The zenith of this trend was John Drummond's complete Mahler cycle in 1995.

For us today, symphonies are a crucial, vital element in many programmes, but they take their place along much other major repertory. The Proms makes a determined effort to introduce works that for one reason or another have escaped audiences, drawing on a thousand years of Western musical history, and we have found over nine hundred of them in the last decade, ranging from large twentieth-century oratorios to tiny medieval motets. But symphonies are still central, especially those by Mahler and Bruckner, which sound so well in the hall. Beethoven is still a reliable draw, as is Brahms to a lesser extent; Sibelius is making a big comeback alongside Nielsen, while the single most noticeable change in the symphonic repertory in recent years has been the rise and rise, with conductors, orchestras and audiences alike, of Shostakovich. Compare the hierarchy of popular composers in the Proms' first decade (p. 69) with that in the Proms' second half century, 1950–94, where the top-ten list reads, in order of number of performances (of all works, not just symphonies): Beethoven, Mozart, Bach, Tchaikovsky, Brahms, Elgar, Stravinsky, Haydn, Wagner and Berlioz.

These changes in taste are formed by a complex interaction of what we want to programme, what conductors want to conduct, and what audiences want to listen to – and what is going on in the rest of the musical world. What orchestras are playing elsewhere, what's on the radio, what's on CD, and maybe soon what's available for downloading onto iPods: none of these things happens in isolation. Gradually, inexorably, taste shifts.

* * * *

A second, complementary exercise is to consider the character of individual programmes, which is much more difficult to summarize fairly. This book has delineated the development of the Proms very much in terms of the changes from conductor to conductor, from director to director. But one observation might be that the two greatest shifts in the style of Proms programmes took place during, not between, two regimes. Henry Wood's programmes moved quickly from the miscellaneous bran-tub approach with which he began – with short items, sometimes accompanied on the piano, jostling together – towards a series that explored seriously the great symphonies and concertos, a change that was stimulated both by the educative intent of the Proms and by the influences of its successive promoters. And from the late 1960s to the early 1970s, William Glock (who, as is abundantly clear from Chapter 5, was no manic modernist but an eclectic planner of amazingly wide taste) moved from the multi-work programmes of his early years to the much more streamlined, bold, high-impact, one- or two-work programmes that provide the template for today's Proms.[14]

This trajectory may be illustrated by looking at selected examples of Proms programming in 1970, 1980, 1990 and 2000: these seasons were chosen at random, but not entirely so, since they each come from well into the periods directed respectively by William Glock, Robert Ponsonby, John Drummond and myself, and show the character of each very clearly. A sample of four programmes given by the BBC Symphony Orchestra in each of these seasons is shown in Table 2 (p. 272); these are not intended to be representative, but to hint at something of the changing shape of the programming and especially the inclusion of new work.

In 1970 there are Glock programmes for the Proms that showed the influence of his early Third Programme Invitation Concerts, for example interleaving Bach Orchestral Suites with Elliott Carter's Double Concerto and music from medieval Florence.[15] Programmes were substantially longer than now, adding to their richness: Elgar's *The Dream of Gerontius* was preceded by Byrd motets, Bruckner's Eighth Symphony by a Mozart Serenade.

TABLE 1 Symphonies at the Proms 1895–2005

The numbers of symphonies by individual composers performed in five-year periods during the history of the Proms. Along the bottom of the graph, 1895 indicates the total for 1895–9, 1900 the total for 1900–04, etc. On the side axis, the figures relate to all symphonies by that composer: for example, twenty for Beethoven in 1895–9 means that in those five seasons there was a total of twenty performances of any of his symphonies (including repeat performances in any season but not part-performances of individual movements).

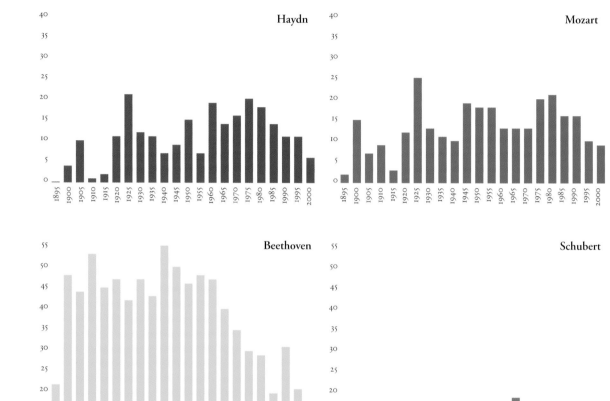

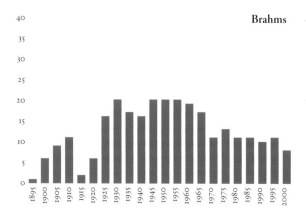

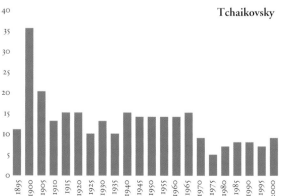

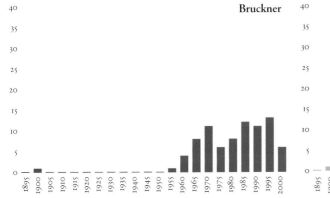

Bruckner

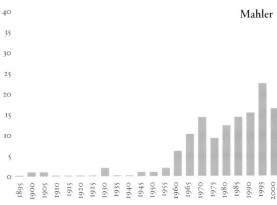

Mahler

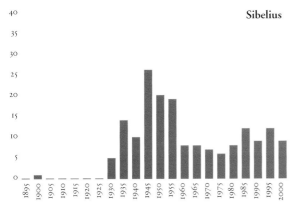

Sibelius

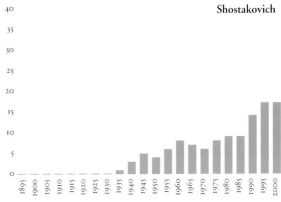

Shostakovich

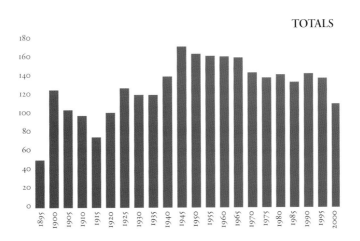

TOTALS

New to the Proms were, among other things, two acts of Rameau's *Hippolyte et Aricie*, Weill's *Der Lindberghflug*, and the famous late-night concert by The Soft Machine (preceded by a Tim Souster première). There was also an increase in the number of big one-work evenings: Beethoven's *Missa solemnis*, opera from Glyndebourne and Covent Garden, a concert performance of Beethoven's *Leonore*, and a bold, Friday First Night of Messiaen's *La Transfiguration de Notre Seigneur Jésus-Christ*. The shape of the 1970 season had other determining factors: the BBC Symphony Orchestra gave twenty-six of the fifty-three concerts, several on successive days and in one case five concerts in a week, including the first complete British performance of Ives's Fourth Symphony, an extraordinary workload. There was only one orchestra from abroad – the Amsterdam Concertgebouw, which gave four concerts. New music was perhaps less prominent than Glock's reputation might suggest: five new works, by Malcolm Arnold, Elliott Carter, Sebastian Forbes, Elisabeth Lutyens and Tim Souster. Of the fifty-three concerts, just eight were televised. There were eight Beethoven symphonies, two of Brahms, two each by Bruckner, Dvořák, Mahler and Tchaikovsky. The Last Night omitted the original Henry Wood *Sea Songs* in favour of a new Malcolm Arnold Fantasy. Glock aptly commented in the prospectus: 'Two main features of the present-day Proms are their greater historical range and a freer composition of the individual concerts.'

A decade on, in 1980, the template used in Robert Ponsonby's time had undergone important developments. The BBC Symphony Orchestra's contribution was now a more realistic nineteen concerts (or would have been, had there not been the Musicians' Union strike that year) out of a planned fifty-seven concerts. The BBC's regional orchestras, represented in 1970 by only one concert by the BBC Northern, were now a key part of the season, and the other UK orchestras were more fully represented. The Concertgebouw was back, still the only orchestra from abroad, although the Toronto Mendelssohn Choir also came to sing. In repertory there was much innovation in early music, reflecting a flourishing revival (there were modern premières of works by Joan Cererols, Alessandro Striggio, Dufay and his contemporaries, as well as pieces by Bach and Handel). One week saw the premières of Rubbra's Symphony No. 11 and Tippett's Triple Concerto; these were the only first performances of new works. (There were also planned British premières of existing new pieces by Harrison Birtwistle, Paul Patterson and David Lumsdaine that fell victim to the MU strike.) The shape of the programmes looks much more familiar to us today:[16] sometimes a new work was placed first, followed by a popular concerto and a symphony; but echoing Proms tradition, Ponsonby complemented Elliott Carter's Piano Concerto and music by Ives with a first half of Bach – played by one of the emerging British period-instrument ensembles that were to become increasingly important to the season. This year there were seven Beethoven symphonies and four of his piano concertos, three Brahms symphonies and two of his concertos, but only one Sibelius symphony.

In 1990 the most striking aspect of John Drummond's wide-ranging season was that it had taken on a wholly new international character, each visiting orchestra bringing something characteristic and interesting: the Concertgebouw (yet again) included Berio's *Rendering* (on surviving fragments of a Schubert symphony) under Chailly; the Swedish Radio Symphony Orchestra with Salonen performed a Sandström première and Mahler's Seventh. The Cleveland Orchestra under Dohnányi brought the Lutosławski Concerto for Orchestra, and juxtaposed Schoenberg's Piano Concerto, played by Mitsuko Uchida, with Bruckner's Seventh. Seiji Osawa's Saito Kinen Orchestra came from even further afield. There was a conscious sequence of major events at the start of the season: Mahler's Second Symphony, Handel's *Belshazzar* and Tippett's *The Ice Break*; and later in the season, Janáček from Glyndebourne and a pioneering period-instrument performance of Mozart's *Die Zauberflöte* under Roger Norrington. Late-night concerts were for the first time all in the Royal Albert Hall, following the main evening concerts, thus enabling sixty-six concerts in the season (of which the BBC SO gave sixteen). By this point of his directorship, Drummond had left behind thematic strands, but there were many big events – Britten's *War Requiem*, Günter Wand in Bruckner's Fifth, Gluck's *Orfeo ed Euridice* with Gardiner – and juxtapositions such as Libor Pešek in Beethoven's 'Eroica' Symphony and Janáček's *Glagolitic Mass*, and Rozhdestvensky conducting the Dvořák Cello Concerto and the Berlioz *Te Deum*. Two important, diverse strands first appeared – non-classical Western repertory, and the featuring of young performers – which have subsequently been developed further: the London All Stars Steelband gave a Prom at lunchtime on Bank Holiday Monday in Kensington Gardens (though this was not broadcast; it was followed at 3.00 pm by a chamber music concert played by the Beaux Arts Trio in the Royal Albert

Three Prom Directors (left to right): Sir William Glock, Sir John Drummond and Robert Ponsonby in the Henry Cole Room of the Royal Albert Hall.

Hall); and children were featured in a staging of Britten's *Noye's Fludde*. The standard repertory was still there: eight Beethoven symphonies, three by Brahms, but only one each by Sibelius and Tchaikovsky, while Table 2 shows how some of the new works by Poul Ruders, Anthony Payne and Roger Marsh were skilfully programmed in mixed contexts. Among the premières, the first performance of James Macmillan's *The Confession of Isabel Gowdie* made the biggest impact. In his preface to the 1990 Proms guide, Drummond put his finger on the 'extraordinary atmosphere which is characteristic of the Proms. This mood of keen expectation and relaxed enjoyment is something we might be tempted to take for granted … we should guard it jealously, because it is, in fact, rare.'[17]

In 2000, my fifth season as Proms Director, the season aimed to highlight youth and make a strong statement about the future of music to mark the turn of the millennium. It featured several major youth orchestras, and there was a collaboration for the Berlioz Requiem under Colin Davis between conservatory students from London and from Paris. The Proms Millennium Youth Day brought together a whole range of youth ensembles – orchestras, jazz, brass bands, wind ensembles – in a day of music-making that culminated in a massive performance of Walton's *Belshazzar's Feast*. This was a new concert format, and there was more experimentation elsewhere in the planning: a new commission for several youth music groups brought together pieces by crossover composers Nitin Sawhney, Alec Roth and Peter McGarr, which were combined in performance by composer Gary Carpenter and pianist Joanna MacGregor. As part of the continuing increase in the number of visiting ensembles, there were ten orchestras from abroad, from the Berlin Philharmonic with Claudio Abbado to the San Francisco Symphony under Michael Tilson Thomas, as well as many other ensembles and early music groups. For the first time since 1970 there was a new pattern to the televised First Night – a choral work in the

second half and a popular first-half concerto. Other major BBC commissions were from Mark-Anthony Turnage, Jonathan Harvey, Rhian Samuel (for the BBC National Orchestra of Wales) and James Dillon (for the BBC Scottish);[18] there were also Bach orchestrations for the 250th anniversary of his death. New to the Proms, in a year that featured music inspired by man's relationship with God, marking two millennia since Christ's birth, were Mendelssohn's *St Paul* and Schmidt's *Book of the Seven Seals*; in contrast, for the anniversary of Kurt Weill's birth were his opera *The Rise and Fall of the City of Mahagonny* and *Street Scenes*. With this plethora of new repertory, what was omitted? There were only four Beethoven symphonies and only one by Brahms, but four by Mahler and six by Shostakovich. There were seventy-two main concerts, plus the now-established weekly Proms Chamber Music of eight concerts and numerous extra events, including the popular Proms in the Park and a Young Composers' Competition. My own statement in the freshly redesigned Proms Guide was: 'What is the future of music? It is nothing if there are not new performers to excite us, new composers prepared to push the boundaries of music forwards, and new audiences with open ears to listen. In this vital process, it is up to the Proms to lead and inspire …'

TABLE 2 Some sample Prom programmes by the BBC Symphony Orchestra:
1970, 1980, 1990, 2000

1970 (Proms director: William Glock)

21 July Colin Davis
Piano Trio in B flat major	Schubert
Tristan und Isolde – Act 3	Wagner

10 August Pierre Boulez
Suite from *The Firebird* (1910)	Stravinsky
Piano Concerto No. 2	Bartók
Ballet: *Daphnis et Chloé*	Ravel

4 September Pierre Boulez
Three Nocturnes	Debussy
Et exspecto resurrectionem mortuorum	Messiaen
The Rite of Spring	Stravinsky

8 September Colin Davis/Norman Del Mar
Symphony No. 40 in G minor	Mozart
Piano Concerto No. 4 in G major	Beethoven
*The Essence of Our Happinesses**	Elisabeth Lutyens
Fantasia and Fugue in C minor (organ solo)	Bach

1980 (Proms director: Robert Ponsonby)

7 August John Pritchard
Symphony No. 4	Mahler
Poèmes pour Mi	Messiaen
La valse	Ravel

25 August Mark Elder
Praeludium for brass, bells and percussion	Tippett
Ringed by the Flat Horizon	George Benjamin
Cello Concerto	Delius
Belshazzar's Feast	Walton

2 September Gennadi Rozhdestvensky
Symphony No. 1 in F minor	Shostakovich
Francesca da Rimini (opera in one act)	Rachmaninoff

6 September Gennadi Rozhdestvensky
Symphony No. 9 in C major	Schubert
Spring Symphony	Britten

1990 (Proms director: John Drummond)

24 July Andrew Davis
Symphony No. 2 in D major	Beethoven
*Time's Arrow**	Anthony Payne
Violin Concerto in B minor	Elgar

31 August Lothar Zagrosek
Prélude à l'après-midi d'un faune	Debussy
Shéhérazade	Ravel
Symphony No. 5 in B flat major	Schubert
*Stepping Out**	Roger Marsh
La valse	Ravel

3 September Michael Schøenwandt
Tapiola	Sibelius
Piano Concerto No. 3	Bartók
Symphony No. 1, *'Himmelhoch jauchzend – zum Tode betrübt'**	Poul Ruders
Le roi Lear, grand overture	Berlioz

2000 (Proms director: Nicholas Kenyon)

19 July Andrew Davis
Symphonies of wind instruments (1947)	Stravinsky
*Fractured Lines**	Mark-Anthony Turnage
Rhapsody in Blue	Gershwin
Daphnis et Chloé – Suite No. 2	Ravel

29 July Donald Runnicles
Symphony*	Robin Holloway
Die Walküre – Act 3	Wagner

2 August Jac van Steen
Prelude and Fugue in C minor (organ solo)	Bach
*Mothers Shall Not Cry**	Jonathan Harvey
Concerto in A minor for violin and cello	Brahms
Prelude and Fugue in E flat major, 'St Anne'	Bach, orch. Schoenberg

1 September Ingo Metzmacher
Piano Concerto No. 3 in C minor	Beethoven
Symphony No. 9 (UK première)	Hans Werner Henze

* BBC commission

What broadcasting created for the Proms was, and is, something extraordinary and precious. Through being relayed to a wider public than those who were concert-goers, the season, along with many other sporting, royal and similar occasions originally designed for a specialist audience, became part of British life. Through broadcasting, the Proms became one of the landmarks of the year, alongside Wimbledon, the Service of Nine Lessons and Carols at King's College, the FA Cup Final, and other events that became available to all. The media historian Paddy Scannell has written memorably that these 'events became, and have remained, punctual moments in a shared national life. Broadcasting created, in effect, a new calendar of national events. Unobtrusively threaded through the continuing daily output was the cyclical reproduction, year in year out, of an orderly and regular progression of festivities, celebrations and remembrances that marked the unfolding of the broadcast year ... this calendar became the expressive register of a common, corporate public life that persists to this day.'[19]

We need look no further than this for the real reason why the Proms, and its televised Last Night in particular, has become so deeply embedded in our national culture and why attempts to change the Last Night, or even to criticize it, rouse such fury. Yet tradition must be refreshed and renewed, for otherwise it will stultify. Our central commitment is still to bring great music to everyone, and it is sometimes difficult to remember how controversial an undertaking that was when the BBC took over the Proms in the 1927. 'It was never meant that the BBC should have the trusteeship of large sums of public

Television goes digital: Charles Hazlewood (right) interviews conductor Christoph Eschenbach for BBC4 TV, 4 September 2006.

money', railed the Hallé's conductor Sir Hamilton Harty in 1930, 'in order to use this money to crush and imperil public enterprise' – words echoed by the BBC's commercial rivals today. But broadcast music changed our culture for ever, and – surely now we can be quite clear about it – unquestionably for the better. I have always loved the words of the historian L. C. B. Seaman, reflecting on the process by which segregated cultures for the few became mass culture for the many: 'Much that was disseminated by the new processes was ephemeral or bad; but the hostility to mass culture so frequently expressed from the 1920s onwards was often the result of a too narrow educational system, a too early hardening of the spiritual arteries, and, above all, of an ingrained distaste for the masses as such.'[20]

* * * *

Eighty years since the Proms and the BBC came together, and over a century since the season began, the Proms remain, to a perhaps surprising extent, unique. (Pierre Boulez remarked in a radio interview, 'It is an eccentricity of London to have that much audience during the summer, and a really joyful eccentricity I must say.'[21]) On one level that uniqueness was achieved by the devastatingly simple stroke of turning on its head the conventional arrangement of the audience in a concert hall, clearing the floor for standing and giving Promenaders the key place both in the layout of the Hall and in the relationship between audience and performers.[22] This crucial aspect of the Proms survived the move from the Queen's Hall to the Royal Albert Hall and is the hallmark of the series – and has been surprisingly little imitated elsewhere. The circular hall gives a remarkable sense of the audience and

Starting young: children sampling instruments during the Proms Out and About event at the Brixton Academy, 2003.

Inspiring children: Bobby McFerrin improvising with members of the African Children's Choir at a Prom, 7 August 2005.

performers being part of a shared community, gathered together in the act of making and listening to music. The intensity of the experience is almost palpable, a demonstration of how active listening can be – an aspect of the Proms that has remained constant through its history.

Henry Wood said in a war-time Last Night message to his audience: 'I am amazed at your stillness and how you listen, and what is more encouraging is that youth is the predominant character of this audience each year.'[23] That commitment to youth is now at the top of our priorities in a world where young people have a very different relationship with classical music – both in audiences and as performers. We face a fundamental challenge: because of rapid cultural change, today's young audiences no longer necessarily come to classical music in the same way as previous generations, who were brought by mothers and fathers, aunts and uncles; nor because of educational changes do they all encounter it naturally at school. Hence the development of what may seem a novel emphasis on outreach work and young audiences at the Proms in recent seasons. The creation of the *Blue Peter* Proms, full of high-impact short pieces, snappily presented; 'Proms Out and About', bringing hundreds of children to the Brixton Academy, jumping and clapping in counterpoint to John Adams's *Short Ride in a Fast Machine*; the Proms Young Composers' Competition, in which teenagers can hear their new works, written just a few weeks previously, played by professionals – these are deliberate innovations to stimulate the interest of new young audiences. And this now extends to young performers: we wanted to bring young players to London and enable them to

Handing on the tradition: Anoushka Shankar, who appeared with her father Ravi Shankar in a sold-out Prom, 3 August 2005.

play alongside professionals. That was the origin of a project in the 2005 Proms that brought four groups of young players from around the country to perform alongside the BBC Symphony Orchestra and to create their own remarkable improvised piece, *Invisible Lines*.[24] From the participatory Choral Day in 1999 has grown a vocal day in the 2006 Proms, with 'rabble' choirs taking part in the creation of new choral work by Orlando Gough.

Because of its sheer visibility, the Proms has become a symbolic institution for the revitalization of classical music, and at the heart of that ethos has been the continuing development of the concerts' accessibility through technological change. New technology has led to the big screens of Proms in the Park, uniting the singing crowds in England, Scotland, Wales and Northern Ireland on the Last Night through television; it has encouraged audiences to phone in a vote for their favourite overture or aria and have it played in the Albert Hall, to email in their comments and reviews to the Proms message-board, or to receive a text message saying who is appearing on at the Proms that night. None of that was possible a decade ago. Others may have differing views as to whether these initiatives are worthwhile, but at the Proms such public service innovations offer the means to reach audiences who in today's increasingly crowded media environment might never have thought of encountering these concerts. Whether, having experienced them, they wish to return or to move from the fun of Proms in the Park to the challenges of the Royal Albert Hall is up to them; but contact has been made. Websites, big screens and interactivity are a natural development of everything the Proms has ever stood for.

Equally, there are many aspects of the Proms that will never change: the commitment to informal, unelitist music-making at the highest level; the hush of the crowded hall as it waits for a great conductor; the intense concentration as a masterwork unfolds; the roar of approval after a great performance of Beethoven's Ninth, or Mahler's Fifth, or Shostakovich's Eighth, or Messiaen's *Turangalîla*. An ever-expanding range of great masterpieces will be reinterpreted and renewed by musicians each season. The interaction of past and present is remarkable: a balance between the long traditions of concert-giving that the Proms did so much to formulate and the imperative of cultural change.

As luck would have it, the Proms is now organized where it began. Just across the road from BBC Broadcasting House, on the south-east side of All Souls, Langham Place, the BBC's Henry Wood House is an ugly postwar building that stands exactly on the site of the Queen's Hall. There is a plaque on a pillar commemorating the Hall, and round the corner, down a small alley off Great Portland Street, you can just see very dimly the words QUEEN'S HALL on a back entrance. Doubtless these relics are ignored by most people who pass by. But the legacy of Robert Newman and Henry Wood endures, and the spirit of the Proms is flourishing: its values and principles remain, their expression transformed by the new world of the twenty-first century. That, surely, is exactly what the founders of the Proms would have wished.

Towards the future: Jiří Bělohlávek, the new Chief Conductor of the BBC Symphony Orchestra, conducting the opening night of the 2006 BBC Proms season, 14 July 2006.

A Proms Chronology

1893 The Queen's Hall opens in November with Robert Newman as its manager; Newman helps run Promenade concerts at Covent Garden conducted by Frederic Cowen.

1894 The Philharmonic Society transfers its concert series to the Queen's Hall; Newman becomes the Hall's lessee.

1895 Newman launches Promenade concerts at the Queen's Hall funded by George Cathcart and conducted by Henry Wood.

1896 Newman begins funding the Proms; 'Animated pictures' shown in the interval and after concerts, at additional cost to the standard ticket price.

1898 Mondays established as Wagner Night.

1900 Season includes a 'Thanksgiving Concert to Celebrate the Victory of the Troops' in South Africa.

1901 Elgar's *Pomp and Circumstance* March No. 1 given a double encore at its Proms première.

1902 Over-extension bankrupts Newman; Edgar Speyer leads syndicate to finance the Queen's Hall Orchestra (QHO); Chappell & Co., under William Boosey, becomes the Hall's lessee.

1903 First English performance of Mahler's First Symphony.

1904 Wood forbids the use of deputies, 40 players leave in protest; Debussy's *Prélude à l'après-midi d'un faune* first performed in Britain, under Wood.

1905 Wood arranges his *Fantasia on British Sea Songs* (with solo spots for orchestral players).

1906 The impact of Sibelius' *Finlandia* encourages repeat at the last night.

1908 Rosa Newmarch takes up role as programme-note writer for the Proms; Parisian conductor Edouard Colonne deputizes for part of the season in Wood's absence.

1912 Proms première of Schoenberg's *Five Orchestral Pieces*.

1913 Wood admits six women players to the QHO but excludes them from the Proms, considering the season too strenuous.

1915 Anti-German sentiment forces Speyer out, but the Proms (now kept afloat by Chappell's) continue to programme German music; QHO renamed 'New Queen's Hall Orchestra'; finances force the discontinuation of the season ticket (until 1927).

1916 Twelve women orchestral members play in the Proms season, replacing men on active service.

1918 Public pressure helps Wood decide to turn down the conductorship of the Boston Symphony Orchestra.

1921 The unknown Malcolm Sargent conducts his *An Impression on a Windy Day*.

1924 King George V and Queen Mary attend a Prom; in the face of financial pressures on Chappell's, Newman and Wood each secretly approach Reith about possible BBC interest.

1926 Newman dies; W. W. ('Tommy') Thompson takes over management of New QHO.

1927 Financial pressure obliges Chappell's to withdraw; the BBC contracts Wood, gains microphone access to the Queen's Hall and takes on the running of the Proms; the first Prom is broadcast on 13 August; the season ticket returns.

1929 The Proms are promoted to the 'Ordinary Listener' with five broadcasts each week and coverage in the *Radio Times*; the Thursday British composer nights have poor attendance.

1930 The new BBC Symphony Orchestra (BBC SO), still in the process of being formed, becomes the Proms orchestra.

1931 Broadcast Prom performances of Webern's *Passacaglia* and six of Berg's *Seven Early Songs*, the first time these pieces are heard in Britain.

1935 Marie Wilson appointed leader of the BBC SO for the Proms seasons.

1936 The BBC begins to air individual works, rather than full halves of concerts, to allow greater variety in its evening schedules.

1937 Refurbishment and redecoration of the Queen's Hall with improved seating and ventilation.

1938 Wood's Golden Jubilee as a conductor is celebrated; Wood's first broadcast speech; Proms are transmitted on the television sound wavelength.

1939 The season abruptly ends on 1 September (on the outbreak of the war) when the BBC withdraws use of the BBC SO, which is evacuated to Bristol.

1940 Truncated season (10 Aug–7 Sept); the Proms are sponsored by Keith Douglas instead of the BBC and fronted by the Royal Philharmonic Society; no Proms are broadcast.

1941 The Queen's Hall is destroyed; the Proms move to the Royal Albert Hall (again with the Royal Philharmonic Society); Basil Cameron is appointed assistant conductor and shares the conducting with Wood; some Proms broadcast.

1942 The BBC resumes management of the Proms, and the season runs in June and July; this is the first Proms season with two orchestras (LPO and BBC SO); Adrian Boult joins Cameron and Wood.

1943 Children admitted free to Prom rehearsals; average nightly attendance at the Proms rises to 4,000; the first Sunday Prom; Wood is ill, so Boult and Cameron do most of the conducting.

1944 Golden Jubilee season; flying bombs force the close of the London season after three weeks; some concerts scheduled for broadcasting continue from Bedford; Wood dies at end of season.

1945 The BBC's first season in sole charge of the Proms; the series is rechristened 'The Henry Wood Promenade Concerts'.

1946 The BBC contracts Julian Herbage to manage the Proms.

1947 Malcolm Sargent joins the Proms; ballots instituted for First and Last Night places; Last Night first televised as an experiment.

1950 Malcolm Sargent appointed chief conductor of the BBC SO; Boult leaves the BBC.

1951 The 'Festival of Britain Proms'.

1953 The Hallé with Barbirolli is the first non-London orchestra at the Proms; First and Last Nights televised.

1954 Diamond Jubilee season.

1957 Sargent is replaced as chief conductor of the BBC SO by Rudolf Schwarz but remains conductor-in-chief of the Proms.

1960 William Glock's first season; the first BBC-commissioned Proms work (Alwyn's *Derby Day*).

1961 The first complete performance of an opera at the Proms (Mozart's *Don Giovanni*).

1963 Reappearance of international conductors with Stokowski, Giulini and Solti.

1964 TV broadcasts ten Proms; end of Friday 'Beethoven nights'.

1965 Large increase in the price of Promming reduces season ticket holders by half.

1966 The Proms' first overseas orchestra (the Moscow Radio Orchestra with Rozhdestvensky); Sargent's last season of Proms conducting.

1967 Sargent makes his adieu in a Last Night speech and dies shortly afterwards.

1968 Sir Malcolm Sargent's Memorial Concert initiates Fridays as the First Night.

1969 Medieval music (Machaut's *Messe de Nostre Dame*) and dancing (in Stravinsky's *Renard*) come to the Proms.

1970 The first Late Night Prom features the crossover sounds of the electro-acoustic group 'The Soft Machine'.

1971 First 'world musics' at the Proms with Imrat Kahn (sitar); Proms also held in Westminster Cathedral and the Round House.

1972 Pierre Boulez appears at the Proms in new role as chief conductor of the BBC SO.

1973 Glock's last season; return of the 'traditional' Last Night.

1974 Robert Ponsonby's first season; introduction of the pre-Prom talks.

1975 Visits by the New York Philharmonic and Cleveland orchestras.

1976 Ponsonby's distinction between programming the 'very popular and the very great' causes controversy.

1977 Financial pressures on the BBC necessitate a significant rise in ticket prices.

1978 The 50th Prom season promoted by the BBC.

1979 Some 5.8 million watch the Viennese Night introduced by Esther Rantzen on BBC1.

1980 Musicians strike against BBC's plan to axe five house orchestras and twenty Proms are lost.

1981 Publication of *The Proms and Natural Justice* fuels controversy over programme planning; first all-night Prom of Indian rāg; reduced audiences in consequence of the strike.

1982 BBC runs a Proms travel offer in a bid to restore audiences to pre-strike levels; Philadelphia Orchestra plays.

1983 Scheme to restrict Last Night attendance to those who have attended other Proms.

1984 Appearance by the Vienna Philharmonic.

1985 Ponsonby's last season as director of the Proms.

1986 John Drummond becomes Proms' director.

1987 Proms season takes dance as its theme.

1988 Proms season takes literature as a theme; five youth orchestras appear; average attendance stands at 79%.

1989 Average attendance at the Proms reaches 85%.

1990 Controversy about the Last Night in view of Gulf War leads to replacement of Mark Elder as conductor.

1991 Berlin Philharmonic Orchestra (with Claudio Abbado) makes its first Proms appearance.

1993 Appearances by the Cleveland, Los Angeles and Pittsburgh orchestras.

1994 100th season celebrated with a retrospective survey of the Proms' contribution to British musical life.

1995 The Proms Centenary season celebrated with new commissions; programming of all the Mahler symphonies; Drummond's last season.

1996 Nicholas Kenyon becomes director and institutes the first Prom in the Park, the first Prom chamber music series and the Prom lecture.

1998 First *Blue Peter* family Prom; Choral Day at the Proms.

2000 Celebration of the new millennium focuses on young musicians, including the 'Proms Millennium Youth Day'.

First interactive digital transmission of the Proms on BBC 4 TV.

2003 Proms in the Park expands across the UK with events in London, Belfast, Swansea and Glasgow.

2005 Access to the Proms expands through the internet and mobile phones; increased education and outreach events, including a concert with young performers playing alongside the BBC SO.

2007 The BBC celebrates the 80th anniversary of its association with the Proms.

Biographical Sketches

Some readers will have easy access to a range of biographical sources, such as *The New Grove Dictionary of Music and Musicians*, the *Oxford Dictionary of National Biography*, web search engines etc. But for those who do not, what follows are brief biographical details for a selective list of individuals and institutions mentioned in the text, focusing on their relations with the Proms. Composers have not been included.

BBC Symphony Orchestra (founded 1930). The BBC established its symphony orchestra in 1930 as the first full-time salaried orchestra in the UK, recruiting some of the country's best orchestral musicians. Adrian Boult was its first chief conductor (1931–50), and many outstanding guest conductors and composers (including Webern) appeared during the 1930s, culminating in Arturo Toscanini conducting the London Music Festivals. The orchestra played under Henry Wood for all Proms until the Second World War, when the orchestra was evacuated first to Bristol and then Bedford. Following the war, the Proms seasons began to be shared with other London and then UK orchestras. After Boult's enforced BBC retirement (1950), the BBC SO prospered less under Sargent, but was revitalized under Antal Dorati, Colin Davis and then Pierre Boulez (1971–5) who re-established the orchestra's international reputation as a performer of new music. Subsequent chief conductors have included Gennadi Rozhdestvensky (1978–81), Sir John Pritchard (1982–9), Sir Andrew Davis (1989–2000), Leonard Slatkin (2000–04) and Jiří Bělohlávek (from 2006).

Balfour, Margaret (d. 1961). A mezzo-soprano whose career was at its height in the 1920s and 1930s, Balfour was one of the original soloists in Vaughan Williams' *Serenade to Music*, and the Angel in Elgar's own recording of *The Dream of Gerontius*. She made 76 Prom appearances (including many last nights) between 1911 and 1940, the largest number of any single singer.

Barbirolli, Sir John (1899–1970). Barbirolli was the youngest member of the Queen's Hall Orchestra when he joined it as a cellist in 1916. He succeeded Toscanini as conductor of the New York Philharmonic Orchestra (1937), and returned to England to become conductor of the Hallé in Manchester (1943). The Hallé (with Barbirolli) was the first non-London orchestra to play at the Proms (1953) and their Viennese nights became a major attraction in successive seasons. Barbirolli conducted some 240 works at the Proms.

Beecham, Sir Thomas (1879–1961). This conductor and mercurial character, described by the critic Richard Capell as 'the most gifted executive musician England has ever produced', was a mover and shaker in British musical life in ways that were the opposite of Wood's systematic and consistent approach. However, Beecham appeared very rarely at the Proms (once in 1915, twice in 1954). He alienated the BBC by involving himself with early plans for the BBC SO (1930) but then leaving them in the lurch and establishing the rival London Philharmonic Orchestra (1932), and later the Royal Philharmonic Orchestra (1946). He was dismissive of Boult and once described Herbert von Karajan as 'a sort of musical Malcolm Sargent'.

Birt, Sir John [later Lord Birt of Liverpool] (b. 1944). Worked in independent television, first at Granada (1966–71) and then at London Weekend (1971–87), where he became Director of Programmes (1982). Moved to the BBC as Deputy Director-General (1987) and controversially was appointed Director-General (1992–2000). His strategic thinking and forward planning enabled the BBC to plan for a digital future, including online activity. He was never perceived as a supporter of the arts, and introduced the contentious internal-market scheme known as 'Producer Choice'. But by forcing the BBC to become more efficient, Birt was able to retain the licence fee and the cultural patronage it allowed.

Boulez, Pierre (b. 1925). Boulez made his Proms conducting début in 1965 (he first featured as a composer in 1961), and as BBC SO Chief Conductor (1971–5) he worked closely with Glock to produce a series of adventurous and innovative programmes that helped establish the Proms as an international festival. These included a celebrated series of late-night avant-garde Proms held at the Round House in London's Camden Town (1971–82).

Boult, Sir Adrian (1889–1983). The young Adrian Boult observed the great German conductor Arthur Nikisch while a student at the Leipzig Conservatory (1912–13), which proved a formative experience. After a period as conductor of the City of Birmingham Orchestra (1924–30), Boult became the BBC's Director of Music in 1930. He was the guiding force behind the foundation of the BBC Symphony Orchestra and nurtured its unrivalled playing standards as its chief conductor (1931–50). He was also associate conductor of the Proms (1942–50) until his enforced retirement, but never enjoyed the conditions under which he had to appear at them, considering them too little rehearsed. But in later years he often returned to the Proms with various orchestras, giving outstanding performances of classical and British repertory until 1977.

Cameron, Basil (1884–1975). After training in Berlin (1902–06), working for a period as an orchestral violinist and spending some years conducting municipal orchestras in Torquay, Hastings and Harrogate, Cameron went to the USA (1930) to direct the San Francisco and later the Seattle symphony orchestras. Returning to the UK in 1938, he became Wood's assistant conductor at the Proms, a reliable conductor with a varied repertory: he directed nearly 2,000 works. He was never a charismatic figure, and suffered in comparison with Malcolm Sargent, but he continued to appear at the Proms until his eightieth birthday year in 1964.

Curzon, Sir Clifford (1907–82). A renowned pianist, whose approach to performance was shaped by contact with Artur Schnabel, Wanda Landowska and Nadia Boulanger, Curzon made 68 Prom appearances between 1924 and 1981. He was especially acclaimed for his performances of Mozart's piano concertos.

Davis, Sir Andrew (b. 1944). A Cambridge organ scholar, Davis enjoyed a meteoric rise to fame as a conductor and worked for some years in Toronto before being appointed chief conductor of the BBC SO (1989–2000). From 1971 Davis became a popular Proms figure, conducting a wide repertory, including many premières, and re-establishing the tradition that the chief conductor of the BBC SO conducted the Last Night.

Davis, Sir Colin (b. 1927). Davis made his early conducting reputation in opera and became chief conductor at Sadler's Wells Opera (1959) and later music director (1961–5). In the 1967 Proms season he took over from Sargent, conducting 14 of the season's 52 concerts (including the First and Last Nights) before being appointed chief conductor of the BBC SO (1967–71). He has continued to appear annually at the Proms with the LSO and a variety of youth orchestras.

De Greef, Arthur (1862–1940). A Belgian pianist and composer, De Greef studied with Liszt after graduating from the Brussels Royal Conservatory (1879). Grieg admired De Greef's performance of his Piano Concerto, which he first conducted on a tour of Belgium (1889), and De Greef made the first complete recording of the work with the 'Royal Albert Hall Orchestra' and Landon Ronald in 1927, which in 2000 was re-released in a digital transfer.

Drummond, Sir John (1934–2006). After reading history at Cambridge, Drummond joined the BBC as a general trainee (1958) and became Assistant Head of Music and Arts at BBC Television (1975). He directed the Edinburgh Festival from 1979 to 1983 and rejoined the BBC as Controller of Music in 1985, planning the Proms from the 1986 season. His post was amalgamated with that of Controller Radio 3 (1987), giving Drummond an unprecedented influence over both the BBC's patronage of music and its broadcasting until he left Radio 3 in 1992; he remained director of the Proms until the centenary season of 1995. His outspoken views, brilliant skills at publicity, and flamboyant planning of an increasingly international season ensured that the Proms remained high in the BBC's priorities and retained its position at the forefront of British musical life.

Glock, Sir William (1908–2000). After an organ scholarship at Cambridge where he read history, Glock studied the piano with Artur Schnabel in Berlin (1930–33), and appeared at the Proms in the 1940s. He worked as a music critic, especially on the *Observer*, before starting the Dartington Summer School of Music (1948), which he directed until 1979. Glock also founded the critical journal *The Score* (1949–61), which focused on twentieth-century music, and he was chair of the ICA Music Section (1954–8). Perceived as an outsider in the British musical scene, his appointment as Controller of Music at the BBC (1959–73) was a surprise. He used the BBC's public service broadcasting mandate to revitalize many aspects of national musical life, especially the Proms. After retiring from the BBC he was, among much else, artistic director of the Bath Festival.

Greene, Sir Hugh Carlton (1910–1987). Brother of the novelist Graham Greene, Hugh Greene opened up the BBC to the influences of the 1960s with programmes that reflected the tone of social and cultural change and caused considerable controversy, such as *That Was the Week That Was*. Greene had joined the BBC as head of the German Service (1940) after a period as a newspaper correspondent in Berlin. He became Director of News and Current Affairs, then Director of Administration, and was appointed Director-General in 1960. He provided both a context and a support for Glock's changes to the Proms, which fitted well with the innovation and controversy of Greene's years at the BBC.

Haendel, Ida (b. 1923). A British violinist of Polish birth, she made her London début with Wood in the 1937 Proms playing the Beethoven concerto. She is credited with the largest number of solo appearances by any violinist at the Proms, playing in 62 concerts between 1937 and 1994.

Haley, Sir William (1901–1987). Joined the *Manchester Evening News* (1922) and rose to become its managing director before entering the BBC as Editor-in-Chief (1943). As Director-General of the BBC (1944–52) he supervised the crucial postwar reorganization of the radio networks, and in 1946 the launch of the Third Programme, which changed the British cultural landscape. In his time the BBC SO was subject to increased competition from new orchestras in London: the number of orchestras at the Proms was increased, as was the budget for the season, to ensure the quality of the performances.

Hely-Hutchinson, Victor (1901–1947). He was a member of the BBC Music Department (1926–33) as a staff pianist and composer, and worked with Edward Clark and Julian Herbage in the music programme building section. After ten years as Professor of Music at Birmingham University, he rejoined the BBC as its Director of Music in 1944.

Herbage, Julian (1904–1976). After working as a theatre musical director Herbage joined the BBC in 1927. In the Music Department, Herbage was acknowledged for his command of repertory (including early music) and his skills in programme building, and he founded the long-running *Music Magazine* (1944–73) with Anna Instone. Herbage fulfilled a particular responsibility for the Proms (planning them, attending auditions of artists, supervising broadcasts and writing a report on each season) from Wood's death (1944) until Glock's appointment as Controller (1959).

Hess, Dame Myra (1890–1965). An internationally acclaimed British pianist, Myra Hess achieved iconic standing among London audiences for her lunchtime recitals at the National Gallery during the Second World War. Her pianistic qualities are less well remembered than those of many of her contemporaries because of her dislike of recording. She was a hugely popular soloist at the Proms, first playing Liszt's E flat Concerto in 1908, and making more appearances than any other single soloist across the years.

Howgill, Richard (1895–1975). Howgill was an amateur composer who entered the BBC as a specialist in musical copyright. He worked his way to become Controller of Entertainment in 1948 (the division which housed the Music Department), and then became Controller of the newly established Music Division in 1952. He was more concerned with administrative than artistic policy, and had to cope with problems surrounding Malcolm Sargent, but he was alert to criticism of the BBC's unadventurousness in the 1950s and played a decisive role in appointing William Glock as his successor as Controller of Music (1959), an act with far-reaching consequences for British musical life.

Hussey, Marmaduke [Lord Hussey of North Bradley] (b. 1923). Hussey was appointed Chairman of the BBC (1986–96) after a management career with Associated Newspapers and Times Newspapers. He knew little about broadcasting, and his appointment was widely seen as an attempt to undermine the BBC's traditional values and bring it closer to the marketplace. But he proved a staunch defender of its independence against attack and helped ensure the renewal of its charter and licence-fee funding in 1996. During his time as Chairman, one Director-General, Alasdair Milne, was sacked (1987), and another, Sir Michael Checkland (1987–92), resigned early.

Jullien, Louis (1812–1860). The publicity generated by the bizarrely self-aggrandizing gestures of this extraordinary character tend to overshadow his significance in the democratizing of music through his Promenade concerts and many concert tours across Europe and the USA (1853–4). Aiming to 'ensure amusement as well as attempting instruction', Jullien's London Promenade concerts (the first of some 24 seasons was in 1840) attracted huge audiences of the 'one-shilling public' and are sometimes considered the forerunners of the Newman–Wood Proms. But Jullien's approach lacked Wood's essential musical quality and seriousness of purpose; he remained the showman, but Wood was the pioneer.

Manns, Sir August (1825–1907). Percy Scholes wrote of Manns that 'more than any other single individual he taught the British people to love the orchestral classics', a judgment indicative of the significance of his Saturday Crystal Palace Concerts (1855–1901), run initially with the help of George Grove, in developing an enthusiasm and knowledge of orchestral music. For these concerts, held in the suburban location of Sydenham and with tickets at popular prices, Manns ran London's first 'permanent' orchestra and set new performance standards, something that was crucial to his achievement.

Moiseiwitsch, Benno (1890–1963). A pianist who built himself a legendary reputation performing the Romantic piano repertory (especially Rachmaninoff), Moiseiwitsch was born in Odessa, studied in Vienna with Theodor Leschetizky and then settled in Britain. He enjoyed a great rapport with the Proms audiences, giving his first and last concerts in 1914 and 1962; apart from Myra Hess, he was the pianist who made the most appearances at the Proms, playing in some 88 concerts.

Murrill, Herbert (1909–1952). A fastidious composer in a neoclassical idiom, he worked in the theatre until joining the BBC (1936). After war service he returned to the BBC, becoming head of the Music Department (1950), where he was a thoughtful and effective administrator until his early death.

Newman, Robert (1858–1926). After early employment as a stockjobber, he studied singing in Italy and then at the Royal Academy of Music (1888–89), singing professionally for several years; he joined the concert agent Farley Sinkins in promoting promenade concerts at Covent Garden Theatre in 1893. He was first manager, then lessee, of the new Queen's Hall and inaugurated the Queen's Hall Promenade Concerts in 1895. Though bankrupted by an ill-advised theatrical venture (1902), he continued as manager of the Queen's Hall Orchestra and the Promenade concerts until his death. His genius in starting the Proms as a foundation for other, interlinked orchestral series in the Queen's Hall ensured him a secure if hidden place in musical history. He changed London's concert life in further ways: the quality of the music-making in the hall reflected his invitations to leading Continental conductors, soloists and orchestras; he pioneered Sunday concerts; and he was innovative in his approach to concert promotion and management, attracting ordinary listeners, educating them, and giving them both familiar and new repertory.

Newmarch, Rosa (1857–1940). A specialist in Russian music, her articles in *Grove's Dictionary* (2nd edn) became a primary source of information in English on a range of Russian composers and their works, including Tchaikovsky. After Russia closed itself off to most visitors, she pioneered interest in Czech composers, particularly Janáček, whom she brought to England (1926). Newmarch was official programme-note writer for the Queen's Hall Orchestra (1908–19) and a frequent contributor until 1928.

Nicolls, Sir Basil (1893–1965). After working for the BBC as Station Director in Manchester and London, Nicolls was appointed General Editor of Publications in 1928. He became Director of Internal Administration (1933), rising to Director Home Broadcasting (1948), and for a year was Acting Director-General before his retirement (1953). He was a key figure in the BBC between the wars and supervised closely the work of the Music Department, which did not always feel that he was a supporter of their activities.

Ponsonby, Robert (b. 1926). Ponsonby read English at Oxford (where he was also an organ scholar) and after a period with Glyndebourne Opera (1951–5) was appointed director of the Edinburgh Festival (1956–60). He became General Administrator of the Scottish National Orchestra (1964) and succeeded Glock as the BBC's Controller of Music (1972–85). He planned some twelve seasons of Proms from 1973 to 1985 (and 1986 in outline), in which he built on Glock's innovations, expanding the international scope of the Proms and the quality of performers. His programming was extremely effective and the concerts were increasingly prestigious events, but he came into conflict with the BBC hierarchy partly because of his resistance to developing television's role in broadcasting the Proms.

Pritchard, Sir John (1921–1989). After early success in opera at Glyndebourne, Pritchard directed the Royal Liverpool Philharmonic Orchestra (1957–63), where he introduced the 'Musica Viva' series of contemporary music concerts, and brought the orchestra to the Proms. He was at the LPO (1962–6), and later became chief conductor of the BBC SO (1982–9), in which role he was a frequent conductor at the Proms. He had a wide concert and operatic repertory, including much new music, giving the premières of operas by Britten and Tippett and introducing many younger composers. He enjoyed less public renown than his professional achievements deserved.

Reith, Sir John (later Lord) (1889–1971). Reith originally trained as an engineer, and after gaining some commercial experience and working in Whitehall he was appointed General Manager of the fledgling British Broadcasting Company (1922), and Director-General when it became the British Broadcasting Corporation (1927–38). His vision for public service broadcasting, combined with a robustly authoritarian management style, established the BBC as a national institution whose significance for the UK's musical and wider cultural life cannot be overestimated. His commitment to music as a central part of the BBC's activities enabled both its support of the Proms from 1927 and the establishment of the BBC SO in 1930.

Samuelson, Christopher (1920–2001). From his appointment as BBC SO Concerts Manager in 1966, Samuelson was the planner chiefly responsible to William Glock, and later to Robert Ponsonby, for the implementation of their Proms programmes. He engaged artists, discussed programming and supervised rehearsals. As well as an indefatigable organizer, he was also a keen photographer whose pictures of Proms rehearsals and artists are an invaluable resource. He retired in 1982.

Sargent, Sir Malcolm (1895–1967). A product of the English cathedral organist tradition, Sargent was encouraged by Henry Wood, who invited him to conduct his own *An Impression on a Windy Day* in the 1921 Proms. Sargent made a strong reputation as a choral conductor of great vigour (premièring Walton's *Belshazzar's Feast* at Leeds in 1931); he was always popular with choral singers, but less so with orchestral players. He was appointed chief conductor of the BBC SO (1950–57) and quickly made the Proms his personal platform. But his reluctance to undertake studio work or new repertory made him unpopular in the BBC, and

he was replaced at the BBC SO in 1957 while remaining Conductor-in-Chief of the Proms (1957–67). Television turned his appearances at the Last Night into national occasions, and he was adored by audiences. In the 1960s William Glock's increasing use of international conductors in the Proms inevitably sidelined Sargent. He made an emotional final appearance, just before his death, to speak to the audience on the 1967 Last Night.

Slatkin, Leonard (b. 1944). His parents were part of the famous Hollywood String Quartet. Slatkin himself came to prominence through his work with the St Louis Symphony Orchestra, whose profile he raised. He was appointed music director of the Washington Symphony Orchestra (1996) and appeared regularly at the Proms with various UK orchestras, speaking directly to audiences about such works as Elgar's *Enigma Variations* and Musorgsky's *Pictures at an Exhibition.* He became Chief Conductor of the BBC SO (2000–04), and his sensitive handling of the 2001 Last Night of the Proms in the wake of the 9/11 atrocity was widely admired.

Solomon [Cutner, Solomon] (1902–1988). A legend with audiences and fellow pianists alike, Solomon was admired for his unforced quality of pianism, in which virtuosity and sheer beauty of tone were always at the command of the music and never displayed for their own sake. He first appeared at the Proms in 1914 and played over seventy times before his career was tragically ended by a stroke in 1965.

Wellington, Sir Lindsay (1901–1985). After Oxford University, Wellington had joined the BBC as a Presentation Assistant (1924), was promoted to Presentation Director (1933) and Director of Programme Planning (1935). As a BBC mandarin, Wellington played an important role in the Corporation's wartime relations with Whitehall and the USA. After the war he became head of the Home Service and then Director of Home Sound Broadcasting (1952–63). As such, Wellington took part in William Glock's appointment as Controller of Music (1959), and was a constant though not uncritical supporter of Glock's innovations.

Wilson, Sir Steuart (1889–1966). After reading Classics at Cambridge (1909) Wilson sang professionally, gaining a reputation as the Evangelist in the Bach Passions. He joined the BBC as overseas music director (1943) and then became the Arts Council's first music director (1948). He briefly rejoined the BBC as its music director (1948–50), where his main legacy was to dispense with the services of Sir Adrian Boult and appoint Malcolm Sargent to the BBC SO. This was followed by unhappy periods at Covent Garden and the Birmingham School of Music.

Wood, Sir Henry Joseph (1869–1944). Wood studied at the Royal Academy of Music but learned about conducting by sitting in on Henry Holmes's orchestral rehearsals at the Royal College of Music. Unknown when Robert Newman asked him to establish the Queen's Hall Orchestra for the first Promenade Concerts (1895), Wood conducted almost every concert and soon gained a popular following as well as international fame; he remained the central figure of the Proms for decades, much loved by the public. He pioneered new standards of discipline (his intolerance of 'deputies' prompted some of his players to break away to establish the London Symphony Orchestra in 1904) and regularly championed new repertory, premiering over 700 works. Following Newman's death, Wood was contracted by the BBC in 1927 when the Corporation also took on the Promenade Concerts; he continued to conduct the Proms until his death in 1944. His bust in the Royal Academy of Music is still taken to the Royal Albert Hall for the Proms season and

decorated on the Last Night, when his *Fantasia on British Sea Songs* remains an evocative tribute to this astonishing man.

Wood, Lady Jessie (d. 1979). As the mezzo-soprano Jessie Goldsack she sang for Wood as soloist in several Proms seasons. In 1935 she and Wood established a permanent relationship; when Wood's wife would not divorce him, Goldsack changed her name by deed poll to 'Lady Jessie Wood'. Her involvement with Wood gave him a domestic happiness that renewed his spirits and energy in his last decade, and she continued to be a staunch defender of his legacy (and Proms traditions) with the BBC after his death.

Wright, Kenneth (1899–1975). Wright was an amateur composer of light music who trained as an engineer at Sheffield University and became involved in early radiotelephony developments with the electricity firm Metropolitan-Vickers. He became the first director of the BBC's Manchester Station (1922), then moved to London and was a vital member of the Music Department as Assistant and Deputy Music Director. He later became Artists' Manager and moved to BBC TV, being involved in music on television until his retirement (1959).

Audience Capacities: Queen's Hall and Royal Albert Hall

The capacity of the Queen's Hall for the Promenade Concerts was 3,274: 1,294 seats, about 1,850 standing and an additional 130 in the orchestra when there was no choir. (The paying attendance at the 1937 Proms season, to give an example, is quoted as 113,000, and 117,150 in 1938.)

With the concerts' change of venue, the Proms could take advantage of the more spacious Royal Albert Hall; calculating the exact capacity, however, is always complicated by the fact that of the Albert Hall's seats just under 1,300 – including most of the boxes in the Grand Tier – are privately owned. This situation has its origins in the way in which the capital for building the hall was raised: in 1865 a prospectus was issued and private individuals were invited to purchase 999-year leasehold on seats at £100 each, and were thus entitled to attend every performance. (At this point the hall's potential capacity was given as 6,500.) A subsequent modification allowed there to be some occasions when a promoter would be allowed an 'Exclusive Let' (with

leaseholders excluded and their seats made available to the promoter), as opposed to the more usual 'Ordinary Let'. At present the official capacity of the hall when the arena is fully seated is 5,222 for an exclusive let and 3,901 for an ordinary let.

However, during the Proms season the arena seats are removed, and a larger number of people can stand. A further complication in attempting to assess audience numbers for the Proms at any given period is the fact that seating capacity for the Royal Albert Hall has varied considerably with the refurbishment of different parts of the hall (the 1996 rebuilding of the circle, for instance, which removed 188 restricted view seats and added 83 better seats) and more recently with restrictions for health and safety reasons. On different occasions some choir seats are not sold, boxes are removed from sale for television cameras or off-stage performers, and for large forces the stage is extended into the arena, thus reducing promming space.

In his book *The Henry Wood Proms*, David Cox gives the total capacity in the Second World War as 7,300 (4,900 seats, including private seats; 1,250 arena standing; 1,150 gallery standing), which is surely a maximum. In 1954 the capacity is quoted as 6,852: 2,756 seats plus 646 in the orchestra for non-choral concerts (totalling 3,402), 1,150 arena standing, and 1,000 gallery standing, making a total of 5,552 for an ordinary let, plus a further 1,300 for an exclusive let. (It is difficult to believe the *Who's Who in Music* for 1913,[1] long before the Proms arrived at the Albert Hall, which indicates 3,000 spaces in the gallery alone, thus making the hall's maximum capacity a staggering 9,087! Perhaps this figure was conjured up to boost the attractiveness of the hall for some of the huge, non-musical gatherings it hosted. Some illustrations seem to show a raked flooring arrangement in the gallery, so people at the back would have been able to see.)

Nowadays capacity for a Prom concert ordinary let is 4,588 and 5,909 for an exclusive let: 3,188 seats (reduced by a maximum of 450 for choral concerts), arena standing capacity capped at around 900 (although it has been fuller on occasions), and gallery capacity 500, plus 1,300 private and other seats for an exclusive let. However, the figures for ordinary lets do not take account of the fact that hall members frequently use, return to the box office or otherwise dispose of their own seats, increasing the attendance considerably. (Whereas in the past it was a frustration to the BBC that there were frequently empty members' seats at sold-out concerts, it is now the case that most are returned when they are not used. Members benefit from the resale of the their tickets and the hall is fuller as a result.) So in a full hall for a BBC Prom there are probably just under 6,000 people present. Because there are more Proms concerts today than in the series' early years, and because they are held in a larger hall, the total attendance at the season is now regularly over 250,000, more than double that at the Queen's Hall.

Note: The number of exclusive lets that can be given to the Proms in the course of the season is regulated by the fact that the hall can grant only twelve for concerts in the course of any year; the BBC usually has the benefit of five or six of these, negotiated in light of the rest of the year's programme in the hall. A semi-staged opera performance can be an exclusive let because it falls outside the definition of a concert. (In 1968 Glock was allocated four exclusive lets instead of the ten he had hoped for.[2] The lettings manager was sympathetic, and remarked to Glock that exclusive lets tended to go to the Brass Band Championship and to Freemason events, because seat holders were less reluctant to give up their rights to those sorts of occasions than they were for the Proms![3])

1 *Who's Who in Music: A Biographical Record of Contemporary Musicians*, ed. H. Saxe Wyndham and Geoffrey L'Epine (London: Pitman, 1913), 288–89.
2 Christopher Samuelson, memo to William Glock, 9 January 1968, WAC R27/1022/2.
3 Samuelson, memo to Glock, 19 October 1967, WAC R27/1022/1.

Contributors

Elisabeth Agate studied music at York University, and has worked as a picture researcher and editor since 1973, enjoying a long association with *The New Grove Dictionary of Music and Musicians* (1980 and 2/2001) and the many related reference works, including the *Man and Music* series. She has worked on a wide variety of projects, and since 1995 has been principal picture researcher on the sixty-book series the *Oxford History of Art*, also acting as picture consultant for the Glyndebourne Festival Opera programmes. She contributed the chapter on 'Pictures and Picture Research' to Lewis Foreman's *Information Sources in Music* (2003).

Jenny Doctor's research into the history of BBC music broadcasting has contributed to two books: her own *The BBC and Ultra-Modern Music, 1922–36: Shaping a Nation's Tastes* (CUP, 1999) and Humphrey Carpenter's *The Envy of the World: Fifty Years of the BBC Third Programme and Radio 3* (Weidenfeld and Nicholson, 1996). With Nicky Losseff she is now preparing *Music and Silence* (Ashgate), and with Sophie Fuller an edition of letters exchanged by British composers Elizabeth Maconchy and Grace Williams (University of Illinois Press). She is currently a Senior Lecturer at University of York.

Alison Garnham was born and brought up in Durham, so it was not until she came south as a student (at Oxford and London universities) that she got the chance to come to the Proms, which she did especially frequently in the 1980s. She became Archivist of the Hans Keller Archive at Cambridge University Library in 1996. In 2003 she published *Hans Keller and the BBC: The Musical Conscience of British Broadcasting* (Ashgate), and her edition of Keller's letters is now in press.

Ivan Hewett had his first brush with the Proms as a very small boy in Peshawar and Delhi, thanks to the BBC World Service. He studied music at Oxford University and composition at the Royal College of Music, and spent a fascinating year in commercial music, where he rose to the dizzy heights of scoring the music for a TV cat-food advertisement. He researched Granada TV's *Man and Music* series and assisted with Jonathan Miller's TV dramatization of Bach's *St Matthew Passion*. In 1993 he was entrusted with Radio 3's weekly magazine show *Music Matters*, and in the 1980s and 90s was a regular contributor to the *Musical Times*, *Prospect* and other magazines. Since the late 1990s he has taught at the Royal College of Music, and in 2003 published a very personal view of twentieth-century music, *Music: Healing the Rift* (Continuum). He now writes on music for the *Daily Telegraph*, and from time to time presents BBC Radio 3's new music series, *Hear and Now*.

Nicholas Kenyon has been director of the BBC Proms since the 1996 season. He was a music critic for the *New Yorker*, *The Times* and the *Observer* and wrote the history of the BBC Symphony Orchestra (1981). He was editor of *Early Music* from 1983 to 1992 and edited the influential volume *Authenticity and Early Music*. He became Controller, BBC Radio 3 in 1992, and was responsible for the award-winning seasons *Fairest Isle* (1995) and *Sounding the Century* (1997–9). He is now Controller, BBC Proms, Live Events and TV Classical Music. He has edited four volumes of BBC Proms Guides to the repertory, and has most recently written *The Faber Pocket Guide to Mozart* (2005).

Paul Kildea is a conductor and writer, born in Australia and educated at the universities of Melbourne and Oxford. A former pupil of Cyril Ehrlich and assistant of Simone Young, his performing career has taken him throughout Europe and Australia. He has written extensively on twentieth-century music and social history, and is a recognized authority on the music of Benjamin Britten, both in print and on the podium. His two books on the composer are published by Oxford University Press: *Selling Britten: Music and the Marketplace* (2002) and *Britten on Music* (2003). He is former artistic director of Wigmore Hall, London.

Tom Service has presented *Music Matters* in BBC Radio 3 since 2003 and writes about music for the *Guardian*, where he was Chief Classical Music Critic. He was made the inaugural ICMP/CIEM Classical Music Critic of the Year in 2005. He was Guest Artistic Director of the Huddersfield Contemporary Music Festival in 2005, having finished his PhD on the music of John Zorn at the University of Southampton in 2004. He has taught at Trinity College of Music, has given lectures and talks, and has written programme notes for Britain's major classical music festivals and institutions, including the Proms. He appears regularly as a guest on BBC television's Proms coverage.

Leanne Langley is a social cultural historian. She has written on the development of English music criticism, the early histories of the Royal Academy of Music and the Philharmonic Society of London, the background and publication of George Grove's *Dictionary of Music and Musicians*, and the British reception of Berlioz, 1870–1920. With Christina Bashford she edited *Music and British Culture, 1785–1914: Essays in Honour of Cyril Ehrlich* for Oxford University Press (2000). Formerly a lecturer with an American university in London and Senior Consulting Editor of the *New Grove Dictionary of Opera*, she is now a research fellow at Goldsmiths College, University of London, completing a book with Simon McVeigh on London concert life, 1880–1914, for Cambridge University Press. She met her husband in the Proms queue in 1980; they live in Southampton with their two sons.

David Wright is Reader in the Social History of Music at the Royal College of Music, London. Recent research has included George Grove's role in establishing the RCM, in *George Grove, Music and Victorian Culture* (Palgrave Macmillan, 2003); the political and cultural significance of the music selected for the 1902 Coronation Service, in *Europe, Empire and Spectacle in 19th-Century British Music* (Ashgate, 2006); and the part played by the South Kensington Music Schools in the development of British conservatories, in the *Journal of the Royal Musical Association* (2005). His account of the institutional history and cultural identity of the London Sinfonietta appeared in *twentieth-century music* (2005).

Abbreviations

Add. MS Additional manuscript
BBC British Broadcasting Company (1922–26);
   British Broadcasting Corporation (from 1927)
BBC call signs in use before the war:
   2LO (London), 5GB (Daventry Experimental)
BBC SO BBC Symphony Orchestra
BL British Library
BLSA British Library Sound Archive
BNOC British National Opera Company
CEMA Council for the Encouragement of Music and the Arts
ENSA Entertainment National Service Association
fol. folio
LPO London Philharmonic Orchestra
LSO London Symphony Orchestra
PRO Public Record Office
QHO Queen's Hall Orchestra
RCM Royal College of Music
RPS Royal Philharmonic Society
WAC BBC Written Archives Centre

Notes

CHAPTER 1 PAUL KILDEA

1 E. M. Forster, *Howards End* (1910; Harmondsworth: Penguin Books, 1989), 51.
2 Henry J. Wood, *My Life of Music* (London: Victor Gollancz, 1938), 68.
3 Friedrich Nietzsche, *The Will to Power*, trans. Walter Kaufmann and R. J. Hollingdale (London: Weidenfeld & Nicolson, 1968), 382.
4 Entry in Forster's diary for 27 January 1908, quoted in Oliver Stallybrass, Editor's Introduction to Forster, *Howards End*, 10.
5 John Carey, *The Intellectual and the Masses* (London: Faber and Faber, 1992), 3.
6 Dan H. Laurence, ed., *Shaw's Music*, ii: *1890–1893* (London: The Bodley Head, 1981), 965.
7 The generic title the 'Proms', although historically inaccurate, will be used in this chapter when reference is made to the concept and execution of the series in its entirety. The different names applied to the series, evoking different historical periods and aspirations, is clarified throughout the course of this book.
8 Wigmore Hall, which opened in 1901, is the only comparable institution, yet this is a recital hall, not a concert hall, and its economy for many years was built entirely on outside entrepreneurs and artists taking the financial risk, still an important aspect of its operation. Their eyes were, of course, on artistic excellence. But so too were they trained on commercial opportunities and good box-office returns. The Royal Philharmonic Society, which was formed in 1813, no longer presents an annual series of orchestral concerts.
9 Wood, *My Life of Music*, 68–9.
10 The origins of the phrase as a cliché most likely date from 1928, when the *New York Times* art critic, Enrico Raffaele, used it in an article about the American Dadaist Bert Lange.
11 Ezra Pound, 'The New Sculpture', *Egoist* (16 February 1914), 67–8.
12 George Gissing, *Our Friend the Charlatan* (London: Chapman and Hall, 1901), repr. in Carey, *The Intellectual and the Masses*, 95.
13 Carey, *The Intellectual and the Masses*, 6–10.

14 Lord Northcliffe, quoted in Carey, *The Intellectual and the Masses*, 6.
15 It is worth remembering how *morally* controversial this work was. After attending a performance of it at the Metropolitan Opera of New York in 1907, the director of Chicago's Law and Order League declared that the opera should be 'classed as vicious and suppressed along with houses in the red light district. I am a normal man, but I would not trust myself to see a performance of *Salome*.' John Dizikes, *Opera in America: A Cultural History* (Yale: Yale University Press, 1993), 315–16.
16 Wood, *My Life of Music*, 185–6.
17 Quoted in David Cox, *The Henry Wood Proms* (London: BBC, 1980), 62.
18 Benjamin Britten, *On Receiving the First Aspen Award* (1964), in *Britten on Music*, ed. Paul Kildea (Oxford: Oxford University Press, 2003), 261.
19 *Ibid.*
20 D. L. LeMahieu, *A Culture for Democracy: Mass Communication and the Cultivated Mind in Britain Between the Wars* (Oxford: Oxford University Press, 1988), 136.
21 'There are many dangers which hedge round the unfortunate composer: pressure groups which demand true proletarian music, snobs who demand the latest avant-garde tricks; critics who are already trying to document today for tomorrow, to be the first to find the correct pigeon-hole definition. … [The composer] may find himself writing more and more for machines, in conditions dictated by machines, and not by humanity.' Britten, *On Receiving the First Aspen Award*, in *Britten on Music*, 258.
22 Wood, *My Life of Music*, 94.

CHAPTER 2 LEANNE LANGLEY

This chapter is an expanded version of a paper given at the Institute of Historical Research, University of London (May 2003), and the University of Nottingham (July 2005). For assistance of various kinds and many stimulating conversations, I am grateful to Simon McVeigh and Eva Mantzourani, my colleagues at Goldsmiths College; the Editors; and especially the late Cyril Ehrlich, who fundamentally shaped my thinking on the Proms. For access to material in their collections, I thank Francesca Franchi, Royal Opera House Archives, Covent Garden; Nicolas Bell, Curator of Music Manuscripts, The British Library; Oliver Davies and Paul Collen, Department of Portraits and Performance History (now the Centre for Performance History), Royal College of Music; Janet Snowman, Royal Academy of Music Archives; Richard Mangan, Mander & Mitchenson Theatre Collection, Trinity College of Music; Edward Bhesania, BBC Proms Office; and the BBC Written Archives Centre, Caversham. For research funding through the London Concert Life project at Goldsmiths, I am happy to acknowledge the Arts and Humanities Research Council.
1 Wood, telegram to John Reith, 27 June 1927, WAC R30/2344/1.
2 Percy A. Scholes, *The Mirror of Music, 1844–1944: A Century of Musical Life in Britain as Reflected in the Pages of the 'Musical Times'*, 2 vols. (London: Novello & Co. and Oxford University Press, 1947), 195–6n; Reith, Diaries, vol. ii/1, 22 October 1924, WAC S60/5/2/1. Newman had confided to Scholes his wish for such an outcome 'some time before' an actual meeting with John Reith was arranged, privately at Scholes's flat on 22 October, four days after the end of the 1924 season. See further in text, p. 63–5.
3 Rosa Newmarch, in her 'Four Phases of the Promenade Concerts' (typescript, August 1927, Henry Wood Papers, BL Add. MS 56442, fols. 19–26), elaborated this theme in a public relations effort to smooth the transition to BBC management, presenting Wood as the unifying influence.
4 H. C. G. Matthew, 'The Liberal Age (1851–1914)', *The Oxford*

Illustrated History of Britain, ed. Kenneth O. Morgan (Oxford and New York: Oxford University Press, 1984), 481–93.

5 'The Victoria Concert Hall, Limited', share prospectus, 18 June 1887, City of Westminster Archives Centre.

6 On Ravenscroft (1829–1902), see 'The Presiding Genius of the Birkbeck Bank', *Bankers' Magazine* 54 (1892), 827–31 [with portrait]; and C. Delisle Burns, *A Short History of Birkbeck College* (London: University of London Press, 1924), 84–5. Related to the family of wig- and robe-makers who were partners in Ede & Ravenscroft, he founded the Birkbeck Bank, Chancery Lane, in 1851 as a building society for students of the London Mechanics' Institution. His original directors on the concert hall project included Viscount Folkestone, Frederic Cowen, Henry Sutherland Edwards and John Hollingshead; the hall's joint architects were Charles Phipps and Thomas Knightley.

7 See the architect's description and plan in 'Proposed New Concert-Hall, Langham-Place', *The Builder* (14 February 1891), 128–9; for reports on the opening see 'The New Concert Hall', *The Times* (27 November 1893), and 'Notes from the Concert Room: London's New Hall', *The Sketch* (6 December 1893).

8 PRO CRES 35/2144, Public Record Office, Kew. On 19 August 1893 Ravenscroft requested a change of name to 'The Queen's Concert Hall', or 'The Queen's Hall' for brevity, and proposed a deferral on the drafting of any lease. See also Robert Elkin, *Queen's Hall, 1893–1941* (London: Rider & Co., [1944]), 11–24.

9 As a youth Newman was 'recognised as one of the best athletes in the country' ('The Queen's Hall Orchestra', *The Tatler* [27 November 1901], 425). He studied at the Guildhall School of Music, worked as a jobber on the London Stock Exchange in 1885 and 1887, and studied singing at the Milan Conservatory and, from 1888 to December 1889, the Royal Academy of Music. As a professional he sang in promenade concerts at Her Majesty's Theatre (1889) and the Crystal Palace (1890) as well as in oratorio, notably the title part for Hubert Parry's *Job* at that work's London première in May 1893 (the work was panned by G. B. Shaw, though 'Mr Newman did what he could with the part … and his performance was entirely creditable to him' [*The World*, 3 May 1893]). Newman entered musical agency work with Farley and C. W. Sinkins around mid-1893; by August they were running promenade concerts at Covent Garden conducted by Cowen.

10 Arthur Jacobs, *Henry J. Wood: Maker of the Proms* (London: Methuen, 1994), 29.

11 See Frederic H. Cowen, *My Art and My Friends* (London: Edward Arnold, 1913), 233–5. Sinkins and Newman had signed their contract to manage the new hall in Cowen's room at Covent Garden Theatre, originally intending him to be conductor of a new orchestra for 'high-class concerts at popular prices' (*The Strad* 4, October 1893, p. 120). By mid-November Sinkins had pulled out; in spring 1894 Newman and Cowen gave only a few choral concerts, not very successful. Cowen's limited means prevented him from taking any further share in Queen's Hall promotions.

12 Henry J. Wood, *My Life of Music* (London: Victor Gollancz, 1938), 62, 65, 67–8; see also the typescript 'Queen's Hall Promenade Concerts now known as The Henry Wood Promenade Concerts', probably by Elsie Newmarch, in BL Add. MS 56421, fol. 76, summarizing events leading up to the founding of the Promenade concerts. The celebrity tour, that of Marie Roze (one of the biggest stars Newman and Cowen had worked with at the Covent Garden proms of 1893), was itself a strong recommendation of Wood's skill and versatility.

13 Wood, *My Life of Music*, 69 (italics original).

14 *Ibid.*, 69–70; and Mathilde Verne, *Chords of Remembrance* (London: Hutchinson, 1936), 238–40, quoting Cathcart's own recollections. These two accounts vary on whether or not sole conductorship was a pre-condition for funding, but the object was

agreed: to show that an Englishman could conduct Wagner.

15 Obituaries of Cathcart in early January 1951 in fact went too far, according to Elsie Newmarch, by suggesting that he 'discovered' Henry Wood or financed all the early Proms; see copies of her letters to Frank Howes and Thomas Russell in BL Add. MS 56421, fols. 70–71.

16 The vocalists were Clara Samuell, Ben Davies, Marian McKenzie and Robert Grice; the planned programme included William Vincent Wallace's Overture to *Maritana*, the Gavotte from Ambroise Thomas's *Mignon*, the Intermezzo from Mascagni's *Cavalleria rusticana*, a selection from Sullivan's operas, the *William Tell* overture, and a selection from Gounod's *Faust* (programme in Mander & Mitchenson Theatre Collection, Trinity College of Music).

17 According to extant promenade programmes in the Royal Opera House Archives, Covent Garden, Eayres was leader in 1873 under Jules Rivière; Ould (violoncello), Hann (viola/second violin), Anderson (bassoon) and Reynolds all played in 1875 under Luigi Arditi.

18 Particularly rich sources include Adam Carse, *The Life of Jullien: Adventurer, Showman-Conductor and Establisher of the Promenade Concerts in England, together with a History of those Concerts up to 1895* (Cambridge: W. Heffer & Sons, 1951); the memoirs of Jules Rivière (*My Musical Life and Recollections* [London: Sampson Low, Marston & Co., 1893]), Luigi Arditi (*My Reminiscences* [London: Dodd, Mead, 1896]), and James W. Davison (*From Mendelssohn to Wagner, being the Memoirs of J. W. Davison*, comp. Henry Davison [London: William Reeves, 1912]); original Covent Garden promenade programmes; and periodicals such as the *Theatrical and Concert Companion* (1838–40), the *Musical World* (1836–91) and the *Monthly Musical Record* (from 1870).

19 Wood, *My Life of Music*, 68: 'I was greatly impressed with Newman over that lunch [Pagani's, March 1894]. I had never met a manager who knew anything about music. Newman did. He possessed both business acumen and artistic ideals. *He wanted the public to come to love great music*' (italics original). Wood refers to this motivating dream several times. While the manager may indeed have conveyed such a message, not least to inspire the workhorse he hoped Wood would be, we may also recall the mature conductor's equivocal position with the BBC in the late 1930s when he was writing his memoirs: wanting the public 'to come to love great music' was Wood's depiction of his own legacy at that date, in the face of curtailment by his current employers whom, unlike Newman, he mistrusted. For a longer view of this rhetorical device in English concert promotion, see Simon McVeigh, '"An Audience for High-Class Music": Concert Promoters and Entrepreneurs in Late-Nineteenth-Century London', in *The Musician as Entrepreneur, 1700–1914: Managers, Charlatans, and Idealists*, ed. William Weber (Bloomington: Indiana University Press, 2004), 162–82.

20 Events from company liquidation to the bombing of Queen's Hall appear to have destroyed all official business files from before 1927. Each proprietor ran the business as a private concern before that date, not necessarily discretely from other concert promotions, such that any tidy handover of Proms records could hardly have been effected, even if considered relevant to the BBC, in 1927. The one continuous source acquired by the BBC at some point is a complete set of programmes, probably the in-house original. The British Library set is incomplete and shows signs of compilation from programmes of individual concert-goers, possibly including Percy Pitt and Rosa Newmarch.

21 First-hand accounts include Eugene Goossens, 'Sir Henry Wood at Rehearsals', *New York Times* (3 September 1944), typescript copy in BL Add. MS 56442, fols. 53–7; Eric Coates, *Suite*

in Four Movements: An Autobiography (London: William Heinemann Ltd, 1953), 136–7; and Bernard Shore, 'Sir Henry Wood', in The Orchestra Speaks (London: Longmans, Green & Co., 1938), 183–218. For Wood's appeal to science in other practical music matters, e.g. the tuning of choral bodies separated spatially, see My Life of Music, 215.

22 Wood, My Life of Music, 101. By 1910 this rank-and-file figure was about 11 per cent higher. According to his Suite in Four Movements, 134, Eric Coates, as outside player at the second desk of violas, was earning £2. 10s. a week in the promenade season (50s. for nine sessions), which was roughly half what he got for weekly Symphony concerts with rehearsal (21s., two sessions) and Sunday concerts without (10s. 6d.). Principal players would have earned more.

23 For a summary see Scholes, Mirror of Music, 406–9, and Wood, My Life of Music, 69–71, where Michael Costa is blamed for having promoted the building of higher-pitched organs and wind instruments in England (up to about a' = 452). August Manns had advocated a lowering of pitch even before Wood and Cathcart did, more for convergence in internationally mixed instrumental ensembles than through worry about voice damage.

24 Joseph Bennett, 'Music of the Day', Daily Telegraph (28 February 1894), reveals Newman's earliest plan for what was to have been a series of nine instrumental and three choral concerts directed by Cowen, using an orchestra of 80 and a chorus 'proportioned to the demands of the building'. Drawn from the Middlesex Choral Union of 1893 with which Newman had sung, the choir first performed Gounod's Redemption on Good Friday 1894 and gave a few more concerts before re-emerging under Alberto Randegger (1895–97), Wood (1898) and then George Riseley (1899) as the Queen's Hall Choral Society, performing Elijah, Samson, Messiah, Sullivan's Golden Legend, The Creation and other large works. Meanwhile choral activity was overtaken by the orchestral side of Newman's plan, which itself split into two related series in 1895: the Promenade concerts and Sunday Afternoon Orchestral concerts (first conducted by Randegger). Any notion of regularly combining choral and orchestral forces at the Proms was thus a non-starter from the outset, for logistical, economic and promotional reasons. Not only was the metropolis deficient in strong, reliable amateur chorus singers (cf. Scholes, Mirror of Music, 34–5), but Wood insisted on adequate joint rehearsal for such occasions (impossible for Proms) and the public were less enthusiastic anyway. Newman's 1902 bankruptcy proceedings indeed revealed that he had found orchestral concerts profitable, but choral concerts loss-making (Jacobs, Henry J. Wood, 83).

25 Richter did more to raise the profile of orchestral music with London devotees than any other conductor since Haydn's day. The Crystal Palace, however, offered a better model for attracting wide audiences and expanding repertory through its garden atmosphere, range of music (military bands, promenades and Saturday orchestral concerts), year-round opening, welcome of new works and young artists (including British), open admission, ticket pricing, music classes and audience training through programme notes. See Michael Musgrave, The Musical Life of the Crystal Palace (Cambridge: Cambridge University Press, 1995).

26 Rosa Newmarch, Henry J. Wood (London: John Lane, The Bodley Head, 1904), 11–13.

27 Ralph W. Wood, 'The Prom. Audience', Music and Letters 11 (1930), 177–81 ('All tastes are catered for, all brands of listener attracted, … due simply to the necessity for filling the hall' [178–9]). See also Constant Lambert, 'Positively the Last on the Promenades', Night and Day (21 October 1937), 188–9, who links changes in his chosen position in the hall, from balcony to promenade to circle, with his advancing age, variable tastes and other kinds of listener.

28 'To Mr. Robert Newman and to Mr. Henry J. Wood undoubtedly belongs a measure of praise, which all who have the true welfare of real music in our midst should be disposed to give them for their great achievement. The credit for first forming a public entirely their own, and for following this up by educating that public to the point where it sees more in music than mere external glitter and glamour, is, indeed, large. … The artistic and the educational worth of the concerts is undoubted, unquestioned. … From the public point of view, they have never previously had their like' (Daily Telegraph, 15 August 1908).

29 Both Manchester and Sydenham had resident orchestras performing at least half the year from the 1860s. Spa towns, most recently Bournemouth, and Glasgow from the early 1890s had also made serious inroads in creating local orchestras and audiences, whereas the Philharmonic Society of London (founded 1813), never a permanent orchestra, was in 1895 still giving only a handful of concerts each year in 'the season'. From about 1906 the success of the Queen's Hall Proms reversed the flow of influence, prompting similar promenade experiments at Birmingham and Blackpool under Landon Ronald.

30 Wood notes in My Life of Music that the manager went through his proposed 1895 programme with him, discussing the relative drawing-power of each item (75); and on the closeness of their working relationship: 'I had never so much as engaged an extra player without having discussed it with him first … we discussed every detail from all angles calmly and in the kindliest spirit' (319–20). In his Introduction to J. Daniel Chamier, Percy Pitt of Covent Garden and the B.B.C. (London: Edward Arnold, 1938), 11–14, Wood quotes Newman as saying to him, on possibly hiring Pitt as accompanist, 'You are my musical boss … I leave purely musical matters to you' (12).

31 BL shelfmark h.5470, programmes for 8–13 September 1919. Landon Ronald was then conductor of the New Symphony Orchestra, giving regular Sunday Afternoon concerts at the Albert Hall.

32 Wood's audition books, 1896–1926, included a final column on each performer, 'whether likely to be of use to Newman' (My Life of Music, 75). The manager's method of popularizing an unknown artist fascinated Wood. It involved a trial at the Promenades, a longer engagement there the next year if successful, then movement away from the Proms by the third year to protect the artist's appeal at the Sunday or Saturday Symphony concerts.

33 After its première in 1905 the Sea Songs achieved 28 performances to 1920, up to four times in some seasons (1909, 1910, 1914) but not at all in others (1906, 1915, 1919). It first appeared on a Last Night in 1908 (as first item in the second half) and occasionally thereafter, but did not become a regular Last Night item until 1922. Wood's other song medleys, Fantasia on Welsh Melodies and Fantasia on Scottish Melodies, both of 1909, reappeared occasionally.

34 Wood, My Life of Music, 133–4, records an incident of 1899 in which a singer who could not find her pitch, twice, drew the orchestra's 'gentle shuffling of feet', their standard expression of disapproval on sensing a lack of musicianship; Wood was then hissed by some of the Prom audience (her friends) because he resorted to accompanying her on the piano. See also C. E. M. Joad, 'Queen's Hall was My Club', in Sir Henry Wood: Fifty Years of the Proms, ed. Ralph Hill and C. B. Rees (London: British Broadcasting Corporation, [1944]), 54: 'you had only to break down once or twice in the performance of your concerto to evoke rounds of sympathetic applause at the end.'

35 Wood, My Life of Music, 211–12; Jacobs, Henry J. Wood, 46, 52, 99–100.

36 Wood, My Life of Music, 94–5. Newman attended every rehearsal, knew every player by sight and what instrument he or

she played, and was especially stringent with percussionists – locking all platform doors at rehearsal (performances too) to prevent their sneaking out. He was the first to break the custom of employing a separate player for each percussion instrument: contracts were given only to players who could play three.

37 Quoted in Eugene Goossens, *Overture and Beginners: A Musical Autobiography* (London: Methuen, 1951), 90. The audition was held in July 1912.

38 Both published and unpublished music was free of any performance fee until at least 1914; see Cyril Ehrlich, *Harmonious Alliance: A History of the Performing Right Society* (Oxford and New York: Oxford University Press, 1989), 1–42. A more obvious issue is whether composers who were asked to provide Wood with a new score and parts received payment for their work (a copy of which then went into Wood's musical library); more likely, a Queen's Hall performance was seen as its own reward, assisting publication and further exposure. In this period, only one work is known to have been commissioned by Newman for a specific occasion and credited – Percy Pitt's *Coronation March*, 23 September 1896, commemorating 'H.M. The Queen's Record Reign'. As Proms accompanist Pitt often contributed short MS works and arrangements as part of the job.

39 Wood, *My Life of Music*, 105. Wood believed that an exciting performance appealed to the wide public more than a careful, 'stolid academic' one. Eric Coates, *Suite in Four Movements*, 134–5, reiterated a similar idea about orchestral membership from separate experience – that an orchestra's responsiveness and sense of abandon were enhanced by an intermingling of national traditions in which players had been trained differently. At no time was there ever an attempt to build an 'all-British' orchestra at Queen's Hall; that aim was more closely associated with Beecham in this period, and with George Halford in Birmingham.

40 *My Life of Music*, 216: 'The preparation for a Symphony concert is at least a degree more leisurely, and therefore more thoughtful than it can ever be for a Promenade concert. Four or five rehearsals for a single Symphony concert is one thing; a morning of rehearsal for tonight's Promenade *plus* a new work down for tomorrow night as well as a bit of the programme for the Strauss concert next week, is quite another. That is, if some composer-conductor does not expect me to give half an hour of my time to let him rehearse a work of his own lasting ten minutes!' Soloists were normally given a piano rehearsal with Wood, not a full orchestral one, which for the vast majority was sufficient. Percy Grainger, who played Liszt's *Hungarian Fantasy* at a Prom in 1906, wrote in a letter: 'Wood conducted excellently. We had no rehearsal' (quoted in Jacobs, *Henry J. Wood*, 40).

41 This is self-evidently true, or the concerts would never have lasted. On loose orchestral playing in this period generally, see Robert Philip, *Performing Music in the Age of Recording* (New Haven and London: Yale University Press, 2004), who is, however, particularly critical of the Queen's Hall Promenade standard.

42 *Overture and Beginners*, 91.

43 *Suite in Four Movements*, 134.

44 *Overture and Beginners*, 90–91.

45 Maurice Sons (1857–1942), originally from Amsterdam and late of the Scottish Orchestra in Glasgow, became principal first violin of the QHO in the main season of 1904, staying until 1927, but never led the Promenade orchestra. A violin professor at the RCM, he preferred to use the long vacation for his annual holiday (Wood, *My Life of Music*, 186); he occasionally appeared as a soloist.

46 *Overture and Beginners*, 92: 'Ten weeks of nightly three-hour symphony concerts, with three rehearsals a week (and Sunday afternoon concerts thrown in for good measure), is a back-breaking – but worthwhile – experience.'

47 'Queen's Hall Promenade Concerts', *Musical Times* 59 (1918),

424. The new status of women – nearly five million were in employment by January 1918 – led to the first stage of their being granted the vote in 1918.

48 *My Life of Music*, 113–14: 'I was delighted when Miriam Timothy came to us as harpist. She was a beautiful girl, and in those days (the wearing of black not being compulsory) she was able to express her sense of artistry in her dress. She certainly made a charming platform picture seated at her harp' (113). In the period of Timothy's membership (*c.* 1896–1904), Wood's harpists sat in front of the second violins.

49 Cathcart later stated there was a loss of not less than £50 on every concert, with the exception of the two at which Sims Reeves sang, when the hall was sold out (Elkin, *Queen's Hall*, 25). This would have made a total loss of around £2,300. Newman however gained something through a benefit concert at the end of the season – the first Last Night, 5 October 1895 – when Wood and the orchestra gave their services. According to Cathcart, 'The hall was crammed and Newman was richer by £400' (quoted in Mathilde Verne, *Chords of Remembrance*, 239).

50 BL shelfmark h.5470, bound at the beginning of the 1902 summer Promenade programmes. A model of simplicity, the leaflet is undated and gives no outline programmes, but refers to the artists engaged and 30 compositions 'to be performed for the first time in London at the forthcoming season of Promenade Concerts at the Queen's Hall'. These include Tchaikovsky's First Symphony and Franck's *Variations symphonique* (which indeed were given) as well as Mahler's First Symphony (which was not, postponed until 1903). The idea of a brief prospectus may well have arisen in the wake of Newman's bankruptcy, to reassure the public and focus attention on an ambitious season; certainly this leaflet links the Promenades to Queen's Hall (not Newman) and the orchestra to Wood in an effective new division.

51 Programmes for 1903 show that 'full particulars' were available from the new QHO Ltd office, 320 Regent Street, at the beginning of the season. Two letters of 1907 (BL Music Misc., Deposit 2003/13, Wood to Rosa Newmarch, 5 and 11 June 1907) suggest that necessary information for the programme-note writer (i.e. the chosen works) would be available in January, and that 'everything' was 'ready and printed' (the prospectus of programmes) in early June. A letter from Wood to Miss Alice Taylor, 18 September 1913 (McCann Collection, Royal Academy of Music), is clearer still: 'I am … sorry that it is not possible for me to comply with your request, … as we send out about forty thousand prospectuses and our subscribers are naturally annoyed if they find alterations are being made.'

52 On 17 September 1907, Liszt's *Totentanz* was substituted for his *Concerto pathétique in E minor* 'owing to the non-arrival of the orchestral parts' from the arranger; on 20 October 1908, Handel's 'Ombra mai fù' was substituted for Three Songs by Somervell because the orchestral parts 'did not arrive in time for the Rehearsal this morning'; more understandably, in 1917 Vasilenko's Violin Concerto had to be cancelled because the parts could not be secured from Russia.

53 For background see Christina Bashford, 'Not Just "G.": Towards a History of the Programme Note', in *George Grove, Music and Victorian Culture*, ed. Michael Musgrave (Basingstoke: Palgrave Macmillan, 2003), 115–42.

54 Wood to Newmarch, 9 July 1908, BL Add. MS 56421, fol. 22: 'I should like you to put a special line in the Promenade programmes whenever we play a Haydn Symphony, to the effect that the symphony will be played without break between the movements.' On Wood's well-known crusade for the suppression of intermediate applause, see Jacobs, *Henry J. Wood*, 132 (citing examples of 1911, 1914, 1923) – a trend read by some 'historically informed' commentators to suggest that Wood was misguidedly trying to inhibit personal enjoyment. Wide of the mark, this assumption fails to understand the nineteenth-century performing and listening context in which coherence of programming was untypical and had to be built through education and consensus. On the contrary, at the Proms in 1908 guiding applause selectively was a tool of modernization in orchestral discipline as well as in corporate listening, and was intended to promote enjoyment.

55 On the left, 'Smoking is permitted at these Concerts, excepting in the seats between doors E and F in the Grand Circle, which are reserved for Non-Smokers [some 168 seats]. Gentlemen are politely requested to refrain from striking matches during the performance of the various items.' On the right, 'These Concerts are advertised to commence at 8 o'clock and terminate at 11 o'clock, but the persistent demands for encores sometimes necessitate the omission of certain items in order to finish within reasonable time.' By 1907 management took an even firmer line, with 'Encores are not permitted in the first half of the Programme', and 'Patrons are earnestly requested to support the Management in carrying out the programme advertised in the Daily Papers.'

56 This was a longstanding problem at prom concerts from at least the 1870s to the 1920s. See Ralph W. Wood, 'The Prom. Audience', 178; and BL h.5470, programme of 19 September 1919, with MS annotation next to 'Morning in my Garden' by F. S. Boville Smith, sung by John Smith (first performance): 'Mediocre song, also accompaniment. His singing also made me want to go into hysterics! Encore.'

57 In 1919 Newmarch asked the 30-year-old Eric Blom to assist her with the notes, a task they shared until 1926. See Jack Westrup, rev. Rosemary Williamson, 'Blom, Eric (Walter)', New Grove 2; Alec Hyatt King, rev. G. R. Seaman, 'Blom, Eric Walter', Oxford Dictionary of National Biography; and Newmarch's published collection The Concert-Goer's Library of Descriptive Notes, 6 vols. (London: Oxford University Press, 1928–48).

58 See the 'Press Proof' for the concert of 25 August 1900 in the British Library set (h.5470), showing a skeletal layout in which some items have the programme-note space filled in with typeset text (where previous notes already existed at Baines & Scarsbrook), while others are blank, stimulating the note-writer's flow of new copy. The final programme follows behind. This proof may itself have been Pitt's, a clue to when he first started helping Jacques. Wood, My Life of Music, 161–2, explains that so many blank spaces had been meant to shock Jacques into speeding up his study of novelties and his note-writing.

59 BL Music Misc., Deposit 2003/13. Wood's proposal included work for the Symphony and Sunday concerts too; but the promenades would be the more challenging assignment in terms of time, intensity and number of novelties.

60 BL programmes, 16 and 24 August 1904; 12 and 14 September 1905; Wood, My Life of Music, 204, 359, and Jacobs, Henry J. Wood, 442; BL programme, 26 October 1906, and Wood, My Life of Music, 205, respectively.

61 My Life of Music, 154. Arthur Jacobs (Henry J. Wood, 74) raises doubt over whether there was a third playing of the march, given that press reports 'record one encore'. But even a letter from A. J. Jaeger describing the event to an absent Elgar called it 'the greatest success I have ever witnessed over a novelty at any concert' (quoted in Jacobs, 73).

62 W. H. Reed, Elgar (London: Dent, 1946), 69. The idea of putting words to the March tune had been Clara Butt's.

63 Programme, 31 October 1902. The Ode was sandwiched between the 'Coriolan' overture and the symphony, both conducted by Arthur Payne in Wood's absence. Besides the QHO and the Band of the Coldstream Guards, forces included the Queen's Hall Choral Society and four soloists: Agnes Nicholls, Edna Thornton, Lloyd Chandos and David Ffrangçon-Davies.

The unusual presence of choir and soloists helps explain why, also unusually, the Ninth was given with its choral finale.

64 He was not above short cuts, pointed advice or tinkering to make things tell in a performance. After the première of Pitt's string piece Aria, on 21 October 1913, Wood wrote to the composer: 'I hope the tympani part was not too awful as I only sketched it in at the last moment, trusting that you might arrive in time to do it yourself', followed by 'Do you think I could do the wind piece of yours, the Mozart, without the repeats? For wind pieces to be effective they must err on the short side and I felt it was a little long' (25 October 1913, BL Egerton MS 3306, fol. 215).

65 Typescript of Music Magazine radio script, 25 February 1945, BL Add. MS 56442, fols. 71–82 at 74. Economics were the key, with the Symphony concerts allotted the most rehearsal time, the best artists and the higher ticket pricing. In the same radio script, Boult surmised that 'Sir Henry himself' always examined British scores and made his choice of them 'single handed'.

66 See Jacobs, Henry J. Wood, 136–41, for events surrounding the performance of Five Orchestral Pieces, a world première although Wood did not realize it. Goossens recalled that the work needed three consecutive one-hour rehearsals and baffled the players, who were hostile ('Sir Henry Wood at Rehearsals'). After further work and increased familiarity, the tide changed: the Symphony concert performance on 17 January 1914 was brilliant and well received. Wood, My Life of Music, 273, reprints the glowing letter Schoenberg sent to Newman ('I must tell you that on the Continent, as far as my knowledge goes, there are only at the most two orchestras which would be compared with you – the Amsterdam Orchestra and the Viennese Philharmonic').

67 Like the summer Proms, both these series introduced substantial new works. The Saturday-only Proms (17 October 1896–10 April 1897) included the British premières of Tchaikovsky's Nutcracker suite, two Dvořák symphonic poems and Rimsky-Korsakov's Scheherazade, for example, though as a weekly series these Proms carried twice the labour cost of nightly Promenades. Newman meanwhile launched his flagship Saturday Afternoon Symphony series in January 1897 with top artists, rendering the Saturday-night Proms less attractive. The winter Proms of 1901–2 (32 concerts), also ambitious, attempted to spin off repertory from the successful Symphony concerts that could not have been accommodated in the summer rehearsal schedule, such as Berlioz's Symphonie fantastique and Strauss's Don Juan (both scheduled for late January 1902); the challenge proved too great (Don Juan was cancelled), and attendance was evidently too small at that time of year.

68 My Life of Music, 156: 'Several bodies were anxious to take over the management of the concerts, but we had to steer a clear course; otherwise we might have found ourselves in the hands of a firm of publishers and have had to study their interests; or, again, some composer. That would have been disastrous.' He does not name names, but among the most likely candidates were: a group of shareholders in the St James's Hall Co., including its chairman, Thomas Chappell (who were hoping to sell the old rival hall to a hotel developer, which they soon did, opening the way for William Boosey to pick up Newman's lease); possibly Henry Balfour Gardiner, the wealthy young English composer with Frankfurt connections; and possibly Ernest Palmer (of Huntley & Palmer biscuit fortune, by 1903 founder of the RCM Patron's Fund to promote British works and performers). Modern guesswork aside, Wood's sentiment is clear: the Promenades' best chance in 1902 lay in an independent, liberal and inclusive policy, not in a promotional link with popular, indigenous or any other particular kind of music.

69 Theo Barker, 'Speyer, Sir Edgar', Oxford Dictionary of National Biography; Edward Speyer, My Life and Friends (London: Cobden-

Sanderson, 1937), 202: 'He told me later that on average it cost him £4000 a year.' The Promenades' portion, £2,000, would have represented an average shortfall, not the whole cost of a Proms season; and indeed the subsidy continued when subscription and box-office receipts were rising (see note 94 below). This suggests a conscious decision to keep prices down even when demand rose, and that Speyer was effectively funding continual improvements to the orchestral standard through the hire of excellent players, visits of European composers and provision of increased rehearsal time. Among his non-commercial philanthropic causes were hospitals and art; he was a founding trustee of the Whitechapel Gallery in 1901.

70 In 1905 Speyer became chairman of Underground Electric Railways of London Ltd (UERL), by 1914 the city's major transport operator. For a fascinating account of issues in the company's finance, public relations, advertising and fare-setting, competition from the petrol bus and the importance of an integrated system in Speyer's period, see T. C. Barker and Michael Robbins, *A History of London Transport: Passenger Travel and the Development of the Metropolis*, 2 vols. (London: George Allen & Unwin, 1963/rev. 1975; 1974), ii, 70–74, 113–17, 137–41, 150–53. The three new tube lines were the Bakerloo, Piccadilly and 'Hampstead' (now Northern), all opened in 1906–7. The Central Line's Oxford Circus station, closest to Queen's Hall, had opened in July 1900.

71 For attacks on Speyer, which continued throughout the war, see Panikos Panayi, *The Enemy in our Midst: Germans in Britain during the First World War* (New York and Oxford: Berg, 1991), esp. 188–91. Edgar had been born of German parents in New York, where his brother James ran the American branch of Speyer's; Leonora, of an American mother and German father, was born in Washington, D.C. Edgar wound up the London branch of Speyer's in 1915 and later defended his British loyalty in court; in late 1921 his naturalization and all honours were revoked.

72 Speyer offered his personal resignation to the prime minister in May 1915, but Asquith declined, replying that the king was not prepared to revoke his baronetcy (letters published in *The Times*, 18 and 25 May 1915). From New York, on 18 June, Speyer wrote to Shaw: 'It was exceedingly kind of you to write and both my wife and I appreciate the thought that prompted your letter which has given us very great pleasure. After Mr. Asquith's letter "honour is satisfied" as they say but I shall never forget nor forgive the treatment I have received. This may not be a fine sentiment but it is the true one at any rate' (G. B. Shaw Papers, BL Add. MS 50527, fols. 256–7). In an attempt to head off final official rejection, Elgar wrote on Speyer's behalf: 'I have the happiest memories of the days when you were connected with the Queen's Hall orchestra and the moving spirit of that splendid organisation. … Your ungrudging support, not confined to any one school, was for years a great uplifting force in London and your influence and enthusiasm were very greatly missed' (draft letter, Elgar to Speyer, 23 October 1921, Elgar Birthplace Museum, Broadheath, ref. 9620). In 1910 Leonora had helped Elgar try out sections of his Violin Concerto; in 1911 Speyer funded the QHO rehearsals and first performance of Elgar's Second Symphony.

73 Rosa Newmarch, 'Queen's Hall in 1914–15', letter to the editor, *Monthly Musical Record* 62 (1932), 36–7, in reply to a recent review of Boosey's memoir *Fifty Years of Music* (London: Ernest Benn, 1931). Newmarch refuted Boosey's unfounded allegation (p. 106) that Speyer's programmes had 'contained nothing but German music'; equally, she credited Boosey and the Chappell firm for stepping into the breach as a guardian of the public taste in music.

74 Speyer gave the title deeds of the QHO to Wood as a parting gift in 1915, forcing Boosey to change the orchestra's name. Though Wood all along appreciated Boosey's magnanimous support and considered his emphasis on Chappell products at the Proms 'an astute stroke' (*My Life of Music*, 320), privately, in the 1920s, he was unhappy about 'Boosey's dictation in the matter of Chappell pianos, Chappell singers and Chappell songs' (John Reith, 'Memorandum of Meeting with Mr. Boosey', 10 March 1927, WAC R30/2344/1). Eric Coates, *Suite in Four Movements*, wrote that Boosey 'was not in the least orchestrally-minded and thought only in terms of popular song-hits' (183–4). Nor was banter about the lucrative conversion of concert halls only frivolous. Boosey joked about converting Queen's Hall into a permanent circus, while St James's Hall was in fact taken down for a hotel in 1904–5 (see Boosey, *Fifty Years*, 102–5). At the very least, Boosey's interior redecoration of Queen's Hall in 1919, acquisition of the Crown lease in 1920, and rebuilding of the organ in 1923 suggest a conscious effort to improve the building as a capital asset.

75 See 'Discussion on the Queen's Hall Promenade Programmes', *Musical Times* 59 (1918), 469–70, recounting several exchanges from September in the *Daily Telegraph*, including an anonymous correspondent's complaint about hearing 'the same old stuff we have heard for years and years … the eternal Tchaikovsky, Grieg, Mendelssohn, Liszt, Saint-Saëns, Handel – the same old "Peer Gynt," Hungarian Rhapsodies, Pathetic Symphony' (469). To Robin Legge's (the *Telegraph* critic's) statement of agreement that too little was being done at the Proms to encourage new English music, Boosey replied, defending the economic reasons for his programming policy: 'The moment we are convinced by receipts that the public prefer Mr. Joseph Holbrooke's music to that of Beethoven, or Mr. Granville Bantock's compositions to those of Tchaikovsky, we are perfectly prepared radically to alter the character of the Queen's Hall programmes' (470). Ultimately concert finance was a serious challenge. And though Boosey, Newman and Wood had different approaches to attracting audiences, they agreed a composer's nationality was of itself irrelevant: 'The average British concert-goer does not care a pin who composes the music, so long as it is found attractive to *him*' (Wood, quoted on 470).

76 See *Ferruccio Busoni: Letters to his Wife*, translated by Rosamond Ley (London: Edward Arnold, 1938), 281, letter of 6 November 1919. Busoni had worked with Newman since 1900, Wood championing his music as well as his playing. On this London visit, Newman purposely called on Busoni to promote the idea of his playing Chappell pianos, presumably to build bridges with Boosey; the war came up in conversation.

77 Edward Speyer (d. 1934) was Edgar's much older second cousin, and both came from an established Frankfurt banking family. Edward arrived in London in 1859, worked in the import business and eventually made his home at Ridgehurst in Hertfordshire. His classical affinities, conservative politics and connections with Brahms, Joachim, Tovey and chamber music are described in his *My Life and Friends*; for his strong advice to Henry Wood in the Boosey crisis, to 'give up the mixed programmes and … make the classics the mainstay of the concerts', see p. 202. Some evidence of the classics he meant – 30 by Bach, 35 by Mozart and 13 by Haydn – may be found in Speyer's 'List of works, in the handwriting of Sir Henry Wood, performed under his direction at the series of Promenade Concerts at the Queen's Hall London, August–October 1924', BL Add. MS 42233, fols. 292–6, dated 19 August 1924. The exact nature of any transaction underlying this list is unclear, but it seems likely that since Speyer was a Saturday Symphony subscriber, Wood approached him for a contribution in the hope of buying time until a longer-term solution could be found: the Proms were fundamental to safeguarding the Symphony concerts, after all, and any external funding, however restricted, would help. See also 'Thirty Years of Promenade Concerts', *The Times* (15 October 1924), alluding to Wood's 'personal action' in ensuring the 1924 season.

78 Wood, *My Life of Music*, 310; 'The Promenade Concerts: Rumours and Facts', *The Times* (9 August 1924), probably by H. C. Colles; and Reginald Pound, *Sir Henry Wood: A Biography* (London: Cassell, 1969), 152–3. Other journalists briefed by Newman would have included Eric Blom, London music critic for the *Manchester Guardian* and a Proms note-writer, and Percy Scholes, music critic of the *Observer* and a known believer in public music education. On the value of royal recognition, more a sign of encouragement than of self-evident success, see Wood, *My Life of Music*, 159, 303. In early February 1902 Edward VII and Queen Alexandra had attended a Sunday Afternoon concert, silencing criticism of that series from Sabbatarians since 1898.

79 Percy Scholes, *Mirror of Music*, 195–6n, documents a confidential conversation in which Newman conveyed his wish to Scholes, an early supporter of broadcasting, that the BBC might take up the Proms (see note 2 above, and Chapter 3, note 55). Certainly it was Newman whose interests depended most heavily on salvaging the Proms as a series. Wood seems to have wanted secure, well-paid conducting work on an ongoing basis that was not necessarily limited, or even linked, to Promenade concerts.

80 Memos, Reith to Pitt, 19 February 1926, and R. H. Eckersley to Reith, 16 February 1927, in WAC RCONT1/Wood/2; memo, Eckersley to Reith, 26 May 1927, and 'Estimate for Six Weeks Promenade Concerts at Queen's Hall' with a projected loss of £3,160 [undated, late May 1927], in WAC R30/2344/1. These documents show that in 1926 Wood was only one of many conductors the BBC were considering for occasional employment, and not in the front rank; that the idea of subsidizing Chappell's Queen's Hall concerts was never seriously considered by the BBC before March 1927; and that as late as late May 1927, the right of entry into Queen's Hall for broadcasting their own symphony concerts was still thought, by Roger Eckersley at least (he was against the BBC's managing the series), more important than the Promenade concerts or any public-relations value associated with funding them. (See also Chapter 3.)

81 Reith, Diaries, vol. ii/1, 22 May 1925, WAC S60/5/2/1. I am grateful to Jenny Doctor for alerting me to this reference.

82 Robin H. Legge, 'Retrospect of Literature, Science, and Art in 1925: Music', *Annual Register* (1925), 74. Boosey was clearly impatient with continual Newman–Wood efforts to attract more finance, including from the BBC, none of which had proven successful.

83 Obituary notices in *The Times* (6 November 1926), and the *Musical Times* 67 (1926), 1134. In the Memorial Benefit Concert programme, Newmarch called him 'a sound man of business and an indefatigable worker'. The secret of his success 'lay quite as much in his heart as in his head: in the fact that he used music for large and honourable ends, and always kept in view the human side of every enterprise he undertook' (programme cutting in BL Add. MS 56442, fol. 11*v*). In a private letter to her son after Newman's funeral, Newmarch wrote: 'He was very experienced and tactful, and knew his press and public. Also he was a strong-minded man and perfectly honest. Such people are not picked up in a week' (quoted in Pound, *Sir Henry Wood*, 155).

84 Chamier, *Percy Pitt*, 14, and Wood, *My Life of Music*, 89. R. H. Eckersley doubted Pitt's positive view of Wood's usefulness, given that the BBC would want to use other well-known conductors (memo to John Reith, 16 February 1927), and B. E. Nicolls was against Wood's last-minute request for a little more compensation: 'he is frankly lucky to find us willing to face the risks of a Season at all' (memo to V. H. Goldsmith, 2 June 1927), both in WAC RCONT1/Wood/2.

85 Memo, Young to Eckersley, 7 April 1927, WAC RCONT1/Wood/2.

86 Reith, 'Memorandum of Meeting with Mr. Boosey', 10 March 1927, and Eckersley to Reith, 26 May 1927, both in WAC R30/2344/1. The press release 'Saving the Promenades', issued in May 1927, is reproduced in David Cox, *The Henry Wood Proms* (London: British Broadcasting Corporation, 1980), 86, where the author accepts without demur that the BBC 'welcomed the opportunity to take over an already famous and musically (if not financially) very successful series'.

87 The first definite offer to Wood, a contract 'on a comprehensive basis', was made in early April (Eckersley to Wood, 12 April 1927, WAC RCONT1/Wood/2), opening the way for negotiation about the Promenade season. In her 'Four Phases of the Promenade Concerts', Rosa Newmarch alluded to Newman, Speyer, Chappell & Co. and the BBC as the four changes of dynasty in 34 years, with Wood as the one 'prime minister' throughout.

88 Wood, *My Life of Music*, 35. Goossens vividly evoked 'the fantastic amount of music heaped in thick orderly masses on the iron music racks of the orchestra' ('Sir Henry Wood at Rehearsals'). According to B. E. Nicolls it was Wood's comprehensive music library that gave him his 'grip on the conductorship' of the Proms (Nicolls to Goldsmith, 2 June 1927, WAC RCONT1/Wood/2). He had charged Boosey 10s. 6d. per item, or something like 20 guineas a week, for the hire of music over and above his Proms conducting fee.

89 The most notable 'British' nights were 11 October 1898 and 22 October 1901. Occasional Scottish (e.g. Macfarren, Mackenzie, MacCunn and Allan Macbeth) or Irish (Stanford, Wallace and Balfe) nights, as in 1895, mixing familiar and new pieces may have been more popular; meanwhile Sullivan often had his own night in the early period. For Wood's general view on programming new British works, see *My Life of Music*, 174, where he discusses the sandwich principle, concluding, 'I knew only too well that a complete programme of native works would mean a very poor audience.' See also Wood's remarks quoted in 'Discussion on the Queen's Hall Promenade Programmes', *Musical Times* 59 (1918), 470: 'British works have always had their chance at the Proms as items of an ordinary programme without too much preliminary fanfare. I believe concerts advertised "All British" a mistake.'

90 Listed with dates in Rosa Newmarch, *Henry J. Wood* (1904), 84–9. Composers included Dora Bright, Coleridge-Taylor, Elgar, German, Holbrooke, Amy Horrocks, Mackenzie, W. H. Reed, Ronald and Stanford.

91 War was declared on 4 August and the season opened on 15 August, when Tchaikovsky's *Capriccio italien* replaced Strauss's *Don Juan* ('much to the loss of musical value and interest', according to the *Musical Times* 55 [1914], 589). On the first Monday (17 August), a Franco-Russian programme was substituted for the usual Wagner under pressure from Boosey, evidently fearing a demonstration by non-musical super-patriots; but by the following Monday Newman had intervened, judging the public mood and restoring Wagner. Newman stated in programmes and in the press his determination to keep to the original scheme as much as possible, declaring that 'the greatest examples of Music and Art are world possessions and unassailable even by the prejudices and passions of the hour'. Even Bartók's 'New Suite' was given on 1 September, though Strauss and Mahler remained off the menu. See also Newmarch, 'Queen's Hall in 1914–15', and Jacobs, *Henry J. Wood*, 148–50.

92 Still a fluke, not the start of a trend; see note 63 above.

93 The end-of-season summary for 1911 (BL h.5470) refers to 'that fine, healthy appreciation of *all kinds* of good music, which has been such a marked feature of the Promenade public, and the admiration of the foreigner in London' (italics original). By the time of the 1927 crisis, public discussion mentioned the admiration of other countries as one reason why the Proms should not be dropped: 'The "Promenades" have such world-wide fame that it would be a very serious thing for our reputation on the Continent

if they ceased. It would indeed give them an opportunity to call us unmusical' (Wood, quoted in Cox, *The Henry Wood Proms*, 84).

94 In 1912 the Proms were 'more popular than ever' and an 'indispensable part of the musical life of Londoners'; in 1913 'a crowded hall, and money refused at the doors' was 'the rule rather than the exception' (end-of-season summaries, BL h.5470).

95 See Wood, *My Life of Music*, 185–6. There was no performance of *Faun* in 1905, but two in each of 1906 and 1907, and four in 1908 (one of those conducted by Colonne).

96 See A. H. Sidgwick, *The Promenade Ticket: A Lay Record of Concert-Going* (London: Edward Arnold, 1914; new edition, 1945), in which the Fifth Symphony is 'much the most important element in the Promenade culture' (91), welding all Promenaders 'in a single mass: the novice is enraptured, the licentiate confirmed in his allegiance, while the most experienced can at least recall, whether with contempt or regret, the emotions of his orchestral nonage' (177).

97 Newmarch, 'Four Phases of the Promenade Concerts', fol. 23.

98 *Ibid.*, fols. 23–4.

99 See Jacobs, *Henry J. Wood*, 148–67 *passim*, for further detail on Wood's wartime concerts and repertory.

100 Newmarch, 'Four Phases of the Promenade Concerts', fols. 21, 24. On her view of the damage done to English musical culture through two centuries of the oratorio industry, see her *Henry J. Wood*, 14–15.

101 'Four Phases of the Promenade Concerts', fols. 21–2.

102 *Overture and Beginners*, 92.

103 *Journey towards Music: A Memoir* (London: Victor Gollancz, 1964), 199.

104 'London Scene: 1895–1944', in *Sir Henry Wood: Fifty Years of the Proms*, ed. Hill and Rees, 17.

105 See 'Queen's Hall was my Club', 51–5.

106 *Ibid.*, 53; Gollancz, *Journey towards Music*, 199–202.

107 London: Edward Arnold, 1914 (repr. 1921, 1928, 1936, 1943, 1945). Arthur Hugh Sidgwick (1882–1917) was a graduate of Balliol College, Oxford, which figures in the story, and a civil servant at the Board of Education. His father was the classical scholar and champion of women's education Arthur Sidgwick, younger brother of the Cambridge philosopher Henry Sidgwick. Even before 1930, J. A. Fuller Maitland believed the Proms' educational value was reflected in *The Promenade Ticket*'s publishing success.

108 *The Promenade Ticket*, 73–4, entry for 'Tuesday, 18th September' by Nigel F. Clarke.

CHAPTER 3 JENNY DOCTOR

1 Marina Warner, Introduction to *World of Myths* (London: British Museum Press, 2003), vi.

2 Peter Childs, *Modernism* (London: Routledge, 2000), 21, 19.

3 Alan Peacock and Ronald Weir, *The Composer in the Market Place* (London: Faber Music, 1975), 51.

4 Cyril Ehrlich, *The Piano: A History* (1976), rev edn (Oxford: Clarendon Press, 1990), 186.

5 Edwin Evans, 'Music and the Cinema', *Music and Letters* 10/1 (January 1929), 67.

6 Evans, 'Music and the Cinema', 65.

7 Ralph Hill, 'The Future of Music-Making', *Musical Times* 80 (February 1939), 93.

8 Peacock and Weir, *The Composer in the Market Place*, 57.

9 Asa Briggs, *The History of Broadcasting in the United Kingdom*, i: *The Birth of Broadcasting* (London: Oxford University Press, 1961), 64.

10 'Licence Figures', *BBC Handbook 1939* (London: BBC, 1939), 129.

11 The Marconi-Reisz carbon microphone 'gave good overall performance and was much smaller and more portable than [predecessors]. By 1927 the Marconi Reisz was in virtually universal use, continuing well into the 1930s'; 'BBC Microphones: Thirty Years of Evolution, 1920–1950s', *History of Public Address*, <http://www.historyofpa.co.uk/pages/ microphones.htm#bbc>, accessed 16 October 2005.

12 Simon McVeigh and Cyril Ehrlich, 'The Modernisation of London Concert Life around 1900', in *The Business of Music*, ed. Michael Talbot (Liverpool: Liverpool University Press, 2002), 99–100.

13 The 'Ordinary Listener' was overtly catered for and much discussed in the BBC and general press throughout the 1920s and 30s. For example, in January 1926 Sir Walford Davies began a series of talks, 'Music and the Ordinary Listener', providing basic instruction on music topics for untrained listeners; see Jennifer R. Doctor, *The BBC and Ultra-Modern Music: Shaping a Nation's Tastes* (Cambridge: Cambridge University Press, 1999), 67.

14 'Finance and Commerce in 1929', *Annual Register* (1921), 69.

15 'Finance and Commerce in 1924,' *Annual Register* (1924), 71.

16 Robin H. Legge, 'Retrospect of Literature, Science, and Art in 1919: Music', *Annual Register* (1919), 62.

17 Kaikhosru Sorabji, 'Some Ideas on the Concert Problem', *Musical Times* 66 (May 1925), 414–5.

18 Cyril Ehrlich, *The Music Profession in Britain Since the Eighteenth Century: A Social History* (Oxford: Clarendon Press, 1985), 204.

19 For example, in 1921 at the Queen's Hall Eugene Goossens conducted 'a superb orchestra' in a series of concerts that was deemed 'the home of the extreme modern in music', while Edward Clark organized and conducted a series of chamber orchestra concerts that introduced 'no little of the most recent English and Continental music as well as old'. Robin H. Legge, 'Retrospect of Literature, Science, and Art in 1921: Music', *Annual Register* (1921), 67.

20 Legge, 'Retrospect of Literature, Science, and Art in 1921: Music', 66.

21 Paul Kildea, 'World War I and the British Music Industry' (MM thesis, University of Melbourne, 1991), 36, 48 and 78.

22 For pre-war attitudes to British music programming and wartime patterns of programming German music, see Chapter 2, 66–70.

23 Robin H. Legge, 'Retrospect of Literature, Science, and Art in 1924: Music', *Annual Register* (1924), 68.

24 Cyril Ehrlich, *The Music Profession in Britain*, 207.

25 The discussion began on 7 September 1918 and is summarized in 'Discussion on the Queen's Hall Promenade Programmes', *Musical Times* 59 (October 1918), 469–70.

26 Anonymous writer, quoted in *ibid.*, 469.

27 Sir Ernest Palmer, quoted in *ibid.*, 470.

28 Chappell & Co., quoted in *ibid.*, 470.

29 Chappell & Co. became lessees of the Queen's Hall in 1902, the same year that Boosey, who had been working for the company since 1894, became managing director. Chappell's took on the management of the Proms in 1915. See Chapter 2, 62.

30 Legge, 'Retrospect of Literature, Science, and Art in 1919: Music', 62.

31 Alfred Kalisch, 'London Concerts', *Musical Times* 61 (October 1920), 689. It was now possible for 'new Wagner excerpts to [be added] to the list of those usually played, but till the end of 1913 Bayreuth had the control of such things and exercised its right to refuse permission. The intervening years [since 1913] were not suitable for experiments. Now, however, there are no obstacles, and on Monday, September 13, a start was made with long extracts from "Götterdämmerung", some at least of which had not before been heard in a London concert hall'.

32 Legge, 'Retrospect of Literature, Science, and Art in 1921: Music', 67.

33 Robin H. Legge, 'Retrospect of Literature, Science, and Art in 1922: Music', *Annual Register* (1922), 79–81; and 'Retrospect of Literature, Science, and Art in 1923: Music', *Annual Register* (1923), 68–70.

34 Reginald Pound, *Sir Henry Wood: A Biography* (London: Cassell, 1969), 157.

35 Cyril Ehrlich, *Harmonious Alliance: A History of the Performing Right Society* (Oxford and New York: Oxford University Press, 1989), 13.

36 William Boosey, *Fifty Years of Music* (London: Ernest Benn, 1931), 174.

37 Boosey, *Fifty Years of Music*, 175. His revised view led him to serve on the Royal Commission that formulated the 1911 Copyright Act, which recognized 'property in copyright beyond the mere right to print and publish, including the right to perform'; Ehrlich, *Harmonious Alliance*, 14.

38 Legge, 'Retrospect of Literature, Science, and Art in 1921: Music', 66–7.

39 Boosey later recalled, 'the more perfect broadcasting became, the more obvious it was that many of the public could sit at home and enjoy the music, for practically nothing'; *Fifty Years of Music*, 177.

40 The Entertainments Industry Joint Broadcasting Committee represented 'every branch of the industry affected by broadcasting', including 'concert givers and concert agents'. Recognizing that the broadcasting of 'plays, music, songs, and other entertainments' was 'prejudicial' to their interests, the committee resolved to take steps to protect them; 'Broadcasting and the Theatres: Entertainment Industry's Opposition', *The Times* (28 April 1923), 8(B).

41 'Entertainment Industry and Broadcasting: Negotiations Broken Off', *The Times* (10 May 1923), 12(C).

42 William Boosey, 'Broadcasting', *Daily Telegraph* (19 May 1923), 11(D).

43 The government first imposed the entertainments taxes in 1916, and they was not abolished until 1953. From 1916–22, the act specified: 'Payment for admission one shilling – rate of tax one penny; payment for admission exceeding one shilling – rate of tax one penny for the first shilling and one half-penny for every sixpence or part of sixpence by which this payment exceeds one shilling.' In other words, the rate started at 20 per cent on 1 shilling admission rates, and increased for higher seat prices.

44 'The Broadcasting Dispute', *The Times* (12 May 1923), 10(B). Negotiations between the BBC and the entertainment industry continued over the next few years; in 1925–6 industry representatives, including Boosey, were invited to give evidence at the government-appointed Broadcasting Inquiry; see 'The Broadcasting Inquiry: Attitude of the Theatres, Artists and the Public', *The Times* (19 December 1925), 23(E).

45 Reith, Diaries, vol. ii/1, 15 May 1923, WAC S60/5/2/1.

46 Letter from the BNOC lawyers to Robert Newman, 14 May 1923, in WAC R34/504.

47 'Occasional Notes', *Musical Times* 64 (August 1923), 548.

48 The first BBC Outside Broadcast took place on 8 January 1923 from Covent Garden, when the BNOC's performance of an act of Mozart's *Die Zauberflöte* was aired; see Doctor, *The BBC and Ultra-Modern Music*, 63.

49 'Broadcasting and Music', *BBC Handbook 1928* (London: BBC, 1928), 85.

50 For more details of these series, see Doctor, *The BBC and Ultra-Modern Music*, 64–5, 87–9.

51 The Programme Board discussed the plans for the series just a few days after this meeting; see Minute 1, 5 July 1924, in WAC R34/600/1.

52 Reith, Diaries, vol. ii/1, 1 July 1924, WAC S60/5/2/1. That is, Wood was contracted with Boosey until May 1925.

53 Reith, Diaries, vol. ii/1, 16 July 1924, WAC S60/5/2/1.

54 Reith, Diaries, vol. ii/1, 22 October 1924, WAC S60/5/2/1.

55 Percy Scholes was then the BBC Music Critic. He did not allude to this meeting in print until 1947: 'The late Robert Newman had some time before confided to the present writer … his wish that this solution could be brought about [i.e. broadcasting the Proms], the difficulty at that time lying in Messrs. Chappell's antagonism to the B.B.C. A meeting was suggested between Newman and the Director of the B.B.C. … But Newman declared that he could not even risk being seen to enter B.B.C. premises. A private meeting between the parties was therefore arranged at the writer's flat. Nothing came immediately of this.' Percy A. Scholes, *The Mirror of Music, 1844–1944* (London: Novello & Co. and Oxford University Press, 1947), 195–6n. Thanks are due to Leanne Langley for bringing this note to my attention.

56 'Entertainments: the Promenade Concerts: Rumours and Facts', *The Times* (24 August 1924), 8(B).

57 [H. C. Colles, probably], 'Thirty Years of Promenade Concerts', *The Times* (15 October 1924), 15(E).

58 Leanne Langley, in a private communication to the author, 2 September 2005, made the following insightful suggestions: 'The royal presence has to be explained: the [King and Queen] didn't go because they wanted to hear the music or see the crowd – do we know of any previous royal visits? In other words, *some* interested party had to have engineered that visit for a purpose. One could speculate that since the royals were obviously specially symbolic & the series was in big trouble, the point was to attract, promote, flush out a national or private sponsor of some kind – maybe a wealthy amateur as Speyer had been, maybe another music concern (like a record company) with something to gain; or, maybe the plan was just to garner public attention & stimulate politicians in hopes that the government would cough up subsidy (as *The Times* hints).'

59 In a press statement in March 1927, Wood estimated: '[Chappell's] must have lost something like £60,000 in the interests of the musical public of London and of England'; see Wood, quoted in David Cox, *The Henry Wood Proms* (London: BBC, 1980), 84. Given inflation and higher annual costs to musicians, who enjoyed improved union representation, it is likely that the losses increased annually.

60 'Letters to the Editor: Thirty Years of Promenade Concerts', *The Times* (20 October 1924), 20(E). Chappell's economizing continued, and in another letter, the heads of the Royal Academy and Royal College of Music called for the establishment of a private fund for Wood to '[use] at his sole discretion' to enable 'more time to rehearse than could be allowed by the prevailing conditions of management'; John B. McEwen and Hugh P. Allen, 'Letters to the Editor: The Promenades: A Rehearsal Fund', *The Times* (31 October 1925), 8(A); and 'Sir Henry Wood', *The Times* (31 October 1925), 13(E). Chappell's once again responded defensively, blaming the 20 per cent war tax; see Chappell & Co., 'Letters to the Editor: The Promenades', *The Times* (6 November 1925), 12(D).

61 See 'B.B.C. and Entertainment Industry: Progress of Negotiations', *The Times* (27 January 1925), 11(G).

62 Reith, Diaries, vol. ii/1, 10 March, 7 April, 22 May and 23 July 1925, WAC S60/5/2/1. 'Rice' was G. V. Rice, then BBC Secretary; and L. Stanton Jefferies produced the music programmes. See Doctor, *The BBC and Ultra-Modern Music*, 60–61.

63 Robin H. Legge, 'Retrospect of Literature, Science, and Art in 1925: Music', *Annual Register* (1925), 74.

64 Memo from Reith to Pitt, 19 February 1926, in WAC RCONT1/Wood/2. Meeting also mentioned in Reith, Diaries, vol. ii/1, 17 February 1926, WAC S60/5/2/1.

65 The contract terms were for £2,000 per annum, to conduct a maximum of 20 concerts with at least 9 in London, and to serve on the Musical Advisory Committee; see draft letter from Reith to Wood, 14 April 1926, WAC RCONT1/Wood/2.

66 Memo from Reith to Lewis and R. H. Eckersley, 9 April 1926, in WAC RCONT1/Wood/2. As Reith explained to Wood, the offer was delayed 'in view of the fact that this concern under its present constitution is being liquidated at the end of this year, and that I had not then reached a satisfactory settlement with the Post Office regarding the financial allocation which we would receive to carry us on in our ordinary work'; see Reith to Wood, 30 April 1926, in WAC RCONT1/Wood/2.

67 Letter from Wood to Reith, 27 April 1926, in WAC RCONT1/Wood/2.

68 Wood, Introduction to J. Daniel Chamier, *Percy Pitt of Covent Garden and the B.B.C.* (London: Edward Arnold, 1938), 13–14.

69 *The Jazz Singer*, dir. Alan Crosland, with performers Al Jolson and May McAvoy, 88 minutes (Warner Bros., 1927). The Vitaphone system of sound-on-disc was used for the synchronized soundtrack. Although it was not the first sound film, and in fact was only part-talkie, this was nevertheless the first Hollywood feature with spoken dialogue (mostly conversational ad-libs) and the first to integrate musical episodes within the dramatic action. In particular, it was Jolson's five musical numbers that made the film an international sensation.

70 A special issue of *Radio Times*, priced at the usual twopence, provided extensive commentary and illustrations: *Beethoven Number, Radio Times* (18 March 1927). Special articles were by Arnold Bennett, Romain Rolland and George Bernard Shaw, and eight full pages were devoted to 'The Story of Beethoven' by Percy Scholes (577–84).

71 George Bernard Shaw, 'Beethoven Broadcast', *Radio Times* (18 March 1927), 575.

72 Thomas Armstrong, 'Wireless and the Concert-Goer', *Musical Times* 67 (December 1926), 1078.

73 'Queen's Hall: Orchestra's Last Season', *The Times* (4 March 1927), 14(F).

74 Announcement quoted in Pound, *Sir Henry Wood*, 156. See also Wood's press statement, excerpt quoted in Cox, *The Henry Wood Proms*, 84.

75 'No More "Promenades"?', *The Times* (4 March 1927), 15(D). See also footnote 89.

76 Sir Bernard Partridge, 'For the Honour of London' [cartoon drawing], *Punch* (16 March 1927).

77 Memo from R. H. Eckersley to Reith, 16 February 1927, WAC RCONT1/Wood/2.

78 Memo from Reith to Eckersley, 18 February 1927, WAC RCONT1/Wood/2.

79 Letter from Reith to Wood, 4 March 1927, WAC RCONT1/Wood/2.

80 For complaints about the acoustics, see for example F. B[onavia], 'London Concerts: The B.B.C. at the Albert Hall', *Music Times* 68 (March 1927), 263.

81 See for example the unusually long Minute 19 of the Control Board, 1 February 1927, WAC R3/3/3; Eckersley expressed the view that purchasing the Covent Garden lease would offer the BBC a chance to satisfy loftier social obligations with good promotional prospects: 'We should get a "National Gallery" of music, where the public could enjoy it at midday for a few pence, and hold that the ultimate reflection of this on the public life – granted the continued publicity we were in a position to secure for it directly and in the Press – would be to create a greater regard for music as one of the fundamental interests of life, and thus directly increase our supporters and our licences.' The following week, the lease was ruled out, since 'it was felt that the maximum the B.B.C.

commitments should be £10,000 per annum' – the exact amount of the Proms estimate prepared several months later; see minutes for 8 February and 31 May 1927, WAC R3/3/3, and note 89.

82 Reith, Diaries, vol. ii/2, 24 March 1927, WAC S60/5/2/2. Previous meetings took place on 7 February and 4 March.

83 Including R. H. Eckersley, Assistant Controller (Programmes), C. D. Carpendale, Controller, and Sir Walford Davies; see Reith, Diaries, vol. ii/2, 6 March 1927, WAC S60/5/2/2.

84 Reith, Diaries, vol. ii/2, 7 March 1927, WAC S60/5/2/2.

85 Boosey, letter to the editor of the *Evening Standard* (8 March 1927), accessed in WAC R30/2344/1.

86 Reith, Diaries, vol. ii/2, 10 March 1927, WAC S60/5/2/2.

87 Memo from Reith, 'Memorandum of Meeting with Mr. Boosey', 10 March 1927, WAC R30/2344/1. This quotation appears on a detailed summary of this strategic meeting that, unusually, Reith compiled afterward. Boosey had had an offer for the sale or lease of the hall, and they discussed options for broadcasting. Reith offered to 'run the Promenade and Symphony Concerts for perhaps two or three years', and agreed to back any arrangement with the potential buyer to make the deal more attractive. But he also suggested that Boosey run the hall himself, with a substantial annual contribution guaranteed from the BBC in return for broadcasting facilities and some control over concerts.

88 A special meeting of the Control Board took place on 11 March to consider the financial options of running the Proms and its Symphony Concerts 'either at the Queen's Hall or elsewhere', as well as the 'future of Queen's Hall'. All alternatives that it considered were 'conditional on the Promenade and Symphony concerts being continued'; WAC R3/3/3.

89 The memo included the costs of a season of twelve symphony concerts (£250 per concert), in addition to the Proms costs, giving a total of £15,000. Of course other costs, such as publicity and management costs, were not included. The final projections for the six-week 1927 season, prepared for the 31 May Control Board, was estimated at the £10,000 previously identified as the BBC's bottom line, including hall rental (£400 per week), orchestra of 70 (£4,200), publicity (£1,000), soloists (£1,000), Wood (£900), administration (£250) and contingencies (£250); WAC R3/3/3.

90 Nicholas Kenyon, *The BBC Symphony Orchestra, 1930–1980* (London: BBC, 1981), 8–15. Other organizations included the Royal Philharmonic Society (Kenyon, 15) and the Columbia Gramophone Company (HMV), with whom the BBC was already allied through a series of recording contracts for existing BBC performance ensembles; Reith, Diaries, vol. ii/2, 10 March 1927, WAC S60/5/2/2; memos from Eckersley to Reith, [18 March] and 9 April 1927, WAC R30/2344/1. See also WAC R22/783/1.

91 Wood, letter to Reith, 26 March 1927, WAC RCONT1/Wood/2.

92 Reith, letter to Wood, 28 March 1927; Wood, letter to Reith, 29 March 1927; WAC RCONT1/Wood/2.

93 Davies, letter to Reith, 30 March 1927, WAC RCONT1/Wood/2.

94 Memo from Eckersley to Reith, 1 April 1927, WAC RCONT1/Wood/2.

95 The BBC's financial dispute with the Albert Hall was not resolved, and it was decided the Corporation would 'have no more dealings with them whilst under present management'; see Minutes, 23 August 1927, WAC R3/3/3.

96 Boosey, letter to Reith, 7 April 1927, WAC R30/2344/1.

97 Reith, letter to Wood, 8 April 1927, WAC RCONT1/Wood/2.

98 Wood, letter to Eckersley, 14 April 1927, WAC RCONT1/Wood/2; see also other correspondence, dated 7–14 April 1927, in same file. Reith responded with an extremely careful, sympathetic letter; Reith, letter to Wood, 25 April 1927, WAC RCONT1/Wood/2.

99 Boosey, letter to Wood, 4 May 1927, WAC RCONT1/Wood/2.
100 C. G. Graves, Assistant Controller, letter to Wood, 12 May 1927; Wood, letter to Assistant Controller, 12 May 1927; WAC RCONT1/Wood/2. The contract terms were a three-year agreement, beginning 1 June 1927, to conduct a maximum of 25 concerts for a salary of £2,500 per year; to help the BBC in an advisory capacity and give it first refusal on services; all non-BBC engagements to include the billing 'by courtesy of the B.B.C.'.
101 Reith, Diaries, vol. ii/2, 19 May 1927, WAC S60/5/2/2.
102 Eckersley, letter to Boosey, 26 May 1927, WAC R30/2344/1.
103 Boosey, letter to Eckersley, 26 May 1927; Eckersley, note to Reith [D. G.], [undated]; WAC R30/2344/1.
104 B. E. Nicolls, letter to Boosey, 28 May 1927, WAC R30/2344/1.
105 Eckersley, telegram to Reith, 31 May 1927, WAC R30/2344/1. The Control Board met that day: 'Further overtures had been made to Mr. Boosey, all those hitherto having been ineffective, and Mr. Boosey having refused co-operation with us on Promenades, it was agreed to make a final proposal to run the Queen's Hall at Boosey's figure of £400 per week for six weeks, and run Promenades ourselves, and for 12 symphony concerts at his figure of £100 each, subject to microphone entry at a reasonable figure otherwise'; Minute 2, Control Board, 31 May 1927, WAC R3/3/3.
106 Reith, Diaries, vol. ii/2, 31 May 1927, WAC S60/5/2/2.
107 Minute 1, Control Board, 15 November 1927; Minute 1, 13 September 1927; WAC R3/3/3.
108 Henry J. Wood, My Life of Music (London: Victor Gollancz, 1938), 321.
109 'B.B.C. and Queen's Hall: a Season of Promenade Concerts', The Times (1 June 1927), 16(F).
110 Within a week of Boosey's and Reith's agreement, the BBC convened what became known as the 'Promenade and Symphony Concerts Committee'; yet the minutes of its first meeting recorded honestly that 'the terms of reference of the Committee had not been formulated very definitely'. Although the remit of the committee eventually grew, that first year it primarily looked after the way the publicity budget was dispersed; Meetings of the Promenade Concerts Publicity Committee, from 25 June 1927, WAC R27/431/1.
111 Memo from Nicolls to V. H. Goldsmith, 'Sir Henry Wood', 2 June 1927, WAC RCONT1/Wood/2.
112 Thompson, 'The Story of the Proms', Sir Henry Wood: Fifty Years of the Proms, ed. Ralph Hill and C. B. Rees (London: BBC, [1944]), 8.
113 'The Promenade Concerts: Successful Opening of the Season', The Times (15 August 1927), 8(E).
114 A. H. Sidgwick, The Promenade Ticket: A Lay Record of Concert-Going (London: Edward Arnold, 1914; new edition, 1945).
115 Ibid.
116 Tom Eadie, 'B.B.C. and the Proms', Glasgow News (17 August 1927), accessed in WAC P452.
117 For details, see WAC R79/115/1.
118 See WAC R79/117/1.
119 Boosey offered 'to allow us [the BBC] to use the name "New Queen's Hall Orchestra" provided we stated after it in every case "by arrangement with Messrs Chappell Ltd." It was decided not to pursue this [because] ... the title "Sir Henry Wood and his Orchestra" was preferable as it bridged the way to a possible future year, where Queen's Hall might not be in question'; Minute 6, Control Board, 14 June 1927, WAC R3/3/3.
120 Admission to the Promenade arena was 2 shillings, available only at the door; seats in the balcony were unreserved, at 3s; the Grand Circle's numbered and reserved seats cost 5s. or 7s. 6d. From 1932, some seats in the Grand Circle were available for 6s. These prices remained the same, even when the series moved to the Royal Albert Hall; WAC R79/117/1. Compared to prices for Chappell's 1926 series of Queen's Hall Symphony Concerts – unreserved seats for 2s. 4d or 3s. 6d., reserved ranging from 5s. 9d to 12s., season subscriptions for each series of four concerts ranging from 20s. to 36s. 6d. – the cost of Proms tickets, especially the season tickets, was undoubtedly a bargain, since from 1927 they were subsidized by BBC licence fees. As incentive for its 1927–8 National Concerts, the BBC chose to reduce tickets prices to 'the same prices as the Proms'; Minute 7, Control Board, 18 July 1927, WAC R3/3/3.
121 The season ticket price from 1928 was 35s. for six weeks, staying the same price when the season increased to eight weeks – the norm for the interwar years – in 1929, but rising to 37s. 6d in 1932. From 1934, a half-season ticket was available at 21s. In 1943 the season rose to 42s., with one-third-season tickets available at 21s. In 1945 the season ticket price returned to 37s. 6d, with half-seasons again available for 21s. WAC R79/117/1.
122 'The Promenade Concerts: Successful Opening of the Season', The Times (15 August 1927), 8(E).
123 Rosa Newmarch, 'The "Proms"', in Promenade Concerts: Programme, Thirty Third Season, 1927 ('Opening Night – August 13') (1927), 9, 11, 13, 15, 17, 29, 31.
124 Newmarch, 'The "Proms"', 31.
125 [Rosa Newmarch], 'The Promenade Concerts', BBC Handbook 1928, 101–4.
126 'The Promenade Concerts: Successful Opening of the Season', The Times (15 August 1927), 8(E).
127 Percy A. Scholes, 'The "Proms" and the "Provinces"', Radio Times 16 (29 July 1927), 161–2.
128 Unfortunately, a surviving transcript of this talk has not been found.
129 Wood was perturbed in 1937 when he realized that the BBC 'was instituting a revolutionary system during the present season of Promenade Concerts, in that you are going to begin the announcements at 8–O'clock, and in consequence, I cannot start my Concert until 8–2.p.m. instead of punctually at 8, as has been my fixed rule for 43 years'; letter from Wood to Thatcher, 6 August 1937, WAC RCONT1/Wood/7.
130 The BBC did not favour the Proms tradition of encores, no longer permitting them in the hall or over the air: 'it was the fault of the microphones that the packed house was not allowed to hear more. Either encore rules or engineers might yield to enthusiasm, but together they can prevail against the will of mere listeners'; Herman Klein, 'The Lure of the "Proms."', Radio Times 20 (9 August 1928), 223.
131 See for example the Programme Board decision, 12 May 1925, WAC R34/600/2.
132 The BBC stations then included London (2LO), Daventry (5XX), Birmingham (5IT), Bournemouth (6BM), Cardiff (5WA), Manchester (2ZY), Hull (6KH), Leeds-Bradford (2LS), Liverpool (6LV), Nottingham (5NG), Plymouth (5PY), Sheffield (6FL), Stoke (6ST), Swansea (5SX), Newcastle (5NO), Glasgow (5SC), Aberdeen (2BD) and Belfast (2BE).
133 'X. Y. Z.', 'The B.B.C. and the "Proms"', Glasgow Herald (17 August 1927), accessed in WAC P452.
134 'The Dawn of a New Era for Listeners: the B.B.C. Announces the First "Alternative Programme"', Radio Times 16 (12 August 1927), 241–2.
135 'The service is experimental and we cannot guarantee the same freedom from breakdown as in the case of our other transmitters'; [P. P.] Eckerley, 'The Great Experiment Begins', Radio Times 16 (26 August 1927), [325].
136 For examples, see 'Which shall we Listen to Tonight? A Note on the New Art of Listening to the Broadcast Programmes', Radio Times, 16 (2 September 1927), 365; P. P. Eckerley, 'The Art of Listening', Eve, the Lady's Pictorial (7 December 1927); St John

Ervine, 'What does the Public Want?', *Radio Times* 20 (10 August 1928), [233]–4; Filson Young, 'The Art of Listening', *BBC Handbook 1928*, 349; 'Good Listening', *The BBC Yearbook* 1930, 61. See also Doctor, *The BBC and Ultra-Modern Music*, 32–7.

137 G. M., 'The B.B.C. and the Proms', in *Promenade Concerts: Programme, Thirty Fourth Season* ('Saturday, August 11th, 1928') (1928), [8–9].

138 Experiments in Listener Research were finally carried out in 1937; 'Notes of the Year, 1937: "Listener Research"', *BBC Annual 1938* (London: BBC, 1938), 25–6. The BBC Listener Research Department, headed by R. J. E. Silvey, was established in 1938.

139 Minute 2, Meeting of the Promenade Concerts Publicity Committee, 12 September 1927, WAC R27/431.

140 G. M., 'The B.B.C. and the Proms', [9].

141 The surviving evidence of Wood's uneasy relationship with BBC management survives in hefty contributor files, WAC RCONT1/Contributors/Sir Henry Wood/1–17, and is interwoven into Arthur Jacobs' admirable biography: *Henry J. Wood: Maker of the Proms* (London: Methuen, 1994).

142 Wellington, memo to Beadle, Director of Programme Administration, 2 March 1936, WAC R30/2428/2.

143 Spike Hughes, 'Music', *Daily Herald* (7 August 1936), accessed in WAC P463.

144 'Radio and the Proms', *Sunday Times* (9 August 1936), accessed in WAC P463.

145 'The Promenade Concerts: End of a Successful Season', *The Times* (26 September 1927), 10(C).

146 For details, see Kenyon, *The BBC Symphony Orchestra*, Chapter 1.

147 N[eville] C[ardus], 'The Queen's Hall Promenade Concerts', *Manchester Guardian* (20 August 1938), accessed in WAC R79/115/14.

148 Wood, *My Life of Music*, 74–5.

149 *Ibid.*, 75.

150 See Chapter 2.

151 The interval was stipulated in the annual contract: 'Procure that at each evening performance entertainment or user there shall be an interval of not less than ten minutes prior to 10 p.m. and that there shall be printed in all programmes relating to each performance entertainment or user a statement that it will continue for the time appointed being not less than ten minutes'; Clause 4(e), Agreement between Chappell & Co. and the British Broadcasting Corporation, 11 February 1938, WAC R30/2383. This was broken only for Toscanini's performance of Beethoven's Mass in D major, in May 1939, by special agreement; see letter from G. M. Stevenson to C. S. Taylor, Queen's Hall, 7 December 1938, WAC R30/2380/1.

152 'The Proms: Record of Consistent Progress', *The Times* (20 August 1927), 8(E).

153 Cruttwell, memos to Wynn, 19 Jun 1934, and Thompson, 'Estimated Cost of Summer Promenade Concerts, 1934', 16 May 1934, WAC R79/115/8.

154 Artists' fees figures derived from 'Promenade Concerts', [undated], WAC R79/115/14; audience figures from WAC R79/236/1. Note that some artists would appear several times in the season for the cumulative fee shown in this table.

155 See for example Wood's detailed letter to Thompson, 18 December 1937, sketching the 1938 season and pointing out that 'if the whole scheme could be completed during the moth of January, you would have first call upon the artists'; WAC RCONT1/Wood/7.

156 By the 1930s, the relationship was social as well as professional, Thompson and his wife dining with Wood and Lady Jessie on occasion; see, for example, letter from Wood to Thompson, 11 March 1938, WAC RCONT1/Wood/7.

157 See WAC RCONT1/Wood/1 (1944).

158 'The Promenade Programmes: Sir Henry Wood's 44th Season: Much New Work', *Daily Telegraph* (8 July 1938), accessed in WAC R79/115/14.

159 'Promenades Once More: The Thirty-Fifth Season', *The Times* (10 August 1929), 13(D).

160 See Doctor, *The BBC and Ultra-Modern Music*, 84–6.

161 'Promenade Concerts: Works of Six Composers', *The Times* (9 September 1938), accessed in WAC R79/115/14. The first half of concerts was still the main focus for composer nights.

162 Wood, *My Life of Music*, 68 (emphasis in original).

163 John Reith, 'What is Our Policy?', *Radio Times* 2 (14 March 1924), [441].

164 See WAC R79/171–315, Concert Organiser's Office/Promenade Concerts/Concerts/Repertoire, orchestrations, etc. (1920–54).

165 The works performed in each Proms season of this period are discussed in detail in Cox, *The Henry Wood Proms*, Chapters 10–16.

166 [no title shown on cutting], *Evening Standard* (25 June 1942); accessed in WAC P468.

167 For BBC music policies during the war, see, for example, Boult's memo, 'Music Policy', 14 November 1939, or more substantially, Arthur Bliss's memo, 'BBC Music Policy', 6 March 1942; WAC R27/245/1.

168 See Chapter 2–63n.

169 'Promenade Concerts', *The Times* (20 August 1928), 13(E).

170 From 1931 it was known as the Wireless Chorus, from 1934 the BBC Chorus.

171 See Programmes & Accounts (1928), WAC R79/184/1.

172 'Promenade Concerts 1935 – Summer Season', [unsigned, undated financial summary], WAC R79/115/9.

173 *Ibid.*

174 See James J. Nott, *Music for the People: Popular Music and Dance in Interwar Britain* (Oxford: Oxford University Press, 2002).

175 In 1932–3, the first halves of the concerts were broadcast, as in the summer; in 1934–5, the first halves of four concerts were broadcast each week, the other two performed only in the hall; and in the final season, 1935–6, three first halves and three second halves were aired weekly.

176 Wellington, memo to Wright, 25 September 1935, WAC R30/2428/1.

177 'Rehearsals for the Concerts', *Manchester Guardian* (26 August 1927), accessed in WAC P452. As Kenyon notes, 'Wood issued a sharp rejoinder: "No work with which I am connected is ever performed in public unrehearsed". … It emerged that the violinist had been able to play through the work at a private rehearsal with Wood at the piano, and then to play "some passages" with the orchestra on the day. This inspired Ernest Newman to a waspish article (28 August). He suggested an advertisement to foreign players: "Do not be afraid to come to England to play your concertos. … Take it from us that you and the orchestra will rehearse – *though perhaps not together*"'; Kenyon, *The BBC Symphony Orchestra*, 13.

178 '"The Solitary Boo": Incident at Promenade Concert', *Manchester Guardian* (21 August 1930), accessed in WAC P456.

179 The BBC was looser with the use of this term than Wood liked. For Wood, novelties were works that had not been performed before in England, whereas for the BBC it could encompass also first London and first concert performances. See Jacobs, *Henry J. Wood*, 349.

180 Wood, 'Appendix', *My Life of Music*, 353–72; Cox, 'Appendix A: "Novelties" at the Proms 1895–1979', *The Henry Wood Proms*, 256–308.

181 Newmarch, 'The Proms', 10; same essay printed as 'The Promenade Concerts', *BBC Handbook* 101.

182 Sacheverell Sitwell, 'When Such Works were New', in *Sir Henry Wood: Fifty Years of the Proms*, 60.

183 See, for example, 'The Promenade Programmes: Sir Henry Wood's 44th Season: Much New Work', *Daily Telegraph* (8 July 1938), accessed in WAC R79/0115/14.

184 Director of Entertainment, R. H. Eckersley, memo to Music Director, Boult, 'Celebrity Artists', 8 February 1935; accessed in WAC R27/432. The debate about the presentation of British versus foreign artists and music on the BBC raged throughout the 1930s, both internally and externally, reaching a climax in written and verbal evidence to the Ullswater Committee in 1935, as part of the rigorous review before the first renewal of the Corporation's royal charter the following year. For details, see Doctor, *The BBC and Ultra-Modern Music*, 292ff.

185 Figures taken from Programmes & Accounts (1929), WAC R79/188/1.

186 [no title shown on cutting], *Musical Opinion* (August 1934), accessed in WAC P460.

187 14 August 1934 was the first Tuesday of the Proms season, traditionally a night with poor attendance, and the Berg, along with Bax's Phantasy for viola and orchestra and Debussy's *La mer*, drew new takings of only £95 (322 tickets sold) – certainly the lowest takings of the season, and among the lowest recorded during the interwar period.

188 Arnold Bax, 'He is a National Institution', in *Sir Henry Wood: Fifty Years of the Proms*, 27.

189 W[illiam] McNaught, 'Retrospect of Literature, Art, and Science in 1943: Music', *Annual Register*, new series (1943), 349.

190 Bax, 'He is a National Institution', 29.

191 W. Rooke-Ley, 'If Stevenson Could Have Listened', *Radio Times* 24 (30 August 1929), 411.

192 Herman Klein, 'The Lure of the "Proms."', *Radio Times* 20 (9 August 1928), 223.

193 Robert Mayer, Chairman of Sir Henry Wood Jubilee 1938 Committee, letter to Central Appeals Advisory Committee, 3 March 1938, WAC RCONT1/Wood/8.

194 This concert took place just after the Proms finish on 1 October 1938. Wood was pleased that his friend Rachmaninoff agreed to perform in the first half of the anniversary concert, but the pianist adamantly refused to broadcast, so only the second half of the concert was aired.

195 Assistant Director of Empire Service, letter to Mrs Beckett, Boult's secretary, 4 March 1938, RCONT1/Wood/8.

196 Wood, transcription of appeal speech, broadcast on 6 August 1938, National wavelength, WAC R79/115/14. Wood had applied for his project to be handled as an official BBC appeal, but the BBC turned down his request. The Corporation allowed the interval speech, but firmly 'dissuade[d] him from his haunting hopes that Sir Walford [Davies] will be allowed to slip into his introductory broadcast of the Jubilee Concert on October 5th a reference to the H.J.W. Appeal', first softening him up with 'the exquisite fare and faultless service of [lunch at] the Langham Hotel'; Wright, memo to Music Executive, 'Lunch to Sir Henry Wood', 22 August 1938, WAC RCONT1/ Wood/8.

197 'Proms on Vision Wavelength: Fidelity of Reception', *Daily Telegraph* (8 August 1938); accessed in WAC R79/115/14.

198 'Broadcasting Concerts: Ultra-Short Waves to be Used', *Sunday Times* (7 August 1938), accessed in WAC R79/115/14.

199 *Promenade Concerts 1938* [season prospectus] (London: BBC, 1938), [3].

200 Rosa Newmarch, 'Sir Henry J. Wood's Jubilee Year', *Promenade Concerts 1938* [season prospectus], [2].

201 Ralph Vaughan Williams, 'Henry Wood', *London Mercury* (October 1938), 499.

202 'Opening of the "Proms": The Concert: Warm Welcome for Old Friends', *Observer* (7 August 1938), accessed in WAC R79/115/14.

203 'Finish of the Proms', *News Chronicle* (3 October 1938), accessed in WAC R79/115/14.

204 'The Proms Conductor Celebrates his Half-Century', *Picture Post* (1 October 1938), 24–9, accessed in WAC P466.

205 *Ibid.*

206 Wood, statement to Prom audience, 1 September 1939, quoted in '"Proms" to Close: Audience Told by Sir Henry Wood', *Daily Telegraph* (2 September 1939), accessed in WAC R79/115/15.

207 'Civil Defence: Full Machinery in Motion: Black-out from Sunset to Sunrise', *The Times* (2 September 1939), 7(A).

208 Jas. Beveridge, 'Promenade Concerts Summer 1938: Final Statement – Summary and Comparison with Estimate', 23 January 1939, WAC R79/115/16. The net profit did not include contractual orchestra or programme preparation costs. With nearly 900 season and over 15,000 single tickets sold, the figures compare to nearly 700 season and 12,675 single tickets in 1937, with a net profit of £5,470. A factor in the net profits was also the discontinuation of certain taxes, increasing income by £2,875 in 1938.

209 '"Proms" Without the B.B.C.: Next Season Sir Henry Wood's Last', *The Times* (5 April 1940), accessed in WAC R79/115/16.

210 *Daily Telegraph* (5 April 1940). The statement was published also in other papers, including *The Times*, where it appeared over Boult's signature: Adrian C. Boult, 'The Promenade Concerts: To the Editor', *The Times* (9 April 1940); both accessed in WAC R79/115/16.

211 Henry J. Wood, 'B.B.C. and the "Proms": Plans for the New Season: To the Editor', *Daily Telegraph* (9 April 1940), accessed in WAC R79/115/16.

212 Jacobs, *Henry J. Wood*, Chapter 21.

213 Boult reported on several occasions to Wood about how little the orchestra was doing: 'as you have no doubt seen our programmes have not yet included any Symphonies'; letter, 14 September 1940, WAC RCONT1/Wood/9.

214 See for example a lengthy telegram Wood wrote to Ogilvie, 15 September 1940, WAC R30/2383/2.

215 See the increasingly irritable correspondence in WAC RCONT1/Wood/9.

216 Wood, letter to Thompson, 10 January 1940, WAC R79/115/16.

217 *Ibid.*

218 There is an enormous correspondence with the Queen's Hall negotiating such payments; see in particular WAC R30/2383/2 and R79/115/16.

219 Chappell's threatened to turn the hall into a cinema (early February), threatened to give the bookings to others interested in running the series (the BBC doubted their existence) and eventually had a solicitor write with veiled threats about what would happen if the hall were not booked for the season. See Nicolls, 'Short Note on Proms Negotiations – 1939/40', 23 April 1940, WAC R79/115/16.

220 Herbage, memo to S. J. Lotbinière, AC(P), 'Promenade Season', 30 May 1940, WAC R79/115/16.

221 See memos in WAC R79/115/16 and R30/2383/2, especially Nicolls, 'Short Note', 23 April 1940, WAC R79/115/16.

222 Nicolls, 'Short Note', 23 April 1940, WAC R79/115/16.

223 Boult, memo to Nicolls, 26 April 1940, WAC R79/115/16.

224 Schuster, ADPA, memo to AC(P), 4 June 1940, WAC R30/2383/2.

225 Control Board Minute, 24 June 1940, quoted in memo from Rose Troup, DPA, to Music Executive, WAC R30/2383/2.

226 Boult to Nicolls, 29 June 1940, WAC R79/115/16.

227 Herbage, 'Suitability of 1940 Promenade Concerts for Broadcasting', [c. 29 June 1940], WAC R79/115/16.

228 R. Jardine Brown, Business Manager, memo to C(A), 20 June 1940, WAC R30/2383/2.

229 Herbage, teleprinter message to Thatcher, 18 July 1940, WAC R79/115/16.

230 Jardine Brown, letter to M. R. Ricketts, 21 April 1937, copy in WAC R30/2383/2.

231 Ricketts, letter to Jardine Brown, copied to Ogilvie, 8 January 1940, WAC R30/2383/2.

232 Jardine Brown, report for Control Board, 'Queen's Hall', 22 February 1940, WAC R30/2383/2.

233 Thatcher, memo to Nicolls, 1 November 1940, WAC R30/2383/2.

234 CEMA was founded in 1940 and was the precursor to the Arts Council, established in 1946. ENSA was founded in 1938.

235 C. S. Taylor, Manager of Queen's Hall, quoted in Robert Elkin, *Queen's Hall, 1893–1941* (London: Rider & Co. [1944]), 71–2.

236 Details may be found in particular in Cox, *The Henry Wood Proms*, Chapters 14–16, and in Jacobs, *Henry J. Wood*, Chapters 21–3.

237 *Promenade Concerts 1940* [season prospectus] (London: 1940), accessed in WAC R79/115/16. Wood suggested 1940 would be his farewell season but continued until his death in 1944.

238 'Promenade Concerts: The New Syllabus', *The Times* (1 July 1940), accessed in WAC P426.

239 'Promenade Concerts: Wagner, Elgar, and Others', *The Times* (28 August 1940), accessed in WAC R79/115/16.

240 For details and more discussion, see Jacobs, *Henry J. Wood*, 355, and plates 32, 33.

241 Herbage, memo to Director of Programme Planning, 8 May 1941, accessed in WAC R30/2343/1.

242 'Sir Henry J. Wood', publicity notes from C. H. Warren to the Editor of *Radio Times*, 12 June 1941, WAC R79/115/17. The Royal Albert Hall was not generally associated with music events before the war. It had been closed since the war's beginning, but was reopened after the Queen's Hall bombing for an LSO concert on 31 May 1941. Even before then, on 24 May, the RPS had announced that the 1941 Proms would take place there; 'Theatres: Concerts &c.', *The Times* (24 May 1941), 8(F).

243 'Albert Hall Acoustics: Some Notes', [undated 1941], WAC R79/115/17.

244 *Promenade Concerts, Forty-Seventh Season, 1941* [season prospectus] (London, 1941), accessed in WAC R79/117/1.

245 William Glock, 'Music', *Observer* (13 July 1941), accessed in WAC R79/115/17.

246 Jacobs, *Henry J. Wood*, 361.

247 Minute 225, Home Board Minutes, 18 April 1941, quoted in 'Extracts from Home Board Minutes: Promenade Concerts', WAC R30/2609/2.

248 Jacobs, *Henry J. Wood*, 361–2.

249 Asst DPA, memo to Director of Programme Administration, 29 August 1941, WAC R30/2609/2. Thompson estimated average takings at £400 per concert gross.

250 D. H. Clarke, Director of Programme Administration, memo to S. S. E., 17 April 1942, WAC R30/2609/2. There is further correspondence about the screen decision. When negotiations with Douglas proved difficult, the BBC Civil Engineer would not agree to make another screen, not able to 'say, from my point of view, that it is <u>essential</u>. A screen exists; it can therefore hardly be in the interests of the national war effort to make another!'; Civil Engineer, memo to S. S. E., 27 April 1942, WAC R30/2609/2. Douglas eventually agreed to sell the screens and canopy to the Royal Albert Hall.

251 See WAC R30/2609/2 for details of all issues leading to the BBC's resumption of Proms management for the 1942 season.

252 The agreement with Thomas Russell, manager of the LPO, was not completed until early June.

253 *Promenade Concerts, Forty-eighth Season, 1942* [season prospectus] (London: BBC, 1942), accessed in WAC R79/117/1.

254 The first British performance of this symphony had been planned for 4 June 1942, but was postponed when the parts did not arrive on time. It was broadcast on 22 June and repeated a week later in the Proms. See Jacobs, *Henry J. Wood*, 369, and *Times* notices for 22 June, p. 8(A), 29 June, p. 6(F), and 30 June, p. 2(F).

255 'Sir Adrian Told Them, Sir Henry Showed Them', *Evening Standard* (19 August 1942), accessed in WAC P468.

256 *Promenade Concerts, Forty-eighth Season, 1942* [season prospectus], Prom 16, accessed in WAC R79/117/1.

257 *Sir Henry Wood's Jubilee Season Promenade Concerts* [1944 season prospectus] (London: BBC, 1944), accessed in WAC R79/117/1.

258 Nicolls, memo to Boult, 'Promenade Season', 3 June 1940, WAC R30/2342/1.

259 Warner, 'Introduction', viii.

CHAPTER 4 ALISON GARNHAM

1 W. W. Thompson, memo to Victor Hely-Hutchinson, 7 May 1945, WAC R30/2345/1.

2 Report by William Haley to the meeting of the Board of Governors held on 9 January 1947, quoted in Nicholas Kenyon, *The BBC Symphony Orchestra, 1930–1980* (London: BBC, 1981), 195. Kenyon noted that '40 out of 90 would have been a more accurate proportion'.

3 See Chapter 3.

4 George Barnes, first Controller of the Third Programme, in a draft statement of intent for 'Programme C', as the Third was known at the planning stage, 14 January 1946, WAC R34/420.

5 William Haley, quoted by Rex Keating, 'Third Programme Problems in Certain Underdeveloped Areas', *UNESCO Reports and Papers on Mass Communications*, No. 23 (December 1956).

6 Haley, 'The Home Programme Policy of the BBC', policy document submitted to Board of Governors, 4 July 1946, WAC R34/420.

7 Haley interviewed by Frank Gillard, BBC Oral History Project, 1978, quoted in Humphrey Carpenter, *The Envy of the World: Fifty Years of the BBC Third Programme and Radio 3, 1946–1996* (London: Weidenfeld & Nicolson, 1996), 9.

8 Haley, handwritten note to Lindsay Wellington, Controller, Programmes, on memo from Basil Nicolls, Senior Controller, to Haley, 9 February 1945, WAC R30/2345/1.

9 Nicolls, memo to Haley, 9 February 1944, WAC R30/2345/1.

10 Wellington, Director of Sound Broadcasting, memo to Mungo Dewar, Head, Sound Broadcasting Administration, 10 July 1956, WAC R27/700/1.

11 W. E. Streeton, Programme Contracts Director, memo to Richard Howgill, Controller, Entertainment, 21 April 1947, WAC R29/195/2.

12 Frederic Dambman, General Secretary of the Musicians' Union, letter to Streeton, 16 June 1947, WAC R29/195/2.

13 See Nicolls, 'Promulgation of the N.A.S.O. Agreement', 13 June 1949, WAC R29/195/2.

14 Wood, letter to Nicolls, 2 May 1944, WAC R30/2345/1.

15 Letters from Wood to Haley, and Haley to Wood, 26 and 30 May 1944, WAC R30/2345/1.

16 Hely-Hutchinson, memo to Wellington, 1 February 1945, WAC R30/2345/1.

17 Nicolls, memo to Haley, 2 February 1945, WAC R30/2345/1.

18 Hely-Hutchinson, letter to Wellington, 1 February 1945, WAC R30/2345/1.

19 Lady Jessie Wood, paper presented to the BBC Chairman at a meeting held on 6 October 1946, WAC R30/2345/1.

20 Lady Jessie, letter to Haley, 20 March 1945, WAC R30/2345/1.

21 Lady Jessie, letter to Herbert Murrill, Acting Deputy Director of Music, 1 November 1947, WAC R30/2345/1.

22 Lady Jessie, paper presented to the BBC Chairman, 6 October 1946, WAC R30/2345/1.

23 Lady Jessie, letter to Murrill, 1 November 1947, WAC R30/2345/1.

24 Lady Jessie, letter to Thompson, 29 November 1947, WAC R30/2345/2.

25 Lady Jessie, letter to Thompson, 21 September 1945, WAC R30/2345/1.

26 BBC Solicitor, memo to Nicolls, 17 March 1952, WAC R30/3742/1.

27 Julian Herbage (in his role as Secretary of the Henry Wood Society), memo to Nicolls, 11 January 1946, WAC R27/124. It is noteworthy that Lady Jessie co-opted both Herbage and Thompson on to the Board of her Henry Wood Society.

28 Haley, annotation dated 14 November 1947, on memo from Nicolls, 13 November 1947, WAC R30/2641/1.

29 Harold Holt, letter to Haley, 8 August 1946, WAC R30/3742/1

30 'Winter Proms: "The Shadow of Cain"', The Times (14 January 1953).

31 Herald (31 January 1953).

32 Harold Rutland, memo to Thompson, 19 January 1953, WAC R30/3742/1.

33 Thompson, Concerts Manager, memo to Howgill, Controller of Music, 11 February 1953, WAC R30/3742/1.

34 Hely-Hutchinson, 'The Rising Tide of Music', BBC Yearbook 1945, 47.

35 Hely-Hutchinson, letter to Arthur J. Beard, Liverpool Philharmonic Orchestra, 29 April 1946, WAC R30/2345/1.

36 Nicolls, memo to Haley, 9 February 1945, WAC R30/2345/1.

37 Hely-Hutchinson, memo to Lindsay Wellington, Controller (Programmes), 10 April 1945, WAC R30/2345/1.

38 Hely-Hutchinson, memo to Wellington, 1 February 1945, WAC R30/2345/1.

39 William Glock, Notes in Advance: An Autobiography in Music (Oxford: Oxford University Press, 1991), 101.

40 Hely-Hutchinson, memo to Wellington, 1 February 1945, WAC R30/2345/1.

41 Boult, memo to Kenneth Wright, 22 October 1947, WAC R30/2345/2.

42 Ibid.

43 Hely-Hutchinson, memo to Howgill, Controller of Entertainment, 21 January 1946, WAC R30/2345/1.

44 Wright, letter to Elisabeth Lutyens, 2 March 1970, British Library, Add. ms. 71144, f. 148v.

45 Ibid.

46 Howgill, memo to Maurice Johnstone, 10 March 1954, WAC R30/2345/7,

47 Wellington, memo to Hely-Hutchinson, 30 September 1946, WAC R30/2345/1.

48 Boult, memo to Hely-Hutchinson, 'Report on Promenade Concerts, 1946', 21 September 1946, WAC R30/2345/1.

49 Ibid.

50 Thomas Russell, unpublished letter to the editor of The Times, 22 August 1946, copied to Hely-Hutchinson, WAC R30/2345/1. According to Russell, he sent this letter to number of different newspapers, and it eventually found its way into the Daily Graphic. Thomas Russell, The Proms (London: Max Parrish, 1949), 68.

51 Streeton, memo to Wright, 30 April 1947, WAC R30/2345/2.

52 Wellington, memo to Nicolls, 2 February 1947, WAC R30/2345/2.

53 Thompson, memo to Wright, 14 October 1947, and memo from Wright to Howgill, 28 October 1947, WAC R30/2345/2.

54 Herbage, Foreword to The Henry Wood Promenade Concerts [1947 prospectus] (London: BBC, 1947), 5.

55 Hely-Hutchinson, memo to Howgill, 21 November 1946, WAC R30/2345/1.

56 Herbage, Foreword to The Henry Wood Promenade Concerts [1947 prospectus], 6.

57 Hely-Hutchinson, memo to Howgill, 15 October 1945, WAC R30/2345/1.

58 Ibid.

59 Herbage, Foreword to The Henry Wood Promenade Concerts, [1946 prospectus] (London: BBC, 1946), 5.

60 Hely-Hutchinson, memo to Howgill, 21 November 1946, WAC R30/2345/1.

61 Ibid.

62 Herbage, 'Report on the Promenade Concerts, Summer 1948', [undated, c. September 1948], WAC R30/2345/2.

63 Paper presented by Lady Jessie to the BBC Chairman, 6 October 1946, WAC R30/2345/1.

64 Hely-Hutchinson, memo to Howgill, 21 November 1946, WAC R30/2345/1.

65 Nicolls, memo to Howgill, 10 February 1947, WAC R30/2345/1.

66 This is the first of a list of 'policy directives' in a memo from Wellington, then Controller, Home Service, to Nicolls and Howgill, 2 February 1947, WAC R30/2345/1.

67 Ibid.

68 Hely-Hutchinson, memo to Howgill, 21 November 1946, WAC R30/2345/1.

69 Nicolls, memo to Howgill, 10 February 1947, WAC R30/2345/1.

70 Ibid.

71 Herbage, memo to Murrill, 'Promenade Concerts 1951: The Festival of Britain Proms', 15 October 1951, WAC R30/2345/5.

72 Murrill, memo to Howgill, 22 October 1951, WAC R30/2345/5.

73 Thompson, memo to Wright, 14 October 1947, WAC R30/2345/2.

74 Wright, memo to Howgill, 28 October 1947, WAC R30/2345/2.

75 Nicolls, memo to Howgill, 16 September 1947, WAC R30/2345/2.

76 The conductor in question was Nino Sanzogno. Although Glock had already engaged him to perform with the BBC SO in the Royal Festival Hall in May 1960, the proposal to bring him back for three or four concerts in the Proms led to letters of protest from Lady Jessie and the President of the Royal Academy of Music, Sir Thomas Armstrong. WAC R30/2345/10. See also Chapter 5.

77 Wright, memo to Howgill, 13 August 1947, WAC R20/2345/2.

78 See Richard Aldous, Tunes of Glory: The Life of Malcolm Sargent (London: Hutchinson, 2001), 100–102.

79 Asa Briggs, The History of Broadcasting in the United Kingdom, iii: The War of Words (London: Oxford University Press, 1970), 292.

80 Briggs, The War of Words, 290–91.

81 BBC Listener Research Report, 29 December 1943, quoted in Briggs, The War of Words, 508.

82 Brains Trust, broadcast on BBC Home Service, 22 and 27 December 1942, transcribed in Charles Reid, Malcolm Sargent: A Biography (London: Hamilton, 1968), 330.

83 Quoted in Aldous, Tunes of Glory, 81.

84 See Streeton, Programme Contracts Director, memo to Wright, 30 April 1947, WAC R30/2345/2.

85 Davis, letter to Reid, quoted in Reid, Malcolm Sargent, 468.

86 Sargent, letter to Thompson, 26 August 1947, WAC RCONT1, Contributors/Sargent/Artist's/4 (1947–9).

87 Aldous, Tunes of Glory, xiv.

88 Alan Bennett, *Untold Stories*, (London: Faber & Faber, 2005), 202–3.
89 *Ibid.*, 411.
90 Chalmers, memo to Murrill, 4 December 1950, WAC R30/2345/4.
91 There had been experimental broadcasts via television of the sound only during the 1938 Proms season. See Chapter 3.
92 Maurice Gorham, Head of Television Service, memo to Murrill, 21 July 1947, WAC T14/836/1.
93 Gorham, memo to Wright, 29 July 1947, WAC T14/836/1.
94 Many thanks to Jeff Walden for this information.
95 Cecil McGivern, memo to the Outside Broadcast team, 15 September 1947, WAC T14/836/1.
96 McGivern, memo to Howgill, 22 September 1947, WAC R34/420.
97 McGivern, memo to Nicolls, 26 September 1947, WAC T14/836/1. Given the small size of the television audience at this date, it is not surprising that this correspondence, though over four times that received for other programmes, was still only seventeen letters!
98 Nicolls, memo to McGivern, 24 September 1947, WAC R34/196.
99 Howgill, memo to McGivern, 25 September 1947, WAC R34/196.
100 Wright, memo to Howgill, 22 September 1947, WAC R30/2345/2.
101 McGivern, memo to Nicolls, 26 September 1947, WAC T14/836/1.
102 Howgill, memo to McGivern, 25 September 1947, WAC R34/196.
103 Orr-Ewing, memo to McGivern, [date] December 1947, WAC T14/836/1.
104 Orr-Ewing, memo to Wright, 4 November 1947, WAC T14/836/1.
105 Orr-Ewing, programme report, [undated], WAC T14/836/1.
106 McGivern, memo to Orr-Ewing, 17 January 1948, WAC T14/836/1.
107 Note by Streeton, Head of Programme Contracts, 21 June 1948, quoted in Briggs, *The History of Broadcasting in the United Kingdom*, iv: *Sound and Vision* (Oxford: Oxford University of Press, 1979), 667.
108 Philip Hope-Wallace, *Time and Tide*, 6 June 1953.
109 Harry Hopkins, *The New Look: A Social History of the Forties and Fifties in Britain* (London: Secker & Warburg, 1963), 295.
110 McGivern, memo to Joanna Spicer, Programme Organiser, Television, WAC T14/836/1.
111 See annotations on memo from Wright to Howgill, 12 March 1953, WAC T14/836/1.
112 Wright, memo to Spicer, 11 March 1953, WAC T14/836/1.
113 Streeton, memo to Spicer, 16 June 1953, WAC T14/836/1.
114 Haley, memo to Nicolls, 21 December 1949, WAC R30/2343/4. See also Julian Herbage's report on the 1949 Proms, and Nicolls' memo, 'Relations between the Programme Controllers and the Music Department', 3 February 1949, in which the Proms head a list of occasions on which the Head of Music was to be given 'plenary powers'.
115 Craxton, memo to Wright, 5 May 1954, WAC T14/836/1.
116 See Chapter 5.
117 Wright, memo to McGivern, 12 May 1953, WAC T14/836/1.
118 Nicolls, memo to Haley, 9 February 1944, WAC R30/2345/1.
119 Nicolls, memo to Howgill, 7 March 1952, WAC R30/2345/5.
120 Richard Marriott, memo [undated], July 1956, WAC R34/1022/2.
121 *Ibid.*
122 Craxton, memo to Orr-Ewing, 30 July 1953, WAC T14/836/1.

123 Franklin Engelmann, memo to the Controller of the Light Programme, 27 July 1953, WAC T14/836/1.
124 Frank Wade, Assistant to Controller, Music, memo to Howgill, WAC T14/836/1.
125 Craxton, memo to Orr-Ewing, 30 July 1953, WAC T14/836/1.
126 Sargent, memo to Nicolls, 17 November 1951, WAC RCONT1/910/Malcolm Sargent/1.
127 Howgill, memo to the Director-General, 3 September 1953, WAC RCONT1/910/Malcolm Sargent/1.
128 Johnstone, memo to Howgill, 6 August 1953, WAC RCONT1/910/Malcolm Sargent/1.
129 Howgill, memo to the Director-General, 3 September 1953, WAC RCONT1/910/Malcolm Sargent/1.
130 Wright, memo to Howgill, 5 October 1954, WAC T14/836/2.
131 Robinson, memo to Wilson, 5 March 1948, WAC R30/2345/2.
132 Thompson, memo to Murrill, 3 December 1947, WAC R30/2345/2.
133 Lady Jessie, memo to Thompson, 29 November 1947, WAC R30/2345/2.
134 Nicolls, memo to Howgill, 11 March 1948, WAC R30/2345/2.
135 Chalmers, memo to Wright, 12 May 1947, WAC R30/2343/3.
136 Chalmers, memo to Howgill, 19 September 1949, WAC R30/2345/3.
137 *Ibid.*
138 Chalmers, memo to Murrill(?), 4 December 1950, WAC R30/2345/4.
139 Adam to Nicolls, memo, 6 December 1950, WAC R30/2345/4.
140 Nicolls, memo to Haley, 20 November 1950, WAC R30/2345/4.
141 Adam, memo, 24 September 1951, WAC R30/2345/5.
142 Typed notice distributed by 'Three Arena Members', 19 August 1953, R30/2345/6.
143 Howgill, memo to Pelletier, Controller of the Light Programme, 8 September 1953, R30/2345/6.
144 Johnstone, memo to Howgill, 21 August 1953, WAC R30/2345/6.
145 McGivern, memo to Director of Television Broadcasting, 20 September 1953, WAC T14/836/1.
146 Johnstone, memo to Howgill, 8 March 1954, WAC R30/2345/6.
147 Willoughby, Report on the 1958 Proms, 23 October 1958, WAC R30/2345/9.
148 Sargent, memo to Howgill, 12 November 1953, WAC R30/2345/7.
149 Quoted in Barrie Hall, *The Proms and the Men Who Made Them* (London: Allen & Unwin, 1981), 131.
150 Sargent, memo to Howgill, 12 November 1953, WAC R30/2345/7.
151 Vaughan Williams, 'First Performances', *The Henry Wood Promenade Concerts*, 1949 [season prospectus] (London: BBC, 1949), 3–4.
152 Murrill, memo to Howgill, 6 November 1950, WAC R30/2345/4.
153 Russell, *The Proms*, 70.
154 Herbage, Report on the 1954 Proms, WAC R30/2345/7.
155 Thompson, memo to Murrill, 19 October 1950, WAC R30/2345/4.
156 Herbage, Report on the 1956 Proms, WAC R30/2345/8
157 Ironically, this incident is also an example of the enterprise of Wood, who had been in correspondence with Britten about performing excerpts from *Peter Grimes* at the 1944 Proms before the opera had even been completed; Arthur Jacobs, *Henry J. Wood: Maker of the Proms* (London: Methuen, 1994), 382.
158 Quoted in Herbage, Report on the 1958 Proms, WAC R30/2345/9.

159 Herbage, Report on the 1952 Proms, WAC R30/2345/5.
160 Thompson and Herbage, memo to Murrill, 25 January 1952, WAC R30/2345/5.
161 Herbage, Report on the 1952 Proms, WAC R30/2345/5.
162 Memo from Howgill to H. J. Dunkerley, Controller, Midland Region, WAC RCONT1/Herbage/Artist's/4 (1954–5).
163 *Ibid.*
164 Herbage, Report on the 1953 Proms, WAC R30/2345/6.
165 *Ibid.*

CHAPTER 5   DAVID WRIGHT
For their help and assistance in different ways, I am most grateful to the following: Robert Ponsonby and Stephen Plaistow for their kindness in giving me interviews and for answering subsequent questions; my co-editors and fellow contributors of this volume; members of the 'Music in Britain Seminar' in the London University Institute of Historical Research; my colleagues in the Centre for Performance History at the Royal College of Music; Nicolas Bell, Curator of Music Manuscripts, and his colleagues at the British Library; and Jeff Walden and the staff at the BBC Written Archives Centre, Caversham. I owe especial gratitude to the late Professor Cyril Ehrlich for the goad of his generous and stimulating friendship, and for the vital role he played in this project in so many important respects.
1 David Pountney et al., 'If We Ran the Proms', *Guardian* (12 July 2002).
2 'Glockenspiel' (the 'Notebook' column), *Spectator* (17 May 1963), 626.
3 Nicholas Kenyon, *The BBC Symphony Orchestra, 1930–1980* (London: BBC, 1981), 292.
4 William Glock, *Notes in Advance: An Autobiography in Music* (Oxford: Oxford University Press, 1991), 101.
5 Personal communication to the author, 27 June 2006.
6 Interview with the author, 27 July 2005.
7 Andrew Smith, *Daily Herald* (19 September 1960) [emphasis added].
8 *Ibid.*
9 Tom Maschler, ed., *Declaration* (London: MacGibbon & Kee, 1957).
10 Lindsay Anderson, 'Get Out and Push!', in *Declaration*, 156–7.
11 *Ibid.*, 155.
12 Maurice Johnstone, Introduction to *The 65th Season of the Henry Wood Promenade Concerts*, 1959 [season prospectus] (London: BBC, 1959), 4.
13 *Ibid.*
14 Roy Porter, *London: A Social History* (London: Penguin Books, 1996), 363.
15 In addition to Roy Porter's vivid account of this period, stimulating discussions can be found in: Peter Clarke, *Hope and Glory: Britain 1900–2000*, rev. edn (London: Penguin Books, 2004); Mark Donnelly, *Sixties Britain* (Harlow: Pearson Education, 2005); Robert Hewison, *Too Much: Art and Society in the Sixties, 1960–75* (London: Methuen, 1986); Stephen Inwood, *A History of London* (Basingstoke: Macmillan, 1998); Kenneth O. Morgan, *Britain Since 1945: The People's Peace*, 3rd edn (Oxford: Oxford University Press, 2001); Arthur Marwick, *British Society Since 1945*, 3rd edn (London: Penguin Books, 1996); Dominic Sandbrook, *Never Had it So Good: A History of Britain from Suez to the Beatles* (London: Little, Brown, 2005).
16 'Challenge of the Proms: Alan Blyth Talks to William Glock', *Music and Musicians* 15/12 (August 1967), 16.
17 Shawe-Taylor, [review], *Sunday Times* (14 August 1960). The performance was on 8 August. See also 'Electronics at the Proms: No Substitute for Live Music', *The Times* (9 August 1960).
18 Reid, 'The Most Exciting Proms for Years', *News Chronicle* (20 August 1960). Reid was later the biographer of Malcolm Sargent.
19 'Prommers Stay for Gerhard', *The Times* (30 July 1960).
20 Glock, *Notes in Advance*, 112.
21 See Chapter 4.
22 Glock, diary entry, 22 September 1967, William Glock Collection, BL MS Mus. 983.
23 Glock, Introduction to *The 66th Season of Henry Wood Promenade Concerts*, 1960 [season prospectus] (London: BBC, 1960), 4.
24 'Enterprise, Not Revolution in the 1960 Proms', *The Times* (10 June 1960).
25 'An Adventurous Programme', *The Times* (19 August 1960).
26 'A Thrilling Oedipus Rex: Cogent Justification of New Proms Policy', *The Times* (24 August 1960).
27 Glock, Introduction to *The 68th Season of Henry Wood Promenade Concerts*, 1962 [season prospectus], (London: BBC, 1962), 4.
28 'Challenge of the Proms', 16.
29 David Cairns, 'Hall of Fame', *Spectator* (9 August 1963), 177.
30 In his diary entry for 4 November 1967, Glock notes, 'Went, unnecessarily as I thought in retrospect, to represent the BBC in a performance of Britten's *War Requiem* in Ypres Cathedral. … Sat in the front row of the "stalls" through a bad performance of this, I'm convinced, pretty bad work. The settings of Wilfrid Owen are tolerable because one can grasp desperately at the poems, some of them superb; but the setting of the Requiem proper is MGM'; William Glock Collection, BL MS Mus. 983.
31 Julian Herbage, 'Henry Wood Promenade Concerts 66th Season – 1960', WAC R79/115/63.
32 Charles Reid, 'The Public and the Proms: Report on the "Spectator" Inquiry', *Spectator* (8 October 1965), 446.
33 *Ibid.*
34 Freda Grove, Concerts Organiser, memo to Glock, '1965 Provisional accounts', WAC, R27/700/1.
35 Humphrey Carpenter, *The Envy of the World: Fifty Years of the BBC Third Programme and Radio 3* (London: Weidenfeld & Nicolson, 1996), 207.
36 Minutes, BBC Governors' Meeting, 27 April, 1961, WAC R27/847/1; passed to Glock by Lindsay Wellington, Director of Sound Broadcasting.
37 Standing, memo to Glock, 18 October 1965, WAC R27/700/1.
38 See Chapter 4–9n.
39 Marriott, memo to Glock, 19 October 1965, WAC R27/700/1; Glock's reply is noted on the memo by hand.
40 Standing, memo to Glock, 28 February 1968, WAC R27/1022/2 [emphasis added].
41 'Enterprise, Not Revolution in the 1960 Proms', *The Times* (10 June 1960).
42 Glock, Introduction to *The 70th Season of the Henry Wood Promenade Concerts*, 1964 [season prospectus] (London: BBC, 1964), 5.
43 An account of the early involvement of BBC2 in music programmes is given in John Drummond, *Tainted by Experience: A Life in the Arts* (London: Faber & Faber, 2000).
44 Helen Cook, memo to Head of Presentation, Radio, 1 August 1969, WAC R27/847/2.
45 Hugh Tattersall, Presentation Organiser, World Service, memo to David Cox, Music Organiser, External Services, 2 October 1968, WAC R27/1022/3. The reference is to the traditional perceptions of social and cultural exclusion on the part of those living in the area around the Royal Albert Hall. In a memo of 7 October, Cox hotly denied the charge that this material was 'aimed at the denizens of Kensington Gore … but [rather] for the very general audiences of the Proms'.
46 Michael Nyman, 'Saucer-shaped', *Spectator* (2 August 1969).

47 Michael Tippett, *Those Twentieth Century Blues: An Autobiography* (London: Hutchinson, 1991), 207.
48 Julian Herbage, 'Henry Wood Promenade Concerts 66th Season – 1960', WAC R79/115/63.
49 Glock, *Notes in Advance*, 121.
50 Glock, diary entry, 16 September 1967, William Glock Collection, BL MS Mus. 983.
51 Chief Accountant, Radio, memo to Managing Director, Radio, 22 March 1971, WAC R101/302/1.
52 Michael Nyman, 'Plain Clothes Don', *Spectator* (16 August 1969), 215.
53 Christopher Samuelson, Concerts Manager, memo to Glock, 16 May 1968, WAC R27/1022/3.
54 Simpson, memo to Glock, 29 August 1969, WAC R/27/847/2.
55 Head of Presentation, Radio, memo to Glock, 9 September 1969, WAC R/27/847/2.
56 Newby, memo to Glock, WAC R/27/847/2.
57 Glock, memo to Samuelson, 28 April 1968, WAC R27/1022/2.
58 Howard Newby, memo to Ian Trethowan, Managing Director Radio, 24 August 1972, WAC R101/302/1.
59 The rehearsal schedule, dated 12 July 1967, survives; see WAC R27/1022/1.
60 Joan Chissell, *The Times* (15 September 1969).
61 Quoted in Barrie Hall, *The Proms and the Men who Made Them* (London: George Allen & Unwin, 1981), 168.
62 Ponsonby, quoted in Nicholas Kenyon, 'Conflicts of Sound and Vision', *The Times* (15 September 1984) [interview with Ponsonby].
63 *Ibid.*
64 Hugh Muirhead, memo to Robert Ponsonby, 5 February 1982, WAC R27/1082. A tabulation of types of advertisers and changing proportions of editorial to advertising matter in Proms prospectuses from 1974 to 1995 appears in Andrew Blake, *The Land Without Music: Music, Culture and Society in Twentieth-Century Britain* (Manchester: Manchester University Press, 1997), 207–8.
65 Carpenter, *The Envy of the World*, 285.
66 Drummond, *Tainted by Experience*, 188.
67 *A Report on Orchestral Resources in Great Britain (1970)*, chaired by Alan Peacock (London: Arts Council of Great Britain, 1970), 52–3, paragraphs 142–5.
68 Humphrey Burton, memo, WAC R27/1081/1.
69 See Carpenter, *The Envy of the World*, 306–7.
70 Singer, memo to Ponsonby, 'The Opening of the Proms', 23 January 1981, WAC R27/1082/1.
71 The intervening Prom offered a popular programme of Franck, Saint-Säens, Dukas and Ravel.
72 Singer, memo to Ponsonby, 'Proms 1982: First Night', 7 October 1981, WAC R27/1083/1.
73 Ponsonby, memo to Singer, 9 October 1981, WAC R27/1083/1.
74 Ponsonby, interviewed by Kenyon, 'Conflicts of Sound and Vision' (1984).
75 Exchange of memos between Kenneth Corden, Executive Producer, Music and Arts, Television, and Ponsonby, 13 and 20 December 1984, WAC R27/1074.
76 Minutes of the 1985 Proms post-mortem meeting, 8 November 1985, WAC R27/1074.
77 Concert Meeting, 6 September 1985, WAC R27/1077.
78 Ponsonby, memo, 7 May 1982, WAC R27/1083. Ponsonby's view contrasts strongly with the proprietorial attitude that Basil Nicolls expressed about the BBC and the Proms in a memo to William Haley, quoted in Chapter 4–17n.
79 Elizabeth Russell, memo to Ponsonby, 16 August 1982, WAC R27/1083.
80 Ponsonby, memo, 9 July 1979, WAC R27/1082.
81 Minutes from Director-General, 23 February 1983; Managing Director Radio, 21 February 1984 and 26 February 1985. WAC R27/1074.
82 Singer, memo to Ponsonby, 'Proms Ticket Prices', 11 October 1979, WAC R27/1081.
83 Asa Briggs, *The History of Broadcasting in the United Kingdom*, v: *Competition*, new edn (Oxford: Oxford University Press, 1995), 402.
84 Briggs, *Competition*, 737.
85 This process is discussed in Michael Tracey, *The Decline and Fall of Public Service Broadcasting* (New York: Oxford University Press, 1998).
86 Briggs, *Competition*, 767.
87 *Broadcasting in the Seventies: The BBC's Plan for Network Radio and Non-metropolitan Broadcasting* (London: BBC, 1969).
88 The issues as they affected the philosophy of music broadcasting are set out in Alison Garnham, *Hans Keller and the BBC: The Musical Conscience of British Broadcasting, 1959–1979* (Aldershot: Ashgate, 2003). See also Carpenter, *The Envy of the World*, 247–63.
89 Letter from John Stonehouse, Paymaster General, to Lord Hill, Chairman of the BBC, quoted in Briggs, *Competition*, 778.
90 Minutes of Board of Governors Finance Committee, 16 November 1972, quoted in Briggs, *Competition*, 779.
91 Howard Newby, *Radio, Television and the Arts* (London: BBC, [1976]), which was the text of a lunchtime lecture given on 15 January 1976; 7, 11.
92 See Kenyon, *The BBC Symphony Orchestra*, 429–34. The affected BBC orchestras were: the Scottish Symphony, the Northern Ireland, the Midland Radio, the Northern Radio and the London Studio Players.
93 Ponsonby, memo to Singer, 'Salvaging the 1980 Proms', 2 April 1980, WAC R27/1081/1.
94 See Chapter 3.
95 Singer, memo to Ponsonby, 'Salvaging the 1980 Proms', 10 April 1980, WAC R27/1081/1. This uncompromising attitude was confirmed in a statement Singer released to *The Times* ('We are not going to do the Proms at the sacrifice of not going through with our intentions'); 'Promenade Concerts may be Sacrificed, BBC Says', *The Times* (18 June 1980).
96 Secretary-General of the Arts Council, letter to the BBC Director-General, 30 June 1980, WAC R27/1081/1.
97 Chief Accountant, Radio, memo, 14 September 1981, WAC R27/1082.
98 Robert Simpson, *The Proms and Natural Justice* (London: Toccata Press, 1981).
99 *Ibid.*, 7–10.
100 Ponsonby, quoted in Kenyon, 'Conflict of Sound and Vision'.
101 This account follows the synopsis of the situation set out in Robert Ponsonby's paper 'The Planning of the Proms: a paper for the Central Music Advisory Committee', dated October 1981 and prepared for CMAC's meeting on 6 November 1981. It has a covering note by Aubrey Singer that refers to the CMAC's discussion of October 1978.
102 These are contained in the issues of 10, 17, 24 September, and 1, 8 October 1981.
103 Carey Blyton, 'Letters to the Editor: Proms Discord', *Listener* (17 September 1981).
104 Robert Ponsonby in interview with the author, 24 May 2005; Carpenter, *The Envy of the World*, 294.
105 Minutes, Central Music Advisory Committee, 6 November 1981; Ponsonby, 'The Planning of the Proms', October 1981.
106 Michael Tippett, letter to Ponsonby, 28 July 1972, quoted in Thomas Schuttenhelm, *Selected Letters of Michael Tippett* (London: Faber & Faber, 2005), 22–3.

107 *The Committee on the London Orchestras* [The Goodman Report] (London: The Arts Council, 1965), and *BBC/Arts Council Review of National Orchestral Provision* (London: Arts Council of England, 1994).

108 These definitions and figures are taken from *The Committee on the London Orchestras*, Appendix B, 20, 26, 27.

109 'Concert Organisers Office: Promenade Concerts Attendances', WAC R79/114.

110 These figures are taken from *BBC/Arts Council Review*, 51–fig. 2, and 104–Appendix 14. The generic label 'classical concerts' is not further defined.

111 For discussion of the Royal Albert Hall seating capacities, see pp. 285–6.

112 *BBC/Arts Council Review*, 51.

113 Robert Ponsonby, Introduction to *The Complete Programme of the 90th Season of Henry Wood Promenade Concerts, 1984* [season prospectus] (London: BBC, 1984), 3.

114 'Listening Report', 7–12 September 1981, LR/81/293, October, 1981, WAC R9/935.

115 The 1973 statistics are included within the 1981 'Listening Report'.

CHAPTER 6   IVAN HEWETT

1 Henry J. Wood, *My Life of Music* (London: Victor Gollancz, 1938, edn 1946), 68.

2 'Promenade Concerts: Opening of the Season', *Daily Telegraph* (10 August 1925).

3 *Ibid.*

4 Malcolm Sargent, Introduction to *The Story of the Proms* (London: BBC, [1955]), 7.

5 Compton Mackenzie, 'Memories of the Proms', *Radio Times* (19 July 1946), 3.

6 Victor Gollancz, 'The Last Night of the Proms', *Radio Times* (17 September 1964), 9.

7 Rees, quoted in Reginald Pound, *Sir Henry Wood: A Biography* (London: Cassell, 1969), 170–71.

8 Horace Thorogood, letter to the editor, *Radio Times* (5 January 1951).

9 Frederick Grisewood, *My Story of the BBC* (London: Odhams, 1959), quoted in Pound, *Sir Henry Wood*, 234.

10 'Promenade Concerts: Opening of the Season', *Daily Telegraph* (10 August 1925).

11 C. B. Rees, 'Happy Recollections', in *The Story of the Proms* (London: BBC, [1955]), 60.

12 Ross McKibbin, *Classes and Cultures: England 1918–1951* (Oxford: Oxford University Press, 1998), 387, 389.

13 Letter from Lady Colefax to Bernard Berenson, [undated] 1945, Bodleian Library, Colefax Papers, C. 3169, quoted in McKibben, *Classes and Cultures*, 386.

14 WAC LR/1093, Listener Research Report, Promenade Concert, Saturday 1 August 1942, 6.30–7.30 pm, Home Service. BBC Symphony Orchestra (Leader, Paul Beard) conducted by Sir Henry Wood. Laelia Finnaberg (soprano), Phyllis Sellick (piano). Programme: Rossini, Overture to *William Tell*; Verdi, Scena and Cavatina, 'Come delay not' (*Macbeth*); Copland, Ballet Suite from *Billy the Kid*; Liszt, *Hungarian Fantasia* for piano and orchestra.

15 WAC LR/1076, Listener Research Report, Promenade Concert Wednesday 22 July 1942 8.00–9.00 pm, Home Service. London Philharmonic Orchestra, conducted by Basil Cameron. Leon Goossens (oboe), G. Thalben-Ball (organ). Programme: Britten, *Sinfonia da Requiem*; Cimarosa-Benjamin, Oboe Concerto; Handel, Organ Concerto No. 7 in B♭.

16 WAC LR/1093. For programme, see note 14.

17 See Chapter 5.

18 Jo Kearney, 'Prom Nerds Facing Last Night Blues', *Independent* (4 September 1994), 8.

19 *The Chesterian*, 1930, quoted in Pound, *Sir Henry Wood*, 53.

20 WAC LR/1018, Listener Research Report, Promenade Concert, Saturday 27 June 1942, 6.30–7.30 pm, Home Service. London Philharmonic Orchestra, conducted by Sir Henry Wood. Joan Hammond (soprano), Pouishnoff (piano). Programme: Ireland, *Epic March*; Verdi, recit. and aria, 'Ah, fors'è lui' (*La Traviata*); Rachmaninoff, Piano Concerto No. 2 in C minor.

21 Goossens, quoted in Pound, *Sir Henry Wood*, 178.

22 Quoted in Michael Wright, 'Flash Harry's Heirs', *Daily Telegraph* (16 July 2004), 12.

23 Letter to the editor, *Daily Telegraph* (13 August 1954).

24 For further discussion, see Chapter 7.

25 'There's this man who comes with an inflatable parrot …' [The Giles Smith Interview], *Independent* (24 July 1995), 'Life' section, 4.

26 Mark Elder was relieved of the post of conductor of the Last Night in 1990, when he questioned, at a time of possible international conflict, the inclusion of what he called its 'jingoistic' elements.

27 *Independent*, 17 September 1994.

28 For example Geoffrey Wheatcroft, 'Why Nostalgia Can be Such a Potent Force for Good', *Daily Mail* (10 September 1994), 8.

CHAPTER 7   TOM SERVICE

1 A phrase used to describe the Proms in the BBC's own literature, including 'Building Public Value through Music' (see <http://www.bbc.co.uk/thefuture/text/music_bpv.html>), as well as a moniker adopted by many commentators and critics when describing the festival.

2 Drummond was BBC Controller of Radio 3 and the Proms from 1986 to 1992, after which he focused solely on the Proms directorship. Kenyon was Controller of Radio 3 between 1992 and 1998, and his first season as Controller of the Proms was 1996. After the 1998 season, the Controllership of Radio 3 passed to Roger Wright. Kenyon remains Proms Controller alongside other BBC responsibilities.

3 Interview with the author, September 2005.

4 Drummond's first real year in charge of the Proms was 1987, since the 1986 season was largely programmed by his predecessor, Robert Ponsonby.

5 The Proms broadcasts on the digital television channel BBC4 since 2003 have become an important part of the changing identity of the Proms seasons. What began as an experiment with the medium, and with new means of delivering information – digital viewers could access a live running commentary to the music – has grown year on year, with more concerts broadcast each season. The broadcasts were presented in a more informal manner than the BBC1 or BBC2 relays, often by Charles Hazlewood, who had become, by the early 2000s, the BBC's face of classical music. The mix of live interviews, interval guests, quizzes with Prommers, and the fact that BBC4 often broadcast every Prom in a two or three week period, offered a new vision of what classical music could look like and sound like (in terms of its presentation) on television.

6 Interview with the author, September 2005.

7 John Drummond, *Tainted by Experience: A Life in the Arts* (London: Faber & Faber, 2000), 419–20. In fact, rather than insisting that the BBC use his name in the title of the series, Henry Wood granted the BBC the opportunity to use it, but there was no legal requirement for the BBC to do so, or any stipulation about how many years they were obliged to use it (see Chapter 4).

8 See Chapter 5, and also Drummond, *Tainted by Experience*, 419–20.

9 Drummond, *Tainted by Experience*, 418.

10 Interview with the author, August 2005.

11 Memo from Drummond to the Director-General, 19 November 1990; BBC WAC (RAPIC).

12 Drummond, *Tainted by Experience*, 450.

13 See the 2002 Proms prospectus for Louise Downes' history of how the Last Night presentation of these works ossified into this sequence during the postwar years.

14 Drummond, *Tainted by Experience*, xv.

15 *Ibid.*

16 *Ibid.*, xvi.

17 *Ibid.*.

18 BBC switchboard log, 16 September 1995; BBC WAC (RAPIC).

19 Drummond, *Tainted by Experience*, xvi.

20 *Ibid.*, 382.

21 *Ibid.*

22 Memo from Sue Brealey to Sue Farr, 4 February 1994; BBC WAC (RAPIC).

23 Drummond, *Tainted by Experience*, 389–90.

24 *Ibid.*, 390.

25 Letter to Liz Forgan (Managing Director of Radio), Colin Browne (Head of Corporate Affairs) and Nicholas Kenyon, 25 March 1996; BBC WAC (RAPIC).

26 All from interview with the author, September 2005.

27 In later seasons, the Proms' own education and outreach work sought to create a different kind of openness and accessibility (see below).

28 This was not, perhaps, the foregone conclusion that it now seems. In terms of promotion, the Proms in the Park had a tentative start: the first event was not announced or even mentioned in the 1996 prospectus. A more obvious way in which the Proms attempted to broaden its appeal to prospective audiences that year was with a free CD that came with the prospectus (an initiative for the 1997 season), in which celebrities such as the tennis player Tim Henman, actress Joanna Lumley, comedian Harry Enfield, and football player and commentator Trevor Brooking introduced some of their favourite pieces of classical music from those Proms seasons. In the 1997 prospectus, however, the Prom in the Park received a brief mention in Kenyon's introduction, and by 1998 it had its own reference in the 'Listings and Bookings' section. The free CD idea was not reprised.

29 'Report by the BBC Broadcast: Radio Strategy and Analysis Team on Proms in the Park 1996/1997', 8–9; BBC WAC (RAPIC).

30 *Ibid.*

31 *Ibid.*

32 See Chapter 6.

33 Interview with the author, September 2005.

34 *Ibid.*

35 Esteban Buch, *Beethoven's Ninth: A Political History* (Chicago: University of Chicago Press, 2003).

36 Interview with the author, September 2005.

37 *Ibid.*

38 *Ibid.*

39 Even if the use of the piece in this way is, as Nicolas Slonimsky describes it, a 'lurid aberration of circumstance'; Slonimsky, *The Concise Baker's Biographical Dictionary of Musicians* (London: Simon Schuster, 1988), 71.

40 A few headlines: 'Music that Rose to the Occasion' (*Independent*), 'An Enlightened Change' (*Guardian*), 'One of the Most Dignified and Musically Intense Evenings of its Kind' (*Sunday Times*).

41 *The BBC Proms* (BBC, 2003), video for internal Corporation use. The fact that the strategy of the Proms was presented as part of a meeting of the BBC's senior management demonstrated its importance within the BBC, and the video was subsequently used at presentations and conferences to demonstrate the achievements of the Proms. A recently distributed booklet, *The BBC Proms in the 21st Century*, had the same aim.

42 Continuing the work of Kenyon's first ten seasons, which presented more than nine hundred pieces that were new to the Proms.

CHAPTER 8 NICHOLAS KENYON

1 See Chapter 3.

2 Thomas Russell, *Philharmonic Project* (London: Hutchinson, 1952), 100–101.

3 This is discussed in Chapter 2.

4 See, for example, Table 2.

5 Elisabeth Lutyens, *A Goldfish Bowl* (London: Cassell, 1972), 128.

6 See Chapter 4.

7 Letter dated 18 October 1914, no. 445 of *The Collected Letters of Peter Warlock (Philip Heseltine)*, ed. Barry Smith (Woodbridge: Boydell Press, 2005), ii: 333–7.

8 See Chapter 7.

9 Neither of these aspects sufficiently covers the question of artists and performers, which would require a separate study.

10 Henry Wood, radio interview, BBC Sound Archives, BLSA 9CL0031032.

11 See Chapter 2.

12 Reprinted in David Cox's *The Henry Wood Proms* (London: British Broadcasting Corporation, 1980); see also Chapter 5.

13 Released as *Mahler: Symphony No. 2*, with Janet Baker, Rae Woodland, BBC Chorus, BBC Choral Society, Goldsmith's Choral Union, Harrow Choral Society, London Symphony Orchestra, cond. Leopold Stokowski; recorded at the Royal Albert Hall, London, 30 July 1963 (CD, BBC Legends, BBCL4136-2, 2004).

14 Of some 45,000 works performed at the Proms since the series began, over 16,000 were given in the first decade (see p. 69). More recent average decades include no more than 2,500 works, even though there are more concerts; this represents a radical change.

15 See Chapter 5.

16 Table 2 illustrates some of the strong combinations.

17 John Drummond, Forward to *Proms 1990* [season prospectus], 3.

18 Table 2 shows how some of these were programmed.

19 Paddy Scannell, 'Public Service Broadcasting and Modern Life', in *Culture and Power: A Media, Culture and Society Reader*, ed. Paddy Scannell, Philip Schlesinger and Colin Sparks (London: Sage, 1992), 135–66.

20 L. C. B. Seaman, *Post-Victorian Britain, 1902–1951* (London: Methuen, 1966).

21 Pierre Boulez, radio interview, BBC Sound Archives, BLSA 1LP0196603.

22 See Chapters 1 and 6.

23 Henry Wood, speech for last night, pre-recorded 12 August 1943 for transmission on 21 August 1943, BLSA 9CS0016140; transcription in BBC WAC R79/115/20.

24 This project was nominated for a Royal Philharmonic Society award.

Select Bibliography

This bibliography lists books and articles referred to in the text and notes. The main books and pamphlets that refer to the history of the Proms are listed first, in summary.

Sidgwick, A. H. *The Promenade Ticket: A Lay Record of Concert-Going* (1914)

Wood, Henry. *My Life of Music* (1938)

Hill, Ralph and C. B. Rees, eds. *Sir Henry Wood: Fifty Years of the Proms* (1944), including: W. W. Thompson, 'The Story of the Proms', 3–12

Russell, Thomas. *The Proms* (1949)

The Story of the Proms ([1956])

Orga, Ateş. *The Proms* (1974)

Cox, David. *The Henry Wood Proms* (1980)

Hall, Barrie. *The Proms and the Men Who Made Them* (1981)

Kenyon, Nicholas. *The BBC Symphony Orchestra, 1930–1980* (1981)

Jacobs, Arthur. *Henry J. Wood: Maker of the Proms* (1994)

The Proms in Pictures: A Pictorial History Celebrating the Centenary of the Proms (1995)

The BBC Proms in the 21st Century (2006)

PUBLISHED SOURCES

General

Aldous, Richard. *Tunes of Glory: The Life of Malcolm Sargent*. London: Hutchinson, 2001.

Arditi, Luigi. *My Reminiscences*. London: Dodd, Mead, 1896.

Ayre, Leslie. *The Proms*. Foreword by Sir Adrian Boult. London: Frewin, 1968.

A Report on Orchestral Resources in Great Britain (1970). Chaired by Alan Peacock. London: Arts Council of Great Britain, 1970.

Barker, T. C. and Michael Robbins. *A History of London Transport: Passenger Travel and the Development of the Metropolis*. 2 vols. London: George Allen & Unwin, 1963/rev. 1975; 1974.

Barker, Theo. 'Speyer, Sir Edgar', in *Oxford Dictionary of National Biography*, ed. Lawrence Goldman. Oxford: Oxford University Press, online edition, <http://www.oxforddnb.com/>, accessed February 2006.

Bashford, Christina. 'Not Just "G.": Towards a History of the Programme Note', in *George Grove, Music and Victorian Culture*, ed. Michael Musgrave. Basingstoke: Palgrave Macmillan, 2003. 115–42.

BBC/Arts Council Review of National Orchestral Provision. London: Arts Council of England, 1994.

'BBC Microphones: Thirty Years of Evolution, 1920–1950s'. *History of Public Address* website, <http:// www.historyofpa.co.uk/pages/microphones.htm#bbc>, accessed 16 October 2005.

Beerbohm, Max. *Fifty Caricatures*. London: Heinemann, 1913.

Bennett, Alan. Introduction to *Hymn*. Broadcast on BBC Radio 4, 22 December 2001.

———. *Untold Stories*. London: Faber and Faber, 2005.

Blake, Andrew. *The Land Without Music: Music, Culture and Society in Twentieth-Century Britain*. Manchester: Manchester University Press, 1997.

Boosey, William. *Fifty Years of Music*. London: Ernest Benn Ltd, 1931.

Boulez, Pierre. Radio interview. BBC Sound Archives, BLSA 1LP0196603.

Boult, Adrian. *My Own Trumpet*. London: Hamilton, 1973.

Briggs, Asa. *The History of Broadcasting in the United Kingdom*. London: Oxford University Press, 1961–95.
i: *The Birth of Broadcasting* (1961); ii: *The Golden Age of Wireless* (1965); iii: *The War of Words* (1970); iv: *Sound and Vision*. (1979); v: *Competition* (1995).

Broadcasting in the Seventies: The BBC's Plan for Network Radio and Non-metropolitan Broadcasting. London: BBC, 1969.

Buch, Esteban. *Beethoven's Ninth: A Political History*. Chicago: University of Chicago Press, 2003.

'Building Public Value through Music'. BBC website, <www.bbc.co.uk/thefuture/text/music_bpv.html>, accessed 30 May 2006.

Burns, C. Delisle. *A Short History of Birkbeck College*. London: University of London Press, 1924. [on Francis Ravenscroft, 84–5]

Busoni, Ferruccio. *Ferruccio Busoni: Letters to his Wife*, trans. Rosamond Ley. London: Edward Arnold, 1938.

Carey, John. *The Intellectual and the Masses*. London: Faber and Faber, 1992.

Carpenter, Humphrey, with research by Jennifer Doctor. *The Envy of the World: Fifty Years of the BBC Third Programme and Radio 3, 1946–1996*. London: Weidenfeld & Nicolson, 1996.

Carse, Adam. *The Life of Jullien: Adventurer, Showman-Conductor and Establisher of the Promenade Concerts in England, together with a History of those Concerts up to 1895*. Cambridge: W. Heffer & Sons, 1951.

Chamier, J. Daniel. *Percy Pitt of Covent Garden and the B.B.C.* With introduction by Henry J. Wood. London: Edward Arnold, 1938.

Childs, Peter. *Modernism*. London: Routledge, 2000.

Clarke, Peter. *Hope and Glory: Britain 1900–2000*. Rev. edn. London: Penguin Books, 2004.

Coates, Eric. *Suite in Four Movements: An Autobiography*. London: William Heinemann Ltd, 1953.

The Committee on the London Orchestras [The Goodman Report]. London: The Arts Council, 1965.

Cowen, Frederic H. *My Art and My Friends*. London: Edward Arnold, 1913.

Cox, David. *The Henry Wood Proms*. London: British Broadcasting Corporation, 1980.

Davison, James W. *From Mendelssohn to Wagner, being the Memoirs of J. W. Davison*, comp. Henry Davison. London: William Reeves, 1912.

Dizikes, John. *Opera in America: A Cultural History*. Yale: Yale University Press, 1993.

Doctor, Jennifer R. *The BBC and Ultra-modern Music: Shaping a Nation's Tastes*. Cambridge: Cambridge University Press, 1999.

Donnelly, Mark. *Sixties Britain*. Harlow: Pearson Education, 2005.

Drummond, John. *Tainted by Experience: A Life in the Arts*. London: Faber and Faber, 2000.

Edmunds, Neil. 'William Glock and the British Broadcasting Corporation's Music Policy, 1959–73'. *Contemporary British History* 20/2 (June 2006), 233–61.

Ehrlich, Cyril. *Harmonious Alliance: A History of the Performing Right Society*. Oxford and New York: Oxford University Press, 1989.

———. *The Music Profession in Britain Since the Eighteenth Century: A Social History*. Oxford: Clarendon Press, 1985.

———. *The Piano: A History* (1976). Rev edn. Oxford: Clarendon Press, 1990.

Elkin, Robert. *Queen's Hall, 1893–1941*. London: Rider & Co., [1944].

Foreman, Lewis and Susan Foreman. *London: A Musical Gazetteer*. New Haven and London: Yale University Press, 2005.

Forster, E. M. *Howards End*, ed. Oliver Stallybrass. London: Penguin Books, 1989.

Garnham, Alison. *Hans Keller and the BBC: The Musical Conscience of British Broadcasting, 1959–1979*. Aldershot: Ashgate, 2003.

Gissing, George. *Our Friend the Charlatan*. London: Chapman and Hall, 1901.

Glock, William. *The BBC's Music Policy*. BBC Lunch-time Lectures, no. 6, 10 April 1963. London: British Broadcasting Corporation, [1963].

_____. *Notes in Advance: An Autobiography in Music*. Oxford: Oxford University Press, 1991.

Gollancz, Victor. *Journey towards Music: A Memoir*. London: Victor Gollancz, 1964.

Goossens, Eugene. *Overture and Beginners: A Musical Autobiography*. London: Methuen & Co. Ltd, 1951.

Grisewood, Frederick. *My Story of the BBC*. London: Odhams, 1959.

Hall, Barrie. *The Proms and the Men Who Made Them*. London: Allen & Unwin, 1981.

Hewison, Robert. *Too Much: Art and Society in the Sixties, 1960-75*. London: Methuen, 1986.

[Hill, Ralph and C. B. Rees, eds.] *Sir Henry Wood: Fifty Years of the Proms*. London: British Broadcasting Corporation, [1944]. W. W. Thompson, 'The Story of the Proms', 3–12; Thomas Burke, 'London Scene: 1895–1944', 13–17; Arnold Bax, 'He is a National Institution', 26–9; C. E. M. Joad, 'Queen's Hall was My Club', 51–5; Sacheverell Sitwell, 'When Such Works were New', 60–64.

Hobsbawm, Eric and Terence Ranger. *The Invention of Tradition*. Cambridge: Cambridge University Press, 1983.

Hopkins, Harry. *The New Look: A Social History of the Forties and Fifties in Britain*. London: Secker & Warburg, 1963.

Inwood, Stephen. *A History of London*. Basingstoke: Macmillan, 1998.

Jacobs, Arthur. *Henry J. Wood: Maker of the Proms*. London: Methuen, 1994.

Keating, Rex. 'Third Programme Problems in Certain Underdeveloped Areas'. *UNESCO Reports and Papers on Mass Communications*, No. 23 (December 1956).

Kenyon, Nicholas. *The BBC Symphony Orchestra, 1930–1980*. London: BBC, 1981.

Kildea, Paul. *Britten on Music*. Oxford: Oxford University Press, 2003.

_____. 'World War I and the British Music Industry'. MM thesis, University of Melbourne, 1991.

King, Alec Hyatt, rev. G. R. Seaman. 'Blom, Eric Walter, in *Oxford Dictionary of National Biography*, ed. Lawrence Goldman. Oxford: Oxford University Press, online edition, <http://www.oxforddnb.com/>, accessed February 2006.

Laurence, Dan H., ed. *Shaw's Music*, ii: *1890–1893*. London: The Bodley Head, 1981.

LeMahieu, D. L. *A Culture for Democracy: Mass Communication and the Cultivated Mind in Britain Between the Wars*. Oxford: Oxford University Press, 1988.

Lutyens, Elisabeth. *A Goldfish Bowl*. London: Cassell, 1972.

McKibbin, Ross. *Classes and Cultures: England 1918–1951*. Oxford: Oxford University Press, 1998.

McVeigh, Simon. '"An Audience for High-Class Music": Concert Promoters and Entrepreneurs in Late-Nineteenth-Century London', in *The Musician as Entrepreneur, 1700–1914: Managers, Charlatans, and Idealists*, ed. William Weber. Bloomington: Indiana University Press, 2004. 162–82.

McVeigh, Simon and Cyril Ehrlich. 'The Modernisation of London Concert Life around 1900', in *The Business of Music*, ed. Michael Talbot. Liverpool: Liverpool University Press, 2002. 96–120.

Marwick, Arthur. *British Society Since 1945*, 3rd edn. London Penguin Books, 1996.

Maschler, Tom, ed. *Declaration*. London: MacGibbon & Kee, 1957. Including Lindsay Anderson, 'Get Out and Push!', 153–78.

Matthew, H. C. G. 'The Liberal Age (1851–1914)'. *The Oxford Illustrated History of Britain*, ed. Kenneth O. Morgan. Oxford and New York: Oxford University Press, 1984. 463–522.

Morgan, Kenneth O. *Britain Since 1945: The People's Peace*, 3rd edn. Oxford: Oxford University Press, 2001.

Musgrave, Michael. *The Musical Life of the Crystal Palace*. Cambridge: Cambridge University Press, 1995.

Newby, Howard. *Radio, Television and the Arts*. London: BBC, [1976].

Newmarch, Rosa. *The Concert-Goer's Library of Descriptive Notes*. 6 vols., London: Oxford University Press, 1928–48.

_____. *Henry J. Wood*. London: John Lane, The Bodley Head, 1904.

Nietzsche, Friedrich. *The Will to Power*, trans. Walter Kaufmann and R. J. Hollingdale. London: Weidenfeld & Nicolson, 1968.

Nott, James J. *Music for the People: Popular Music and Dance in Interwar Britain*. Oxford: Oxford University Press, 2002.

Orga, Ateş. *The Proms*. Newton Abbott: David & Charles, 1974.

Panayi, Panikos. *The Enemy in our Midst: Germans in Britain during the First World War*. New York and Oxford: Berg, 1991.

Peacock, Alan and Ronald Weir. *The Composer in the Market Place*. London: Faber Music, 1975.

Philip, Robert. *Performing Music in the Age of Recording*. New Haven and London: Yale University Press, 2004.

Porter, Roy. *London: A Social History*. London: Penguin Books, 1996.

Pound, Reginald. *Sir Henry Wood*. London: Cassell, 1969.

The Proms in Pictures: A Pictorial History Celebrating the Centenary of the Proms. Ed. George Hall and Matías Tarnopolsky. With text by Andrew Huth. London: BBC Books, 1995.

Reed, W. H. *Elgar*. London: Dent, 1946.

Reid, Charles. *Malcolm Sargent: A Biography*. London: Hamilton, 1968.

Rivière, Jules. *My Musical Life and Recollections*. London: Sampson Low, Marston & Co., 1893.

Russell, Thomas. *Philharmonic Project*. London: Hutchinson, 1952.

_____. *The Proms*. London: Max Parrish, 1949.

Sandbrook, Dominic. *Never Had it So Good: A History of Britain from Suez to the Beatles*. London: Little, Brown, 2005.

Scannell, Paddy. 'Public Service Broadcasting and Modern Life', in *Culture and Power: A Media, Culture and Society Reader*, ed. Paddy Scannell, Philip Schlesinger and Colin Sparks (London: Sage, 1992), 135–66.

Scholes, Percy A. *The Mirror of Music, 1844–1944: A Century of Musical Life in Britain as Reflected in the Pages of the 'Musical Times'*, 2 vols. London: Novello & Co. and Oxford University Press, 1947.

Schuttenhelm, Thomas, ed. *Selected Letters of Michael Tippett*. London: Faber and Faber, 2005.

Seaman, L. C. B. *Post-Victorian Britain, 1902–1951*. London Methuen, 1966.

Shore, Bernard. *The Orchestra Speaks*. London: Longmans, Green & Co., 1938.

Sidgwick, A. H. *The Promenade Ticket: A Lay Record of Concert-Going*. London: Edward Arnold & Co., 1914; new edition, 1945.

Simpson, Robert. *The Proms and Natural Justice: A Plan for Renewal*. Foreword by Sir Adrian Boult. London: Toccata Press, 1981.

Slonimsky, Nicolas. *The Concise Baker's Biographical Dictionary of Musicians*. London: Simon Schuster, 1988.

Smith, Barry, ed. *The Collected Letters of Peter Warlock (Philip Heseltine)*, 4 vols. Woodbridge: Boydell Press, 2005.

Speyer, Edward. *My Life and Friends*. London: Cobden-Sanderson, 1937.

The Story of the Proms. London: BBC, [1955]. With introduction by Malcolm Sargent, 7–8.

Tippett, Michael. *Those Twentieth Century Blues: An Autobiography*. London: Hutchinson, 1991.

Tracey, Michael. *The Decline and Fall of Public Service Broadcasting*. New York: Oxford University Press, 1998.

Verne, Mathilde. *Chords of Remembrance*. London: Hutchinson, 1936.

Warner, Marina. *World of Myths*. London: British Museum Press, 2003.

Westrup, Jack , rev. Rosemary Williamson. 'Blom, Eric (Walter)', in *The New Grove Dictionary of Music and Musicians*, 2nd edn, ed. Stanley Sadie and John Tyrrell. London: Macmillan, 2001. iii: 712–13.

Who's Who in Music: A Biographical Record of Contemporary Musicians, ed. H. Saxe Wyndham and Geoffrey L'Epine. London: Pitman, 1913. [Capacity of Royal Albert Hall, 288–9.]

Wood, Henry J. *About Conducting*. London, 1945.

_____. *My Life of Music*. London: Victor Gollancz, 1938.

_____. Speech for last night, pre-recorded 12 August 1943 for transmission on 21 August 1943. BBC Sound Archives, BLSA 9CS0016140; transcription in BBC WAC R79/115/20.

Wood, Jessie. *The Last Years of Henry J. Wood*. London: Gollancz, 1954.

Journal, newspaper etc. citations (ordered chronologically)

'Proposed New Concert-Hall, Langham-Place', *The Builder* (14 February 1891), 128–9.

'The Presiding Genius of the Birkbeck Bank', *The Banker* liv (1892), 827–31. [on Francis Ravenscroft, with portrait]

G. B. Shaw. [Review of the first performance of Parry's *Job*], *The World* (3 May 1893).

The Strad 4 (October 1893), 120.

'The New Concert Hall', *The Times* (27 November 1893).

'Notes from the Concert Room: London's New Hall', *The Sketch* (6 December 1893).

Joseph Bennett. 'Music of the Day', *Daily Telegraph* (28 February 1894).

'The Queen's Hall Orchestra', *The Tatler* ([27 November 1901]), 425.

Daily Telegraph (15 August 1908).

Ezra Pound. 'The New Sculpture', *Egoist* (16 February 1914), 67–8.

Letters to the Editor, *The Times* (18 and 25 May 1915).

'Queen's Hall Promenade Concerts', *Musical Times* 59 (1918), 424.

'Discussion on the Queen's Hall Promenade Programmes', *Musical Times* 59 (1918), 469–70.

Robin H. Legge. 'Retrospect of Literature, Science, and Art in 1919: Music', *Annual Register* (1919), 60-63.

Alfred Kalisch. 'London Concerts', *Musical Times* 61 (1920), 689–90.

'Finance and Commerce in 1921', *Annual Register* (1921), 69–80.

Robin H. Legge. 'Retrospect of Literature, Science, and Art in 1921: Music', *Annual Register* (1921), 66–8.

Robin H. Legge. 'Retrospect of Literature, Science, and Art in 1922: Music', *Annual Register* (1922), 79–81.

'Broadcasting and the Theatres: Entertainment Industry's Opposition', *The Times* (28 April 1923), 8(B).

'Entertainment Industry and Broadcasting: Negotiations Broken Off', *The Times* (10 May 1923), 12(C).

'The Broadcasting Dispute', *The Times* (12 May 1923), 10(B).

William Boosey. 'Broadcasting', *Daily Telegraph* (19 May 1923), 11(D).

'Occasional Notes', *Musical Times* 64 (1923), 548–51.

Robin H. Legge. 'Retrospect of Literature, Science, and Art in 1923: Music', *Annual Register* (1923), 68-70.

John Reith, 'What is Our Policy?', *Radio Times* 2 (14 March 1924), [441].

'The Promenade Concerts: Rumours and Facts', *The Times* (9 August 1924).

'Entertainments: the Promenade Concerts: Rumours and Facts', *The Times* (24 August 1924), 8(B).

[H. C. Colles, probably]. 'Thirty Years of Promenade Concerts', *The Times* (15 October 1924), 15(E).

'Letters to the Editor: Thirty Years of Promenade Concerts', *The Times* (20 October 1924), 20(E).

'Finance and Commerce in 1924', *Annual Register* (1924), 71–83.

Robin H. Legge. 'Retrospect of Literature, Science, and Art in 1924: Music', *Annual Register* (1924), 68–70.

'B.B.C. and Entertainment Industry: Progress of Negotiations', *The Times* (27 January 1925), 11(G).

Kaikhosru Sorabji. 'Some Ideas on the Concert Problem', *Musical Times* 66 (May 1925), 414–6.

'Promenade Concerts: Opening of the Season', *Daily Telegraph* (10 August 1925).

John B. McEwen and Hugh P. Allen. 'Letters to the Editor: The Promenades: A Rehearsal Fund', *The Times* (31 October 1925), 8(A).

'Sir Henry Wood', *The Times* (31 October 1925), 13(E).

Chappell & Co. 'Letters to the Editor: The Promenades', *The Times* (6 November 1925), 12(D).

'The Broadcasting Inquiry: Attitude of the Theatres, Artists and the Public', *The Times* (19 December 1925), 23(E).

Robin H. Legge. 'Retrospect of Literature, Science, and Art in 1925: Music', *Annual Register* (1925), 73–4.

The Times (6 November 1926). [obituary notice for Robert Newman]

Thomas Armstrong. 'Wireless and the Concert-Goer', *Musical Times* 67 (1926), 1078–80.

Musical Times 67 (1926), 1134. [obituary notice for Robert Newman]

'No More "Promenades"?', *The Times* (4 March 1927), 15(D).

'Queen's Hall: Orchestra's Last Season', *The Times* (4 March 1927), 14(F).

William Boosey. [Letter to the Editor], *Evening Standard* (8 March 1927).

Sir Bernard Partridge. 'For the Honour of London' [cartoon drawing], *Punch* (16 March 1927).

Beethoven Number, *Radio Times* (18 March 1927). Including articles by Arnold Bennett, Romain Rolland; George Bernard Shaw, 'Beethoven Broadcast', 575–6; Percy Scholes, 'The Story of Beethoven', 577–84.

F. B[onavia]. 'London Concerts: The B.B.C. at the Albert Hall', *Music Times* 68 (1927), 263.

'B.B.C. and Queen's Hall: A Season of Promenade Concerts', *The Times* (1 June 1927), 16(F).

Percy A. Scholes, 'The "Proms" and the "Provinces"', *Radio Times* 16 (29 July 1927), 161–2.

'The Dawn of a New Era for Listeners: the B.B.C. Announces the First "Alternative Programme"', *Radio Times* 16 (12 August 1927), 241–2.

Rosa Newmarch. 'The "Proms"', in *Promenade Concerts: Programme, Thirty Third Season, 1927* ('Opening Night – August 13') (1927), 9, 11, 13, 15, 17, 29, 31.

'The Promenade Concerts: Successful Opening of the Season', *The Times* (15 August 1927), 8(E).

Tom Eadie. 'B.B.C. and the Proms', *Glasgow News* (17 August 1927).

'X. Y. Z.' 'The B.B.C. and the "Proms"', *Glasgow Herald* (17 August 1927).

'The Proms: Record of Consistent Progress', *The Times* (20 August 1927), 8(E).

[P. P.] Eckerley. 'The Great Experiment Begins', *Radio Times* 16 (26 August 1927), [325].

'Rehearsals for the Concerts', *Manchester Guardian* (26 August 1927).

Herman Klein. 'The Lure of the "Proms."', *Radio Times* 20 (9 August 1928), 223.

'Which shall we Listen to Tonight? a Note on the New Art of Listening to the Broadcast Programmes', *Radio Times*, 16 (2 September 1927), 365.

'The Promenade Concerts: End of a Successful Season', *The Times* (26 September 1927), 10(C).

P. P. Eckersley. 'The Art of Listening', *Eve, the Lady's Pictorial* (7 December 1927).

Herman Klein. 'The Lure of the "Proms."', *Radio Times* 20 (9 August 1928), 223.

St John Ervine. 'What does the Public Want?', *Radio Times* 20 (10 August 1928), [233]–4.

G. M. 'The B.B.C. and the Proms', in *Promenade Concerts: Programme, Thirty Fourth Season* ('Saturday, August 11th, 1928') (1928), [8]–9.

'Promenade Concerts', *The Times* (20 August 1928), 13(E).

'Broadcasting and Music', *BBC Handbook 1928*, [83]–7.

[Rosa Newmarch]. 'The Promenade Concerts', *BBC Handbook 1928*, 101–4.

Filson Young. 'The Art of Listening', *BBC Handbook 1928*, 349.

Edwin Evans. 'Music and the Cinema', *Music and Letters* 10/1 (January 1929), 65–9.

'Promenades Once More: the Thirty-Fifth Season', *The Times* (10 August 1929), 13(D).

W. Rooke-Ley. 'If Stevenson Could Have Listened', *Radio Times* 24 (30 August 1929), 411.

Ralph W. Wood. 'The Prom. Audience', *Music and Letters* 11/2 (April 1930), 177–81.

'"The Solitary Boo": Incident at Promenade Concert', *Manchester Guardian* (21 August 1930).

'Good Listening', *The BBC Yearbook 1930*, 61.

Rosa Newmarch. 'Queen's Hall in 1914–15', Letter to the Editor, *Monthly Musical Record* 62 (1932), 36–7.

Spike Hughes. 'Music', *Daily Herald* (7 August 1936).

'Radio and the Proms', *Sunday Times* (9 August 1936).

Constant Lambert. 'Positively the Last on the Promenades', *Night and Day* (21 October 1937), 188–9.

'The Promenade Programmes: Sir Henry Wood's 44th Season: Much New Work', *Daily Telegraph* (8 July 1938).

Rosa Newmarch. 'Sir Henry J. Wood's Jubilee Year', *Promenade Concerts 1938* [season prospectus], [1]–2.

'Broadcasting Concerts: Ultra-Short Waves to be Used', *Sunday Times* (7 August 1938).

'Opening of the "Proms": The Concert: Warm Welcome for Old Friends', *The Observer* (7 August 1938).

'Proms on Vision Wavelength: Fidelity of Reception', *Daily Telegraph* (8 August 1938).

N[eville] C[ardus]. 'The Queen's Hall Promenade Concerts', *Manchester Guardian* (20 August 1938).

'Promenade Concerts: Works of Six Composers', *The Times* (9 September 1938).

'The Proms Conductor Celebrates his Half-Century', *Picture Post* (1 October 1938), 24–9.

'Finish of the Proms', *News Chronicle* (3 October 1938).

Ralph Vaughan Williams. 'Henry Wood', *London Mercury* (October 1938), 497–501.

'Notes of the Year, 1937: "Listener Research"', *BBC Annual 1938*, 25–6.

Ralph Hill. 'The Future of Music-making', *Musical Times* 80 (February 1939), 93–5.

'Civil Defence: Full Machinery in Motion: Black-out from Sunset to Sunrise', *The Times* (2 September 1939), 7(A).

'"Proms" to Close: Audience Told by Sir Henry Wood', *Daily Telegraph* (2 September 1939).

'"Proms" Without the B.B.C.: Next Season Sir Henry Wood's Last', *The Times* (5 April 1940).

[BBC statement], *Daily Telegraph* (5 April 1940).

Adrian C. Boult. 'The Promenade Concerts: To the Editor', *The Times* (9 April 1940).

Henry J. Wood. 'B.B.C. and the "Proms": Plans for the New Season: To the Editor', *Daily Telegraph* (9 April 1940).

'Promenade Concerts: the New Syllabus', *The Times* (1 July 1940).

'Promenade Concerts: Wagner, Elgar, and Others', *The Times* (28 August 1940).

'Theatres: Concerts &c.', *The Times* (24 May 1941), 8(F).

William Glock. 'Music', *Observer* (13 July 1941).

'Sir Adrian Told Them, Sir Henry Showed Them', *Evening Standard* (19 August 1942).

W[illiam] McNaught. 'Retrospect of Literature, Art, and Science in 1943: Music', *Annual Register*, new series (1943), 349.

Hely-Hutchinson, Victor. 'The Rising Tide of Music', *BBC Yearbook 1945*.

Compton Mackenzie. 'Memories of the Proms', *Radio Times* (19 July 1946), 3.

Horace Thorogood. Letter to Editor, *Radio Times* (5 January 1951).

'Winter Proms: "The Shadow of Cain"', *The Times* (14 January 1953).

'Orchestra Saves the Proms', *The Herald* (31 January 1953).

Philip Hope-Wallace. *Time and Tide* (6 June 1953).

'Enterprise, Not Revolution in the 1960 Proms', *The Times* (10 June 1960).

'Prommers Stay for Gerhard', *The Times* (30 July 1960).

'Electronics at the Proms: No Substitute for Live Music', *The Times* (9 August 1960).

Burston Armagh. Letter to Editor, *Daily Telegraph* (13 August 1954).

Desmond Shawe Taylor. [Review], *Sunday Times* (14 August 1960).

'An Adventurous Programme', *The Times* (19 August 1960).

Charles Reid. 'The Most Exciting Proms for Years', *News Chronicle* (20 August 1960).

'A Thrilling Oedipus Rex: Cogent Justification of New Proms Policy', *The Times* (24 August 1960).

Andrew Smith. *Daily Herald* (19 September 1960).

'Glockenspiel' (the 'Notebook' column), *Spectator* (17 May 1963), 626.

David Cairns. 'Hall of Fame', *Spectator* (9 August 1963), 177.

Victor Gollancz. 'The Last Night of the Proms', *Radio Times* (17 September 1964), 9.

Charles Reid. 'The Public and the Proms: Report on the "Spectator" Inquiry', *Spectator* (8 October 1965), 446.

'Challenge of the Proms: Alan Blyth Talks to William Glock', *Music and Musicians* 15/12 (August 1967), 16.

Michael Nyman. 'Saucer-shaped', *Spectator* (2 August 1969).

Michael Nyman. 'Plain Clothes Don', *Spectator* (16 August 1969), 215.

Joan Chissell. *The Times* (15 September 1969).

Carey Blyton. 'Letters to the Editor: Proms Discord', *Listener* (17 September 1981).

Nicholas Kenyon. 'Conflicts of Sound and Vision', *The Times* (15 September 1984). [interview with Robert Ponsonby]

Jo Kearney. 'Prom Nerds Facing Last Night Blues', *Independent* (4 September 1994), 8.

Geoffrey Wheatcroft. 'Why Nostalgia Can be Such a Potent Force for Good', *Daily Mail* (10 September 1994), 8.

'There's this man who comes with an inflatable parrot…' [The Giles Smith Interview], *Independent* (24 July 1995), 'Life' section, 4.

David Pountney et al. 'If We Ran the Proms', *Guardian* (12 July 2002).

Michael Wright. 'Flash Harry's Heirs', *Daily Telegraph* (16 July 2004), 12.

BBC Publications

Each season since around 1902, an annual Proms prospectus has been prepared, under different titles and in different formats. Since 1927 these have been published by the BBC.

BBC Handbook 1928. 'Broadcasting and Music', [83]–7. [Rosa Newmarch], 'The Promenade Concerts', 101–4.

BBC Annual 1938. 'Notes of the Year, 1937: "Listener Research"', 25–6.

BBC Handbook 1939. London: BBC, 1939. 'Licence Figures', 129.

BBC Yearbook 1945. London: BBC, 1945. Hely-Hutchinson, Victor. 'The Rising Tide of Music'.

The BBC Proms in the 21st Century. London: BBC Prom Publications, 2006.

In addition, the Proms pages on the BBC website (accessible from the Proms home page <http://www.bbc.co.uk/proms/>) provide important sources of information.

ARCHIVE SOURCES

BBC WAC – Radio and television files

R3/3/3, Control Board/Minutes (1927).

R9/935, LR/81/293, Promenade Concerts 1981/Attenders in the last week/Research.

R9, LR/1018, Listener Research Report, Promenade Concert, Saturday, 27 June 1942, 6.30–7.30 pm, Home Service.

R9, LR/1076, Listener Research Report, Promenade Concert Wednesday 22 July 1942 8.00–9.00 pm, Home Service.

R9, LR/1093, Listener Research Report, Promenade Concert, Saturday 1 August 1942, 6.30–7.30 pm, Home Service.

R22/772/1, Legal/Promenade Concerts/Wood, Henry/Use of name (1944).

R22/783/1, Legal/Columbia Gramophone Company/Agreements (1926–36).

R27/124, Music General/Henry Wood Concert Society (1946–53).

R27/125, Music General/The Henry Wood Proms Jubilee (1943–4).

R27/214, Music General/Music Dept Meetings (Monthly)/Minutes (1941–5).

R27/245/1, Music General, Music Policy (1930–43).

R27/247, Music General/Music Policy/Surveys & reports (1922; 1939–49).

R27/250/2–3, Music General/Music Programme Advisory Panel (1936–9).

R27/431/1, Music General/Promenade and Symphony Concerts Committee (1927–33).

R27/432/1, Music General/ Public Concerts/Policy (May 1933–Apr 1935).

R27/523/1, Music General/Wood, Sir Henry/General Correspondence (1940–43).

R27/700/1, Music General/Promenade Concerts (1955–65).

R27/847/1–3, Music General/ Music Policy (1955–70).

R27/1022/1–3, Music General/Promenade Concerts (1967–8).

R27/1073–5, Music General/Henry Wood Promenade Concerts/Seasons (1984–6).

R27/1076–7, Music General/Henry Wood Promenade Concerts/General (1966–83, 1984–6).

R27/1081–3, Music General/Henry Wood Promenade Concerts (1978–80, 1978–82, 1979–83).

R29/192/1, Orchestral General/Orchestral Meetings (1929–30).

R29/194/1–3, Orchestral General/Orchestral Policy (1933–9, 1940–41, 1941).

R29/195/1–2, Orchestral Policy/Public Concerts (1933–46).

R29/212/1, Orchestral Policy/Scottish Promenade Concerts (1931).

R30/2342/1, Outside Broadcasts/Promenade Concerts (1939–44).

R30/2343/1–4, Outside Broadcasts/Promenade Concerts/General (1939–49).

1 (1939–44), 2 (1945–6), 3 (1947–8), 4 (1949).

R30/2344/1, Outside Broadcasts/Promenade Concerts/Negotiations (1927–8).

R30/2345/1–10, Outside Broadcasts/Promenade Concerts/Policy (1944–7).

1 (1944–7), 2 (1947–8), 3 (1949), 4 (1950), 5 (1951–2), 6 (1953), 7 (1954–5), 8 (1956–7), 9 (1958), 10 (1959–60).

R30/2379/1, Outside Broadcasts/Queen's Hall (1939–40).

R30/2380/1, Outside Broadcasts/Queen's Hall/London Music Festival 1939 (1938–9).

R30/2381/1, Outside Broadcasts/Queen's Hall/Promenade Concerts (1938).

R30/2383/1–2, Outside Broadcasts/Queen's Hall/Agreements, Rehearsals, Bookings (1935–8).

R30/2416/1–2, Outside Broadcasts/Queen's Hall Promenade Concerts/Internal memos (1939, 1940).

R30/2417/1, Outside Broadcasts/Queen's Hall Proms/Letters & Station Memos (1939–40).

R30/2428/2, Outside Broadcasts/Queen's Hall/Winter Proms (1935–9).

R30/2607/1–3, Outside Broadcasts/Royal Albert Hall/Promenade Concerts (1942–3, 1943, 1944)

R30/2609/1–2, Outside Broadcasts/Royal Albert Hall/Promenade Concerts/Internal memos (1941–2).

R30/2641/1, Outside Broadcasts/Royal Albert Hall/Promenade Concerts/Winter (1946–52).

R30/3742/1, Outside Broadcasts/Royal Albert Hall/Promenade Concerts/Winter/Policy (1946–53).

R34/196, Policy/Anniversaries/BBC Silver Jubilee.

R34/420, Policy/Home Services (1944–47).

R34/504, Policy/ Opera/British National Opera Company Ltd (1923–5).

R34/600/1–4, Policy/Programme Board/Minutes (1924, 1925, 1926, 1929).

R34/1022/2, Policy/Future of Sound Broadcasting in the Domestic Services Working Party.

R79/114/1, Concert Organiser's Office/Promenade
Concerts/Attendances (1956–74).
R79/115/1–108, Concert Organisers Office/Promenade Concerts/
Correspondence (1927–1977).
Esp. 1 (1927), 8 (1934), 9 (1935), 14 (1938), 15 (1939), 16 (1940),
17 (1941), 63 (1960).
R79/117/1–2, Concert Organisers Office/Promenade
Concerts/Prospectuses and handbills (1923–50, 1951–66).
R79/0171–315, Concert Organiser's Office/Promenade
Concerts/Concerts/Repertoire, orchestrations, etc. (1920–54).
R101/302/1, Central Registry Management Section/Promenade
Concerts (1971–6).

T14/836/1, TV Outside Broadcasts/Promenade Concerts/1
(1947–53).
T14/836/2, TV Outside Broadcasts/ Promenade Concerts (1954).

In addition a number of recent BBC files cited in Chapter 7 have
not yet been given identifying file numbers by the BBC Written
Archives Centre; these have been designated BBC WAC (RAPIC).

BBC WAC – Contributors and special collections
RCONT1/Julian Herbage/Artist's File/4 (1954–5).
RCONT1, Contributors/Malcolm Sargent/Artist's File/4 (1947–9).
RCONT1/910/Malcolm Sargent/1.
RCONT1/Contributors/Sir Henry Wood/1–17 (1926–44).
1 (1944), 2 (1926–8), 3 (1929–32), 5 (1933), 6 (1934–6), 7 (1937),
8 (1938), 9 (1938–44), 10 (1937–44), 11 (1936–66), 12 (1928),
13 (1940), 14 (1941), 16 (1944–5), 17 (1943–4)

S60/5/2/1–2, Reith Diaries, vol. ii/1–2.

BBC WAC – Press cuttings
P111–15, Press Cuttings/Broadcasting & War: Miscellaneous
(1939–42, 1939–42, 1943–4, 1945–6).
P116–18, Press Cuttings/Miscellaneous (1947–8, 1949–50, 1951–2).
P426–31, Press Cuttings/Music (September 1939–1940, 1941, 1941,
1942, 1943, 1944)
P452–3, Press Cuttings/Promenade Concerts (1927–8).
P454–5, Press Cuttings/Promenade Concerts (1929).
P456, Press Cuttings/Promenade Concerts (1930).
P460–61, Press Cuttings/Promenade Concerts (1934).
P463, Press Cuttings/Promenade Concerts (1936).
P466–7, Press Cuttings/Summer Promenade Concerts (1938,
1939).
P468–9, Press Cuttings/Promenade Concerts (June-August 1942,
1943).
P470, Press Cuttings/Promenade Concerts/Jubilee Concerts 1944.

Bodleian Library, Oxford
Lady Colefax. Letter to Bernard Berenson, [undated] 1945. Colefax
Papers, C. 3169.

British Library, London
Boult, Adrian. Typescript of *Music Magazine* radio script,
25 February 1945. Add. MS 56442, fols. 71–82 at 74.
Glock, William. Diaries. William Glock Collection, BL MS
Mus. 983.
Goossens, Eugene. 'Sir Henry Wood at Rehearsals', *New York
Times* (3 September 1944), typescript copy. Add. MS 56442,
fols. 53–7.
[Newmarch, Elsie (probably)].
Letters to Frank Howes and Thomas Russell, Add. MS 56421,
fols. 70–71.

'Queen's Hall Promenade Concerts now known as The Henry
Wood Promenade Concerts', Add. MS 56421, fol. 76.
Newmarch, Rosa.
'Four Phases of the Promenade Concerts', typescript, August
1927. Henry Wood Papers, Add. ms 56442, fols. 19–26.
Programme cutting. Add. MS 56442, fol. 11v.
Speyer, Edgar. Letter to George Bernard Shaw. G. B. Shaw Papers,
Add. MS 50527, fols. 256–7.
Speyer, Edward. 'List of works, in the handwriting of Sir Henry
Wood, performed under his direction at the series of
Promenade Concerts at the Queen's Hall London,
August–October 1924', 19 August 1924. Add. MS 42233, fols.
292–6, dated.
Wood, Henry J.
Letters to Rosa Newmarch, 5 and 11 June 1907. Music Misc.,
Deposit 2003/13.
Letter to Newmarch, 9 July 1908. Add. MS 56421, fols. 11 to 22.
Letter to Percy Pitt, 25 October 1913. BL Egerton MS 3306,
fol. 215.
Wright, Kenneth. Letter to Elisabeth Lutyens, 2 March 1970.
Lutyens Papers, Add. ms 71144, fol. 148v.

Promenade Concert Programmes
8–13 September 1919, shelfmark h.5470.

City of Westminster Archives Centre
'The Victoria Concert Hall, Limited', share prospectus, 18 June
1887.

Elgar Birthplace Museum, Worcester
Elgar, Edward. Draft letter to Edgar Speyer, 23 October 1921. Elgar
Birthplace Museum, Broadheath, ref. 9620.

Public Record Office, Kew
PRO CRES 35/2144.

Royal Academy of Music, London
Wood, Henry J. Letter to Miss Alice Taylor, 18 September 1913.
McCann Collection.

Acknowledgments

The editors would like to acknowledge and thank a number of people and organizations without whom this book would not have been possible. First and foremost, our fellow contributors – Alison Garnham, Ivan Hewett, Paul Kildea, Leanne Langley and Tom Service – who have devoted so much time and effort to researching, thinking and writing in new and invigorating ways about a subject as well known and yet as deeply complex as the Proms. Similarly, for the pictures selected with such care and diligence, we owe enormous thanks to Elisabeth Agate, and also to Rowena Alsey for the book design. We would especially like to thank the family of Christopher Samuelson for making his unique photo archive available. We are very grateful to Sam Wythe for his care and patience throughout the editorial processes, and thank Jamie Camplin not only for perceiving the potential of the book in its initial stages but for his support of the project. We greatly appreciate the support and assistance that the contributors and we have received from the BBC Written Archives Centre, and would particularly like to thank the Archivist, Jacqueline Kavanagh, for her support of the project, and Jeff Walden for his invaluable advice and quiet but consistent help. In the BBC Proms Office, Yvette Pusey has provided wonderful and efficient support, for which we thank her, and we are also grateful to Victoria Bevan for her assistance with the photograph illustrations. For the index we thank Christopher Dell, and also appreciate the financial support of the Royal College of Music towards its preparation. Finally, in dedicating this book to the memory of Cyril Ehrlich, we would like to acknowledge the sense of inspiration, excitement and direction that he gave to us when embarking on this project.

Photo Credits

Frontispiece Chris Christodoulou; 9 Haywood Magee/Hulton Archive/Getty Images; 19 London Transport Museum. © Transport for London; 21 BBC Proms; 23 Chris Christodoulou; 24 Christopher Samuelson; 26 Reproduced with the permission of Punch, Ltd. www.Punch.co.uk; 27 Alex von Koettlitz; 28 BBC Proms. Alex von Koettlitz. Poster photo Painton Cowen; 31 BBC Photo Library; 32 Peter Joslin Collection; 33 Peter Joslin Collection; 36 Royal Institute of British Architects. A. C. Cooper; 37 City of Westminster Archives Centre (above). Peter Joslin Collection (below); 38 Private collection; 43 The Tully Potter Collection; 45 Royal College of Music, London; 47 BBC Proms; 49 From Rosa Newmarch, *Henry J. Wood* (London: John Lane, The Bodley Head, 1904); 51 From J. Daniel Chamier, *Percy Pitt of Covent Garden and the B.B.C.* (London: Edward Arnold, 1938); 53 Private collection; 54 BBC Proms; 55 London Transport Museum. © Transport for London; 56 Private collection; 58 From Reginald Pound, *Sir Henry Wood* (London: Cassell, 1969); 60 Rischgitz/Hulton Archive/Getty Images; 61 From *Max Beerbohm, Fifty Caricatures* (London: Heinemann, 1913)/Berlin Associates; 67 BBC Proms; 73 The Illustrated London News Picture Library; 75 Painton Cowen; 77 Reproduced with the permission of Punch, Ltd. www.Punch.co.uk; 81 From William Boosey, *Fifty Years of Music* (London: Ernest Benn, 1931); 82 Painton Cowen; 86 Reproduced with the permission of Punch, Ltd. www.Punch.co.uk; 87 Reproduced with the permission of Punch, Ltd. www.Punch.co.uk; 89 Painton Cowen; 90 BBC Photo Library; 91 Painton Cowen; 93 Painton Cowen; 95 Painton Cowen; 96 Painton Cowen; 99 BBC Written Archives Centre. Painton Cowen; 103 Musical Opinion; 104 Painton Cowen; 105 London Transport Museum. © Transport for London; 106 The Advertising Archives; 111 Reproduced with the permission of Punch, Ltd. www.Punch.co.uk; 113 Reg Speller/Hulton Archive/Getty Images; 115 Felix Man/Stringer/Hulton Archive/Getty Images; 121 BBC Proms; 122 Fox Photos/Hulton Archive/Getty Images; 123 Raymond Kleboe/Hulton Archive/Getty Images; 124 Painton Cowen; 125 Royal Albert Hall Archives; 127 BBC Photo Library; 128 Horace Abrahams/Hulton Archive/Getty Images; 130 BBC Photo Library; 132 BBC Photo Library; 133 Reproduced with the permission of Punch, Ltd. www.Punch.co.uk; 135 Dr David Adderley Collection; 137 BBC Photo Library; 138 Royal Albert Hall Archives; 143 Keystone Features/Hulton Archive/Getty Images; 147 Painton Cowen; 148 Painton Cowen; 149 Monty Meth/Hulton Archive/Getty Images; 151 Ron Burton/Hulton Archive/Getty Images; 155 Reproduced with the permission of Punch, Ltd. www.Punch.co.uk; 157 Godfrey MacDomnic; 158 Malcolm Crowthers; 161 Topfoto; 163 BBC Photo Library; 166 BBC Proms and EMI; 169 Chris Davies/ArenaPAL; 171 Godfrey MacDomnic; 176 BBC Proms and Lewis Foreman (1960); 181 Christopher Samuelson; 185 Edward Miller/Hulton Archive/Getty Images; 186 Christopher Samuelson; 187 Godfrey MacDomnic; 188 Brooks/Hulton Archive/Getty Images; 189 BBC Proms; 190 Christopher Samuelson; 191 Christopher Samuelson; 192 BBC Written Archives Centre. Painton Cowen (above). Christopher Samuelson (below); 193 Christopher Samuelson (above). Alex von Koettlitz (below); 194 BBC Proms; 195 Alex von Koettlitz (above). Christopher Samuelson (below); 197 Godfrey MacDomnic; 201 Christopher Samuelson; 203 Central Press/Hulton Archive/Getty Images; 210 Godfrey MacDomnic; 211 Alex von Koettlitz; 212 Alex von Koettlitz; 214 Alex von Koettlitz; 215 Thurston Hopkins/Hulton Archive/Getty Images; 219 Godfrey MacDomnic; 222 BBC Proms; 223 BBC Proms. Barney Newman; 224 BBC Proms. Barney Newman; 225 Timothy Allen/© *The Independent* (above). Milein Cosman (below); 226: BBC Proms. Barney Newman (above). Godfrey MacDomnic (below); 229 Godfrey MacDomnic; 230 Alex von Koettlitz (above and centre). BBC Proms (below); 232 Kinetic (below); 233 BBC Proms. Barney Newman (below); 235 Alex von Koettlitz; 236 Simon Jay Price; 239 Alex von Koettlitz; 240 *Private Eye*; 242 Alex von Koettlitz; 243 BBC Proms; 247 © BBC/Tim Kavanagh; 248 © BBC/Tim Kavanagh; 252 Chris Christodoulou; 254 Chris Christodoulou; 255 Sisi Burn (above right). Chris Christodoulou (below left); 256 Royal Academy of Music, London; 257 Alex von Koettlitz; 258 Godfrey MacDomnic; 259 Chris Christodoulou; 262 Godfrey MacDomnic; 269 Alex von Koettlitz; 270 BBC Proms; 271 Mark Chilvers/© *The Independent*; 273 Chris Christodoulou; 274 Zak Waters; 275 Sisi Burn; 276 Chris Christodoulou; 277 Chris Christodoulou.

Index